MOUNTAINEERING
TRAINING
– AND –
PREPARATION

Carlton Cooke, PhD
Leeds Metropolitan University

Dave Bunting, MBE
My Peak Potential

John O'Hara, PhD
Leeds Metropolitan University

Editors

Human Kinetics

Library of Congress Cataloging-in-Publication Data

Mountaineering : training and preparation / Carlton Cooke, Dave Bunting, and John O'Hara, editors.
  p. cm.
 Includes bibliographical references.
 ISBN-13: 978-0-7360-8469-7 (soft cover)
 ISBN-10: 0-7360-8469-X (soft cover)
 1. Mountaineering. 2. Mountaineering--Training. 3. Mountaineering--Psychological aspects. I. Cooke, Carlton, 1958- II. Bunting, Dave, 1968- III. O'Hara, John, 1976-
 GV200.M687 2010
 796.522--dc22

                              2009035774

 ISBN-10: 0-7360-8469-X (print)
 ISBN-13: 978-0-7360-8469-7 (print)

This publication is written and published to provide accurate and authoritative information relevant to the subject matter presented. It is published and sold with the understanding that the author and publisher are not engaged in rendering legal, medical, or other professional services by reason of their authorship or publication of this work. If medical or other expert assistance is required, the services of a competent professional person should be sought.

Acquisitions Editor: John Dickinson; **Developmental Editors:** Amanda Eastin-Allen and Laura Floch; **Assistant Editors:** Laura Podeschi and Michael Bishop; **Copyeditor:** Alisha Jeddeloh; **Permission Manager:** Martha Gullo; **Graphic Designer:** Fred Starbird; **Graphic Artist:** Tara Welsch; **Cover Designer:** Keith Blomberg; **Cover photo:** Everest West Ridge 2006 Team Collection; **Photographer (interior):** Neil Bernstein, pages 157-159, 162-169, 171-174, 176-183; all other photos courtesy of Everest West Ridge 2006 Team Collection; **Visual Production Assistant:** Joyce Brumfield; **Photo Production Manager:** Jason Allen; **Art Manager:** Kelly Hendren; **Associate Art Manager:** Alan L. Wilborn; **Illustrator:** TwoJay!; **Printer:** United Graphics

Human Kinetics books are available at special discounts for bulk purchase. Special editions or book excerpts can also be created to specification. For details, contact the Special Sales Manager at Human Kinetics.

Printed in the United States of America   10 9 8 7 6 5 4 3 2 1

The paper in this book is certified under a sustainable forestry program.

Human Kinetics
Web site: www.HumanKinetics.com

United States: Human Kinetics
P.O. Box 5076
Champaign, IL 61825-5076
800-747-4457
e-mail: humank@hkusa.com

Canada: Human Kinetics
475 Devonshire Road Unit 100
Windsor, ON N8Y 2L5
800-465-7301 (in Canada only)
e-mail: info@hkcanada.com

Europe: Human Kinetics
107 Bradford Road
Stanningley
Leeds LS28 6AT, United Kingdom
+44 (0) 113 255 5665
e-mail: hk@hkeurope.com

Australia: Human Kinetics
57A Price Avenue
Lower Mitcham, South Australia 5062
08 8372 0999
e-mail: info@hkaustralia.com

New Zealand: Human Kinetics
P.O. Box 80
Torrens Park, South Australia 5062
0800 222 062
e-mail: info@hknewzealand.com

                                                      E4897

MOUNTAINEERING
TRAINING
– AND –
PREPARATION

Contents

PART I

PLANNING AND TEAM SELECTION

PART II

CONDITIONING AND NUTRITION FOR EXPEDITIONS

PART III

EXPEDITION LEADERSHIP AND PSYCHOLOGY

Preface

Many people enjoy being in the outdoors mountaineering and spending time with friends and fellow enthusiasts. It could be a simple weekend trip or a major expedition lasting months. Motives will vary: rest and relaxation, physical and mental well-being, escape from busy work schedules, or achievement of goals. Much has been written about mountaineers all over the world, ranging from success stories of climbing new summits to detailed accounts of peril and tragedy. However, what is not so well documented are the principles, processes, methods, and experiences of training and preparing for mountaineering expeditions. With *Mountaineering: Training and Preparation*, whether you are a recreational participant or a seasoned mountaineer, you will find much that will interest and inform you on what goes into devising, planning, preparing for, training for, experiencing, and returning from expeditions of any length or complexity.

In this book, the two main areas of focus are undertaking physical and mental training and preparing well so that you have a safe, enjoyable, and successful expedition. Strong emphasis is placed on accepting that even the best-laid plans can fall by the wayside when conditions and events dictate, but it is still possible to predict and prepare for those situations. Throughout the book, but particularly in chapter 3 on extreme preparation, you'll also find advice on training and preparing for pioneering expeditions, which are reserved for only the most serious, committed, and experienced mountaineers, *not* weekend enthusiasts.

You can use the book in various ways. You can read the entire book to cover the full breadth of material in order to prepare and train for mountaineering expeditions, or you can refer to specific chapters that cover aspects that are of particular relevance to you in your preparation or training for expeditions.

Part I of *Mountaineering: Training and Preparation* contains a wealth of insights on the numerous aspects of planning for expeditions. Chapters focus on selection of teams and equipment, extreme preparation for extreme expeditions, logistics and planning, and first aid. Regardless of the scale of your expeditions, you will have a unique insight into how the experts do it and what lessons you can apply based on their considerable experience.

Part II presents the aspects of physical training required for success in mountaineering: endurance, strength and power, and acclimatisation. Training can be effective only if you are mindful of your nutrition habits and other lifestyle habits such as rest and recovery. Chapters 9 and 10 cover the specifics of nutrition to help you achieve effective outcomes in training and expeditions; those chapters also give consideration to general health and well-being.

Part III covers aspects of psychological skills training and leadership. These skills are essential when preparing for and coping with various situations in extreme environments.

The contributing writers bring a breadth and depth of experience and expertise to this book. Included are some of the very best professionals in mountaineering and sport and exercise science; they have lifetimes of experience participating in, leading, and collecting data from some of the most demanding expeditions to remote locations around the globe. The contributors formed a special partnership on the British Army Everest West Ridge Expedition (EWR) in 2006. All of the authors either were major players in the main expedition team or were part of the group of sport and exercise scientists from Leeds Metropolitan University who provided support in the two and a half years leading up to the expedition, throughout the expedition, and after the team's return from the expedition. This book contains many insights, lessons, stories, and anecdotes from the EWR 2006 expedition as well as from many other ventures of the team members. The details of planning, preparation, and training of mountaineers have never been presented in this way before.

Whether you are new to mountaineering expeditions, a recreational enthusiast, or an experienced campaigner, you should benefit from this book. For those starting to plan their first expeditions the book provides a blueprint for effective training and preparation. The recreational enthusiast will find a wealth of detailed information on specific aspects of training and preparation for mountaineering that they weren't able to access previously. Finally, all serious mountaineers acknowledge the ben-efits to be gained from sharing the experiences and expertise of other seasoned campaigners. Whether it is in specific aspects of preparation or training, there will be great insight to be gained from the combined experience and expertise of the team of mountaineers and sports scientists who have authored the various specialist chapters of this book to provide a complete guide to preparation and training for mountaineering expeditions.

Acknowledgments

First, we are grateful to the participating authors for their contributions and the hard work, patience, and understanding that they have displayed throughout the production of this book. We would also like to acknowledge the contributions of Jamie Harley and Bengamin Taylor for the production of the glossary and research in support of the sports science chapters and Dr. Nick Monastiriotis (ASCC, UUA) for his valuable comments and suggestions on the Endurance Training chapter. We are also in debt to all members of the Everest West Ridge 2006 expedition who have contributed photographs, comments, anecdotes, and quotations to the book. We would also like to acknowledge the support from Leeds Metropolitan University for the Everest West Ridge 2006 expedition and all the staff and students of the University that contributed to the partnership, without which this text could not have been produced. Finally, we would like to express our thanks to Human Kinetics for their support and hard work in the production of this book.

Carlton Cooke, Dave Bunting,
and John O'Hara

Credits

Table 4.1 Table courtesy of Summit Oxygen International Ltd. (www.summitoxygen.com).

Figure 5.3 Adapted from the algorithms for the *Resuscitation Guidelines 2005*. [Online]. Available: http://www.resus.org.uk/pages/gl5algos.htm [August 18, 2009]. Used with permission from the Resuscitation Council UK.

Table 5.4 Adapted from *Clinics in Sports Medicine* 24(2), T. Reilly, J. Waterhouse, and B. Edwards, "Jet lag and air travel: Implications for performance," 367-380, copyright 2005, with permission from Elsevier.

Figure 6.1 Adapted, by permission, from M. Burtscher, M. Flatz, and M. Faulhaber, 2004, "Prediction of susceptibility to acute mountain sickness by SaO_2 values during short-term exposure to hypoxia," *High Altitude Medicine & Biology* 5(3): 335-340. The publisher for this copyrighted material is Mary Ann Liebert, Inc. publishers.

Table 8.1 Adapted from T.R. Baechle, R.W. Earle, and D. Wathen, 2000, Resistance training. In *Essentials of strength training and conditioning*, 2nd ed., edited by T.R. Baechle and R.W. Earle (Champaign, IL: Human Kinetics), 395-426.

Table 9.2 Reprinted, by permission, from Committee on Medical Aspects of Food and Nutrition Policy (COMA), 1991, *Dietary reference values for food energy & nutrients for the United Kingdom* (London: Her Majesty's Stationery Office). Reproduced under the terms of the Click-Use Licence. Data for 60-74 year olds from B. Thomas and J. Bishop, 2007, *Manual of dietetic practice*, 4th ed. (Oxford, UK: Blackwell), 858.

Table 9.3 Reprinted, by permission, from Committee on Medical Aspects of Food and Nutrition Policy (COMA), 1991, *Dietary reference values for food energy & nutrients for the United Kingdom* (London: Her Majesty's Stationery Office). Reproduced under the terms of the Click-Use Licence.

Table 10.2 Source: http://www.complanfoods.com/nutrition_complan_original.php.

Introduction:
From Derbyshire to Everest

Dave Bunting

The British Isles are a haven for adventure, offering some of the most exciting and challenging mountains available. I was lucky enough to grow up in the Derbyshire countryside, running wild and looking for the most exhilarating challenges to pass my time. I was part of a country family where getting dirty, cold, and wet were the norm for what was a fabulous upbringing, but with three brothers to compete against, nothing came without a good battle. Country life was an awesome adventure, especially with my best mate Leigh, but we both wanted something more and thought it might be exciting to join the Army

Cadets as teenagers. This opened our eyes to a wider world of experiences, including the Duke of Edinburgh award scheme and other exciting ventures around the country and sometimes further afield. Our teenage years became filled with a variety of outdoor challenges, which further exposed me to the excitement of the outdoors.

I became hugely inspired by the hills, and my first real mountain experience came when I was lucky enough to go to Scotland with the Cadets and found myself in the Cairngorms. Although only skiing on piste, the trip allowed me to experience the winter mountains, see how harsh conditions could be, and deal with the intricacies of keeping warm and motivated in this environment. My experiences as a schoolboy remained relatively tame in the grand scale of things, but I had a desire even at that time for experiencing new places and challenges, especially when some excitement and danger were involved.

TAKING EVERY OPPORTUNITY

I know so many people who regret not taking up mountaineering and climbing earlier in life. It's never too late, but if you can start early and grasp every opportunity available to enhance your all-round experience, there is a huge amount to do in the outdoors. I was lucky enough to join the Army Cadets, which opened my eyes and led to me joining the army full time, following in the footsteps of both my father and grandfather. I was only 16 when I signed up, and each leave period I would return to Derbyshire and often go walking with my older cousin, Ant. He introduced me to the bigger hills of Derbyshire and taught me how to navigate and prepare myself for the hills, inspiring me to become more involved in the outdoors.

Dave Bunting scrambling in North Wales.

I was well suited to the routine of army life and revelled in the physical training, discipline, and competitiveness required to survive each day. I have many great memories from my training, but a week of leadership training in the mountains of North Wales was my favourite. Focussed on character building and teamwork, the 2 weeks of climbing, canoeing, and hill walking were magnificent, and climbing Moel Siabod was the highlight for me. The steep climb, physical effort, and last 30 minutes in thick mist all added to the adventure.

For a time, another outdoor activity became my passion. Kayaking was my priority, and like the hills, it offered tough challenges and adventure, although I leaned towards the long-distance events, which probably further instilled my love for endurance and long-term commitment over speed and sprinting.

I started to improve my outdoor expertise by doing more walking in my own time. I became more proficient with the techniques required to be in the mountains and took confidence in my performance. Annual adventurous training with my regiment became my next focus. I loved all of the activities from skiing to winter mountaineering, and even though I had spent most of the year kayaking, now climbing and the mountains were beginning to captivate me. Inspired by my friend, Taff Rees, I was encouraged to push myself and realised that I might have found something to which I was really suited. On my first trip to the sea cliffs of Scotland, I realised that I could excel with climbing, and I managed to tick off all of the challenges I was set by Taff. He became a role model for me: capable, knowledgeable, and at the same time inspiring to be around. He also had an air of confidence about him and a fantastic way of encouraging people with his style of leadership. It was during this time that I started to experience the adrenaline buzz and satisfaction from being scared and overcoming that fear, putting myself in the face of danger but being able to handle it.

GAINING EXPERIENCE

I am a believer in taking on things progressively rather than running before you can walk, and following short weekend expeditions as a schoolboy on the Duke of Edinburgh's Award, I thought it would be sensible to take the next step. The Pennine Way or any of the other U.K. long-distance paths offered a chance to cut my teeth on some of the skills required to undertake longer physical challenges. Dealing with the organisation and day-to-day difficulties on such journeys offered a firm grounding for the bigger expeditions that would follow in the future, from the requirements for planning and training before departure to the way you take care of yourself and adjust your plan each day to the prevailing conditions during the journey. My experience on the 12 days and 435 kilometres (270 miles) of the Pennine Way laid a foundation and gave me the desire to achieve something more demanding.

When you spend enough time in the outdoors, you will thoroughly test yourself, sometimes in situations you didn't mean to get into, and some of these lessons may be painful. On my home turf in 1988, I learned some hard lessons that would help shape my future and teach me to respect how serious accidents can be in the outdoors. My climbing ability and strength far outweighed my technique at that time. Whilst climbing, I took a rest on a poorly placed piece of protection. It popped and I plummeted to the rocks below, landing on my feet and breaking my ankle in two places, as well as damaging various joints. My lesson was a realisation of how difficult it can be to extricate a casualty in the outdoors even from a location relatively close to a road.

Thankfully, this accident did not deter me and in 1989 my climbing really started to take off. Along with my close mate Chris Collett, I ventured to North Wales and also pushed the grades on the limestone outcrops of Europe. These mini-holidays were great for my development and were one of the most memorable times of my life, pushing limits, building trust, and above all just having great fun.

Experience in the outdoors is essential and progression is built on it; however, there is huge value in formalising your knowledge and gaining qualifications to confirm your ability. I had spent time self-teaching, reading books, and then going out to practise. The downside of this approach is that it can end in accidents and offers you no confirmation of whether you are doing the right thing. I was lucky enough to attend my first structured training courses through the army and headed off to Norway to fill a vacant slot on an alpine mountaineering course. The course provided me with an excellent introduction to the skills that I required to fill the gap between the climbing and mountaineering.

Years later I was posted to instruct in the Joint Service Mountain Training Centre (JSMTC), where I could consolidate my skills, and combined with activity delivery, I was starting to understand the bigger picture. Risk assessment, programme development, and decision making all helped me to become a more rounded outdoorsman. My enthusiasm for climbing led me to being selected to complete a course attached to the German Army Mountain Troops, where after a year of varied and arduous training I became a German Army Mountain Guide.

MY FIRST REAL EXPEDITION

My course in Norway led to greater opportunity when I was invited to take part in a Himalayan expedition to Pisang Peak. The scary thing about that trip was that because of my technical climbing ability, the leader had chosen me to be the climbing leader, putting me in charge of the technical climbing even though my experience on snow and ice was limited to a little in Scotland and my Norway course. On reflection it was horrendous that I was in charge of this important area of decision making with no experience of altitude. Clueless about acclimatising but a fit hill walker, I set a swift pace and on occasion arrived at our destination well ahead of others, not rehydrating as I should and not setting an appropriately steady pace for acclimatising. Inevitably, as we got to higher altitudes I began to suffer, and on the side of our mountain at around 4,200 metres (13,780 ft) I was feeling terrible.

Once we settled into camp I felt a little better, but by the morning my headache was painful. With no knowledge and only foolish determination, I elected to head up with everyone else.

I plodded on, playing down how bad I really felt, and by the time we reached our next camp at over 5,000 metres (16,405 ft), I was unable to hide my discomfort. We did not know that I should have gone back down immediately, and it turned out to be the worst night of my life as severe acute mountain sickness (AMS) kicked in: Nausea, vomiting, rejection of any food or drink, diarrhoea, and my continuing headaches collapsed my confidence and made for a debilitating night. My tent partners were brilliant but with the ensuing heavy storm, frequent trips outside to be sick and go to the toilet in a whiteout couldn't be shared with anyone and I felt very lonely.

The next morning it was clear I had to go down, and my trusted friend Chris volunteered to accompany me even though he could have continued upwards. His completely unselfish approach to it all was simply superb and it was an amazing lesson for me in descent—with each step I took down the mountain I began to feel better. Three hours later I was scoffing a big pile of food, feeling much better and totally relieved. The team was sadly kept from the summit by severe snow. Thankfully, once everyone was

Dave Bunting and brother, Andy, on the summit of Island Peak (6,200 m [20,340 ft]) with Makalu in the background, 1997.

safely off the mountain, the expedition had to proceed over the high Thorong Pass and onto Pokhara, so I was able to test my ability at altitude once again and all went well.

The Pisang Peak episode was enough to put me off for life, but thankfully it didn't. I look back at it as one of my greatest lessons. Since then I have ensured that my pace on the approach march to high altitude has been slow and enjoyable, and I usually aim to be the last to get to our destination each day. Education in the risks, preparation before departure, and sound judgement whilst on expedition are fundamental to the success and safe return of the team.

My motivation was undeterred by this expedition, and I wanted to learn more and achieve something significant on these fabulous mountains. My pride had been dinted, especially when one of the older members of the team had walked past me as I lay suffering; I did not want this to happen again. Thankfully there was so much more to the expedition than my 48 hours of hell on the mountain, and I was able to focus on the positive rather than negative elements of my experience.

This first expedition was enough for me to realise that bigger expeditions were much more interesting and complex with so many more elements to consider. The bigger expeditions leave far less room for poor preparation, which at best will cause you to suffer memorably and at worst risks serious injury or loss of life. In contrast, short day or weekend excursions can often be poorly planned and prepared but your survival will rarely be at risk. I now wanted another trip to the Himalayas, and this time I wanted to do things right.

GETTING IT RIGHT

Less than 2 years after my first Himalayan expedition, an opportunity came up to go back to Pisang Peak and I jumped at it, thinking there would be no better trial than to attempt the same mountain armed with all I had learned during and since my first attempt. Since my 1990 experience, I had climbed in Central Europe and Yosemite, been to the Alps for glacier and ice experiences, and worked as an instructor in Norway. One thing I noticed during this time was that my first Himalayan trip had gained me

some respect amongst other military climbers. It was a place people aspired to visit and at a young age I had been lucky enough to already have that tick in the box.

With these experiences behind me, I headed back to Pisang Peak on what I saw as a personal rerun to prove to myself that I could operate effectively in this harsh environment. This time I was team medic, which felt a little less imposing than climbing leader, but nevertheless this was still in at the deep end and I learned many lessons about organisation and care of team members on expeditions. The whole experience could not have been better. After a paced approach, enjoying the surroundings, we arrived at the mountain in top condition. I was teamed up with Chris again and a friend named Pete, and everything went swimmingly well right up until a rope length below the summit. Pete was much more experienced on ice than both Chris and I, and he led out the relatively steep final ice pitch as Chris and I belayed him from a small ice step only centimetres wide. The poor ice conditions did not allow us to secure ourselves, and as Pete ran out the rope with no protection, we both became more concerned about our position and what might happen were he to fall. We prepared ourselves to unclip, knowing we would have absolutely no chance of arrest. Thankfully he didn't, and we all stood proudly on the summit with our ice axes held high in celebration. It was an amazing moment and my ghosts had been laid to rest. In 1990 I had been so far out of my comfort zone, but now I felt confident and strong and I wanted more.

This was not the only memorable part of the expedition; we then chose to cross the more remote Tilicho Pass to link over to the opposite side of the Annapurna Circuit. This offered a superb 4-day unsupported challenge as the Sherpas crossed the easier Thorong Pass with the heavier equipment, leaving us to fend for ourselves. This may have been the first time I trod somewhere only a handful of people had been before, and I loved the seriousness of our situation and the hostile landscape with no one else around to help. We had little information about the pass apart from some details in Chris Bonington's *I Chose to Climb* (1985), and we had to deal with problems as they arose, including remote camping, climbing a dangerous gully, and a full-day diversion to avoid a semifrozen lake. Another hard and memorable personal lesson came when I tried to jump a frozen stream and my leg went through the ice! Escaping with painkillers and anti-inflammatory tablets rather than snapping my leg, which could easily have happened from my launch from what I thought was solid ice, is a lesson I often reflect on. Such a remote and high helicopter rescue would not have been possible from this location and a long carry evacuation by my team would have certainly cut down on my list of friends. This lesson taught me that before doing anything in the mountains, you must always consider the consequences for everyone if it goes wrong.

LEARNING HOW TO ORGANISE AN EXPEDITION

Around 1996 I was planning a small venture to Island Peak and we were joined at the last stages of preparation by my brother, Andy, whom we invited along for the travel experience. This expedition still stands today as one my favourite trips, a small uncomplicated team, loads of laughter, and above all standing on the summit with Andy and a climbing friend called Ewen was such a satisfying experience. Taking care of Andy made me feel more confident with both my mountaineering skills and leadership ability.

It soon became apparent from these early experiences that success was all about preparation and planning. If you do all the preparation properly, the expedition will run smoothly; if you neglect your preparation and are lazy before departure, it will result in inescapable discomfort and frustration. A massive investment of energy in the preparation and planning stages will provide for a much more enjoyable experience on the expedition itself, something I have been aware of since my early outdoor experiences.

A TOUGHER CHALLENGE

During the Island Peak trip we had not only viewed the stunning slopes of Mount Everest, but we had also spotted an inspiring peak called Mount Pumori (7,165 m, or 23,505 ft).

On return to Europe in 1997, we immediately began planning the next trip. The Pumori trip was pulled together very quickly, in just 12 months, and it was during that time that I met one of my greatest personal inspirations, John Doyle. He had been posted to the British Alpine Centre in Bavaria, where I worked, to prepare for the next German Army course. John had already completed the impressive Cassin Ridge on McKinley as well as Gasherbrum 1, the 11th highest peak, without oxygen. I revelled in his stories about the bigger peaks, wondering what it must be like to go to these mountains. John was very different to the majority of other people I had met, focussed and strong but also quiet and understated. John was highly respected in mountaineering circles, and within the Army Mountaineering Association he had already reached legendary status.

I felt I could learn from him, and so when he joined our Pumori expedition we were delighted and departed with a very capable team. Pumori

Pumori Base Camp with Everest in the background, 1998.

John Doyle and Dave Bunting at Camp 1 on Pumori, 1998.

is impressive and serious with no easy routes. It turned out to be a great trip for many reasons, a key one being that we took the right people, which is ultimately the foundation for any great expedition.

Climbing each day on relatively technical ground with a clear view up Everest was mind-blowing, and the pull to be on those infamous slopes began to build in me. Being so close to so much history, disaster, and triumph stirred my desire. It was like being in a bubble with history being made around me; there were stories developing over my shoulder on the slopes of Everest that would make up the front covers of British climbing magazines in weeks to come.

Strangely, I remember at that point that I did not have the immediate desire to stand on the summit of Everest, just its slopes. Maybe the poor performance on my first trip had knocked my confidence to perform, but I certainly wanted to be part of a team to climb the mountain.

On Pumori, the climbing was considerably more dangerous than on previous expeditions and it was here that I had one of my closest

calls. After some good progress leading out the route by a variety of team members, John and I were now the two lead climbers. The team had established Camp 3 on a promontory at around 6,300 metres (20,670 ft), where we had chiselled out a small exposed step in the snow to place our tent. We settled in, admired our route above, and picked out the line we would be taking.

Suddenly there was a huge noise from above and we looked in horror as a huge ice serac peeled away from the summit ridge and began to avalanche down the mountain. As it hit the open reentrant way above our camp, it was redirected and steered onto a track heading straight for our position. We both looked on, frozen by what we were witnessing. The only thing to do was get down behind the pathetic 1.2-metre (4 ft) wall that had been carved out during the placement of our tent and hope it would offer some protection from this growing mass of snow and ice. We watched the approaching avalanche in slow motion and 50 metres (55 yd) from our position, behind the only pathetic protection we could use, the mass of debris hit a mound

John Doyle and Keith Jenns climbing to Camp 2 at 6,200 metres (20,340 ft) on Pumori, 1998.

of ground and dissipated down either side of the promontory, leaving a large cloud of ice particles to completely engulf our camp but do no damage. I remember just looking at John, kneeling calmly with me behind this wall, clearly not convinced that it would protect us, but what could we do? It was one of the only times in my life that I genuinely thought for a split second that we were going to die.

As the afternoon progressed, smaller avalanches continued to break free with the warm conditions, but having seen such a big one have little impact on us, we felt protected. The route above, however, was not protected and our line of ascent to the next camp headed directly up the barrel of the gun down which anything from above would be forced. We observed the terrain but settled down for the night, knowing that there was little option than to be exposed to huge danger if we wanted to make the ascent. By daylight, having listened to the frequency of avalanche, I was convinced that with such warm conditions any progress was going to be hit by something, and escape from its path would be

impossible at that altitude on that part of the route.

John and I discussed the realities of our situation, including the length of exposure we would have in the danger zone at 6,300 to 7,000 metres (20,670-22,965 ft). We would be moving exceptionally slowly; something was bound to come our way. Everything we knew and had learned during our time in the mountains said to turn back, but after all the effort to get up there, the money, the sponsorship, and the desire to summit, it was not an easy choice. Desire could not overcome the stark reality, however, and on the morning radio call I announced our decision to turn back. The expedition leader understood, having witnessed the previous day's activities, and the attempt was abandoned.

It was a thought-provoking experience for me and one that could have easily resulted in the wrong decision. It was also a lesson in analysing risk and I was happy with our performance. As we stood looking at the mountain from a distance, having already packed up Base Camp, something happened that was almost meant to be. An even bigger avalanche swept down the mountainside, taking the line straight through our route and camps. The right decision had been made! Mount Pumori remains one of the deadliest mountains, predominantly due to the avalanche risks in the same area where we had our incident. In 2001, five young Spanish climbers were killed just above the site of our incident, and by 2005, 472 climbers had summited the mountain with 42 deaths, 13 of those after summiting—statistics that are far worse than those on Mount Everest.

THE NEXT LEVEL: AN 8,000-METRE PEAK

During 1998, the next big British Services 8,000-metre (26,245 ft) trip was being organised to Kanchenjunga, the world's third highest peak, and John was already in the frame for selection after his performance on the 1996 Gasherbrum trip. The leader of this next trip, Steve Jackson, had been with John in 1996 and had seen his impressive contribution firsthand, and he knew John's involvement would be key. John encouraged me to attend the selection weekend and at the same time, unbeknownst to me, spoke to Steve about my inclusion. John's recommendation had worked; Steve liked me and the route was set for my biggest challenge yet.

The training for this trip was different. The members were already highly experienced with Alpine and Himalayan routes to their names, and the training focus was never on pushing limits. A great atmosphere was created, and meets focussed on the team, getting to know each other, and making sure we would get on when the chips were down. This mindset was developed by Steve, who was a fabulous character, and I could see why he was the man for the job. When I first met him, I did not know what to expect but probably had an image of a towering physical specimen who was going to drag us to the top of this mighty peak. Quite the opposite transpired as the 152-centimetre (5 ft), rosy-cheeked, slightly overweight bloke from Mansfield appeared. His intention was to organise, direct, and inspire the team to achieve

something special, and with his sense of humour and down-to-earth style he soon had the team hanging on every word.

In the interim, in 1999 I became part of a huge expedition to take 180 army personnel to the Himalayas to climb the 18 so-called trekking peaks. The name gave no clue to the difficulty; I was signed up for the technically hardest peak, set in the Everest region—Kusum Kanguru, just over 6,300 metres (20,670 ft). The leader of my team was Dave Wilson and I took on the role of climbing leader. The expedition was brilliant, and sadly we were denied the summit by atrocious snow conditions that sent a wave of extreme storms across the Himalayas, killing a number of people and stranding others in base camps and villages. The experience on Kusum Kanguru added to my all-round confidence for Kanchenjunga, although I was quite nervous but also immensely excited about this expedition.

For the first few weeks of the expedition I felt strong, reaching Camp 1 quickly, carrying loads and with plenty of strength to spare. With my three climbing team partners, we then worked up to Camp 2 at 6,800 metres (22,310 ft), where we stayed for a couple of nights acclimatising and did a short carry before returning to Base Camp. Back at Base Camp we needed a rest, but in the night I woke with a crippling headache. I have never had anything like it in my life. I couldn't move with the excruciating pain until it came light enough to find some paracetamol. When I got up it became clear there was something wrong with my eye, and as I looked down the valley I could only see a distorted image. Using an ophthalmoscope, the doctor soon discovered that I had a severe retinal haemorrhage. He made it clear that going back up the mountain carried a risk of it getting worse. This was incredibly upsetting; my chances of achieving much beyond what I already had were over. However, I did not want to damage my eyes, so I took the commonsense decision and withdrew from the climbing teams. There was still a lot to keep me occupied as I assisted Steve at Base Camp and kept involved with progress. Back home the doctors confirmed a double retinal haemorrhage on my macula, so I was content with my decision.

Dave Bunting and John Doyle at Camp 1 on Kanchenjunga with Jannu in the background, 2000.

The climbing teams went on to set up higher camps and eventually, after an unbelievable effort, John, Ady Cole, a Royal Marine climber, and two of our Sherpas reached the 8,586-metre (28,170 ft) summit. At Base Camp I stood next to our leader, Steve, as the climbers spoke from the summit, and it was an incredibly proud moment I will never forget. I was captured by the whole experience and inspired by the people around me. One big lesson was learned here as Ady pulled off an incredible achievement. Although a talented and physically strong person, he had never been to altitude—he hadn't even done Mont Blanc in the Alps—yet here he was standing aloft the third highest mountain on earth without oxygen. This was a lesson that strong character and determination are key to overcoming adversity, but also I had seen John's experience and confidence help carry Ady forward to success. The seed was planted, and after Kanchenjunga I decided I wanted to organise and lead a big expedition myself.

Nima Sherpa, Ady Cole, and John Doyle on the summit of Kanchenjunga (8,586 metres [28,170 ft]), 2000.

FILLING IN THE GAPS

I felt there were still skills I needed to learn as a leader, so I decided to organise a smaller expedition with novices to the Annapurna area of the Himalayas. My childhood best mate Leigh set up the trip. I was the climbing leader and the experienced member of the team making the decisions on the ground. This experience was outstanding and proved to me that I both enjoyed the planning and preparation elements but also took huge satisfaction from introducing novices to life-changing mountain experiences. My confidence was growing to commit to my own big challenge; all I needed to do was decide on what, where, and when.

MY BIG CHANCE: EVEREST WEST RIDGE

The answer fell on my lap when in 2003 a good friend of mine, Dave Pearce, reached the summit of Everest as part of a Royal Navy expedition. This was enough to send me into action. Overnight I finalised my thoughts of the idea that had been brewing since 2000 and, approaching my boss, I announced that I intended to organise an Army Mountaineering Association trip to scale Mount Everest. Getting John Doyle involved was key, and with our combined qualities I felt confident we could gain both support and interest. John's high-altitude and hard-climbing background and my expedition background and mountain centre experience combined to create quality training and a realistic leadership team for the mountain.

Gaining support from my best mate Leigh further bolstered the plan. Leigh was a trusted friend, and during the 2002 trip to Chulu West he had proved to be a great expedition team member. I became heavily focussed on producing a project that could not fail to inspire and interest, and whereas it was my idea to head for Everest, John's interest in the West Ridge would cause a stir. I realised, however, that there would need to be more in this project to encourage sponsors, and we wanted it to be something that was both groundbreaking and historical. I pushed for the inclusion of some less experienced mountaineers and the involvement of both youngsters and women in the project. This decision was one of the best I made. It gained us unrivalled support from all areas and made for a fabulous project that would cover all angles and involve a junior and development team in addition to the main team on Everest itself.

Dave and Leigh on the Thorong Pass, Annapurna Circuit, during the Chulu West expedition, 2002.

The junior team would be aimed at teenage recruits led by experienced mountain leaders. So long as the team members were kept safe, their experience was going to be unrivalled during their young lives. I wanted them to experience the wonders of Nepal and the Himalayas and give them a flavour of expedition mountaineering and trekking.

I saw the development team as the next generation of high-altitude mountaineers and leaders who could take the place of the experienced climbers in the future. Their main aims would be to have an expedition experience, learn the intricacies of planning, and gain some extreme altitude experience by standing on top of a 7,000-metre (22,965 ft) peak, giving them the confidence to go further in future expeditions.

Six months after the idea had begun, I gained the full support of the Army Mountaineering Association, which was awesome and boosted my confidence hugely. I was keen to quickly recruit real help and gained confirmation that John could fill the role of climbing leader whilst my Kusum Kanguru partner, Dave, was recruited into the deputy leader position. The leadership team—along with Leigh, whom I had asked to head up the sponsorship and finances—now had to become salespeople, getting everyone to share our vision.

In 2004 I was already due to be part of the Joint Services Makalu expedition that was attempting the hugely committing Southeast Ridge, which had seen little action, and almost untrodden ground beckoned our team. This was a superb opportunity to test myself again as I took up the role of deputy leader and climbing leader with a friend from the Kanchenjunga expedition as the expedition leader. Colin and I worked well together, and in this important decision-making role I took advantage of viewing the big picture, in addition to being involved in front-end climbing.

The experience was invaluable, and although we had to turn back at 7,300 metres (23,950 ft) due to running out of time after prolonged extreme bad weather, I still gained much from the expedition. My confidence was boosted because I felt comfortable at our highest point, and my excitement for Everest was now unstoppable. The biggest disappointment was that I believe we could have completed the route; a French team who joined us did so only days after we left. We were going as strongly as they were and had we been able to stay a little longer, I think the summit would have been within our grasp. The French climbers were great and they paid a compliment to us in their national climbing magazine, stating that they could not have achieved it without us. Colin's leadership style was very good but also very different from Steve's on Kanchenjunga, and I took lessons from both expeditions with me to Everest.

The application for the Everest team involved a CV of background experience in key areas of winter and alpine climbing, as well as expedition and high-altitude experience. To gain a feel for character and determination, the obvious question was included: Why do you want to be part of

A panoramic image of Everest West Ridge from above Tilman's camp.

Dave Bunting and Ian Venables at Camp 1 (5,800 metres [19,030 ft]) on Makalu in 2004.

this expedition? I vetted every single application form, of which we received around 160, and split people into those who were appropriate for interviews for either the main or development team. By this stage I had gained permission for the development team to be headed by its own leadership team of trusted and experienced expedition leaders, and although I maintained overall control, I needed to focus now on the main team selection.

We held two selection weekends to give everyone the best opportunity to attend and gave a 20-minute interview to everyone who had applied. I had a strong feeling about how I wanted to run the selection weekends, having been on both sides of the fence in the past. A friendly and relaxed atmosphere was essential to uncovering the real person, and from the outset I tried to be down to earth with everyone involved. For the process to be enjoyable, it could not be too intimidating and our questions had to address what we wanted to know about each person. The panel were carefully compiled

and included myself and Dave as the leadership team, along with three highly experienced climbers from past Everest expeditions. The questions ranged from 'How did you start climbing?' to 'What do you know about the route you are signing up to?' I focussed on what skills each person might bring to the team, and Dave set scenarios to see how the person would react in awkward situations. The other panel members focussed on the question of commitment, not only of the interviewees but also of their family and bosses since this was going to be a 3.5-year project that would require the highest level of focus and drive to ultimately achieve our task on the mountain. No one was going to get released from daily work, so weekends, evenings, and leave periods would be the time commitment to consider, and over such a long time, this could put strain on families and relationships. At the end of the second selection weekend, we found ourselves with around 38 names, twice that of the team we planned to take with us, but ideal for the squad since we expected some drop out.

We retained the squad for 8 months, so early training meets were still part of the selection of our ultimate team.

Under John's direction as climbing leader, an exciting array of training meets was designed, ranging from the Peak District to the Alps. Each meet was enjoyable but at the same time challenged and tested people, uncovering their strengths and weaknesses and allowing me to determine their roles for the mountain. We tried to approach things differently to other expeditions I had been part of, and a professional standard was set on all training. This style of preparation was boosted even further when we began working with Leeds Metropolitan University, which not only offered us a degree of financial support but also became our closest expedition partner. Bringing expertise in nutrition, physiology, and psychology, the university took our training to new levels and became heavily committed to supporting us to reach our goal, as well as carrying out some valuable research into new areas for themselves. The partnership

The North Face of Everest at sunset.

was rewarding for all involved and set a new gold standard for expedition preparation.

During this phase, roles and responsibilities were handed out and I had the chance to assess each person's suitability for the project. In addition, we planned weekends with families and social events, ensuring a well-bonded and fully committed team. It was during this phase that I started to get to know people well and identify my lieutenants whom I could rely upon to help maintain direction, offer advice, and steer the ship in the right direction. This built a better bond with me and made those people feel a big part of the decision-making process. I also canvassed thoughts of all team members to see whom they enjoyed working with. When the time came to select my team, the decisions were not easy. By this time everyone had become incredibly passionate about the expedition and wanted to be included, so the announcement of the team was going to be emotional. I phoned

Dave Bunting at Camp 1 at 5,800 metres (19,030 ft) on Everest.

every member myself once we had made the final decisions, dealing with the disappointments first and then the celebrations.

With the selection behind me and the high-performing team on the start line, a series of training and planning meets filled 2005 and early 2006, along with numerous media opportunities supported by the army, which had come to recognise that the expedition was something quite special. We could not have been given more support, and though all team members continued their full-time jobs, the encouragement for our expedition was outstanding and came from all levels of the army, including the very top.

We departed on the expedition in March 2006 and I began the most amazing journey of my life, leading this superb and highly trained team on a dream route on the highest mountain on earth.

The journey from Derbyshire to Everest had taken 18 busy years from that first experience

Team member arriving back at Camp 2 (6,400 metres [21,000 ft]) on Everest with the summit in the background.

on the Pennine Way. The long learning period suited me, allowing my methodical nature to gain the required knowledge, skills, and confidence to undertake such a big challenge. I felt fully prepared with a quality team around me, and we had placed a large emphasis on picking the right group of people to face this ultimate goal.

As they say, it's history now, and as I reflect back on this once-in-a-lifetime trip, I have no regrets. We were unable to make the summit of the mountain and had to retreat with dignity after the avalanche danger at 8,200 metres (26,900 ft) became so overwhelming that I refused to allow any of the team members to venture back into the Hornbein Couloir area where the worst danger lay.

However, I do not look back at this experience as a failure but as a great success. If I were to write down the positives gained from this expedition, the list would be as high as the mountain itself, whereas the negatives would have only one item on the list.

For me, it is the quality of the journey that counts on every single expedition and the return of each and every team member in good health to enjoy the memories and be able to share the experiences with others. My expedition experiences, particularly my 10 trips to the Himalayas, have created the core of my development in life and I would not change the outcome of any of them. Each was a huge learning experience for the next exciting venture, whether we stood on the summit or not.

KEY IDEAS

▸ *Take every opportunity.* Life is made for living, so don't let opportunities to gain valuable experience pass you by.

▸ *Develop your experience progressively.* Too many people try to run before they can walk, and this will lead to being easily put off or to accidents. Building blocks are the secret to creating a platform to secure your development.

▸ *Allow time to prepare and plan.* Leave no stone unturned when planning expeditions. It's better to train and prepare in the

Guy Homan and Paul Chiddle at Everest Camp 5 at 8,000 metres (26,245 ft), waiting to set out for the summit. Both were in excellent physical and mental shape, but the stress of functioning at this altitude is clear in their faces.

comforts and safety of the preexpedition phase than to try to deal with problems when you are there. Meticulous, detailed planning takes time, so start early.

▸ *Validate your development by gaining qualifications along the way.* It is important to confirm you are doing things right, and by undergoing qualifications you can monitor safe progress. I have a number of climbing friends who have amassed a vast amount of experience in the big mountains, and later in life they regret that not having gained qualifications stands in the way of leading their own simple activities with groups.

▸ *Test yourself.* It is important to put yourself under some pressure to develop yourself in life. Staying in your comfort zone will never allow you to enjoy the possibilities that are at your fingertips.

▸ *When setting up an expedition, take the time to select your team.* The success of any expedition lies with how good your team is, and taking a methodical, well-considered approach to selecting each member can pay dividends in the long run.

▸ *It's all about the journey!* It's no good reaching your goal if the trip along the way has not been challenging, rewarding, and enjoyable. Too many people focus on the goal, and considering that the goal is usually minutes within any length of expedition, it seems foolish to not enjoy the whole experience.

PLANNING
AND
TEAM SELECTION

CHAPTER
1
Logistics and Planning

Pete Longbottom

Amateurs talk about tactics, but professionals study logistics.

General R.H. Barrow,
U.S. Marine Corps, 1980

One wet spring day in 2003, I received a phone call from a guy whom I'd heard of by reputation but never met. He had acquired my number from a mutual friend, and in the course of the following 15 minutes, he put forward a proposition. He painted a picture of high mountain peaks in faraway places with long, sometimes technical routes. There was no doubt that the images were appealing. As a mountaineer, I wanted to be part of this vision. I clearly remember wondering how I was going to be able to wangle the 3 months required for the trip, time I would need to have off work. Worse than this, I had trouble with my knees. Too many years of carrying heavy loads in arduous terrain and too many skiing trips had taken their toll. I was simply not capable of fulfilling the physically demanding role that I was being invited to accept. I had no choice but to decline. 'But . . . ,' I heard myself saying, and it was a very big *but*, "if you need a base camp manager . . .' I was also going to offer my services to one of the other two development teams, but I didn't have chance to speak another word. It was already a done deal—my fate was sealed.

The caller was Dave Bunting, the mutual friend John Doyle, and the audacious undertaking was Everest West Ridge from the Tibetan side (the north). Little did I realise that on that typically British, miserable autumn day, I had let myself in for four of the most frenetic but ultimately most satisfying, rewarding, and unforgettable years of my life. In becoming the baseman, I had effectively forgone my beloved climbing. At that moment, I had given up that rare and privileged possibility of standing in the only place on the planet where every other earthly thing lies beneath you—the summit of Mount Everest. The only heights I could reach now were personal achievements associated with doing the best one can do in one's job. This led me to another realisation: I had never been on an expedition anywhere near as large as this before. I had never even been a base camp manager before. What did a base camp manager do?

Despite these obvious shortcomings, I did have a solid background in climbing and mountaineering, and at the time of asking, I had served with the British Army for over 20 years. Mountaineering, logistics, and planning were what I had spent an awful lot of my time doing. Furthermore, I was in a fortunate position of drawing on 50 years of British Services mountaineering experience. This meant that despite my lack of experience, I had a good knowledge base to draw from.

Some of the ideas I put forward here are those of my predecessors in British Services expeditions. Some of the ideas I have absorbed from 20 years of work in an organisation that has to get planning and logistics right as an absolute imperative. Some of the ideas came from the Everest West Ridge team members. Everyone had input at some level.

This process was an enormous team effort. The team included members far beyond the

20 climbers. Many of this extended team never even left Britain. In some ways, dealing with the extended team was as rewarding as any other area of my responsibility. It showed me just how big our expedition was. Although I rarely mention it, a large part of this chapter is about the extended team away from the climbing team. It was these silent team members who enabled me to deliver those 70 days in Tibet. For all of us, this trip was the most important thing in our lives at that time, and we all were united in the hope that some of the 20 would stand on top of the world in early summer 2006.

My brief was to produce a chapter on expedition planning and logistics, specifically how they become crucial in enabling an expedition to achieve its aim—in other words, how they enable team performance. Though I draw heavily on the Everest West Ridge expedition as my example, the principles, processes, procedures, and practices are relevant to any expedition of any size. The core of this chapter is the planning that goes into delivering those logistics. This planning is closely associated with other aspects of expedition planning, such as team selection, training and command, and decision-making processes. However, these areas are detailed in other chapters and so I have made a conscious effort to avoid overlapping into them, although at some stages, it is simply not possible to avoid doing so. I make no apologies for this encroachment; in fact, it demonstrates two key aspects of logistics. First, logistics is at the heart of expeditionary planning. It is simply impossible to separate it from any key area because it is a fundamental component. Second, it demonstrates the level of cooperation that is required to make an expedition work. No element can stand alone; each is dependent on every other. This close cooperation is how an expedition develops strength.

We were a British Army expedition. Therefore, all of our team thought in military terms. A large part of the presentation of this chapter is based on this military background, and some of the terminology is obviously military. I feel this is appropriate because it is how we actually thought whilst planning this expedition, but more important, it is a proven system. The opening quote demonstrates this—if you look through any source of quotes about military strategy, the same theme is continually repeated. The military is an expeditionary logistics machine.

This chapter is an account of the experience I gained on our expedition through my role of being the base camp manager on Everest West Ridge in 2006. I hope this information is enlightening for any person undertaking any type of expedition of any size.

IMPORTANCE OF LOGISTICS

Before it is possible to detail exactly how we accomplished our logistical plan, it is worthwhile to consider the role of logistics in enabling an expedition. Again, as mentioned, even though our expedition was a reasonably large affair set in the Himalayas, the ideas that I will discuss are applicable to all types of expeditions in all environments.

For anyone undertaking an expedition at any level, logistics should be considered at the very onset of planning. It develops hand in glove with all other aspects of expeditionary planning. Every major decision has an impact on the logistics plan. For example, stating intent to get one extra person to the top of Mount Everest, which is at the top of an exponential pyramid of logistics, is not as easy as adding one to all the requirements. It is a complex power function. Changes that seem small can have a large effect on the logistics of big expeditions. For this reason, the logistics management and the overall expedition management team work closely together. Indeed, in some expeditions, one person will fulfil both functions. We were unusual in that our expedition did not use this approach.

On a low-level expedition, good logistics will make the trip more cost effective, more efficient, and more enjoyable for the participants. At the higher end of expeditionary activity, logistics takes on a strategic importance. Good logistics becomes critical to achieving success. Cost effectiveness, efficiency, safety, and enjoyment have serious logistical consequences on such expeditions—failure to deliver in any one of these areas could lead to overall failure. Therefore, logistics comprises two components. On the one hand, it deals with real items or kit: equipment, clothing, vehicles, food, toilet paper, transport, freight, and every other physical element of an expedition and the means of delivering it. On the other hand, it deals with people. The whole point of logistics is to provide these physical items to satisfy people's needs. Logistics is about helping people to do something. Poor logistics may have a detrimental effect on the morale of participants and their ability to perform. In turn, this will have a detrimental effect on the expedition. The maintenance of morale becomes a logistical effort. To deliver these physical and personal components in an appropriately integrated function, therefore, defines the overall logistics capability that is required. The job of the logistics manager is to deliver this capability to the expedition in a coherent and effective way—to provide the conditions that allow the team to perform.

It is useful to consider some guiding principles. They act as a reminder so that effort is not wasted in fruitless areas or isolated avenues. They are the checks and balances of logistical planning. Every decision, change, or idea should be judged against these principles to ensure that the criteria of the principles are met. They also act as a reminder that at the base of every element of an expedition, there should be an efficiency of effort. For those with an extensive familiarity with logistics, these principles become second nature—often, they are simply gut feelings. For those who are still developing that level of experience, I advise continually thinking in terms of the following.

Planning Planning is the most crucial principle of expeditionary logistics. Complete plans must be made to cover all likely courses of events. Furthermore, contingency plans should be made for the most likely problems, such as excessively inclement weather. Planning effort should be given to what-if questions. What if we lose a camp through bad weather? What if a team becomes stranded at a camp for more than a couple of days? The type of expedition will determine these questions. Whatever the expedition, the most likely what-ifs need contingency plans and preparations. Finally, plan-

Pre-expedition planning meeting.

ning should include numerous decision points that act as balances against possible drift. This keeps the expedition streamlined, promotes momentum, and ensures good anticipation. To place the importance of this planning element in context, the total duration of our expedition was 4 years from the moment of conception to the completion of the expedition itself. By far the greatest time was spent on planning and preparation—3 years.

Expediency The word *expedition* derives from the Latin *expeditus* (unimpeded). In its English verb form, *expedite*, it simply means to process a task in a quick and efficient fashion. At the heart of an expedition is an ethos of expediency—fulfilling the logistics efficiently with as little fuss as possible. I used to teach ski mountaineering, and I conveyed this principle in terms of energy conservation. Even though an expedition is a different beast to a ski tour, the same ideas are applicable here. They are the five Es of energy conservation:

1. *Economy.* This is the correct amount of effort without duplication or waste.

Exactly the correct amount of resources is used to achieve the aim. It is important not to overly burden an expedition with a massive resource schedule, most of which will never be used.

2. *Efficiency.* For big expeditions, enormous quantities of equipment and resources may be required. Additionally, the systems for deploying and managing these resources may be complex. For this reason, every resource and the way it is used must produce the maximum positive impact possible. Resources that are used infrequently, such as luxuries, will burden the expedition and make logistical management slow and unresponsive.

3. *Effort.* There is no doubt that an expedition such as the one we undertook requires an enormous amount of effort. Four years of effort went into ours, but *where* this effort was made was also critical. Pushing hard at the wrong time can lead to an overly exhausted logistical effort and an exhausted team. Therefore, knowing when to push hard, when to coast, and when to relax becomes crucial in executing expedition logistics.

4. *Easy.* Expeditions are not supposed to be easy. They often deliberately seek out the most difficult terrain in the most difficult environments. However, there is no point in making a difficult situation worse. So long as the expedition stays within the bounds of the style, ethics, route, and so on, it should aim to make each individual element within the expedition as easy as possible.

5. *Effective.* There has to be a reason for every logistics effort, and this reason has to promote the success of the expedition or enable an objective or goal that will promote overall success. There is no point in pushing many resources at an effort that will have negligible positive impact on the expedition. Every resource and the way it is used must have an effective impact on the progression of the expedition towards its conclusion.

Simplicity In times of stress or difficult conditions, a simple logistics plan is more likely to survive than a complex one. Because expeditions seek out these very conditions, simplicity makes sense. In project management terms, this simplicity can be achieved by identifying a critical path with as few links as possible. Effort should be made to achieve this critical path.

Teamwork An expedition is a complicated project. It is impossible for one person to take responsibility for it all. Developing a good team with a good work ethic and good lines of communication is essential.

Flexibility Despite the best planning, things will not always develop in the way that they were envisaged. For this reason, a flexible approach to the management of logistical effort is required. The ability to anticipate and react to situations in an appropriate and timely fashion is essential.

Team planning meet at Tilman's Base Camp on Everest.

These principles make it abundantly clear that it is not only impossible to produce a logistics capability that provides for every eventuality, but it is counterproductive and undesirable to even try to do so. For this reason, there is an element of risk involved with every logistical and planning decision. A balance must exist that allows logistics to be robust enough to be effective yet not so cumbersome that it becomes an uneconomical burden. Erring too far in either direction places an expedition at risk. Achieving a good balance reduces overall risk of failure. The primary responsibility of the planning and logistics team is to achieve and maintain this balance. The logistics manager must control this balance, especially when responsibility is devolved to area or function managers. It is easy to become so engrossed in one's own responsibility that one forgets the overall picture.

ROLE OF LOGISTICS IN THE EXPEDITION

To understand how logistics fits into the expedition, it is necessary to discuss where it lies in the higher management functions. On a complicated expedition such as ours, it is impossible for one person to deal with every area. Therefore, large expeditions are often divided into hierarchical areas or functions. In our case, this hierarchy enabled the overall capability of the expedition. Each hierarchical function had a manager who was responsible for delivering that function to the expedition. Figure 1.1 shows how the logistical element fitted in with the overall expedition hierarchy. The whole logistics effort was too large for one person to manage, so we divided this effort further into subfunctions. Figure 1.2 shows how these individual areas were linked.

The lines of communication for our expedition were extensive. Logistics had a central role within the expedition hierarchy and for those who were delivering the details that would make the expedition work. Just about every decision made in any of the other functions and areas influenced the logistics plan. As such, it is fundamental to expedition success to get logistics right. It is also important to ensure that the team works together efficiently. Finally, expeditions by nature involve a group of people from various occupations and geographic locations. Most of the necessary teamwork has to be conducted at a distance. We rarely met as an entire team during the preparation phase of the expedition,

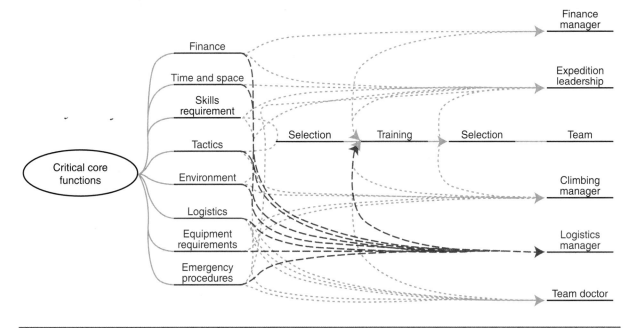

Figure 1.1 Expedition management hierarchy—functional responsibilities.

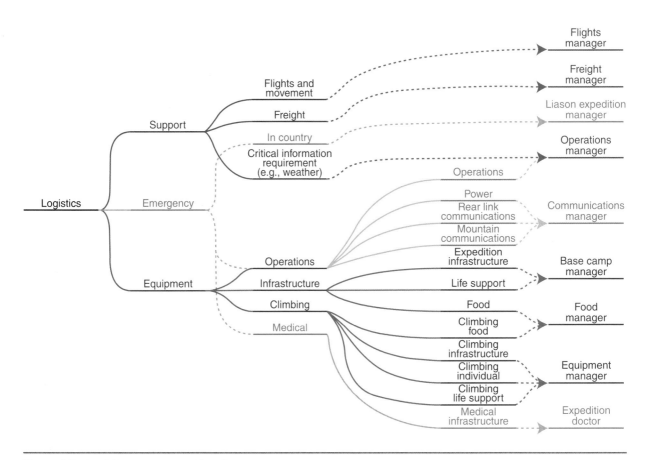

Figure 1.2 Logistics management functions.

and therefore communicating intent to the team became a serious issue.

Logistics should be considered as a series of bases and dumps placed in such a way as to enable the overall effort of the expedition. Careful consideration should be made as to where logistical command and control should sit amongst these operational bases during various expedition phases. This is likely to vary during the course of the expedition.

For our expedition, we had two strategic bases—one in the United Kingdom, where we prepared and deployed all-out logistical effort, and one in Nepal, where all the logistical effort was consolidated in theatre. Then, we established three operational bases—the camp where vehicle transport terminated (Road Head Camp, or RHC), the location where the yak lift had to stop (Tilman's Camp, or TC), and the camp where the heavy portage (mostly Sherpas) had to stop (Camp 1 at the foot of the mountain, where the climbing began). Resources were then deployed in a set order through the operational

bases to allow the tactical effort of climbing the mountain to begin without pause. There were an additional four tactical camps.

SUSTAINABILITY

In the last section, I mentioned that the whole point of logistics is to provide resources for people's needs. In this section, I will develop this theme further. In particular, I am going to develop the idea of sustainability, which is the provision and delivery of resources over a given time in order to achieve the aim of the expedition. A number of factors can influence the sustainability of an expedition, including the following.

Environmental Attrition Expeditions by their nature seek out those areas where environments tend to be extreme. The rate of attrition for materials, resources, and people can be immense. The ability to sustain an expedition through environmental hardship is essential to achieve success.

Tilman's Camp on Everest West Ridge, 2006.

Rates of Consumption and Expenditure These rates are the demand on the logistics framework. However, consumption rates are affected by the environment. As an example, take the effect of altitude on an Everest expedition. In this extremely harsh environment, more calories are required just to sustain normal performance, and in the rarefied air, more fuel is required just to boil a given volume of water. The demand during an expedition can vary enormously to that of normal life. Estimating this demand, therefore, is a primary task to achieve sustainability.

Equipment and Resource Availability An expedition should have all the infrastructure resources available to achieve the overall objective. However, delivering those resources at the right time and in the correct order is critical to sustaining expedition momentum. The team driving the expedition forward must be sustained with a continuous flow of resources. Failure to meet demand means the expedition stops.

Equipment Utility, Redundancy, Regeneration, and Self-Help Every resource is an asset to the expedition, but it is also a liability.

It has to be transported by something or someone, and transport is a limitation. Therefore, each resource should be assessed for utility. Specialised equipment and resources should be minimised as much as is possible without compromising the expedition. However, in some areas they are a necessity, such as certain medical equipment and oxygen. In contrast, some resource items can fulfil multiple functions. (A similar ethos can be extended to expedition team members, too.) Furthermore, once a resource has fulfilled its intended function, it should be available to be redeployed in some other logistical effort. We used the tents from our development team (after its expedition was complete) to establish Camp 1. Additionally, an expedition should have the capability to repair damaged resources (to a certain degree) and put them back into service quickly.

Quantifying Equipment and Resources

One of the fundamental questions early in the planning phase of an expedition is how many equipment items and consumable resources will be required and for how long. Being able to deliver these resources at the correct time and at the correct levels will significantly enhance the probability of achieving the objectives of an expedition.

Quantifying resources is an essential aim of the planning phase, and it cannot be accurately completed until most of the other expedition parameters have been set. Determining an exact quantity of all our resources, especially consumables, took 1,000 hours of work (by two people at about 500 hours each) over 2 years. Even then we got some things wrong, but generally, this amount of preparation paid enormous dividends to the sustainability of the expedition.

To quantify the resources requirement of an expedition like ours, one must answer four questions:

1. *Where are the resources needed—what is their destination?* Environments change demand. They also change the equipment required simply to exist and operate there. High-level mountains are extremely hostile environments, and the equipment and resources of an expedition must take this into account.

2. *What is the demand for these resources?* In its simplest terms, demand is the rate of consumption or the utilisation of resources. However, demand is not usually uniform. It is the product of three demand profiles: The steady state is the uniform consumption of a resource, cyclic demand is a predictable demand over time such as team rotation through camps, and surge demand is caused by unpredictability of the environment or other factors.

3. *How far is it to get the resources to the destination—what is the distance?* Distance should be considered not in terms of actual distance but as a level of effort required to move resources around. Actual distances on a high mountain may be only a few hundred metres, but the level of effort required to move resources these distances is comparatively large.

4. *How long will the demand be—what is the duration?* When considered with demand, the duration of effort will provide the overall volume of resources to be used.

The volume is the product of rate of consumption and duration. The volume of sustainability can be represented in three ways depending on the resource:

▸ *Days of supply (DOS):* This represents the volume of consumption of nonhuman assets, such as vehicles or generators.

▸ *Man days (MD):* This is the volume of consumption of people and includes food, water, and fuel (for cooking).

▸ *Infrastructure supplies:* These are all nonconsumable resources that are required to provide the life-support and resource framework. It includes technical equipment, accommodation, and operational resources.

Part of the sustainment effort involves creating a resupply system and quantifying resources. We used two methods on our expedition:

▸ *Just in case (JIC):* This is a system where resupply is held close to where it is needed. It is very responsive but may slow the overall effort because it requires additional effort to transport.

▸ *Just in time (JIT):* This is a system where resupply is held to the rear in operational bases. It is slower to respond but requires less logistical effort to maintain.

For our expedition, we used a hybrid system where a first line of resupply was held JIC on the mountain itself, but the majority of resupply was held at RHC on a JIT basis.

Creating a Sustainability Statement

Once sustainability has been quantified, it needs to be expressed to the relevant managers so that they can commence the practical process of securing resources. They need a directive that states what the expedition requires in terms of equipment, consumable items, and other materials. For this step, I produced a sustainability statement. Following are the headings I used for this statement along with an explanation of what each directed the team to deliver. This statement gave my team the parameters needed to do the job.

General

These areas dictated volumes (demand × duration) and infrastructure requirements:

▸ *General statement.* Summarised how many DOS and MDs were required for the three teams.

▸ *Rations.* A breakdown of MDs for various phases of the expedition was required because different foods were consumed at different stages and the food manager needed to know how much was required at each stage.

▸ *Oxygen.* Referred to the total MDs required for this specialist high-altitude consumable.

▸ *Fuel.* Fuel had two elements. First, it had a DOS element for infrastructure requirements such as group cooking and generator power. Additionally, it had an MD element for individual climbing needs.

▸ *High-altitude equipment.* Quantified how many high camps were required, what each contained, and how many anchors and metres of fixed rope were required to connect them.

▸ *Medical and environmental health.* Included DOS of general medical requirement and MD for individual requirements.

▸ *Supply systems.* Described how I would hold resupplies in reserve. In our case, I opted for leaving them at the first operational base and operated a JIT resupply system—that is, if the team needed supplies, we fetched them.

▸ *Tentage.* Included the tent requirement for every base or camp and who was to provide it (we had an in-country provider who facilitated some resources at our operational bases).

Sustainability Planning Parameters

These areas gave guidance on how various factors would affect the expedition:

▸ *Environment.* Detailed the facts about the environment and how it would affect the logistical effort of the expedition.

▸ *Duration and activity levels.* Expressed the anticipated ratio of work to rest for the total duration of the expedition.

▸ *Essential equipment.* Listed in order of priority all equipment and resources that were critical to the success of the expedition.

▸ *Attrition.* Detailed which equipment and resources were likely to suffer greatest attrition rates and how this would be dealt with.

Good logistics promote morale, and high morale promotes success. It is worth emphasising once more that ultimately, it is people who make an expedition a success. Logistics has a key role in setting the conditions that sustain people and enable them to perform. The logistics effort is essential for success.

PLANNING

By now it should be clear that in order to produce a sound logistics platform for a complicated expedition, an enormous planning effort is required. Most of the 4 years spent getting ready for the Everest West Ridge expedition were taken up by planning and preparation. This planning phase is the subject of this section. I will use our expedition as a model unless otherwise stated.

Developing the Idea and Building the Team

It is easy to state an intention to organise a major expedition. However, if one is serious, one needs to begin developing details very early. Usually, these details will have developed to a certain degree before the intention is even made public—someone probably has been mulling over the expedition as a pet project. This was the case with our expedition, where Dave Bunting had been doing just this, first alone and then with John Doyle. Dave's vision and John's additional details set the foundation for what was to become the 2006 Everest West Ridge expedition.

At some stage, providing details will become too much for the initial visionary to sustain. As the idea develops, the core team must develop to maintain momentum. Over a few months, Dave built a core team that encompassed the following roles:

▸ *Expedition leaders.* Roles included planning, operations, liaison, travel, marketing, selection, coordination, command and control, and leadership.

▸ *Finance manager.* Roles included sponsorship, marketing, insurance, budgeting, and paying bills.

▸ *Climbing manager.* Roles included subject-matter expertise, planning, environmental requirements, training, and selection.

▸ *Logistics manager.* Roles included planning, logistics, equipment and resources, communications, power, freight, and liaison.

These people formed the core team. Over time as the team took shape and was finalised, this hierarchy developed into the expedition establishment seen previously in figures 1.1 and 1.2 on pages 23 and 24. The core team developed ideas in the following key areas that helped set the scope of the expedition.

Expedition Aim   The details of this area were critical. They included ascent from which side (Tibet or Nepal), exact route, style of climb, with or without oxygen, pre- or postmonsoon season, and how many people we intended to summit.

Cost   Expeditions are enormously expensive. Those that are as large as ours was are far too expensive for the entire cost to be borne by the participants. Of course, we all contributed. We also received funding from a number of self-sustaining military organisations (such as the Army Mountaineering Association). However, the vast majority of funding for the expedition had to come from private sources—through sponsorship.

Team Composition   The size, composition, and experience of the team had to be decided, as did the Sherpa support requirement. The desired number of summiteers was critical. Every additional summiteer would exponentially increase the base of the logistics pyramid. Finally, we had to decide whether this would be a stand-alone expedition (that is, we provided everything ourselves) or whether we would enlist the assistance of a trekking facilitator to get the expedition to the climbing. In the end, we used Jagged Globe as a facilitator. They also facilitated our sponsors' visiting team.

Liaison   At an early stage, Dave decided that we would ascend from the north—Tibet. This presented host-nation issues that required liaison and communication.

Subject-Matter Expertise and Research
This was the largest information requirement. Of course, we had a core of expertise ourselves; however, only one of the climbing team and three of the film production team had been on Everest before. Only one (a climbing partner for one of the cameramen) had been on the route before. Therefore, we had to research almost every aspect of planning for the route. We also enlisted the help of diverse experts (mostly through sponsorship) to provide subject-matter expertise in every field, from mountaineering to training to dietary needs. This is how we became involved with Leeds Metropolitan University, which has ultimately led to the production of this book.

Emergency Procedures   We had to plan for every conceivable eventuality, and accidents and emergencies were obviously an important consideration. Not only did these include trauma and clinical medicine on the mountain, but also evacuation and repatriation processes. Fortunately, through a combination of excellent preparation, training, and good judgement, the expedition doctor was never truly called upon. This suited him entirely—he spent the whole trip demonstrating to the world just how mad he was!

EWR 2006 doctor in a reconstruction of a famous Mallory photograph from Everest.

The development of some of these conceptual ideas is the responsibility of other chapters. From here, I will only demonstrate how we developed those ideas that led to the climbing plan and the logistics that fell out from that. However, it is worth reiterating that to move forward with the logistics planning, I needed detailed information on every one of these key areas.

Developing Your Logistics Plan

Once you've built your team and determined the key ideas of your expedition, it's time to start developing your logistics plan. Our expedition was fortunate in that the deputy leader, Dave Wilson, had an analytical, engineering background and was one of the most thorough planners I know. We were also fortunate in inheriting a proven planning tool from Merion Bridges (also an engineer) that had an established track record in mountain logistics. Both of these people were as much responsible for the logistics plan as I was—without them, I may never have developed such a robust logistics

plan. Our planning process followed a workflow, as described next.

Estimating the Logistical Requirement This process began immediately—about 3.5 years out. All the critical information mentioned previously was factored into an estimate process balanced against a set of constraints. This led to a number of possible courses, which were reviewed individually before elimination led to a coherent plan. Figure 1.3 provides a diagram of this process. Possible courses included various forms of alpine style versus siege style and launching from Tibet versus from Nepal. In the end, we opted for a large-scale, siege-style expedition, with oxygen, launching from Tibet.

Logistics Support Plan This process began about 3 years out. It was the fundamental tool used to quantify the total resources above TC. It included the four Ds mentioned in the logistics section of this chapter—destination, demand, distance, and duration. This planning process required a great deal of effort, and it resulted in the total volume of equipment and resources represented as loads (a load being

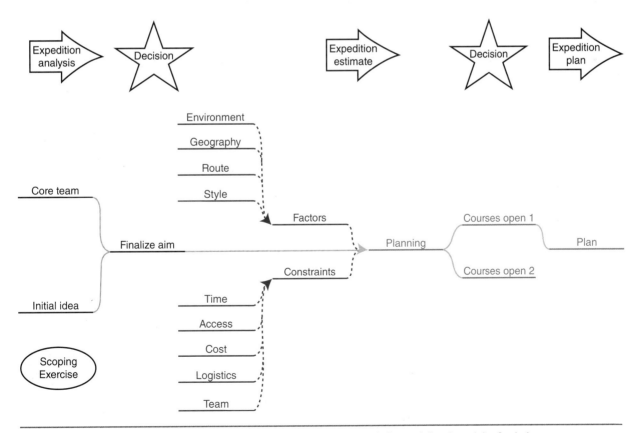

Figure 1.3 The process by which Everest West Ridge 2006 took the initial idea and developed the final plan.

the amount a climber could carry) that must be transported to each camp. Every item carried up the mountain was weighed. Therefore, the total resources in-loaded was divided by the amount a climber could carry to give the number of loads required. Additionally, it provided the total logistical effort (represented in MDs) required to transport this demand. If the number of MDs of effort surpassed the number available, the plan could not work. Therefore, the aim was to achieve the total effort in about two-thirds the available MDs. The remaining third became the reserve for bad weather and other issues leading to lost days of effort. The logistics support plan was developed using a single spreadsheet that is too large to demonstrate here. However, figure 1.4 illustrates how the spreadsheet worked.

Each camp had a table similar to that shown in figure 1.4. The variable factor was supply and demand. In-loading stores also required the consumption of other stores (food and fuel). Therefore, this model was developed to assist in achieving the most efficient in-load profile.

The camp location gives details of the camp and how many climbers it should be able to accommodate. The route-making column details every item of equipment that must be in-loaded to establish the camp and develop the next part of the route—this is consumption neutral. The transit–living column details work that is carried out at the camp—this is a net consumer. The in-loading column shows additional loads to completely stock the camp to enable the next level of development. It is a consumer and supplier, but it has to be a net supplier.

If the net-supplying element falls below the consumption rates of the transit–living element, then the logistics plan will fail. The final column then gives a running total of loads that must be in-loaded and levels of effort to achieve this.

Date	Day	R-H Camp			Tilman's				Camp 1					Camp 2					Camp 3					Camp 4					
		Load	Pax	MVT	Load in	Total loads	Man days	Load bal	Load in	Total loads in	Used/Consumed	Man days	Load bal	Load in	Total loads in	Used/Consumed	Man days	Load bal	Load in	Total loads in	Used/Consumed	Man days	Load bal	Load in	Total loads in	Used/Consumed	Man days	Load bal	MN
16-Apr-06	26					26	LLS		10	126			94	6	18			18											
17-Apr-06	27					18	LLS		10	136	0.5	6	97.5	6	24	0.5	6	16.5		*									
18-Apr-06	28					14	LLS		10	146	1	12	94.5	12	36	0.5	6	28		0									
19-Apr-06	29						LLS		4	150	1.5	18	79	18	54	0.5	6	33.5	12	12			12						
20-Apr-06	30					14				146	1.5	18	77.5		36			33.5		12			12						
21-Apr-06	31					26				146		6	77.5		36			33.5		12			12						
22-Apr-06	32					22				146	0.5	6	77		36			33.5		12			12						

*Note: C2 balance reduced by 7 loads used for fixing to C3.

Figure 1.4 Sample element of the logistics support plan (A, B, C, and D refer to climbing teams).

Climbing-Movement Plan   Once we established how many loads needed to be in-loaded to each camp, a movement plan was required to achieve this task. This movement plan was produced concurrently with the logistics support plan and began about 3 years out. The two plans had to be continually cross-referenced to ensure that one was not getting out of proportion with the other. Adding a single extra team in a camp would throw out the figures in the logistics support plan. For this reason, a change in one had to be reflected by appropriate changes in the other. The expedition was based on four teams, each team comprising four expedition members and two Sherpas. Teams worked on a rotation, including the preparing team, supporting team, developing team, and resting team. This equated to a level of effort of about 4 to 1 (working to resting). Therefore, above Camp 1, each team could carry six loads. A team in a camp for one night consumed about half a load. From this, it was possible to produce simple formulas that would track the net accumulation of loads in each camp. These planning figures were based on what we anticipated a team member could carry—around 11 kilograms (24 lb). The Sherpas could carry significantly more than this amount. This provided a buffer against performance variables, such as fatigue.

Using this approach, the route was developed with a pyramid of logistics. The foundation at Camp 1 was extensive, with each subsequent camp requiring fewer in-loads. The top camp—Camp 5—required only one initial in-load to establish it. The summit team then carried all consumables from Camp 4.

To demonstrate how this planning process worked, consider the plan for 17 April (see figure 1.4). (It is important to realise that this is not actually what happened on 17 April. It is purely a tool.

Everest West Ridge 2006 Sherpas.

The most it can tell us about 17 April is where we wanted to be at that time. When 17 April arrived, we could see whether we were ahead or behind schedule.) Team C is in C1 (Camp 1) and is in-loading into C2, and team B is in C2 developing towards C3. Team C in-loads 6 loads to C2 (first figure in C2—load-in column). This increases the total in to 24 (from 18 on the previous day). However, team B consumes half a load that day, working from C2 to C3. This half-load equates to 6 MDs. The load balance in C2 becomes 24 minus .5 minus the 7 loads team B use to develop the next stage to C3, which equals 16.5. This process is continued throughout the spreadsheet until the summit bids are reached. We also factored in weather days (the hatched areas). These were deliberately placed to account for bad weather or other environmental factors. The total weather days were our best guess based on previous experience. Reading down each column gives the totals for that camp. Reading left to right, C1 will have greater totals than C5. This is evidence of the logistics pyramid that was built.

Load-Movement Plan   This plan began about 6 months out. The load-movement plan can best be described as the desired order of dispatch of loads. It was based on predicted (steady-state and cyclic) demand. To ensure that loads were dispatched in the correct order, a spreadsheet was developed that charted load destination extrapolated against dispatch.

Load-Tracking Plan   This plan was developed in the final month and a half before departure. It was a process for monitoring where loads were and whether they were at their final destination. It was based on reporting the load numbers to the base camp and checking against the predetermined load-movement plan.

Preparation Process

Whilst producing the planning work, I was also busy receiving all the equipment and resources. Although this was a straightforward process of receipt, unpack, account, and repack in a way that allowed ease of freighting and management on the mountain, it was the most time-consuming aspect of the whole expedition. We had a lot of equipment to freight and transport

to RHC—13 metric tonnes (14 short tonnes), including a Jagged Globe package. The aim of this phase was to arrange the logistics in a fashion that promoted efficiency on the expedition. RHC is at 5,000 metres (16,405 feet). Even when acclimatised, working on logistics here was hard work. For this reason, I wanted to complete as much preparation ahead of time as possible to minimise this effort. The following preparations were made in the United Kingdom; all that was required in Tibet was ensuring that loads were dispatched in the correct order.

▸ *Individual issue.* A great deal of personal equipment was provided by sponsors (especially the high-altitude clothing). It was important that the team members had access to this equipment prior to deployment to allow issues to be resolved more efficiently.

▸ *Freight.* Ten metric tonnes (11 short tonnes) of freight left the United Kingdom. Every container (barrel) had to be individually

Packing the kit in the UK.

The barrels containing the kit at Road Head Camp

packed and manifested, and a complete freight manifest had to be produced. This included the anticipated recovery plan for equipment that needed to be returned (about half the outgoing freight).

▸ *Yak transportation.* The equipment deployed above RHC had to be transported by yak. The limit of yak portage is 40 kilograms (88 lb). Therefore, individual bundles or barrels had to be exactly 20 kilograms (44 lb) each, two barrels per yak. If they weighed any more, the yak herders would have refused them; if they weighed less, we would have lost valuable yak capacity to fresh air.

▸ *Desired load order of dispatch.* From the RHC base, I developed a desired order of dispatch for the barrels to be moved to TC and for each load to be dispatched to the mountain. Loads were contained in barrels numbered for each camp (C1 all began with 1, C2 began with 2, and so on). This meant that load organisation was possible without having to open too many barrels at once.

▸ *Load numbers.* Each load was given a load number from the load-movement plan that allowed it to be tracked. The numbers followed the numbering system mentioned previously.

Yak transportation between Road Head Camp and Tilman's Camp.

Key Elements of the Everest West Ridge 2006 Expedition

I would like to detail some key elements of the plan and logistics framework that affected the way we operated on our expedition. Did our preparation have a positive impact on the expedition, and were there areas where we were not prepared?

Momentum

The team was extremely well prepared for the expedition, from individual physical performance to the way that Dave Bunting led the team. Every climber on the expedition ascended to at least Camp 4—over 7,500 metres (24,605 ft), and many went above this point. The momentum of the team was incredible. By the time I had dispatched the last yak from RHC to TC, the team had already established Camp 1. This momentum enormously stretched our ability to keep up with demand. However, our system for deployment was simple, flexible, and robust. A less prepared effort could have easily fallen down, and this would have lost the momentum that the climbers were developing.

Logistics Command

Logistics command became a real issue for me. The distance from RHC to TC was 8 kilometres (5 mi), and from TC to Camp 1 it was another 8 kilometres, in combination a day's worth of movement. I had roles to fulfil in each of these locations, some of them concurrently. I needed to be where the main effort was, but often I simply could not be. For this reason, I was reliant on a core of logistically aware team members. In hindsight, with the length of these lines of communication, I ideally needed a second (deputy) logistics manager who, like me, was not part of the climbing team.

Environment

High-altitude mountaineering is a difficult working environment where simply existing is hard work. For this reason, we needed a logistics plan that placed the minimum burden on the team members. This was the main driver during preparation. Even though some loads did not get to the correct places, our logistics platform was flexible enough to accept the changes that were necessary to prevent system failure.

Weather Days

We anticipated a lot of bad weather. We were lucky and only had two incidents of stormy weather. However, both instances led to the situation we were trying to avoid, with teams stranded in camps, consuming stocks and performing no work. The teams stayed for the right operational reasons. However, both occasions had a negative effect on the logistics effort and on team morale. Even though we couldn't know it at the time, the snow that these two storms deposited led to the avalanche conditions that ultimately thwarted our summit attempt.

Load Tracking

Load tracking became my single biggest problem. The problem arose from momentum and the extended lines of communication previously mentioned. As the key dispatch point for all climbing loads was Camp 1, we really required someone to control this. However, the team was busy developing the route and in-loading, and I was needed elsewhere. In the end, a lot of the load tracking was organised by the powerhouse of our load carrying, the Sherpa team. Often, the Sherpa team would respond to lead-team demand and in-load on this basis. From a logistical point of view, this led to deficiencies in critical equipment at critical times. The people who rescued the effort were the Sherpas, making their own superhuman effort in-loading.

Sherpas preparing to load carry on Everest.

Logistics Support Plan and Climbing-Movement Plan

The logistics support and climbing-movement plans were our single most important planning tools, allowing us to predict the demand for equipment, resources, and consumables on the expedition. However, the translation of this plan to reality was different. We had anticipated a smooth cumulative ascent of the route, but we spent far more time on the lower mountain than predicted. This was due to bad weather, all the steep technical climbing, the need to acclimatise, and plain hard work. Camp 1 unintentionally became an operational base, but it was not resourced as such. Camp 2 became an acclimatisation camp and saw more people living there than was anticipated. Finally, Camp 3 became a key logistical node. Once Camp 4 was established, this is where further effort was launched from. The smooth pyramid we had planned changed and became an even effort up to Camp 3, after which a faster, quasi-alpine style was used.

(continued)

Resource Consumption and Availability

The amount of activity from camps 1 through 3 became a major concern. The consumption rates, especially in fuel (gas), were far greater than anticipated. Although we organised a resupply, the consumption rates in this area were balanced by the reduced rates above Camp 3 (due to the more alpine approach). However, it had the potential to jeopardise the expedition. Additionally, the consumption of mountain rations changed with climbers simply selecting from stocks at Camp 3 based on personal preferences, resulting in a logistical waste of effort carrying up rations not consumed.

Finally, the amount of fixed rope and particularly anchors became a concern. A double rope system was employed (to allow two climbers to ascend simultaneously) on the lower section of the route. Additionally, the anticipated spacing of anchors was grossly underestimated. All of the reserve was used. Fortunately, because of the critical nature of the fixed ropes, that reserve was substantial.

Team members load carrying above Tilman's Camp.

APPLICATION TO OTHER EXPEDITIONS

In this chapter I have given some insight into the principles and process of logistics and planning using Everest West Ridge as my example of an expedition. The level of complexity will not be replicated in most expeditions for weekends away or low-level trekking expeditions lasting a week or two. However, due consideration should be given to the elements of logistics and planning, whether the trip involves 2 people or 20, a garage or an aircraft hanger, yaks or mountain bikes, mountains or an ocean.

Logistics is a never-ending cycle. Much of the equipment that we returned was destined to become the foundation of someone else's logistical plan, which brings me to my final thought—my role as base camp manager for the British Army Everest West Ridge 2006 expedition. I had now become part of that experience reservoir that the next base camp manager would want to tap. Therefore, I had a duty to put something back into that system. I had to provide my experiences and lessons identified so that the next poor soul who volunteered by accident would have a starting point.

This chapter is an extension of that responsibility. It is my repayment to the climbing world—the world that gave me the core skills even to be considered for the expedition in the first place. It is also a form of solace for those people with dodgy knees who think that expeditions are past. Beyond the climbing, this is a world that takes you to the places you love and provides a different form of fulfilment. My time as a baseman took me to the very heart of an expedition. For that experience, I thank my dodgy knees.

KEY IDEAS

▶ Logistics and planning are critical for delivering cost effectiveness, efficiency, safety, and enjoyment on expeditions.

▶ Logistics deals with both kit and people.

▶ Planning is crucial in preparation, but flexibility is a key element of good logistics—be prepared for the unexpected to happen, because it will.

▶ Logistics also involves teamwork and relies on effective communication.

▶ Sustainability is a key focus of logistics and planning to facilitate delivery of an expedition.

▶ Supply and demand of kit and other resources are central components of logistics and planning.

▶ Planning permeates all aspects of expedition preparation and delivery.

▶ Monitor resource consumption as the expedition unfolds and build in some contingency plans, allowing for worst-case scenarios.

▶ Recycle as much kit and knowledge as you can; this will assist others with their logistics and planning.

CHAPTER
2
Team Selection

Stevan Kenneth Jackson

Think where man's glory most begins and ends,
And say my glory was I had such friends.

W.B. Yeats

In this chapter I will draw on my four decades of experience as a member, organiser, leader, adviser, and planner of expeditions in an attempt to pass on my knowledge of how to select a team to achieve a particular goal. I will not be prescriptive about what is right or wrong in putting together a team to tackle any particular objective, apart from saying that first, life is too short to go on expedition with people you don't like, and second, if my experience is anything to go by, the friends you make through expeditions will remain friends for life.

I have been fortunate (though fortune favours the brave) to take part in expeditions that have climbed in the United Kingdom, France, Switzerland, Italy, Austria, Germany, Spain, Gibraltar, Norway, Lofoten Islands, Kenya, Tanzania, California, Peru, Bolivia, Brazil, Argentina, Pakistan, Nepal, and Tibet. I conceived, planned, organised, and led most of the expeditions and have always believed that in achieving personal goals, you are only constrained by lack of imagination. I have enjoyed terrific support from the Royal Navy and Royal Marines Mountaineering Club, the Army and Royal Air Force (RAF) Mountaineering Associations, and many brilliant people from all three of those organisations. I have also been involved in the selection process for a large number of expeditions in every role from being an unsuccessful applicant, to being a successful applicant, to being selected as a reserve, to being a selection team member, and ultimately to being chairman of the selection team. I have had my share of successes and disappointments in the selection process and have been involved in pleasing or disappointing a great many aspiring expedition members. But in doing either, I have always tried to be fair and to treat others as I would like to be treated myself.

I invite you to reflect upon the material in this chapter and draw your own conclusions and put them into your own context. But above all else, I would suggest that expeditions are about people and the interactions amongst them. Teams are made up of people, people are all different, and therefore all teams are different and require unique management. People are driven by emotions, and therefore the key to managing people is to understand and manage their emotions effectively. Preparing a team for any expedition will inevitably involve gaining and maintaining hard skills such as climbing, placing fixed ropes, and so on, but it is just as important to help the team bond using fun activities such as 10-pin bowling, paintball, or go-kart racing. It doesn't matter what vehicle is used as long as the aim of bonding the group into a close-knit team is achieved. To do that, you need the correct raw material in your team and the right approach. Hopefully you'll get some ideas of what that might mean from this chapter.

SELECTORS

The Joint Himalayan Committee was the name given in 1947 to the body that was previously known as the Mount Everest Committee. The Joint Himalayan Committee was composed of senior members of the Alpine Club and the Royal Geographical Society and was responsible for organising and financing British attempts on Mount Everest, including the first ascent in 1953. The Joint Himalayan Committee originally selected Eric Shipton as the 1953 Mount Everest expedition leader. Shipton probably knew Mount Everest better than any other Briton at the time, having been on expeditions to the mountain that included Hugh Ruttledge's expeditions in 1933 and 1936. He also led the 1935 Everest expedition, which included a 19-year-old Sherpa Tensing on his first outing, and he led the 1951 expedition that first identified the route up the Khumbu Glacier. However, apparently as a result of his preference for small-scale, lightweight, alpine-style ascents as opposed to military-style siege tactics, the Joint Himalayan Committee decided to replace him with an army officer, Major John Hunt, and the rest, as they say, is history.

Nowadays few expeditions, aside from those mounted by the armed services to the highest and hardest peaks or to particularly remote regions, appoint a higher management committee (HMC). Perhaps the military persists in having an HMC because it has a slightly different agenda to others when it comes to adventurous training, and this needs to be borne in mind. The army objectives of adventurous training are not simply to get to the top of a mountain, for example, but include the development of knowledge, skills, abilities, and attitudes that will enhance operational capability by developing leadership, teamwork, physical fitness, and resilience (moral and physical courage).

Adventurous training is an ideal mechanism for achieving those objectives because aside from the practical, military-related skills that can be learned (e.g., map reading, crossing difficult terrain, operating in challenging conditions), it uncovers the behaviour patterns and interpersonal skills of participants and how they relate to others. In taking risk whilst being challenged and supported, participants can explore their limitations, how they react to others, and how that affects their behaviour. In this way participants can develop increased self-awareness, an important aspect of emotional intelligence and a key component of leadership.

There is also the unavoidable fact that military expeditions are representing their country; whether they like it or not, they are ambassadors for the United Kingdom and the military needs to ensure that an appropriate management structure is in place to avoid any potential embarrassment and that this structure is integral to the team selection process. The HMC will want to ensure that the expedition leader will be capable of realising the aims and objectives of the expedition whilst protecting the reputation of the Armed Forces. I have been on two HMCs, and they work well for the Armed Forces.

If an HMC is going to be used, those who are selected to serve on it should have a reasonable understanding of the activity that is being undertaken. As the top-level committee, they should have a strategic leadership role and should be looking upwards and outwards, whereas the leader and the operational leadership team should be looking downwards and inwards. The leader should be the link between the two, briefing and updating the HMC on a regular basis and taking the committee's direction, guidance, and encouragement back to the leadership team. The HMC needs to be in a position to support the leader in areas such as selecting the team, fund-raising, obtaining necessary diplomatic clearances and permissions, and helping to deal with obstacles in the planning phase.

Additionally, in this age of instant communication, committee members should be adept in areas such as public relations and handling the media, particularly if bad news emerges in preparation for or during the expedition. When the expedition is taking place, the HMC provides the point of contact in the home country in the event that something goes wrong, especially if it becomes newsworthy. Things will inevitably go wrong; it is just a question of the magnitude. To quote Moltke the Elder, 'No battle plan survives contact with enemy,' though Moltke was not suggesting that plans are a waste of time. On every expedition it is vital that the leader has a written plan, but I can confirm from my own experience that the plan never survives contact with the mountain.

In summary, there needs to be an early decision about whether the expedition warrants an HMC. If so, then its members need to be selected with care, taking into consideration what their role will be during the planning phase and whilst the expedition is taking place.

EXPEDITION LEADER

Whether it is the job of the HMC or others to select an expedition leader, there are two ways of doing it. The first is to identify a leader and let that person decide the objective; the second is to identify an objective and then find a leader capable of selecting, preparing, and leading a team to success. If you have lots of potentially good leaders, you can identify your objective and then find a suitable leader, but if you have a limited number of leaders, then you might have to match your expedition ambitions to the abilities of the available leaders.

Steve Jackson at Base Camp on Kanchenjunga (8,586 metres [28,169 ft]) in 2000.

An alternative approach is for the team to select the leader, as often happens in sport teams. In the rugby and football teams I played in, the season usually started with the players electing their leader or captain for the coming season. The problem was that they would often simply elect the best player rather than the best leader. Sometimes the best player was the worst leader because he had little patience with or understanding of those who could not perform as well as he could. The leader does not need to be the best performer on the team, but it is useful if he is (I was never anywhere near the best climber on any of the numerous expeditions that I led). What is more important is for the leader to be able to stand back, appraise the situation, and give direction and guidance to the team and motivate them to achieve.

If pressed to list the ideal qualities of an expedition leader, I would identify the following characteristics:

▸ Has a good track record in the activity being undertaken.

▸ Is committed to and focussed on the success of the expedition.

▸ Has integrity and is respected and trusted.

▸ Remains calm in a crisis and acts logically and decisively.

▸ Communicates confidently in speech and writing.

▸ Is persuasive and a motivator.

▸ Gives clear direction, sound guidance, and sensible advice to team members.

▸ Has good self-awareness and insight into personal strengths and weaknesses.

▸ Is well organised, well prepared, and punctual.

▸ Is a creative thinker and has a good imagination.

▸ Is able to cooperate with partners, other expeditions, sponsors, and so on.

▸ Is a good listener.

▸ Has an empathic nature.

▸ Delegates effectively.

▸ Challenges team members but is also supportive.

▶ Is capable of rational analysis and interpretation.

▶ Retains a good sense of humour under all conditions and is able to laugh at self.

▶ Is modest and happy for others to take credit.

▶ Acts the part, incorporating the above into the performance of the role.

This list looks rather daunting, and it might seem that the ideal leader needs to be a cross between Admiral Lord Nelson, Mother Teresa, and Dr. Martin Luther King. Some people are naturally better leaders than others, but leadership is a skill, and like any other skill it can be improved with study and hard work. The more effort you put into leadership, the easier it becomes. Leadership is a bit like luck; as Liverpool football manager Bill Shankly once said, 'It's all down to luck and I find the harder we work, the luckier we become.' I learned my expedition leadership skills through trial and error and observing other leaders at close hand, notably Meryon Bridges on Gasherbrum I (Himalayas, Karakorum, Pakistan, near K2) in 1996. In recent years I have seen Dave Bunting, who writes and lectures on the subject, blossom into someone who closely matches the competences listed here. If you want to better understand leadership, you could do a lot worse than to listen to one of Dave's lectures on the subject.

COMPONENTS OF A WINNING TEAM

One of my favourite anecdotes on the subject of winning teams involves the England football team manager, Alf Ramsey, when he selected Jack Charlton, the Leeds United central defender, for the England team in the lead-up to the 1966 World Cup. It wasn't an obvious choice, and Jack was apparently a bit surprised at finding himself in the company of such stellar talents as Bobby Moore, Martin Peters, and Jack's own brother, Bobby Charlton. When he asked Alf Ramsey why he had been selected, he probably didn't expect Ramsey's response: 'I'm selecting a team, I don't necessarily pick the best players, (slight pause) Jack.' Ramsey's focus on compatibility and balance within the team resulted in

England's only ever success in the football World Cup and is a perfect illustration of the approach that is needed for success on any expedition. In Ramsey's view, the keys to success were selflessness, a strong team ethos, and willingness on the part of each member to work hard for the benefit of the team.

It might be useful to give some background information about army expeditions so you can see why I have formed some of the views expressed here. Between 1976 (when Bronco Lane and Brummie Stokes reached the summit of Everest) and 1992, the Services attempted many expeditions to big mountains, including to the West Ridge of Everest in 1988 and 1992, and they didn't succeed in reaching any of the summits. Brigadier David Nicholls, then chairman of the Joint Services Mountaineering Committee, tasked me, the expedition secretary of the Royal Navy and Royal Marines Mountaineering Club, to identify factors that might explain why those teams hadn't been successful and what lessons could be learned to improve the situation. Indeed, the whole question of whether the Services should give up the idea of going to 8,000-metre (26,245 ft) peaks was raised.

I spoke to a number of people who had been on expeditions during that time and to others who would have liked to have been but were not. It seemed that one of the problems was the team selection. A familiar story emerged—the same people went on the expeditions and were in danger of becoming a bit of a clique. You couldn't get on a Himalayan expedition unless you had Himalayan experience, and you couldn't get Himalayan experience unless you went on a Himalayan expedition—a classic catch-22. It was also suggested that some members of these expeditions had been accustomed to failure and were confirming American football coach Vince Lombardi's maxims:

Winning is a habit. Unfortunately, so is losing.

Confidence is contagious. So is lack of confidence.

Once you learn to quit, it becomes a habit.

Astonishingly, one person admitted that his motivation was to be a member of an Everest expedition to enhance his CV, but once he got to base camp, his enthusiasm for doing anything on the mountain disappeared because he got psyched out by the sheer scale of the mountain. He said he was looking to do just enough and then find a respectable place to quit, which is not much help to a leader and other team members who are focussed on reaching the summit. Another issue raised was that some of the expeditions had large, unwieldy numbers of climbers, over 30 in some cases, and more than one person admitted that there were team members whose names they did not know even at the end of the expedition.

Clearly, the Services needed a new approach to climbing the big mountains that retained the experience of the old Himalayan hands but introduced some new blood into the gene pool, and selection needed to be open and fair. There were some amongst the Services mountaineering community who did not think we should continue with extreme high-altitude mountaineering. The alternative view was that not to do so would be like athletes not wanting to play in their national team or go to the Olympics and test themselves against the world's best. David Nicholls decided that what was needed was to get a quick win on one of the 14 8,000-metre (26,245 ft) peaks. We needed a success somewhere, anywhere, and that proved to be on Gasherbrum I (Hidden Peak) in 1996, the 11th highest mountain in the world, under the leadership of Colonel Meryon Bridges and a team of 12 climbers, of whom Dan Carroll, John Doyle, Andrew Hughes, and Steve Hunt reached the summit.

The Gasherbrum expedition had several particularly interesting aspects that subsequent expeditions used as a model. Meryon and the HMC decided that there would be two teams of climbers—the main team, who would attempt Gasherbrum I, and a junior team, who would do something in the same area but would train with and learn from the main team and become the mountaineers of the future. The main team was made up of experienced Himalayan hands along with some very good climbers such as John Doyle, who blossomed into a fantastic Himalayan performer on that trip.

The selection of the Gasherbrum expedition team was a good example of how to choose a team. The expedition was advertised widely throughout the Services in 1993, and people were invited to complete an application that asked them about their climbing experience and what they felt they could bring to the team that would make a difference. These applications were sifted and the likely candidates invited to attend a weekend in North Wales in the company of the selection team. During this time they underwent a formal interview. By the end of the weekend everyone had been given a score between 1 and 5 (1 being the best and 5 being the worst). The leader then selected a team of 12 climbers plus half a dozen reserves (people always drop out of expeditions for various work-related or personal reasons).

Here is a true story about the weekend of the Gasherbrum team selection that illustrates the importance of attitude in a potential team member. I was organising and managing the Gasherbrum team selection at the Ministry of Defence camp at Capel Curig in North Wales. On the first day I was tasked by the camp commandant to find a couple of people to man the main gate security post for half an hour whilst the gateman had his lunch hour. I asked one person if he would mind doing it, and he said he hadn't come all this way to stand on a main gate checking car passes and ID cards, even for half an hour. I should point out that he didn't realise that I was involved in the selection process. This person's experience and climbing ability was such that I think he would have been assessed as a good candidate for the expedition. First impressions are important and his poor understanding of the situation and lack of enthusiasm to contribute to the common cause spoke volumes. I could have insisted that he do the duty, but I wanted to present the situation as an opportunity for someone to demonstrate personal commitment. In the end, a Royal Marine claimed responsibility for the situation and solved the problem.

I advised the selection team of the incident and of my firm view that I didn't think the first person I asked was the sort of individual we should take on an expedition; he was obviously not a team player. They agreed. Being a team player and putting others before yourself is one of the most important characteristics to look for when selecting team members for an expedition, because if you are going to live with people in difficult and dangerous circumstances for many weeks, you need to be able to get on with them.

At the end of the Gasherbrum selection process, people were advised in a personal letter whether their application had been successful or not. For most of those who had not been selected, no feedback was given other than the statement that they had not been successful on this occasion. However, a few people were given some feedback to encourage them to continue to gain the experience necessary to improve their chances of success on future expeditions. One person who got this level of feedback was Royal Marine Darren Swift, who was advised to gain more alpine experience and get some expedition experience on smaller mountains. If he did so, I said he would get a place on a future trip. He went about this with significant effort and determination, and in 1999 he reminded me of what I had said. As a result, he got a place on an expedition in 2000 to Ramtang Peak, adjacent to Kanchenjunga in northeast Nepal. Darren was subsequently selected for the 2003 expedition to Everest led by Lieutenant Colonel Nick Arding of the Royal Marines. He could never have imagined how that trip would involve him in one of the most dramatic episodes in the history of climbing on that mountain and test him to his limits.

This chapter is concerned with team selection, and my point here is to communicate the qualities needed to succeed on a serious expedition, as well as how to conduct the expedition in a morally responsible and ethical manner. The following is an extract from the Royal Humane Society that tells the story of Darren Swift's experiences on the 2003 Everest expedition, and it says a lot about the qualities and attitudes leaders should be looking for in team members. Put yourself in the place of expedition leader Nick Arding, Darren Swift and his fellow climbers, and Peter Madew and you will get a good idea of the character, attitudes, and decision-making skills displayed by the players in this episode.

On 14 January 2004, Royal Marine Darren Swift went for the first time in his life to Buckingham Palace. He was there to receive his Royal Humane Society Silver Medal—the only one awarded in 2003— from the Society's president, HRH Princess Alexandra. Seven months earlier, in May 2003, 30-year-old Swift, from Plymouth, had achieved another first: He'd set foot on Mount Everest. 'I've climbed a lot of mountains,' he says, 'but never Everest—and it's always been my dream.'

After 6 weeks climbing and acclimatising in the Himalayas, the Royal Navy expedition was just days away from the summit. Then disaster struck. News came that a climber on another expedition had broken a leg—a serious injury at the best of times, but life-threatening when you're 8,500 metres (27,890 ft) up Everest. With the help of a fellow climber, the injured man had managed to struggle 200 metres (655 ft) down to Camp VI. But now his helper, Peter Madew, an Australian, was suffering from dehydration, snow blindness, and frostbite and urgently needed help himself. Lieutenant Colonel Nicholas Arding, leader of the Royal Navy expedition, decided he had to divert Summit Team 2 away from the summit to a double rescue operation. Marine Swift—since promoted to Lance Corporal—admits to an initial feeling of disappointment. 'It was hard being so close to the summit and then having to turn back,' he says. 'But I did think,' he goes on, 'if I was in the injured man's position, I would like someone to help me.' One group of men was allocated to help the climber with a broken leg, who would have to be brought down on a stretcher. Marine Swift volunteered to get Peter Madew down on his own.

The weather conditions were grim: a gale of about 35 knots (40 mph) was blowing and the effective temperature was –30 degrees Celsius (–30 degrees Fahrenheit). The route down the treacherous North Col of Everest meant going down near-vertical ice slopes—and Madew could neither see nor use his hands. 'I roped myself to him,' Swift recalls, 'and we set off down the mountain. Because of the wind, our fixed ropes had been blown away and at times there were 2,000-metre (6,560 ft) drops on either side. It was very, very scary,' he says, 'but I knew I had to stay calm because Peter was getting panicky. He couldn't see where he was going and there were times when I had to place his feet in holds.' To make matters worse, Madew was considerably taller than his rescuer. 'I just told him to put his hands on my shoulders,' says Swift, 'and to trust me.' The 1,200-metre (3,940 ft) descent back to Advanced Base Camp took Swift 7 long and exhausting hours. From there, Madew was accompanied back to Base Camp and then taken by truck to hospital in Kathmandu. For this outstanding rescue, Swift was awarded a Royal Humane Society Silver Medal. Christopher Tyler, Secretary of the Society, says: 'Marine Swift showed enormous personal courage in guiding a seriously injured man to safety on the world's most inhospitable mountain. He put the life of a fellow human being before his own and richly deserves his medal.' Swift himself seems surprised at the accolade. 'I'm gobsmacked,' he says, 'I really

didn't think I'd done anything worthy of an award.'

I now invite you to compare the attitudes and actions of Nick Arding and his team with those displayed in similar circumstances by a different group of climbers on Everest 3 years later on 15 May 2006, when David Sharp got into serious trouble high up on the same mountain. In doing so, consider the ethical dimension of climbing 8,000-metre (26,245 ft) peaks, decide whether there is any moral obligation to help others who have got themselves into difficulty on a big mountain, and perhaps draw up a list of the qualities to look for in someone you would want to be on an expedition with. I am not going to go through the details here; it is better that you do the research yourself and draw your own conclusions.

If you are looking for a summary of the attributes needed by an ideal team member, then Dave Bunting's Everest West Ridge team gave a perfect example when they came up with such

The Kanchenjunga 2000 team that made the second British ascent of the mountain via the Southwest (Yalung) Face at Oktang.

a list. Dave mentions it in his chapter on leadership, so I won't labour the point. The list they came up with was as follows:

- ▶ Total commitment to the task
- ▶ Honesty in yourself
- ▶ Tolerance of others
- ▶ Loyalty
- ▶ Teamwork
- ▶ Communication
- ▶ Physical fitness
- ▶ Mental robustness
- ▶ Attention to detail
- ▶ Sense of humour

The important thing to note in this list is that climbing ability is not mentioned. The only item in the list with any element of knowledge and skill is physical fitness; the rest are emotional competences (EQ), illustrating the point that emotional intelligence is the most important quality to be found in a good team member. To put it another way, attitude is more important than knowledge and skills.

SELECTION TIPS

I have included here what I hope will be some useful thoughts based on my experiences. All are commonsense but not, unfortunately, always common practice.

Using Cheese as a Selection Tool   In preparing for one expedition I led, we went to the Swiss Alps for some training and stayed overnight in a mountain hut. When the food comes out from the kitchen in an alpine hut, it always perfectly equates to the number of people in your group. When our breakfast came out on this particular morning, a quick scan showed that there were two pieces of cheese each on the plate. The first member of my group took three pieces of cheese and passed the plate to me. I now had a dilemma—was I going to say something to that person, was I going to take my two pieces and pass on the problem, or was I going to take one piece and thereby solve the problem? I did the latter and passed the plate on to the next person, who even asked the first person if he had enough cheese, but the point was missed. This episode contributed to my decision not to

Kanchenjunga from the southwest.

select the first person for the expedition because if he couldn't work out something as simple as how much cheese is available to share equally for breakfast, then I would question his judgement at extreme high altitude on an 8,000-metre (26,245 ft) peak. It was a useful insight into someone's thought processes or lack thereof.

Doing the Critical Nonessentials The story about the cheese might sound slightly extreme, but it illustrates how small things are important and count for a lot. If you get enough of the team doing the *critical nonessentials*, as Sir Clive Woodward calls it in his book *Winning!* (which chronicles the story of England's rise to Rugby World Cup victory), then you might stand a good chance of success in whatever you are striving to achieve. Sir Clive emphasised that attention to minute detail is essential, and he would doubtless agree that team members need to think about others before themselves and put the welfare of their colleagues ahead of their own. It is a hard thing to do, but if everyone thinks in that way, it will make for an effective team.

Stickability The selection process needs to identify team members who are prepared to continue when they are below par. This is what my late father called *stickability*, the determination to carry on. It is inevitable that all team members will spend some time feeling below their best for all sorts of reasons, some physical and some psychological, on any expedition. It's also important for the team to accept that some people will be below par on some days and to do what they can to support their team members.

Working in Bad Weather It is also important to look for team members who are willing and able to operate in bad weather. Kanchenjunga is notorious for its bad weather, and in 2000 the fact that my team had the courage to work in bad weather, which was almost every other day, was a major factor in explaining why we became only the second British expedition to succeed in reaching the summit via the South West Face. If you are to succeed on the big mountains, then you need team members who will venture out in conditions that you would not go out in if you were in the Alps.

Bad weather on Kanchenjunga.

The bad weather reduced our ability to work on the mountain for almost a third of the expedition, although there were days when the weather at base camp did not stop activity higher up on the mountain. From our experience on Gasherbrum I in 1996, we knew that if we were to be successful on Kanchenjunga, we would have to be prepared to work in marginal weather conditions.

Hewers of Wood and Drawers of Water There is an adage that Himalayan mountaineering is characterised by carrying heavy loads for long distances in dangerous conditions so that someone else can reach the summit. There is a degree of truth in this, and it is important to select some team members who are prepared to be the hewers of wood and drawers of water and do the unglamorous but essential tasks such as load carrying, stocking camps, trail breaking, hauling out fixed ropes, digging the tents out when it has been snowing, and so on. Selecting a team of prima donnas who all think that they should be preserved for the summit bid is a surefire way to guarantee failure.

Being Prepared to Leave Your Safety Margin Behind When tackling the world's highest mountains, you need people with the confidence and courage to leave their safety margin behind them on their way to the top. It is what separates those who have the drive to get to the summit of a mountain like Everest, particularly on a route such as the West Ridge, where there is unlikely to be any chance of help outside of your own team's resources if things take a turn for the worse. It also takes courage to admit that you don't want to make a summit attempt. I have had that experience and can only say that as a leader, it is better that people admit they are not up for it than to make a half-hearted attempt to reach the summit whilst subconsciously looking for an acceptable place to quit.

Being a Leader and a Follower A well-balanced team needs leaders, followers, and people who can fulfil both roles during the expedition. You can be a leader today because you are particularly good at what is being attempted and then a follower tomorrow, when others' expertise comes to the fore.

Sacking the Juggler It is important for the leader to have the courage to change the team if it becomes necessary. If someone is unable or unwilling to change behaviours or attitudes that are having an adverse impact on the ability of the team to achieve its objectives, then the leader needs the courage to sack the juggler if it is in the best interest of the team.

Laughter Is the Best Medicine One of the most important elements of good performance that I always looked for when selecting a team is sense of humour. In any successful team you will find a fund of good stories, but there is a balance to be struck between selecting a team that performs like the Keystone Cops and

John Doyle, leaving his safety margin behind, climbs high on Kanchenjunga with Everest in the far distance.

selecting a team that is serious about achieving the objective. Humour is the best antidote to negative thoughts and can break the downward spiral that leads to failure. It can be used to expose serious issues within the team, bringing them into the public domain where they can be addressed without rancour and disagreement. To achieve this, you need people who can tell amusing tales or recycle popular TV comedy shows. On Gasherbrum we were lucky to have Larry Foden, a Royal Marine officer now and one of the best storytellers I know. On Kanchenjunga I had selected Larry, Dave Pearce, and Ady Cole in the team, and they provided a never-ending stream of dittys and stories. Dave inherited his storytelling abilities from his father, Mike, with whom I went on expedition to Arctic Norway in 1978 and whom I would pay to listen to.

Ady Cole brought the house down on Kanchenjunga when I was doing my daily radio communications from base camp at 1700 with all the teams on the mountain at Camps 1, 2, and 3. Also on the same route as us was Alan Hinkes, the foremost high-altitude mountaineer in the United Kingdom and the only Briton amongst the 13 climbers to have summited all 14 of the world's 8,000-metre (26,245 ft) peaks. Alan is a Royal Marine Commando reservist; in other words, he is a part-time soldier and gives up his time in the evenings and at weekends to do military duty in support of regular forces. Alan came up on the radio and asked me if it was okay to use our Camp 2. Before I had a chance to respond, Ady (himself a Royal Marine Commando) piped up on the radio and said, 'Yes, after 1600 and weekends only.' It is that sort of humour that helps to ignore the discomfort and danger that you have been experiencing and build morale. It is rare for a team to be unhappy and to succeed.

Dave Pearce digging out Camp 2 on Kanchenjunga. Dave's storytelling is legendary and was an important contribution to team morale.

Avalanche on Jannu seen from Base Camp Kanchenjunga. The avalanches often got very close to the route in and out of base camp on the Yalung Glacier.

Reflections on the Kanchenjunga Expedition

I will end with the reflections of a member of the Kanchenjunga expedition that I led in 2000. James Raitt's words capture the essence of what I have attempted to convey in this chapter regarding team selection.

7 June 2000

Dear Steve,

I hope that all is well with you, and that you are coping with the return to normal life. I wanted to thank you for all the hard work and effort that you have put in over the last three years that made [the expedition] such a success. I am sure that there must have been times when you wondered if it were all worth it, and I am glad that it has all worked out so well. I feel that this is largely due to the thoughtful team selection. I never thought at the outset that we would all get on so well for such a long time in a very cloistered environment.

I had a truly excellent time, and although when we departed in March I was very focussed on reaching the summit, I was more than happy to return home a member of a successful expedition. Thank you again and I look forward to seeing you again in July.

Yours,

James Raitt

Note: At the time of the expedition, James was a captain in the Royal Marines. He is now training to become a doctor.

KEY IDEAS

▶ Selecting a team to attempt a challenging objective such as climbing one of the world's highest mountains requires a process that is conducted with professionalism and integrity. It might be overseen by an HMC that will need the appropriate skill sets, experience, and network to be effective in such a role, especially if the expedition experiences circumstances that thrust it into the public arena and the merciless attention of the media. The selection process needs to be carefully thought out, as simple as possible, and clearly understood by the selectors and the applicants so that everyone knows what the selectors are looking for and the mechanism that will be used to give all applicants a fair chance of putting themselves forward in the best possible light.

▶ The leader needs to have a vision of success and be capable of communicating that vision lucidly and with energy and motivating the team to achieve it. The leader needs to demonstrate the qualities of curiosity, enthusiasm, courage, and insight. The main role of the leader is to give the team direction, guidance, and encouragement. The leader also needs strong lieutenants who can support and give advice on specialist areas.

▶ The team should have balance and consist of a strong core of experienced people who can act as role models and coaches for the others, a cadre of technically competent performers who are striving to learn from their more experienced counterparts and take on that role in the near future, and a small number of talented people who will have the middle role next time around and hopefully become the leaders of the future.

▶ Every team member should have strong intrapersonal leadership skills and be able to lead themselves. Most should also have interpersonal leadership skills and be able to lead others. All should have the awareness to know when leadership is required and have the confidence and courage to deliver it and make a difference when needed. EQ is more important than IQ, and team members need to know when it is more appropriate to use followership skills and let others lead. A sense of humour needs to pervade the team, and team members should look out for each other and meet the needs of the team, the task, and the individual. Where necessary, team members may be required to leave their safety margin behind in order to achieve the team goal. Success has many guises and should be celebrated accordingly.

Preparation

Chip Rafferty, John O'Hara, and Carlton Cooke

A life without adventure is likely to be unsatisfying, but a life in which adventure is allowed to take whatever form it will is sure to be short.

Bertrand Russell

This chapter will deal with extreme training techniques that Paul (Chip) Rafferty first used to secure a top-20 place in the London marathon in 1981 and that have been adopted ever since in preparations for personal challenges. These challenges have included some of the world's deepest caves (Gouffre Berger, France; Badalone, Pyrenees; Alpazat, Mexico), summits and attempts on several high-altitude mountains (Mount Shishapangma, Himalayas; Mount Chimborazo, Ecuador; Mount Aconcagua, Argentina), substantial climbing experience in the Alps, and other assorted endurance events. Chip has also used these training techniques in the preparation of mountaineers for high-altitude summit attempts, including the Army Everest West Ridge 2006 climbing team. These training techniques and concepts have been developed through his experiences as a mountaineer and a high-performance triathlon coach, as well as more generally through his career in the outdoors. Some of the concepts introduced in this chapter are based on a mountaineering practitioner approach rather than that of sport science in practice. However, the coauthors (John O'Hara and Carlton Cooke) have supported the ideas and training concepts with scientific evidence where it is available.

Read any of the high-altitude mountaineering books and, with few exceptions, little is mentioned about training for the big mountain other than getting fit on the walk in or on the mountain itself. This concept has always bemused me because I (Chip) have been involved all my life in endurance sport—fell running, triathlon, mountain biking, and mountaineering—and I have always trained before an event! So why not train for high-altitude mountaineering? If you draw the analogy of the summit of Everest being the equivalent of an Olympic gold medal in respect of effort and achievement, then why do so many people go to the mountaineering equivalent of the Olympics without appropriate training? I have never heard of Olympic marathon runners doing the bulk of their training at the Olympic Village in preparation to win a gold medal, but thousands of mountaineers do the equivalent. I would suggest that so many of them have failed to achieve their objectives on the big mountains because of this.

This chapter is about extreme training and preparation for extreme expeditions. The high mountains are an extreme environment and people get stopped when they are unable to cope with the cumulative effects of such an environment. A high-altitude environment is an alien one. It includes extreme cold and heat as well as a reduced ability to utilise oxygen, which offers physical challenges that a normally resilient body may not be able to cope with. I believe that only through training evolutionary physical responses using scientifically appropriate training methods can a mountaineer begin to prepare for a high-altitude expedition. So when the bystander asks me at the side of the lake on a freezing cold morning what the hell open-water swimming for an hour has got to do with climbing a mountain, my answer is cold tolerance and increased vasodilatation to the hands and feet, both of which will enable me to perform better in the extreme conditions experienced on the mountain.

Getting up big mountains is as much about climbing smart as it is about logistics and planning. I have read so many postexpedition reports that illustrate weaknesses in the planning and preparation of the expedition. Attention to fitness and the ability to tolerate extremes is key. This chapter looks at subjects ranging from specific physiological adaptations to transferable lessons from other extreme sports. Advancement in what is being achieved and what is possible in the high mountains is about using vision, thinking outside the box, and not being afraid to contradict current practice, as well as using the tried and tested scientific approaches to training. Be aware—what is about to be suggested is not for the fainthearted!

OVER-DISTANCE DAYS

The often-used strategy of getting fit once you get on the mountain is flawed because high volumes of training are needed over a long time, and the body needs to adapt. The analogy of training kilometres as an investment in a bank and the expedition as withdrawal of that investment helps explain how many mountaineers fail due to the debt that results when the withdrawal far exceeds the investment in training.

Extensive endurance days (over-distance days) have long been the remit of endurance athletes and should be considered by mountaineers of all levels. The idea is to simulate the long days a mountaineer might experience during an expedition so that you are aware of how hard you can push your body. It is not unusual to end up with days lasting beyond 16 hours in the mountains, and the energy systems required at these prolonged durations need training. For example, a summit attempt and descent of Kilimanjaro (5,895 m [19,340 ft]) may take from 10 to 17 hours depending on the speed of ascent and descent, whereas the 2006 Everest West Ridge

team planned for a summit attempt that could take up to 36 hours. Their summit plan was to leave Camp 3 in the morning for Camp 4 and then head for Camp 5 late that night. Then they would depart at midnight to reach the summit of Mount Everest between 8 and 9 a.m., giving them the rest of the day to get down to the relative safety of Camp 4.

A prime example of an over-distance day is the Bob Graham Round, a 105-kilometre (65 mi), 42-peak Lakeland challenge to be completed in less than 24 hours. A less extreme example is the Yorkshire Three Peaks, to be completed in less than 12 hours. Runners such as the legendary Billy Bland, who holds a record of 13 hours and 53 minutes for the Bob Graham Round, may be compared with the average fell runner, who may take up to three attempts to complete the round in less than 24 hours. Now let's say these two are mountaineers setting off on a long endurance day, attempting to reach the summit of a mountain, and one takes twice the time, 24 hours instead of 12. You can understand the rationale behind training for long endurance days to enable you to travel faster and safely. (Note that these extreme over-distance days should be carried out only periodically in a training programme, with sufficient time for the body to recover prior to the expedition.)

One of the most likely occurrences in high-altitude mountaineering is multiple extensive endurance days, or days that deplete the body's reserves for many reasons—the body works progressively harder as altitude is gained, using more energy and creating more products such as lactic acid in the muscles; environmental conditions such as weather and difficult terrain can prolong the time taken to achieve daily objectives; cold creates an inefficiency in the way the body works and taxes the system; and minor injuries through accidents have the effect of slowing the body down. All experienced mountaineers have had long days on the hill, and many tales of mountaineering describe extreme examples of these long days, such as the story of Joe Simpson surviving for more than 3 days as he crawled down a mountain with a badly broken leg in the Peruvian Andes, or Jean-Christophe Lafaille's epic on the south face of Annapurna during which he spent 5 days alone down-climbing one of the biggest alpine walls in the world after seeing his climbing partner Pierre Béghin fall to his death, taking most of their climbing gear with him (Twight & Martin, 1999). Not withstanding the aforementioned extreme examples, it is not unusual for each day to be long and high in volume and intensity of exercise, and the safety implications of not being able to carry on due to lack of training are far greater in the mountains than in any other endurance event. Preparing for such days in training is a prudent if not essential part of any mountaineer's training programme.

In preparing for extreme expeditions, particularly to high altitude, it is not unusual to lose body mass, including both fat mass and muscle mass. With each kilogram of mass lost, there is an increase in the body's ability to utilise oxygen with each breath of air. However, that advantage comes with a cost—inability to cope with the stresses associated with losing body mass, be it from inadequate diet, reduced muscle mass, depleted energy stores, or the extra work required in high-altitude mountaineering. Therefore, replicating the stresses of an extensive endurance day in training is essential.

The training strategies for replicating an extensive endurance day start with early morning fat-burning runs or other activities such as a bike ride or swim. Training the body to become efficient at burning fat is essential to any endurance athlete, whether mountaineer, marathon runner, or triathlete. The early exercise doesn't have to be prolonged. Twenty minutes a day of running before eating, when the liver has reduced glycogen stores, enables free fatty acids to become more easily mobilised, therefore increasing fat oxidation in comparison to the fed state. Additionally, fat burning continues even after exercise, adding to the training effect.

Once a week, an over-distance training day that replicates the intensity and volume of a long hill day should be done. It may take the form of a 4-hour hilly bike ride or a 2-hour run on hilly countryside. My favourite strategy is to do this training after a day's work in outdoor activities on the hill or better still, in the cave. When I get to the transport after the day's caving or hill walking, I bike or run home. The distance and time increase as the training programme

progresses, leading up to a high point of 6 hours plus of biking or 3 hours of running after a tiring day of caving, climbing, paddling, and so on. The result is often extreme fatigue, which is exactly the experience required for those long depletion days on high-altitude mountains.

On one day in the training programme, I carry out an extreme depletion day to simulate the worst-case scenario on the mountain. In the many training programmes I have done, these long depletion days have varied from an Ironman Triathlon (4-km [2.4 mi] swim, 180-km [112 mi] bike ride, and 42-km [26 mi] marathon) to Bob Graham's 24-hour challenge. I have also used long caving trips such as the Cueto-Coventosa route in Spain, which took 32 hours and included 900 metres (984 yd) of abseiling underground, climbing and crawling for something like 10 kilometres (6 mi), and finally swimming 3 kilometres (2 mi) underground in freezing cold lakes before emerging into the daylight 32 hours later.

My employment in the military has resulted in my leading some of the world's classic underground caving and canyoning trips and has been of direct benefit in developing my capacity for extreme endurance challenges. Caving techniques often produce long days in the cold and wet, working in physically arduous conditions whilst crawling and dragging ropes and equipment. I would rank caving as one of the most effective training activities for developing extreme endurance. Also, because of the added implications of working in enclosed areas, as well as the dark and unknown environment, it develops a psychological resilience that serves well on the high mountains, especially on the hard days when problems occur and that extra bit of physical and psychological capacity is essential.

TRAINING IN SOME STATE OF GLYCOGEN DEPLETION

The research literature unequivocally supports the consumption of carbohydrate during endurance exercise to sustain performance (see Jeukendrup, 2004, for a review). However, triathletes and marathon runners may train in a carbohydrate-depleted state as an alternative strategy to stimulate endurance training adaptations. As a marathon runner in the 1980s, I accidentally came across the results of training without eating during one of my many 12-week training programmes. On the base mileage phase of training, I could only train in the morning before breakfast to get the easy base miles in. The result of this regular 30-minute morning run was one of my best marathon results, 19th in the London marathon, taking 3 to 4 minutes off my personal best. Because the early runs without breakfast were the only difference from all the other 12-week build-ups I had done, I was certain that they were the main reason for the improvement in time.

It is now accepted that during acute steady-state exercise following an overnight fast (Bergman & Brooks, 1999) or in a glycogen-depleted state, fat oxidation is increased due to the lower amount of available glucose. Producing adaptations that facilitate the ability to burn fat as efficiently as possible is the holy grail of the endurance athlete since increased fat metabolism for a given exercise intensity is related to better endurance performance (Hawley, Brouns, & Jeukendrup, 1998). Furthermore, there is evidence to suggest that carbohydrate intake can limit important fat metabolism adaptations. Therefore, it is logical to assume that training in a glycogen-depleted state can enhance physiological adaptations that ultimately benefit endurance performance. (However, though I stand by this hypothesis, the effects of long-term training—10 weeks or more—in a glycogen-depleted state are yet to be investigated.) The other good news is that this form of training may mean greater glycogen sparing during endurance training, which is further supported by the consumption of carbohydrate (De Bock et al., 2008).

This form of training prepares the body for a specific scenario that you may need to deal with whilst undertaking your mountaineering challenge. It is likely that at some point during your expedition, you will find yourself in a glycogen-depleted state for one reason or another but you still will be required to perform. Therefore, preparing for this specific scenario may prove to be beneficial.

The increased fat metabolism associated with training in a glycogen-depleted state may be advantageous for those wanting to reduce their fat mass in the preparation phase for a mountaineering challenge. When fat mass is lost, endurance fitness relative to weight improves without any improvement in training status. The power-to-weight ratio is also improved, as long as muscle mass and the associated capacity for energy expenditure are maintained or increased at the same time. Therefore, high-altitude mountaineers are likely to perform better with a reduction in body fat. The laws of physics dictate that all other things being equal, a mountaineer carrying 6 kilograms (14 lb) of weight in the form of excess fat mass is going to use more energy and probably go slower up the mountain than a person without that extra weight. Lance Armstrong, six-time winner of the Tour de France, only became successful in the Tour de France mountain stages after he had trimmed off a good percentage of his body mass (Armstrong & Carmichael, 2006).

However, reducing body mass is more complex than just reducing fat mass. When reducing body mass, you need to target fat mass whilst maintaining muscle mass through strength training and an adequate intake of dietary protein (see chapter 9). Otherwise, you may lose fat mass and muscle mass, which will mean a loss of strength and power. In addition, such strategies may be useful during training, but carbohydrate is essential for optimal endurance performance. Therefore, whilst undertaking your challenge, you should still consume sufficient carbohydrate (see chapter 10).

The feeding and energy systems of the body are delicately balanced mechanisms, and as many dieticians will tell you, tinkering with them often results in unexpected outcomes. Some effects can be beneficial to mountaineers, such as supercompensation trends whereby if you reduce body fat by fasting, your body will attempt to get it back at the earliest opportunity. Fasting was once a common practice for marathon runners; they would fast and then binge on carbohydrate to gain a supercompensation effect of increased muscle and liver glycogen before the race. A mountaineer's ability to supercompensate with mass gain when needed on the mountain is no bad thing; it is far better than retreating off the high mountains looking like a skeleton.

My personal observations suggest that there are limitations to the efficiency of the practice in that without careful balance between training and diet, even highly motivated athletes can spiral into a downward trend of disordered eating, which in some cases can result in profound eating disorders that may take years to control.

The old saying that there is no such thing as bad training—'If it doesn't floor you, it will make you hard'—may sound naive, but nevertheless in my experience it carries a lot of truth. After 25 years of training using these methods, at 57 years old I personally have still biked under an hour for 40 kilometres (25 mi), ran 10 kilometres (6 mi) in 34 minutes, and completed an Ironman Triathlon in less than 11 hours, and I haven't had a day off in sickness for as long as I can remember. (An alternative view of his coauthors is that Chip is a relative of Superman!) The consequences of such training are exactly what are most likely to be encountered on the mountain, and being exposed to them in training is crucial to success.

Having said that, let me offer this advice: This form of training can involve complex responses that vary depending on the person and may include the mobilisation of different types of fat for energy production and the suppression of muscle glycogen breakdown, to mention just a couple. These are responses that are associated with the body's survival mechanisms. Each of these responses can have unexpected consequences. Any protocols of depletion training, including training without eating, should only be carried out under the close supervision of a coach or adviser who understands the implications of such training, especially with young people or developing mountaineers. As with all good ideas, most have been tested and the limitations have been discovered, but often the hard way.

TRAINING FOR DEHYDRATION

Inadequate hydration can have a marked effect on most physiological and metabolic functions, negatively influencing performance. At altitude,

reflected ultraviolet (UV) rays from the snow create intense heat, air is drier, and performance clothing (e.g., down suits) produces more thermoregulatory stresses. All of these factors result in greater fluid loss, and thus the high-altitude mountaineer is a prime candidate for dehydration and its consequences, which may include greater susceptibility to heatstroke, increased prevalence of hyponatraemia (electrolyte disturbance), increased heart rate, reduced cardiac output, reduced stroke volume, and attenuated blood flow, which can limit oxygen delivery to the exercising muscles and accelerate increases in core temperature. However, the ultimate consequence of dehydration is reduced exercise performance, both physically and mentally.

Measuring true hydration status is not as simple as just measuring change in body mass; reconciliation of lost body mass in terms of sweat loss and effective body water loss (itself determined by changes in fuel oxidation, the production of metabolic water, and drinking strategies) needs to be made. In other words, changes in body mass do not directly reflect changes in body hydration. However, loss of body mass is probably the only realistic proxy measure of dehydration in the field since precisely establishing sweat loss and effective body water is so complex (King, Cooke, Carroll, & O'Hara, 2008).

The general consensus within the literature is that body water loss, equivalent to 2 percent of body mass, is tolerable by some athletes, but exceeding this amount in cold (5-10 degrees C [41-50 degrees Fahrenheit]) and temperate (21-22 degrees C [70-71.6 F]) environments may impair performance (Coyle, 2004). Whilst a loss of 5 percent can decrease performance by 30 percent (Armstrong, Hubbard, Szlyk, Mathew, & Sils, 1985; Saltin & Costill, 1988) in hot environments (greater than 30 degrees Celsius [86 degrees Fahrenheit]), dehydrating by the lesser figure of 2 percent of body mass is potentially dangerous.

An example of the potential for dehydration and impaired performance is highlighted from a recent mountaineering expedition to Peru with the Special Air Services. By monitoring body mass daily, I would estimate average body-mass losses to be 3 to 5 kilograms (6.5-11 lb), or 4 to 7 percent body mass, on the high-altitude mountain days. Fluid intake in terms of both volume and frequency was also monitored and recorded. The results illustrated the extent of dehydration, as well as the problem of inadequate drinking strategies, which compounded the effect of water loss. Hydrating on the move has always been a problem for me during long endurance events such as the 2-day Original Mountain Marathon and Ironman Triathlon, especially during hot weather. In those events, gastric emptying becomes greatly reduced as the intensity of exercise increases, which means that over a given duration the body can only use a small amount of the fluids swilling about in the stomach. Even though the general advice should be to drink little and often, you also need to consider the extra effort of carrying excess weight in water or sport drinks.

Some of the pioneer climbers of the big North Face alpine routes that took longer than 18 hours used to train without water in an effort to adapt and therefore have to carry less weight on the difficult, long climbs. I therefore began a regimen of controlled water depletion training, minimising water intake to simulate the effects of dehydration, yet continuing to perform on the mountain. I adopted a strategy whereby once a week, during an over-distance session, I reduced water intake. Furthermore, on one extra-long over-distance day not less than 1 month before the challenge, I would carry only emergency water and would try to perform without any water intake. (I would recommend that you attempt this only under the control of a coach or fellow mountaineer and monitor your reactions, dizziness, and rate of sweating.)

Incredulity was the response from the majority of sport scientists, who have encouraged a spongelike regimen for athletes, the opposite of the minimalist approach I had undertaken. Now, this strategy may seem like complete madness; however, Noakes (2007) has proposed that exercise performance may be impaired by increased thirst sensations caused by inadequate fluid replacement, or an anticipatory response to the body knowing it is not going to receive an adequate amount of fluid, rather than dehydration in itself impairing exercise performance. Therefore, a regimen to develop a tolerance to these factors may explain why the marathon

winners who drink sparingly are the fastest yet most dehydrated (Cheuvront, Carter, & Sawka, 2003) and why the top Ironman Triathlon finishers are able to tolerate body-mass losses in excess of 10 percent (Sharwood, Collins, Goedecke, Wilson, & Noakes, 2002, 2004).

Though training for dehydration will create resilience to dehydration and probably thirst sensations, it is important to hydrate adequately in order to maximise performance once on the mountain, especially at higher altitudes. Therefore, the conclusion is that not drinking at all during exercise will impair performance, but drinking to more than one's pleasure may not provide any additional benefits (Noakes, 2007); drinking enough to avoid the development of thirst may be the key.

TRAINING TO TOLERATE COLD

It was a bemused and somewhat confused Everest West Ridge team of elite service climbers that stood at 5:00 in the morning as the sun rose on an icy cold lake, preparing themselves for 20 minutes of open-water swimming immediately followed by a psychological ability test and a motor task of rethreading a knot. The results varied from cold-water shock to general muscle fatigue to inability to walk and balance after the swim to difficulty doing the tests. Several of the group commented that the only time they had previously felt the same effects was when getting dangerously cold in wintry mountaineering situations, which was exactly the reason they were doing this training. However, by the fourth swim of the early open-water swimming regimen, their physical and psychological tolerance was such that they could do the training without the uncomfortable side effects and, therefore, they gained a number of valuable training benefits.

Training in cold situations can improve tolerance to the cold, especially cold-water submersion. The Japanese Ama pearl divers are a good example. They regularly tolerate average surface water temperatures of 27 degrees Celsius (80 degrees Fahrenheit) in the summer and 10 degrees Celsius (50 degrees Fahrenheit) during the winter, thus being exposed to strong thermal stresses (Ferretti & Costa, 2003). They are able to tolerate the cold through elevation of the shivering threshold and greater body insulation. According to Ferretti and Costa (2003), this is due to either stronger peripheral vasoconstriction or more effective countercurrent heat exchange. The effects of improved cold tolerance are independent of the breath holding associated with diving and are specifically related to cold exposure. Increased cold tolerance due to an elevated shivering threshold has also been highlighted in Australian Aborigines, who used to sleep naked in cold air.

Therefore, in every training preparation for a high-altitude mountaineering expedition, I include regular open-water swimming in temperatures as cold as can be tolerated. Training without a wetsuit is more effective for short-exposure cold tolerance. However, to gain some of the other benefits associated with longer sessions (more than 15 minutes) in water below 8 degrees Celsius (46 degrees Fahrenheit), I would recommend using a wet suit (without head, foot, and hand protection) whilst swimming two or three times a week, which will bring about the relevant adaptations. In any case, if you are thinking of adopting this strategy, you need to adhere to the appropriate safety guidelines associated with open-water swimming, and such sessions should always be monitored with appropriate back-up to deal with any adverse responses that may occur.

Open-water swimmers tend to have a higher percentage of fat than bikers or runners, which helps insulate their bodies against the cold. Rather than a training response, this is more likely a conscious decision by the swimmers that is achieved through dietary manipulation. An increase in body-fat percentage for insulation against the cold in lean climbers may be of particular benefit in the run-up to any mountaineering expedition. Overall, the trend in open-water swimming is to visit environments that are similar to the evolutionary environments that we first developed from. In so doing, the hope is to recreate the strong defences and tolerances we used to have to cope with these harsh environments, therefore better preparing ourselves for the harsh environments of high-altitude mountaineering.

Plunging your hands into icy water in preparation for cold climbs at altitude is another technique used by mountaineers to develop tolerance to the cold. Throwing snowballs with bare hands may be just as effective and potentially more fun! These strategies help to develop changes in peripheral circulation to the hands, which protects against the development of frostnip or frostbite. Blood flow to the fingers in extreme temperatures is reduced (vasoconstriction) to retain heat, but then paradoxically it is increased (vasodilatation) every 15 to 30 minutes, which is commonly known as *hot pulses*. Vasodilatation has been shown to occur more frequently in fishermen who regularly have their hands in cold water. It also lasts longer with acclimatisation (Stroud, 2004), as well as eliciting a reduced vasoconstriction response and higher peripheral skin temperatures. Cold-water swimming also has the same benefit by increasing capillarisation at the extremities of feet and hands. When the body becomes cold, the warm blood migrates to the vital organs for survival reasons. However, in cold-water swimming, the range of movement and continuous activity of the arms, hands, legs, and feet forces the blood back to the extremities and encourages healthy capillarisation of the extremities. On the mountain, this may be important to the preservation of fingers and toes with the ever-present danger of frostnip or frostbite.

In addition to improving cold tolerance, cold-water swimming has other benefits for the mountaineer. Cold-water submersion reduces the heart rate and produces hyperventilation in the same way that working at altitude does. Swimming creates pressure on the rib cage and lungs that feels similar to the constricted feeling of working in thin air, especially if Cheyne-Stokes respiration is also present (rapid and irregular breathing). Initial exposure to cold water can bring on cold shock, resulting in reduced cognitive and physical capability, which can be improved through repeated exposure to cold-water swimming. An additional side effect in training is a slightly hypoxic state as poorer swimmers never seem to get enough air, a tactic also used by some elite swimmers to enhance the anaerobic training effect.

Further training effects include an improvement in the respiratory muscles, which will ensure normal lung function, and increased respiratory muscle strength, which will help to prevent premature respiratory fatigue. Swimming bilaterally, drawing breath with every other stroke, is the best way to train the respiratory muscles, especially for poor swimmers, which many mountaineers tend to be. Training respiratory muscles is extremely important for people who are going to be exposed to altitude because the reduced partial pressure of oxygen in the ambient air increases the demands on the respiratory muscles, including increased respiratory rate and depth, which can be equivalent to maximal exercise at sea level. Interestingly, the respiratory systems of high-altitude Sherpas are highly developed and have adapted to support their regular journeys at high altitude. Sherpas from the Khumbu area (Everest Valley) in Nepal have been shown to have forced vital capacities of 4.7 litres at an altitude of 3,840 metres (12,600 ft), which is significantly higher than that of visitors to the region (Havryk, Gilbert, & Burgess, 2002).

Another effective way to develop your resistance to respiratory fatigue is through the use of a device called the *POWERbreathe*, which isolates the respiratory muscles. The *POWERbreathe* training device could be advantageous to mountaineers of all levels and is discussed more in chapter 7.

HYPOXIC TRAINING

The greatest limiting factor in climbing big mountains is coping with and adapting to the effects of altitude. If this factor could be completely overcome, we would probably see Mount Everest climbed from Base Camp by a well-trained endurance athlete in under 4 hours. At the present time of writing, efforts to overcome the effect of altitude have seen some remarkably fast attempts. Notably, in May 2003, Sherpa Pemba Dorjie climbed Mount Everest from Base Camp in 12 hours and 45 minutes, and Sherpa Lakba Gelu made the same climb in less than 11 hours. Also, in the last decade alpine-style fast ascents have become fashionable for super-fit, well-acclimatised alpine mountaineers such as Jean-Christophe Lafaille and Anatoli Boukreev.

I first approached the concept of using hypoxic training to improve performance back in the 1990s whilst working with triathletes and other endurance athletes. At that time, the person at the cutting edge of hypoxic training was Dr. Arkadi F. Prokopov, who had worked with Russian athletes. The hypoxic training system he adopted could be partly responsible for Russian dominance in endurance events at Olympics and world championships over the last two decades. In the field of athletics, only runners from Ethiopia, Kenya, and Morocco who live at altitude were able to challenge Russian dominance. Ark was consultant adviser to Hypoxico, a company selling hypoxic training systems that were slept in (tents), cycled in and run in (chambers in gyms), and lived in (hypoxic living quarters, used by the Swiss cross-country skiing team, amongst others).

There had been a lot of interest by high-altitude climbers in the hypoxic systems, but at that time it was a new dimension and Ark had not addressed the protocols for such training. The key to unlocking the door and creating a programme that would overcome the acclimatisation problem for mountaineers and produce the climber who could scale Everest in less than 4 hours was a complex one. Very little field research had been done on mountaineers because of the obvious difficulties in reproducing laboratory conditions on the mountain. However, a commonsense approach along with scientific evidence, which I had gathered from research on three high-altitude expeditions in 2006, 2007, and 2008, produced useful data, including blood lactate concentrations, heart rates, blood oxygen saturations, haemoglobin levels, body mass, hydration status, stress, fatigue, and muscle soreness. After each of these expeditions, comparisons were made between those who had used hypoxic training before the expedition and those who hadn't. The effects on the previously mentioned criteria allowed me to untangle the maze and find a starting point from which to help our staff design programmes for high-altitude mountaineering using hypoxic training.

The starting point in designing a preacclimatisation programme was to look at the known physiological adaptations to hypoxic training that would benefit a mountaineer prior to going on a mountain. Repeated exposure to hypoxia interspersed with periods of normoxia has been shown to produce adaptations in the cardiovascular, respiratory, and skeletal muscle systems. This ultimately allows better oxygen extraction and more efficient utilisation of oxygen for metabolic processes, which would be beneficial to a mountaineer. The idea was to then balance these findings with the field research and my personal experiences. I concluded that the best training for high-altitude mountaineers wanting to improve their physical performance on the mountain would be to use a preacclimatisation strategy that integrated a variety of hypoxic training protocols. The use of these strategies will accustom you to hypoxia before your arrival at high altitude. This will enable you to move more comfortably and safely once you reach altitude, and it will make you stronger and able to recover more quickly on the mountain. Other potential benefits include decreased chances of developing acute mountain sickness (AMS). Even though there is a logical argument to support the following recommendations, research is needed to establish the best preacclimatisation programmes for high-altitude mountaineers.

Hypoxic training as a preacclimatisation strategy should include exposure to normobaric hypoxia at rest (sleeping in a hypoxic tent for prolonged lengths of time at various oxygen levels to simulate altitude or intermittent hypoxic training [IHT] at rest), as well as during and following exercise (in-load and postload hypoxic training). These programmes should be used in conjunction, as described later, since the acclimatisation process for each protocol results in different physiological adaptations that are beneficial for those attempting to climb mountains at high altitude.

The hypoxic training programme must be carefully tailored to the person, which is best done after a full physiological assessment that measures variables such as maximal oxygen uptake, lactate tolerance, peak heart rate, peak power, respiratory function, body composition, and blood measurements for haemoglobin and haematocrit levels. Once all data from these tests have been collected, areas for improvements can be better identified, such as poor tolerance for lactic acid or a weak aerobic base. These factors will help determine how much time is spent in the various protocols described next.

Sleeping in a Hypoxic Tent

Athletes have slept at altitude (2,500 m, or 8,200 ft) and trained at sea level (live high, train low) for many years. This form of training has been shown to improve aerobic power, mainly due to an increased oxygen-carrying capacity of the blood. Levine and Stray-Gunderson (1997) showed that 4 weeks of sleeping at a moderate altitude (2,500 m) is sufficient to stimulate erythropoiesis, the process by which red blood cells are produced. This strategy increased red blood cell mass and haemoglobin by 10 percent, thereby increasing the oxygen-carrying capacity of the blood, with an associated 6 percent increase in maximal oxygen uptake ($\dot{V}O_2$max).

These physiological adaptations may be beneficial for training prior to an expedition, as well as assisting the in-country acclimatisation process. Therefore, I recommend sleeping at simulated altitudes (normobaric hypoxia) using a hypoxic tent in the weeks before an expedition to high altitude. Even though this method is different to sleeping at real altitude (hypobaric hypoxia), there is evidence to support improvements in the oxygen-carrying capacity of the blood at sea level (Brugniaux et al., 2006; Robach et al., 2006). This is an area where further research is needed because the research findings are equivocal, with some studies showing no significant changes (Hinckson et al., 2005; Robach et al., 2006). Regardless, the literature does support sleeping at altitude (normobaric hypoxia) as an effective preacclimatisation strategy for athletes wanting to train or compete at altitude; therefore, it must be of benefit to mountaineers.

Maximal oxygen uptake is not a predictor of performance at high altitude. As altitude increases and the partial pressure of oxygen decreases, maximal oxygen uptake is significantly reduced, which may mean that people with a low maximal oxygen uptake may struggle at high altitudes. Nevertheless, the associated haematological adaptations could be crucial in terms of high-altitude performance. Unpublished research by a military team of doctors on Mount Everest in 2007 showed that at 6,000 metres (19,685 ft), maximal oxygen uptake was similar across a number of climbers. This suggests that the more endurance-trained climbers were susceptible to a greater fractional decrease in maximal oxygen uptake in comparison to those less-trained climbers, which is supported by Ogawa Hayashi, Ichinose, and Nishiyasu (2007). It seems that as altitude increases, the absolute decrease in maximal oxygen uptake may be greater for well-trained mountaineers who begin with the advantage of a higher test score. The reason for this might be explained by the fact that endurance-trained athletes tend to have a lower hypoxic ventilatory response (HVR) at altitude in comparison to less well-trained and more sedentary people.

Sleeping at a simulated altitude of 2,650 metres (8,695 ft) has been shown to improve HVR (Townsend et al., 2002), with a well-functioning HVR necessary to perform at intermediate altitudes (Bernardi, Schneider, Pomidori, Paolucci, & Cogo, 2006). This is a positive adaptation because it increases minute ventilation on exposure to hypoxia, which facilitates arterial oxygen saturation. Bernardi and colleagues (2006) suggested that HVR should only be increased moderately to allow high but sustainable ventilation at extreme levels of hypoxia. This adaptation is crucial—a negative outcome of preexpedition endurance training at sea level will result in a decrease in HVR. A blunted HVR may mean you need to spend longer in country acclimatising because it may affect your ability to acclimatise effectively and perform at altitude.

These facts highlight the importance of sleeping at attitude as part of a preacclimatisation strategy. Furthermore, they help explain why some trained athletes perform poorly at altitude in comparison to their relatively untrained counterparts. Lower arterial oxygen saturation in the trained athletes means a lower ability to utilise oxygen. During maximal exercise, this is not helped by the trained athlete's higher cardiac output, which can reduce the transit time of blood in the pulmonary capillaries and thus reduce the time available to reoxygenate the blood. This situation was also evidenced from the blood oxygen saturation measures taken from my previous research showing that super-fit climbers, who wanted to race up the mountain, had consistently low arterial oxygen saturation readings throughout their expeditions at altitude. Therefore, a slower pace on the

mountain and a preacclimatisation strategy may have been beneficial for those climbers, whom I call *low-pulse racing snakes*.

A well-functioning HVR should also be accompanied by a high ventilatory efficiency to maintain adequate arterial oxygen saturation, despite lower increases in minute ventilation. Therefore, including slow breathing training in your preparations may be extremely useful in assisting adaptation to high altitude.

Rather than sleeping at 2,500 metres (8,200 ft) for a prolonged time, it is better to simulate the high-altitude mountaineering situation as best as possible. A typical programme would last 4 weeks starting at an altitude of 2,500 metres (8,200 ft) or so—equivalent to an ambient oxygen percentage of 15 percent. However, a longer programme of sleeping at altitude would be better. The altitude for sleeping is increased incrementally over the 28 days, usually to a maximum of 6,000 meters (19,685 ft, or 10 percent of oxygen); no further benefits will be gained from going above 6,000 metres. A word of warning: Do not go too high too soon; this adjustment needs to be progressive. An oxygen meter should be in the tent at all times to monitor oxygen levels even though the hypoxic generators have safety mechanisms, which should include a safety alarm.

According to anecdotal information from the climbers in the Everest West Ridge team, who utilised this preacclimatisation strategy, they perceived that they acclimatised more quickly and felt physically stronger on the mountain in comparison to other expeditions to high altitude where they had not used such a programme.

This programme should not interfere with normal training, however, because of the effects already mentioned and the intrusive nature of the protocols on the body. Tiredness and overtraining can be felt, in which case a night off or longer break from the tent would be recommended. Tests to monitor any physiological or psychological changes should be carried out at regular intervals during the training, especially on haematocrit and haemoglobin counts—these can quickly become high, dangerously affecting the viscosity of the blood. It is useful to wear a heart rate monitor to record maximum and minimum heart rates whilst in the hypoxic tent.

It is not unusual for the first few nights to be restless as the body adapts, and occasional gasping for air and even Cheyne-Stokes respiration (rapid and irregular breathing) may appear, in which case the answer is simply to ventilate the tent and turn off the generator.

The effective sleeping altitude is the same as living high and training low, which promotes the physiological adaptations required for living and working at altitude whilst using the normal oxygen environment during the day to allow full recovery from the stress and to complete regular training under normoxic ambient conditions. Furthermore, as exposure to altitude increases the energy demands placed upon the body, it is advisable to increase the food consumed. This is especially important because you can lose a lot of body mass in a short time, including muscle mass, which is likely to be detrimental to your preparations. Monitor your body mass, fat mass, and muscle mass regularly during this phase and alter your training and dietary intake accordingly.

Intermittent Hypoxic Training at Rest

Sleeping in a hypoxic tent for prolonged amounts of time is my preferred resting preacclimatisation strategy. However, if you do not have access to a hypoxic tent, another option is IHT, which can be accessed commercially. IHT is a hypoxic training strategy developed in the former Soviet Union. It is a system whereby you are progressively exposed to higher simulated altitudes (4,000-6,600 m, or 13,125-21,655 ft) through increased hypoxia (13 to 9 percent oxygen) for short amounts of time using a face mask or hypoxic chamber or tent. This protocol is interspersed with ambient air and is performed at rest. Typically the air changes every 5 minutes, and sessions initially last 60 minutes, progressing to 90 minutes after at least 15 days (see table 3.1 for more details).

An oxygen-saturation oximeter, or pulse oximeter, should be used when undertaking IHT. There are certain oxygen-saturation levels

TABLE 3.1 Sample IHT Programme

Day	Effective oxygen percentage	Arterial oxygen saturation (±2%)
1	13%, or 4,000 m (13,125 ft)	86%
2	13%, or 4,000 m (13,125 ft)	86%
3	13%, or 4,000 m (13,125 ft)	86%
4	12%, or 4,500 m (14,765 ft)	84%
5	12%, or 4,500 m (14,765 ft)	84%
6	12%, or 4,500 m (14,765 ft)	84%
7	11%, or 5,200 m (17,060 ft)	82%
8	11%, or 5,200 m (17,060 ft)	82%
9	11%, or 5,200 m (17,060 ft)	82%
10	10%, or 5,800 m (19,030 ft)	80%
11	10%, or 5,800 m (19,030 ft)	80%
12	10%, or 5,800 m (19,030 ft)	80%
13	9%, or 6,600 m (21,655 ft)	78%
14	9%, or 6,600 m (21,655 ft)	78%
15+	9%, or 6,600 m (21,655 ft)	78%

you should not go below for each simulated altitude (see table 3.1). Once your oxygen saturation decreases to the recommended safety limit, you should then breathe ambient air, with the recovery of oxygen-saturation levels indicating when to start breathing hypoxic air again. As with sleeping at altitude, IHT protocol benefits are similar, potentially improving the oxygen-carrying capacity of the blood, as well as cellular adaptations.

In-Load and Postload Hypoxic Training

Once you have completed a reasonable acclimatisation phase (a minimum of 3 weeks, reaching a simulated altitude of 5,000-6,000 m, or 16,405-19,685 ft) using the sleeping-at-altitude protocol or the IHT-at-rest protocol, I recommend integrating in-load hypoxic training (ILHT) and postload hypoxic training (PLHT). It is important to reach a simulated altitude of 5,000 to 6,000 metres (16,405-19,685 ft), because this will accustom you to the environment you are likely to operate in during a high-altitude expedition. Furthermore, no additional acclimatisation benefits are likely to be gained above 6,000 metres (19,685 ft).

ILHT and PLHT complement the resting protocols by enabling skeletal muscle adaptations associated with exercise, and this requires certain levels of physical exertion. Skeletal muscle adaptations include increased capillary density, which enhances the ability of the exercising muscles to extract oxygen from the blood; increased myoglobin and mitochondrial activity; and greater lactate tolerance. The implications of these adaptations are that there is a greater likelihood of improvements to better tolerate work at altitude. The more specific the physical exertion is to the activity to be undertaken (e.g., running on a ramped treadmill to simulate climbing steep mountains), the better the training suits the needs of the mountaineer. It becomes apparent after using these ILHT protocols that the volume and intensity often mirror normal training protocols of endurance athletes, starting with the high-volume aerobic base (i.e., sleeping in a tent, training lactate tolerance and endurance using ILHT, and stimulating muscle adaptations and power output through PLHT).

With careful cross-referencing to the physiological tests carried out before hypoxic training, which should determine the requirements of the person (e.g., poor lactate threshold or deficiencies in strength and power), a hypoxic training programme can be designed to suit the needs of the individual. Having listened to Ark Prokopov discussing preacclimatisation strategies and applying his experience, I can recommend the following ILHT sessions as part of your preacclimatisation programme. A sample session may include a warm-up for 5 minutes at an easy pace at normoxia. Then at an altitude of around 3,000 metres (9,840 ft) and 14.5 percent oxygen, carry out continuous exercise at a moderate intensity of 60 to 70 percent of heart rate reserve (see chapter 7). The duration of the session should be progressive, starting at approximately 15 minutes and building slowly to 50 minutes as the sessions become easier. This is obviously dependant on your fitness and previous hypoxic training. At the end of the session, remove the mask and cool down for 5 minutes. Again, you should use a pulse oximeter; oxygen saturation should not drop below 84 percent at any point whilst exercising. If it reaches this safety limit, you should stop exercising and wait for your oxygen saturation to return to normal before continuing.

Maximising lean mass before departing for an expedition is crucial in combating the muscle loss associated with high-altitude expeditions. Therefore, PLHT is essential because anecdotal evidence suggests that such sessions may stimulate the growth of the muscles that were physically loaded during the exercise prior to the hypoxic inhalation. The sessions should be performed after intense exercise bouts and are best used with an intermittent type of training session. A sample session would be 3 to 5 minutes of exercise at normoxia, progressively increasing exercise intensities with 5 minutes of rest under normobaric hypoxic conditions, followed by a bout of exercise, followed by 5 minutes of rest, and so on. The total duration of each session should be approximately 60 minutes. Each rest phase should include inhalation of 12 to 10 percent oxygen, preferably whilst lying down or reclining comfortably with all muscles unloaded. Start with 12 percent oxygen (up to 4,500 m, or 14,765 ft) and then decrease it as you feel the session becoming easier. When performing these sessions, the volume of other exercise during the day should be reduced. It is also recommended to include adequate protein and carbohydrate in your diet to ensure effective muscle recovery and growth.

Hypoxic Training Summary

Hypoxic training is a complex method of training that exposes the body to physiological adaptations that can only be experienced in the unique environment of high-altitude climbing, where no one is able to survive for any great length of time. It is therefore not a natural human environment, with its only parallels being the oxygen-limited existence of a child in the womb before birth or diving without breathing apparatus, which offer other dimensions of study in the use of hypoxic training. However, extreme activities require extreme methods of preparation, and from an ethical standpoint using hypoxic training methods at sea level is no different than going to the high mountains of Chile or Kenya and training to gain some of the benefits experienced by the indigenous athletes from these countries. Simulated training is arguably a cheaper, more convenient form of training, especially for countries such as Finland that have no mountains to use for altitude exposure, and because high-performance athletes do not necessarily thrive in a mountain environment away from home like the leading mountaineers and climbers of the world do.

Nevertheless, hypoxic training does not seem to work for everyone. Some have suggested that being a responder or nonresponder may be due to genetics, initial iron storage status, training level, and initial haematocrit and fatigue level (overtraining status). There are limits on how these protocols can be used, and because of the complexity of hypoxic training effects, such training should only be carried out by experts in the field.

'Train hard, climb easy' is a mantra that underpins the methods illustrated in this chapter. The only caveat to that saying is to train smart, and know why you're delving into these physical extremes.

KEY IDEAS

▸ Over-distance days are important because they prepare you for the long days a mountaineer may experience and develop your awareness of how hard you can push your body.

▸ Including training sessions in some state of glycogen depletion will prepare you for a scenario where you might have to perform in a glycogen-depleted state.

▸ Dehydration will negatively affect your physiological and cognitive function. Therefore, training to tolerate dehydration and drinking frequently during mountaineering should help to maintain performance.

▸ Acclimatising to the cold will increase your shivering threshold and therefore your ability to tolerate the cold conditions you may experience during your expedition.

▸ Hypoxic training will enable you to start adapting to the effects of altitude prior to your expedition, which should assist your in-country acclimatisation and overall performance.

CHAPTER 4

Equipment

John Doyle and Chip Rafferty

Carrying a heavy rucksack, sleeping fitfully in a hut, too hot and then too cold, probably hungry, undoubtedly thirsty, climbing in the mountains takes place in extreme conditions compared with most sports. A runner or rugby player, however serious they are, can always retire from the field of play. . . . In contrast, mountaineering is not the sort of sport which can be stopped at any time. Even if you are at the limits of endurance, if your feet feel like lead, your head is swimming with exhaustion, you cannot sit down and say, 'I've had enough, I'm giving up.'

Gaston, 1975

I (John) had read these words as a young boy new to climbing and enthusiastic to learn from and experience the mountains. I was blessed with a mother who had a considerable gift as a sewing machinist, being able to turn a black-and-white photo of the day's most technically efficient article of outdoor clothing into home-made attire that any 14-year-old mountaineer would envy. It was this steep learning curve, with many days (and nights) spent perfecting the equipment, that would allow me to experience the magic of the outdoors, from the Yorkshire moors to the Himalayas, from the Arctic to the tropics.

We now live in an age of abundant information about most subjects, including expedition equipment, which is also easy to acquire from a range of sources. Literature and Internet sites are plentiful, as are manufacturers and designs. Many articles on outdoor clothing can be found in catalogues, magazines, and newspapers. Cost, quality, and functionality are all important considerations that are related to the intended end use. For the enthusiast either lacking or unwilling to part with large amounts of hard-earned cash to simply keep up with the latest trends, equipment will come down to good old-fashioned practicality, versatility, and reliability.

Stripping down and minimising equipment is important for the elite performers of our sport. However, adopting an article of clothing that will enable speed and success on one route and then dropping it straight into the recycling bin is not something most people can afford to do.

In many ways, choosing clothing and equipment for a specific mountain and route, such as the West Ridge of Mount Everest, can be a far simpler task than trying to select a waterproof shell that will be just as capable for a low-level valley walk as a beautiful alpine climb. In a similar way, the journey to the summit of a large Himalayan peak will have many phases, starting with the drive to the airport, flight to a possible tropical destination, and transfer to your onward destination. The approach trek may be through the Tibetan plain, followed by climbing the lower mountain, then the final push over 8,000 metres (26,245 ft). All phases will require careful thought and consideration as to the equipment and clothing requirements of yourself and the team.

The aim of this chapter is not to sell specific products but to pass on hard-earned experience and advice as to what works in various situations, never forgetting that what is optimal for one person may not work so well for another. Clothing and equipment should be tried and tested before committing it to a serious expedition or making a major purchase for outdoor activities on the weekends and holidays.

LEAVING HOME

Before leaving home, keep in mind the six Ps: Prior planning and preparation prevent poor performance. Few of us would set off for a day in the Lake District or a weekend alpine ski trip without adequate thought for our intended itinerary. Driving licence, passport, inoculations, insurances, and currency would all be seen as essentials. Regardless of final destination, the breakdown of the journey for a serious expedition might look something like this:

▸ Initial travel to location
▸ Trek to base camp
▸ First steps on the mountain
▸ Establishment of route and camps
▸ Summit push

The journey starts as soon as you leave home, and depending on your destination, it might not end for many months. Every item of equipment, whether individual or team kit, will need to be put through its paces before you even consider packing it for the mountain. I once witnessed a climbing partner almost break down in tears when gearing up in a small bivi tent at over 7,000 metres (22,965 ft), preparing for the summit bid, only to discover that his newly purchased neoprene overboots would not facilitate the use of his crampons—an emotional and avoidable experience, to say the least!

My advice is to break the journey into stages and identify what will be needed and when. I have undertaken numerous weekend climbing trips to Scotland and the Alps, driving or using one of the many convenient low-cost airlines,

Make sure everything is checked and accounted for before you leave home. Once you've departed, it's too late.

wearing pretty much my entire climbing outfit, willing to accept the discomfort of the initial journey and the embarrassing aroma of the return trips in order to grasp the opportunity of a weekend climb. I obviously wouldn't recommend this solution for an extended trip.

On a serious expedition, arguably the most important equipment items will not be seen after being packed at home until they reach base camp. If these items are to be freighted by sea, this could take weeks, if not months. It is for this reason that we start with the end in mind.

At high altitude, the sudden variations between being cold or overheating may be dramatic, especially when considering reflected ultraviolet rays from the snow or windchill in gale-force winds. On any single day, clothing may need to be warm and protective or light and cooling. Furthermore, it has to be efficient in thermoregulation so as not to create greater energy expenditure whilst climbing, especially on the more technical mountains.

At 8,000 metres (26,245 ft), early morning temperatures may well be –25 degrees Celsius (–13 degrees Fahrenheit), yet by midday the sun can produce an ambient temperature through radiation off the snow of 20 degrees Celsius or more (68 degrees Fahrenheit). The one-layer down suit is difficult to strip down or vent whilst on technical ground, and heart rate will be increased with the heat and the inefficiency of climbing in the full suit. Tests at sea level have shown that, timed over 100 metres (328 ft) on a 30-degree gradient, the difference between moving in a full down suit versus an articulated pair of trousers is a rise of 20 percent in heart rate in the down suit compared with very little change in the trousers. Such examples demonstrate how all the hard training to increase fitness may come to nothing just by selecting the wrong type of clothing or layers and not having it modified for your needs.

These same variables must be considered when working at lower altitudes on peaks of

Enjoying, or enduring, a food break at 6,500 metres (21,325 ft). Plan for the worst scenario; forgotten goggles can prevent all activity, even eating.

1,000 metres (3,280 ft) or less. For example, fell runners normally wear shorts and a T-shirt. However, they also have to deal with windchill, rain, and cooling of air with increasing altitude, which may produce ambient temperatures below freezing even on a moderate day in the valley.

An important factor common to both mountaineering and fell running is dealing with the heat produced during physical work. Most mountaineering activities involve enough movement to produce heat. In exercise, approximately 75 percent of the energy associated with muscle contractions is heat, so the challenge for clothing is dissipating the excess heat when you are working hard, but also keeping warm when you are doing little physical work. A fell runner who can set off for a day on the mountain wearing little clothing has to maintain a fine balance between warmth generated from movement and the use of appropriate clothing and shelter. When the run is going according to plan, all is well, but if something happens that is not expected, such as an injury, then extra clothing will be required, so it should be carried for safety.

Choose layers for effective performance in combination.

LAYERING CLOTHING

Regardless of summit height or likely conditions, it is always wise to expect the unexpected and plan for the what-if scenario. Basic layering principles are fundamental either on a walk in Snowdonia in North Wales or on summit day on Everest, where shedding or putting on extra clothing is not always viable.

Inner Layer

Lightweight, midweight, heavyweight, long sleeved, short sleeved, round neck, zipped—the choice of next-to-the-skin layers is endless. Once on the mountain, my preference is for long, midweight, synthetic underwear, although wool is now back on the market and is much more comfortable to wear than it used to be. Regardless of your choice of material, ensure that it's not so heavy as to take away its wicking properties but still heavy enough to keep out the chill when

needed—it must be capable of dealing with the expected fluctuations in temperature and conditions. Higher on the mountain, I have often opted for a heavyweight legging to make up for excessively skinny legs, but this will depend on the person. Although most modern underwear is easy to wash, plan on wearing it for extended work sessions, often days at a time, and carry a spare set. On a long trip, I would take at least three sets. Finally, lighter colours provide better protection from sun and heat when used as the outer layer.

Midlayer

The choice of a good functional midlayer will depend on the environment in which it will be used. For a wet and windy U.K. climate, it will almost certainly need to incorporate insulation and a windproof and showerproof layer. Many items now fit this bill, including the newer technologies of Polartec Power Shield and Schoeller Dryskin, both of which offer exceptional warmth, comfort, breathability, and durability.

Valuable Lessons Learned

I set off on the Lakeland Mountain Marathon, two laps of 22 kilometres (13.5 mi) over hilly terrain. All but two of us were in T-shirts and shorts, but having noticed a sprinkling of snow on the high ground, I had decided to wear full leg cover and a full-length LIFA shirt under shorts and a vest. By lap 2, most of the runners in shorts and vests were slowing, and by 32 kilometres (20 mi), many of them were walking. They were visibly distressed with the cold as their decreased work rate had reduced their ability to produce heat. Furthermore, the energy needed to keep warm and increase speed required more fuel, particularly in the form of carbohydrate, which compounded their problems.

—Chip Rafferty

Load carrying through the rocks from Tilman's Camp to Camp I on EWR 2006.

For colder and drier environments, technical fleece jackets are the best way to keep out the chill, yet they also provide a lightweight and comfortable option. A windproof fleece gives added protection and in some cases may cut out the use of an outer layer, but it also adds to weight. If choosing to add a leg layer, ensure it has appropriate-length zips to facilitate going over boots and crampons.

Outer Layer

An outer layer may consist of a hard shell or a soft shell. Both should be windproof, waterproof, and breathable. Considerations in selection include, comfort, fit, weight, and the time and location of your expedition. On a wintry day in Scotland, you are likely to face much more rain and snow than on a higher but much colder arctic peak. Gore-Tex XCR and my personal favorite for the U.K. environment,

Páramo, provide great waterproof performance and excellent wicking properties. When extra warmth is required in a damp environment, opt for one of the synthetic insulation options, such as Primaloft or Polarloft jacket and trousers. These are exceptionally versatile and offer great warmth and protection. Remember to buy a size that is large enough to go on over all your other layers in the worst conditions. As the altitude increases and you experience colder, drier conditions, there is less need for full-on protection from the rain, but more protection will be needed from the wind and cold. It is here that the softer stretch fabrics of Schoeller and Power Shield come into their own, providing good fit and comfort. These items now come well designed with lots of convenient pockets for storing route topos (sketches of the route), small items such as a hat and gloves, and snacks. The designs also allow for neat fitting and wearing of a climbing harness.

Approaching 8,000 metres (26,245 ft) at 7 p.m. can still be warm work; make sure you can vent if needed.

Being Prepared for a Changing World

At extreme altitudes, you operate in a world of inconsistency. On a midafternoon load carry, you may suffer the unbearable sun and heat that can turn in minutes to a full-on Himalayan storm, quickly bringing temperatures and windchill down to an equally unbearable level at the opposite extreme. I have often used a universal outer layer in these conditions that is a one-piece, lightweight, windproof Pertex suit. A midweight base layer and a windproof suit provided me with an ideal arrangement, light and breathable, comfortable and nonrestrictive, but I also carried a down duvet jacket to supply extra warmth should the weather suddenly change, or to put on during breaks. This has been my preferred combination for 90 percent of the climbing I have undertaken; only in extreme conditions (when most progress is halted anyway) or on a summit day have I donned full down protection. Full down protection will normally be provided as either a one-piece or two-piece suit.

A two-piece suit provides a little more versatility, especially lower on the mountain at a belay or food break where the down jacket can be quite useful. Some might also argue that when worn with the bottoms, two-piece suits are easier to vent to stay cool when necessary. However, my own personal preference has been for the one-piece suit. I have found it to be more comfortable and easier to wear (any piece of clothing at 8,000 metres [26,245 ft] is never going to be totally comfortable), it provides significant warmth that has enabled me to spend a number of nights above 7,500 metres (24,605 ft) without a sleeping bag, and it is able to vent when necessary. The key is to get the layers below just right. This has invariably been minimalistic (i.e., a midweight inner layer).

—John Doyle

FOOTWEAR

There are no excuses for getting footwear wrong. Poorly fitting boots, cold feet, or blisters come down to poor preparation, such as not breaking in the footwear before leaving home. When choosing a boot, choose something comfortable that you are happy to wear all day for extended amounts of time. Feet come in all sizes and shapes, and the number of manufacturers and designs available can cater for all. Again, for the high-altitude mountaineer the choice is not as bewilderingly extensive as for the trekker or lower-altitude climber, where marketing and fashion feature as much as functionality due to the larger market.

Lightweight approach shoes or boots provide a good fit, are comfortable, normally require little breaking in, and are now available to suit all shapes and sizes. Those with a Gore-Tex membrane add greater waterproofing and dry relatively quickly. They are available in a choice of low or higher ankle support, and when combined with a lightweight gaiter they provide great flexibility. A lightweight leather boot will provide added durability and improved water protection, but often at the cost of extra weight.

For longer days with snow, ice, and glacier crossings, as well as climbing, lightweight insulated single boots are available in plastic, leather, and various fabric combinations. These boots are appropriate for technical climbing and the use of crampons, but special consideration should be given to fit in order to avoid problems with restricted circulation, especially in cold conditions.

Cold-weather, high-altitude technical boots are invariably going to be a double or even triple boot. A thermal insulating inner boot is combined with a synthetic insulated outer boot, and an integral breathable gaiter gives all-around protection.

Long days on the go will require regular attention to both your footwear and your feet. A consideration for all footwear is moisture build-up; feet perspire even at 8,000 metres (26,245 ft). Single boots can become as wet on the inside as they are on the outside. Drying in the sun or overnight will not only assist in the performance of the boot but also one's feet. A Dampire Dryzone can be used to absorb moisture from within the boot, and the advantage of an inner boot is that it can be removed and dried inside a tent or sleeping bag at night. Keeping feet dry and changing socks regularly will help. I have often worn vapour-barrier socks (essentially waterproof bags) that keep the inner

boot dry but require a disciplined approach to changing and drying socks. This may entail using two to three socks varying in thickness, with the thinnest sock next to the foot. Don't have anything around the foot that is tight or cramping, because this constricts the blood flow. A good tip is to wear a technical marathon running sock; in my experience, the design minimises blistering and overheating. A quality walking sock is paramount, and investment in this item is well worth it. Make sure you take enough pairs to last a long trip. Even when washed at base camp, they never feel the same, so I always take plenty of spares.

Finally, consider a lightweight electric foot-warming system such as the Cozy Feet foot warmer. Twenty years ago, Sharon Wood, the first Canadian and only woman to climb Everest by its West Ridge, used the foot warmer to combat frostbite. The latest version of this system includes a lightweight foot bed with a flexible plastic lead connected to a lightweight power supply of lithium batteries, which without a doubt produces a real safeguard from the cold and the potential for frostbitten toes.

Heading off for a day's work! Note the climbers are roped together and headwear, eye protection, and gloves are all in place. It is important to check all gear with each other before you leave the relative safety of camp.

GLOVES AND HATS

I choose and adjust gloves and hats in a similar fashion to the layering system used with other clothing. A lightweight power stretch glove is suitable in a wide range of conditions, from protecting against the sun on a warm glacier crossing to handling metal objects in extreme cold conditions when dexterity is the key. These will wear out quickly, so take a few spares and don't spend a fortune. The next layer is a midweight alpine climbing glove that is windproof, waterproof, insulated, and reasonably hard wearing, and that provides good grip in the palms for climbing and the use of ice axes and so on. Don't be surprised to go through a few pairs of these on a 3-month expedition, when daily use will take its toll. Finally, when the cold really starts to bite, a mitt is best for keeping your hands warm. A combination of a removable inner layer with a windproof and waterproof outer layer works well. In extreme cold, you might opt for a down-filled version, but beware—you will experience a dramatic loss in your ability to perform even the most straightforward tasks. For this reason I often wear a thin (and dry) inner glove to enable quick removal of the outer mitt for performing tasks whilst protecting the fingers at the same time.

Headwear can also be approached in a similar way. First, use a lightweight hat with a large brim to help keep you cool and cut down on the amount of sun protection you need to wear, which invariably will be sweated off and irritate your eyes. As conditions change, I prefer a hat either in fleece or wool that combines warmth with windproof ability. Make sure the hat covers the ears, or if you're working really hard, opt for a WindStopper headband to protect the ears but allow adequate cooling. If wearing a helmet, consider a skullcap liner for extra warmth. Finally, for extreme cold and wind protection, a lightweight balaclava should provide full neck coverage and protection for chin and nose whilst maintaining good visibility.

RUCKSACKS

Your choice of rucksack depends on a number of variables such as length and type of route, duration, technical difficulty, and approach trek. No

Carrying heavy loads between camps is hard on you and your equipment. Make sure your pack is loaded correctly, well-fitted, and adjusted before you begin steep ascents.

one pack will cover all options, so invariably you will end up taking a combination to suit the various parts of the expedition. You wouldn't want to undertake your approach walk and acclimatisation with a heavy load, so a smaller pack makes sense. A 40-litre (10.5 gal) pack or similar will give you the ability to carry all you need for a day's trek: food, drink, and clothing, with enough spare room for the extra camera lens and tripod. If you are going to be separated from your main supplies for the whole day, ensure you have enough to survive in case the planned reunion is delayed. I once spent a cold and uncomfortable night when my warm clothing and sleeping system failed to make the next camp. If a lightweight alpine style is to be used on the mountain, this size of pack would double up.

If a more traditional approach to the climb is planned with numerous camps and load carries in between, something larger will be required. Here the balance is between being able to transport larger, bulkier objects (i.e., tents, sleeping bags) and weight. With the best will in the world, carrying in excess of 20 kilograms (44 lb) is unlikely to be sustained for many days, especially at altitude, so a pack of 100 litres (26.5 gal) is unlikely to be beneficial. A better choice is a more conservative pack of 60+15 litres (16+4 gal).

Regardless of size, a number of factors will need to be considered. Your rucksack is part of your climbing system and will need to be compatible with your clothing to allow access to pockets and vents. Your climbing harness and rucksack hip belt must not interfere with each other, and due consideration must be given to carriage and accessibility of climbing gear. A water system also needs to be considered, whether that is a bladder and drinking tube or a pouch on the hip belt, not forgetting appropriate insulation. Last but not least, keeping the contents of your rucksack waterproof and separated in stuff sacks (compression straps for reducing volume are useful) will help to keep items separate and easily identifiable.

TENTS

Tents can be divided into four stages of requirement for large expeditions: trek, base camp, mountain camps, and summit assault. On many approach treks in the Himalayas, it is possible to use tea house–type accommodations, consisting of basic shared sleeping space and provision of food and drink. Although convenient, these don't always offer the best night's rest and acclimatisation. For this reason, on the approach I have often used tents earmarked for higher on the mountain.

Once at base camp, something a little more substantial and spacious is recommended for prolonged amounts of time to allow good rest and recuperation after hard climbing days. On the 2006 Everest West Ridge expedition, the Terra Nova Cosmos proved ideal. Designed for eight people, it can be a comfortable and luxurious base camp tent for three or four, providing lots of space for personal equipment and room enough to stand and stretch (as long as you're under 183 cm, or 6 ft), along with the strength to withstand the worst of weather.

No camp on the mountain itself is going to be particularly comfortable. Your tent, normally a two-person tent, will need to be strong, durable, and as light as possible. Single-skin tents are the lightest, but if you are looking to have something placed precariously for longer amounts of time, a double-skin tent will prove more resilient. We combined the Ultra Quasar with double poles for extra strength (although also extra weight) that withstood the worst of Himalayan storms in locations where, previously, only snow holes dug with much time and effort had survived.

Finally, if route and duration are totally unknown for the summit push, plan for the worst and have an emergency back-up. Something as simple as a small two-person bothy bag will be a lifesaver in the worst-case scenario and weighs in at 0.3 kilograms (.7 lb). We went a step further in designing the climber's high isolation pod (CHIP) shelter, a one-off design made specifically for the Everest West Ridge 2006 expedition. The idea for this shelter came from hard-earned experiences of surviving in canyons,

A modern two-person tent design at camp 2 on EWR 2006.

caves, and mountains. Ultralightweight and compact, it can provide shelter for up to four, offering a haven for resting, eating, drinking, and warming up. When used in conjunction with a small stove, it could quickly turn –34 degrees Celsius (–30 degrees Fahrenheit) to –1 degrees Celsius (30 degrees Fahrenheit), no mean feat at over 8,000 metres (26,245 ft).

SLEEPING SYSTEMS

Browse any good equipment catalogue or retail shop and the vast array of choices for sleeping bags will soon become apparent. However, no one sleeping bag will suit all situations. From bag design (mummy or tapered) to filling (down or synthetic), the choice may seem endless. Often you will find yourself on a trip requiring a long approach trek, possibly starting from low altitude in warm, humid conditions and rising to the freezing temperatures of base camp, which means more than one sleeping system may be required. Carrying only one light bag and intending to add clothing as you get higher will not always be ideal, especially for longer trips. You may be happy to rough it for a few days on an alpine-style ascent, but if you're planning an extended trip, a warm and comfortable night's sleep will be much needed.

Insulation comes in the form of down or synthetic; both have pros and cons and your choice will depend on the environment for intended use. In cold, dry conditions, down is hard to beat. Lighter in comparison to synthetic insulation, down packs into a reasonably small size, even for a heavier fill weight, but you will need to look after the bag, treating it with greater care. Down won't perform as well as synthetic material if damp or wet, which will be inevitable in extended use. Make sure to dry and air the bag as often as you can.

Synthetic bags can be much more forgiving. They are generally cheaper, but more filling is required so they tend to be heavier. Importantly, they have the advantage of keeping you warm even when they are wet. So when conditions are a little more unpredictable, synthetic could be the best option.

Regardless of fill type, make sure that all bags have good all-around insulation—you don't want to find any cold spots. The fit needs to be comfortably snug; if it is too big, it won't be as efficient in keeping you warm and will add extra weight. If you're hot bagging, or sharing sleeping systems at various camps with other team members (not normally at the same time), size will be a consideration if one team member is 198 centimetres (6 ft, 6 in.) and another is 152 centimetres (5 ft). Sleeping bags specifically designed for females are also now available. Make sure zips are working well and have a baffle; a good hood and draw cord system will also help you to get a good night's sleep. Added warmth and protection can be gained by using a bivi bag. Choose one that is waterproof and breathable—otherwise you will end up as wet inside as out.

A good sleeping bag will perform at its best if used with an appropriate sleeping mat. Choose between closed-cell and self-inflating mats. Closed-cell mats are durable, forgiving, light, and flexible and can be rolled or folded flat to fit inside a rucksack. Ensure that the mat has a nonslip surface, or you will find yourself sliding off in the night. Closed-cell mats can also be cut down to minimise weight and space. If more comfort is desired, consider a self-inflating mat. Often best used at base camp, these provide far better insulation and comfort at an added cost of weight. I have used Therm-a-Rest mats successfully in all conditions, but always carry a repair kit—you never know!

STOVES

I doubt there is a single serious mountaineer who has never had a severe drama with a mountain stove. It can be the pleasure or pain on any mountain or route. Get it right, fantastic; get it wrong, and it will become your worst nightmare. Give careful thought to the intended objective, height, length, altitude, temperature, country, and availability of fuel, as well as whether it is for personal use or will be shared by expedition members.

Easily maintained and most commonly used are the screw-in cartridges that come in butane or a butane–propane mix. For the majority of low-level objectives, they will prove the easiest and most forgiving options. Make best use of heat exchangers and windbreaks to optimise performance. If placed on the floor, make sure you provide some kind of insulation, especially if using directly on snow. Hanging stoves are now popular, and the Jetboil system provides a compact, neat, and efficient stove. Consider insulating the fuel because it will lose efficiency when getting low and cold; even adding hand warmth will make a difference. I have also witnessed climbers using an external heat source for a hanging stove, but be warned, this can have serious consequences.

At altitude, or when it starts to get really cold, I have sworn by my old MSR XGK for many years. As long as you can get the right fuel (make sure it's not contaminated if it's from an unreliable source), it is remarkably robust, blasts out great heat, and is fast. Regardless of final choice, I can't emphasise enough the need to check your stove, fuel, and intended lighters before setting off and to always carry a small repair kit. Better

still, carry a back-up stove amongst the team. A PocketRocket comes in at 85 grams (3 oz) and will provide instant warmth and a drink, even inside a two-person bothy bag at 8,000 metres (26,245 ft)!

CLIMBING GEAR

Every climb and every route will require a different approach, and to that end the equipment needed will vary immensely. Experience is the key to deciding preferences and what gear is required. Here we will give some insight into the personal climbing gear used on the 2006 Everest West Ridge expedition and similar objectives.

With all climbing gear, compatibility with other gear items and the route is essential. Boots and crampons must match the conditions on the mountain. On Everest, we were unlikely to encounter grade VI ice, so a technical crampon would be inappropriate; more suitable in most

Paul Chiddle, climbing the French Spur up to the West Ridge of Everest, tackling steep ice at 6,300 metres (20,670 ft).

It's Not How Well You're Dressed But How Well You Climb

Well over 20 years ago, I shared a base camp under Mount Kenya's Diamond Couloir with a team of Polish climbers. With my youth and naivety, kitted out in homemade climbing clothing and secondhand boots and ice tools, we shared a passion to climb at any cost. I watched in awe as this bunch of bedraggled climbers would tackle anything and everything in front of them with passion and ease, from hard rock to steep ice, all in preparation for an impending Himalayan trip. It was a valuable lesson for a young lad. Climbing is not about shiny new gear in the latest trends and colours but approach and attitude combined with an ability to improvise, adapt, and overcome.

—John Doyle

cases is a quality mountaineering crampon. Select something strong and reliable in steel, make sure points are sharpened for the best performance, and always use an antiballing plate (plastic plates are lighter than rubber). Ensure the crampons fit your boots well, even when using gaiters, and experiment with various attachments—clip-on, toe bail, heel lever, and plastic harness. Try them in all conditions and whilst wearing gloves and mitts; fitting crampons to boots at 8,000 metres (26,245 ft) can be a major challenge.

A harness needs to be comfortable and adjustable over a wide range of clothing, from a thin base layer on the lower mountain to a full down suit higher up. Consider how the harness fits with your intended rucksack and waist belt (if worn), the adjustment range of waist and leg loops, access to gear loops, and the all-important emergency toilet stop. Though full-body harnesses will have their benefits when travelling through heavily crevassed areas, especially with heavy loads, they tend to be uncomfortable and can cause problems when adding or removing layers. Perhaps a more useful option is to use a separate chest harness if and when required.

Ice tools need to have a balance between technical ability and practical use. For leading initial steep sections, a pair of well-balanced,

performance curved ice tools will give you confidence to tackle hard, steep, mixed terrain, and at least one pair of these for the lead climbers is useful. For the rest of the team following on fixed ropes, a lighter, more versatile tool is appropriate. Something like the Grivel Air Tech Evolution combines a practical approach on moderate terrain with featherweight performance. Choose a length of 50 to 55 centimetres (20-22 in.) and when the going gets less steep, combine it with a telescopic walking pole.

Don't underestimate the value of good head protection, even on easier angled terrain; falling rock and ice can rapidly ruin your day. Ultralightweight modern helmets are constructed of compressed foam, and though they offer protection, they will not stand up to the rigors of a long trip and inevitable wear and tear, kit dumps, and abuse. Opt for a hard-shell helmet, which is perhaps not as stylish but is practical, durable, and sure to last the course.

When ascending fixed ropes, a good expedition ascender will be hard to beat. Normally on all but the steepest of terrain, you will need only one, and a good handle will provide a positive grip even when wearing mitts. Attached with a short sling or daisy chain to your harness, it will also provide safety when passing fixed anchors on steep ground. For descending ropes, a good abseil device can double up for both. Make sure it can handle the rope chosen; many now will cover 8 to 11 millimetres, but it is worth checking, especially on icy ropes. Both ascender and descender should be used with locking karabiners. I prefer screw gate as opposed to twist lock and suggest you carry a couple.

Rope can be categorised by that used for general climbing and fixed lines. A general climbing rope will be dynamic in construction and anywhere between 8 and 11 millimetres in diameter. The terrain (glacier, easy snow slope, or hard mixed rock and ice ground) will dictate the best length, diameter, and weight. When fixing large sections of a route, consider the difficulty of the terrain and the amount of use the ropes will get. If on a popular route, use could involve hundreds of ascents. Because we were the only expedition on the West Ridge of Everest, we had total control over how the fixed lines were to be used and thus chose a heavier 9-millimetre static rope on steeper sections that

required lots of hard Jumar work. On the easier sections we used a much thinner, lighter 7.5-millimetre cord to act mainly as a hand rail in poor weather. Whatever combination you choose, don't underestimate the amount of fixed line you will need to secure your intended route—it could well be in excess of 5 kilometres (3 mi) on an 8,000-metre (26,245 ft) peak.

When it came to securing ropes, 90 percent of the anchors used were in snow and ice, with only a small number of rock pegs. Sixty-centimetre (2 ft) snow pickets were a good length to carry and place in steep snow, and all had been prefixed with small tie-in loops to speed up fixing of rope. Titanium ice screws, although more expensive, are considerably lighter when you have to carry large numbers. Make sure they are nice and sharp to penetrate the hardest ice.

Last but not least in terms of personal climbing gear are Prusik loops. Carry a couple of 6-millimetre loops that will provide for a potential multitude of uses, from crevasse rescue to abseil back-up.

Don't underestimate how much wear and tear fixed ropes will take with team members performing multiple ascents and descents with heavy loads over many weeks of climbing during a long expedition.

SUPPLEMENTARY OXYGEN EQUIPMENT

As with all equipment choices, supplementary oxygen must fit in with the objectives of the chosen peak and route. Many of the 8,000-metre (26,245 ft) peaks are now climbed using supplementary oxygen. Arguably all but the highest (Everest, K2, and Kanchenjunga) are quite feasible without supplementary oxygen, if the expedition team has prepared correctly beforehand. However, many commercial guiding companies will insist on the use of supplementary oxygen. There is no question that using supplementary oxygen will greatly increase your chance of success, and having previously climbed two 8,000-metre peaks without it, I was absolutely amazed at the difference it did make. Donning an oxygen system for the first time at Camp 4 on the West Ridge, I romped across the North Face to over 8,000 metres in less than 2 hours, feeling like I was back at Camp 1. For smaller expeditions, don't underestimate the logistical problems that using oxygen will bring.

Supplementary oxygen systems can be divided into two types. The first and more traditional is the constant-flow system. It is simple to operate, and when used in conjunction with a modern facemask, it provides the best results in terms of physical performance for the climber. With the constant-flow system, oxygen flows all the time the regulator is open. As a climber exhales, the inlet valve in the facemask is closed by the increased pressure. The breath exits the facemask via the exhalation valve. At this point the oxygen is still flowing and starts to fill a reservoir that expands to accept the increasing volume of oxygen. As the climber then inhales, the contents of the reservoir are drawn into the facemask and then the climber's lungs. With older facemask styles, this basic system has not worked reliably, with valves leaking oxygen to the atmosphere and even freezing in the closed position, preventing oxygen from flowing into the facemask. The fit of the facemask is vital to ensure a good seal for efficiency, as well as to prevent the fogging of goggles.

The second system available is the pulsed-dose system. This is a demand-based system that, as the name suggests, doses oxygen to the body on inhalation only. This system offers great savings in the quantity of oxygen used, therefore extending the duration of an oxygen cylinder by at least three times. The other benefit of the pulsed dose is that the oxygen is delivered via a nasal cannula, which allows the climber to eat, drink, and communicate whilst still receiving supplemental oxygen. It also allows a climber to sleep on oxygen without creating vast amounts of condensation in the face mask that then seeps into the sleeping bag. Pulsed-dose systems sense a person's inhalation and deliver a precisely metered dose of oxygen at the leading edge of inspiration. This allows the oxygen to go deep into the lungs, thus realising the best therapeutic benefits. Because the oxygen is only delivered in precise doses and only at the start of inhalation, no oxygen is wasted by filling the anatomical dead spaces in the upper lungs, upper respiratory tract, and mouth where oxygen cannot be absorbed into the body. This is how the pulsed-dose system extends the endurance of the oxygen cylinder for so much longer. Table 4.1 compares the endurance offered by the two systems.

Enjoying a good night's rest at 7,300 metres (23,950 ft).

TABLE 4.1 Oxygen Flow Rates

Cylinder pressure	Flow rate (l.min⁻¹)					
	1	2	3	4	5	6
4 L (1 GAL) CYLINDER ENDURANCE TABLE—PULSED DOSE						
50 bar	10 hr, 6 min	5 hr, 3 min	3 hr, 22 min	2 hr, 32 min	2 hr	1 hr, 40 min
100 bar	20 hr, 12 min	10 hr, 6 min	6 hr, 43 min	5 hr, 3 min	4 hr	3 hr, 22 min
150 bar	30 hr, 20 min	15 hr, 9 min	10 hr, 6 min	7 hr, 35 min	6 hr, 3 min	5 hr
200 bar	40 hr, 25 min	20 hr, 12 min	13 hr, 28 min	10 hr, 6 min	8 hr, 4 min	6 hr, 43 min
250 bar	50 hr, 30 min	25 hr, 15 min	16 hr, 50 min	12 hr, 37 min	10 hr, 6 min	8 hr, 25 min
300 bar	60 hr, 20 min	30 hr, 10 min	20 hr, 12 min	15 hr, 9 min	12 hr, 7 min	10 hr, 6 min
4 L (1 GAL) ENDURANCE TABLE—CONSTANT FLOW						
50 bar	3 hr, 20 min	1 hr, 40 min	1 hr, 10 min	50 min	40 min	34 min
100 bar	6 hr, 40 min	3 hr, 20 min	2 hr, 15 min	1 hr, 40 min	1 hr, 20	1 hr, 10 min
150 bar	10 hr	5 hr	3 hr, 20 min	2 hr, 30 min	2 hr	1 hr, 40 min
200 bar	13 hr, 20 min	6 hr, 40 min	4 hr, 25 min	3 hr, 20 min	2 hr, 40 min	2 hr, 15 min
250 bar	16 hr, 40 min	8 hr, 20 min	5 hr, 30 min	4 hr, 10 min	3 hr, 20 min	2 hr, 45 min
300 bar	20 hr	10 hr	7 hr, 30 min	5 hr	4 hr	3 hr, 20 min

Table courtesy of Summit Oxygen International Ltd. (www.summitoxygen.com).

A number of factors were key to our decision to go with Summit Oxygen's pulsed-dose system:

1. The usage time per bottle was almost triple that of the Russian constant flow system due to the oxygen being on demand rather than constant flow. This meant that the cost, mountain logistics, and number of bottles to be carried were all much lower.

2. The system is far more user friendly because it uses a nasal cannula to deliver the oxygen instead of a large face mask and reservoir bag, thus enabling users to speak, eat, drink, and see where they are going. For those who preferred, a smaller mask was available for use with the system. The mask was tried, but almost all but a few Sherpas preferred the ease of the cannula.

3. All the equipment is compatible, meaning that if climbers want to optimise their performance on the mountain, then the

Dave Wilson at over 8,000 metres (26,245 ft) using a silicone nasal cannula for oxygen on demand.

Breathing With or Without Supplementary Oxygen

It is often assumed that it is best to get as high as possible on the mountain before using supplemental oxygen. This made good sense in days gone by when only constant-flow systems were available. With the advent of pulsed-dose technology, however, supplemental oxygen can now be used in sparing quantities on the lower reaches of the mountain and still reduce the logistical burden of oxygen cylinders on the mountain. A good example of this is our use of oxygen for sleeping at camps above 7,300 metres (23,950 ft) on Everest, which meant that at 7,300 metres, we had acclimatised as much as physiologically possible. Using oxygen when sleeping allows the climber a good night's sleep since apnea is eliminated. This in itself will greatly improve performance, and in my case, after a good night's sleep at Camp 3, the following day I had more than enough energy to allow progress along the entire West Ridge without the use of supplementary oxygen, thus easing the logistical supply problems immensely. It was only on leaving camp 4 at 7,600 metres (24,935 ft) that the pulsed-dose system was used continually, and as previously stated, it made a phenomenal difference. Without any shadow of a doubt, never have I seen a group of high-altitude climbers perform so well both physically and mentally. I only wish we could have controlled the snow conditions as effectively!

—John Doyle

pulsed-dose system could be used on the lower sections of the mountain and then climbers could switch to constant flow before departing the top camp for the summit.

MISCELLANEOUS ESSENTIALS

Last but not least, here is a little food for thought on a number of essential equipment items. As previously stated, the aim of this chapter is not to sell specific products but to pass on hard-earned experience and advice as to what works in different situations. Only by getting outdoors in all conditions will you really appreciate the pros and cons of your equipment and what works best for you.

Eye Protection Never underestimate the effect that the outdoor elements can have on your eyes, from glaring sun reflected and intensified from the surrounding snow to the cold, biting, and drying winds of high altitude. Neglect good eye protection at your peril—I have witnessed how debilitating and potentially catastrophic the effects of snow blindness can be on both an individual and a team.

A vast array of eye protection is now available. Gone are the days of old-fashioned glacier glasses with dull and uncomfortable designs. The new sport-type sunglasses have sleek, face-hugging designs that should provide everyone with an almost perfect fit to prevent unwanted light and wind penetrating to the eyes. One important factor to consider is misting up of the lenses, especially when working hard. Experiment before you depart and look for a balance of protection and ventilation. Glasses are useless if you can't see through them due to misting.

Interchangeable lenses give the option to get the best out of the many light combinations, including clear, amber, brown, grey, and traditional darker lenses. Make certain the protection from UV rays is adequate; different tints provide different levels of protection. During training runs, bike rides, and mountain days, I have found the ability to change lenses quite useful, but once I'm on serious, long mountain routes, I'm unwilling to stop and change lenses to suit the conditions for passing cloud cover.

Once the winds start to blow hard with spindrift, quality goggles will become essential. Don't be tempted to buy cheap goggles; double lenses and good ventilation will ensure the best performance in the worst conditions. Choose a robust yet flexible design because they may well spend most of the trip stuffed in a rucksack pocket, and as with glasses, take spare lenses with you—they are often broken or misplaced.

Hydration Failure to stay hydrated dramatically increases risk to mountaineers as both physical and cognitive performance are negatively affected. Maintaining the ability to take in fluids during a long day is essential. During Everest West Ridge 2006, we developed the complete hydration internal pouches (CHIP) system that has been used successfully above 8,000 metres. The design has two 1-litre fluid bladders winterized with neoprene-covered tubes and nozzles. These tubes are shortened such that when they are placed in a fixed pouch inside a waistcoat, one on each side of the front of the chest, the nozzles are only accessible by a flap in the down suit. With careful management they are only momentarily exposed to the freezing conditions during drinking and are kept liquid by body heat so that fluid is always readily accessible. On a cold night the system makes a great hot-water bottle and gives you a warm start. Equally as effective on warmer days at altitude, the system can be worn over a thermal base with no other layers. As with all new innovations, there are some limitations due to freezing, potential leaks, or pipes coming adrift, but with good husbandry and a repair kit, such

as plumbers tape and strong plastic glue, these limitations can be minimised.

Navigation Tools Map, compass, and GPS all have their place. Once on the route itself, most of the navigation problems are solved. It's now down to technical route-finding ability, and there is no substitute for experience. On the lower mountain, glacier approaches, and easier terrain, marking the route with wands will save you a lot of time and grief after a long day in poor visibility when, for example, searching for a small camp in the middle of a glacier. Always carry a map, compass, and GPS just in case; know bearings and distance to key features; and mark the features as waypoints in your GPS, especially when operating in large, open areas. I would also recommend a good watch with alarm, stopwatch, backlight, and altimeter capability; it is as much a useful navigation aid as a timepiece. Make sure it is waterproof; can stand up to the knocks; and, as with all electronic equipment, has fresh batteries (and spares).

Trekking Poles Poles are a great aid to crossing the variety of terrain you can expect to encounter on expedition, from jungle to deep snow. A trekking pole is great for rough terrain in ascent or descent, and when carrying heavy loads it will help take the strain from aching joints. I prefer a three-piece collapsible pole because it packs neatly onto the side of the rucksack when hands are needed for climbing or scrambling. Trekking poles have also been useful in helping to splint the odd leg sprain.

Headtorch If you can't see the map, guide, or topo, you can't navigate. Now with the latest mini-LED (light-emitting diode) torches, there is no excuse to be caught out. These come with a long battery life, are small and light, and give enough illumination for easier night travel and awkward situations. If you require something a little more substantial, choose a halogen lamp to give a powerful searching beam for serious route finding, although such lamps go through batteries quite quickly and weigh considerably more.

Skis and Snowshoes I have seen more than one expedition grind to a frustrating halt after heavy snowfall. In some areas you should expect a lot more snow than in others, so plan accordingly. Teams are not always stopped due to avalanche conditions, which should never be underestimated, but more often due to the inability to wade through thigh-deep snow above 5,000 metres (16,405 ft). For this reason you should plan on giving yourself the option of skis or snowshoes to operate in such conditions and not waste valuable time.

Skis sound like a fun option, but don't underestimate the effort and skill required for skiing safely at altitude. You will also need to consider the terrain you will encounter, the group's ability, carrying even more equipment, and how often you think you will be able to use the equipment to justify its inclusion. Unless you are taking a team with a main objective to ascend or descend a route on skis (the feasibility and methods would require a chapter of their own), I would recommend snowshoes.

Snowshoes are a much simpler option for the majority of team members and require little training. They are now available in many designs, but opt for a robust model with a universal binding that will fit a wide range of shoe sizes. Look for a toe-crampon system for icy sections, as well as to prevent sideslipping on traverses. They should be able to pack down flat and should be reasonably light—there's no point in carrying more weight than is necessary, and they are often sized for the weight of the climber, including rucksack. The main aim after snowfall is to reopen the route on the mountain as quickly as possible, so you probably won't need to equip every member with a pair of snowshoes, but take a few pairs for the hardy trailbreakers.

Repair Kit Making sure all your equipment is 100 percent serviceable before you leave will pay dividends. However, there will be the odd unforeseen blowout that will have to be dealt with, so balancing the need to carry a small repair kit against all that might happen is worthwhile. A small multitool with a selection of knife blades (make sure they are sharp), screwdriver attachments, small metal file, and pliers is essential. Carry a selection of plastic zip ties in various sizes for fast and efficient repairs, a few metres of 3-millimetre cord, and some superglue for those small, awkward repairs. At base camp on larger expeditions, a more extensive kit can be held to cover larger repairs to tents and so on when time permits.

Eating and Drinking Utensils Use a large, plastic measuring beaker of at least 1 litre to keep track of fluid intake and help you stay hydrated so you can perform at your best. Mark it so you know it's yours—people will be jealous! For eating, I prefer a plastic spoon. Attach a cord to the spoon and beaker so they can be hung in the tent for ease and convenience.

Urine Bottle Another essential piece of equipment that will keep you warm and sane during the night and in any unexpected tent time is the urine bottle. It should be a wide-mouthed plastic container of at least 1 litre, and make sure it's recognizably different from any drinking bottle, even in the dark. Some prefer the collapsible type; I opt for something a bit sturdier to avoid any accidents. Practice makes perfect!

Malcolm Russell replacing fluids at 7,300 metres (23,950 ft) by collecting snow, which is then melted on a stove.

KEY IDEAS

▸ Remember the six Ps: Prior planning and preparation prevent poor performance.

▸ Check and test everything; leave nothing to chance.

▸ Put your equipment through its paces and in all conditions.

▸ Be practical. Whether on a weekend in Scotland or a Himalayan expedition, the best and most expensive equipment won't guarantee success.

▸ Ask questions and take advice, but remember it is ultimately your decision.

First Aid, Travel, and Acclimatisation

Adrian Mellor and John O'Hara

Life is *not* a journey to the grave with the intention of arriving safely in a pretty and well-preserved body, but rather to skid in broadside, thoroughly used up, totally worn out, and loudly proclaiming, "*Wow, what a ride!*"

Anonymous

Planning medical care for a party encompasses everything from a small group out for a day's walk to a major expedition to a remote, high-altitude objective. A chapter in a book of this sort cannot cover the vast array of techniques, background knowledge, and skills involved, nor can it replace common sense or provide the judgement required. However, the basic principles of approach to a casualty, priorities, and recognition of serious illness are covered, along with basic options for treatment. Details will also be provided on specific high-altitude problems and on preparing a medical kit for expeditions. The last part of the chapter deals with travel and acclimatisation to altitude, both of which can cause performance and health problems if not planned for and managed appropriately.

FIRST AID IN A WILDERNESS ENVIRONMENT

The approach to a casualty in a remote location differs little from that in other areas. It is in planning the response and appropriate levels of kit, equipment, and expertise that the real challenges occur.

Approach to the Casualty

Mountain environments present unique challenges for a would-be rescuer. A relatively trivial injury may cause great difficulties in terms of access to and extrication of the patient.

It is of paramount importance to assess the scene of the injury for further risks. The casualty may have been hit by falling rocks that still represent a risk to any rescuer. This situation occurs with winter climbing and avalanche situations where residual avalanche threat may pose a risk to rescuers. It is the responsibility of the rescuer to perform a risk assessment at the scene of the injury. For example, it may be more appropriate for the casualty to come to the rescuer than vice versa.

Calling for Help

An essential part of expedition planning is knowing how to contact local rescue services (e.g., in the United Kingdom, telephone number 999 connects to the emergency services, and in the United States the emergency number is 911). Where applicable, it should be stated that the accident has taken place in a wilderness environment and mountain rescue will be required. In the United Kingdom, the ambulance controller will then make a decision to call out the RAF search-and-rescue services or local air ambulance services. In other countries there may be a choice of numbers for rescue services or even direct lines to private helicopter services. These numbers can usually be found at local guide offices or in guidebooks and should be located as part of the preparation for any international visit to a wilderness environment.

Though mobile phone coverage is good in most areas of Britain and Europe (especially high on the hills rather than in the valleys), this may not be the case in many international locations. For more remote expeditions, consider taking a satellite phone, even though coverage is not complete, especially in steep valleys. There is an international convention for signalling distress with a whistle (six blasts followed by a minute interval) or signalling with a torch (six flashes followed by a minute interval). All expedition members should be aware of the emergency contact numbers and signalling procedures; an aide memoir or reminder can be produced and carried.

Priorities

Once the casualty has been reached, carry out a quick primary survey. The aim of this survey is to identify and provide first aid treatment for life-threatening problems. Treatment priorities are based on the order in which injuries create a threat to life; hence, injuries are treated in the following sequence:

- ▸ Airway
- ▸ Breathing
- ▸ Circulation
- ▸ Disability
- ▸ Exposure

Addressing injuries in this way also provides a framework for reporting the injuries (without necessarily knowing any underlying diagnoses) to ambulance control and other rescuers as they arrive. A logical approach is to assess the scene, approach the casualty, kneel by the head, and with a hand on the forehead and shoulder, gently shake the patient and shout to elicit a response. Airway, breathing, circulation, disability, and exposure—ABCDE—are then assessed.

Airway (and Cervical Spine Control)

Without a patent airway, even with respiratory effort the patient cannot get oxygen in and out of the lungs and death will ensue in approximately 4 minutes. The airway comprises the passages from the mouth and nose to the pharynx and down through the larynx to the trachea. The airway should first be inspected for any foreign bodies (e.g., teeth, dentures, food), which should then be removed. Second, listen for breathing noises. If the mouth is clear of obstruction and no air is passing in and out, then the airway needs to be opened.

The airway is most commonly blocked by the tongue moving back in the mouth to obstruct the air passages. Because the tongue is attached to the jaw, moving the jaw forward will clear the airway and allow breathing. This can be achieved with a manoeuvre known as a *jaw thrust*. The jaw thrust consists of placing the fingers behind the angle of the jawbone (mandible) and lifting the jaw forward (figure 5.1).

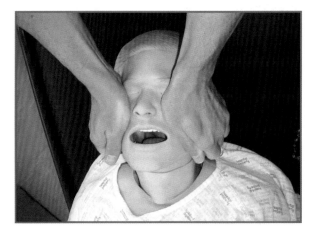

Figure 5.1 Performing a jaw thrust. Note the fingers under the angle of the jaw and hands against the facial bones.

This manoeuvre is of minimum risk to the cervical spine, which can often be injured in falls, resulting in unconsciousness. The cervical spine consists of the vertebrae running through the neck and contains the spinal cord. If the cervical spine is fractured and the usual alignment of the bones disrupted, then damage to the nerves supplying the rest of the body can occur. In the most severe cases, this can cause paralysis of the breathing muscles and death within a few minutes. For this reason every effort must be made to minimise movement of the cervical spine. This can be difficult for a single rescuer, and although the combination of supporting the head and performing the jaw thrust is relatively easy with practice, it effectively ties the rescuer to the patient's head until help arrives (figure 5.2). If there are two or more rescuers, then one should perform manual in-line stabilisation of the cervical spine, gently supporting the sides of the neck in a neutral position, until rescuers arrive and can immobilise the spine.

Various airway adjuncts are available to help keep an airway patent. Most commonly used is a Guedel oropharyngeal airway. This plastic curved tube is inserted over the back of the tongue and keeps the airway patent. For inexperienced rescuers, a simple jaw thrust will suffice.

Breathing

After assessing the airway and performing simple opening manoeuvres as necessary, breathing must be assessed. Breathing can easily be examined by placing one's head close to the casualty's mouth. Important things to note include the following:

1. The rate and rhythm of breathing (normally 10-20 breaths per minute)
2. Whether there are any abnormal noises suggesting secretions or blood in or damage to the airway
3. Whether the chest is moving equally on both sides

If no breathing is noted after opening the airway, it should be established whether there are any signs of life. If there are no signs, basic life support (BLS) commences (see figure 5.3). It is not appropriate to describe BLS techniques in

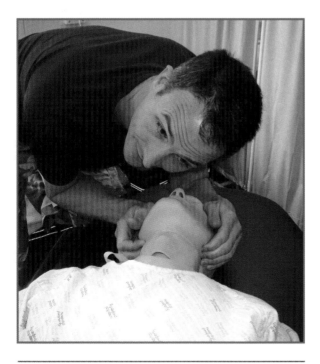

Figure 5.2 Performing a jaw thrust and checking for signs of breathing.

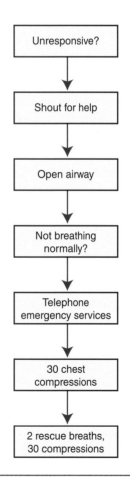

Figure 5.3 Basic life support (BLS) guidelines.
Adapted from Resuscitation Council UK 2005.

detail in a text of this sort; see Suggested Readings on page 108 for suitable references.

Circulation

The initial assessment of the patient should produce some evidence of the adequacy of circulation. For example, to be able to talk coherently, the casualty must have adequate blood flow to the brain. An otherwise healthy person can compensate for a loss of up to 40 percent of blood volume before becoming severely unwell. As part of the assessment of circulation, any bleeding points should be examined and dressed. An elastic pressure dressing (sometimes sold as first field dressings or military-type dressings) consisting of a pad and elasticated bandage is ideal for stopping bleeding from a limb or head wound. Fractures can bleed significantly, especially fractures of the femur (thigh bone) and pelvis. This bleeding can be reduced by gentle alignment and splinting. Treatment of internal bleeding for all but the best equipped and trained rescuers will consist of recognition of the seriously injured patient and expedited transport to a hospital.

Shock is the medical state in which inadequate oxygen is supplied to the body. This may be because of a problem with the heart (e.g., as the pump), a lack of oxygen in the blood (e.g., high-altitude pulmonary oedema), or a problem with the blood supply (e.g., haemorrhage from wounds, internal or external). In the extreme case, a shocked patient will appear cold, clammy, sweating, and unwell with a fast pulse (greater than 120 beats per minute) that may not be felt as a pulse anywhere other than in the neck. Rapid assessment of the circulation

is made by noting the patient's appearance and taking a pulse. The pulse should be measured over 15 seconds and the result multiplied by 4 to get a rate per minute. Absence of a pulse is an important sign—with falling blood pressure, the pulse tends to disappear in the smaller arteries, so it will disappear at the wrist, then in the groin, and then in the neck as blood pressure falls.

Adequacy of circulation can be further assessed with the capillary refill test. This is performed by pressing with a finger on, for example, the breastbone (sternum) for 5 seconds and then releasing; in an uninjured person the skin should flush pink again within 2 seconds. Capillary refill is a useful test, but it can be difficult to interpret, especially in the extremities of a cold patient. Table 5.1 shows the progression of shock with degrees of blood loss. It is imperative to be able to recognise a patient who is in shock, provide any possible first aid, and arrange for urgent evacuation to a hospital.

Disability

Realistically, little can be done to reduce disability in an injured patient other than applying the principles described thus far, ensuring a patent airway and breathing, and stopping any haemorrhage.

In terms of communicating with emergency services, disability can be assessed using the AVPU scale:

Alert—The patient is talking and aware of surroundings.

Verbal—The patient responds to verbal questioning.

TABLE 5.1 Degrees of Shock

Blood loss	<15% lost	15%-30% lost	30%-40% lost	>40% lost
Heart rate	<100 bpm	>100 bpm	120-140 bpm	>140 bpm
Respiratory rate	10-20/min	20-30/min	30-40/min	>35/min
Capillary refill	Normal	>2 s	>2 s	Prolonged or absent
Mental state	Normal	Agitated, frightened	Confused, hostile	Confused, unresponsive

Normal blood volume for an adult male is approximately 5,000 millilitres (5 qt); bpm = beats per minute.

Pain—The patient responds to a painful stimulus (e.g., pressing on the bony area of the eyebrow will produce a response even if the casualty has a spinal cord injury).

Unresponsive—The patient does not respond.

Exposure

Injured patients will quickly become cold and lose heat for various reasons. They may be laid on the ground, losing heat directly; they may have less blood in their circulation; and they will lose more heat by breathing more quickly. Additionally, the emotional component to a significant injury tends to make casualties feel cold and shiver. For these reasons, it is necessary to provide warmth. This can be done in a variety of ways depending what is available, but it is important to try to get the person off cold ground (on a rucksack, spare jacket, or foam mat) and covered as much as possible, especially the head.

Note on Basic Life Support

The decision to start BLS in a wilderness environment can be challenging. It is difficult to rapidly assess what injuries are simply not survivable, in which case BLS is inappropriate. BLS is extremely tiring and once started, it should be continued. For a single rescuer, this is exhausting and limits the ability to call for help. Points for consideration are as follows:

1. If the casualty is seen to collapse rather than suffer any injury, BLS may be appropriate (e.g., the cause may be a preexisting heart condition).

2. If a casualty has multiple injuries and BLS cannot be started for several minutes due to difficulties with access, BLS is futile.

3. Hypothermic casualties may do better than expected because cold tends to protect the brain; thus, BLS should be started if it can be continued whilst the patient is warmed. This is usually only reasonable if evacuation times are short, and it will depend on the number of rescuers available to perform cardiopulmonary resuscitation (CPR). If there is no hope of

rescue within 2 hours of a patient who has a normal temperature, then CPR should not be started.

TREATMENT FOR SPECIFIC INJURIES

The spectrum of medical problems requiring first aid in a wilderness environment is huge and beyond the scope of this chapter. It is important to consider preexisting conditions, illnesses unrelated to the environment (e.g., an expedition member may have the misfortune to develop appendicitis), and injuries due to trauma and the activities undertaken. The immediate management of a few specific injuries is considered next.

Lacerations and Cuts

First aid for any bleeding wound is to apply pressure and elevate the limb above the level of the heart. A dressing should be applied that is firm but not tight enough to cut off the blood supply

Stitching a head wound after a close call in a rock fall on Everest.

to the limb. This can be assessed by looking at the limb beyond the injury and testing capillary refill; if the blood supply to the limb is intact, it should flush pink again within 2 seconds. If stitching is required and the expertise and kit are available, it can be completed. In exceptional circumstances, a tourniquet can be used to stop bleeding. This is usually only required in major limb injury, such as traumatic amputations. A tourniquet (which can be bought already made or fashioned from a rolled triangular bandage) can be applied above the injury, and it needs to be tight enough to prevent any blood flow into the limb. The danger with tourniquets is that because the blood supply to the limb is cut off, the limb is effectively dying. For this reason the casualty needs to be evacuated urgently. If evacuation is delayed, the tourniquet should be eased hourly to assess whether it is still required.

Fractures and Sprains

In the field, it is often impossible to tell the difference between a fracture and a sprain. The treatment for simple sprains consists of RICE: rest, ice, compression (with a crepe or tubular bandage), and elevation. More severe sprains will need splinting in the same way as a fracture.

There can be significant bleeding from fractures, so splinting is important for both reducing pain and preventing bleeding. When assessing a fracture, it is essential to look at blood supply to the limb beyond the break using the capillary refill method described previously. If the limb has very delayed or absent capillary refill, consider applying gentle traction to realign the limb before splinting if adequate pain relief can be given.

The principle of splinting fractures is that the joint above and the joint below the fracture should be splinted. For example, a fracture of the lower leg would need splinting at the ankles and above the knees. The uninjured leg can be used as a splint for the injured leg, paying attention to padding between the legs and ankles. Material such as a foam mattress or spare clothing can be used for padding. Bandages used to splint should be broad (ideally, folded triangular bandages) and tied on the noninjured side. Once again, capillary refill should be checked

before and after splinting. Upper-limb fractures can be treated in a sling made from a triangular bandage.

Open fractures should first be dressed with a sterile dressing and adequate padding around a protruding bone if the fracture cannot be reduced. If possible, the dressing against the wound should be soaked in dilute iodine, potassium permanganate, or a similar antiseptic solution.

Pain relief should be given early in the form of an appropriately strong painkiller. A casualty who does not have to be moved and is well splinted may be surprisingly comfortable, whereas moving will be painful. A casualty should not be fed after an injury (in anticipation of an operation on arrival at hospital), but sips of water with painkillers are entirely appropriate.

Burns

Burns may occur on expeditions due to the use of petrol or gas stoves in tents or other confined spaces. As with all medical problems, prevention is better than cure and every effort must be made to comply with the manufacturer's guidelines. Wherever possible, avoid using stoves inside tents.

First aid for burns is relatively straightforward and consists of three phases:

1. Stopping the burning process
2. Cooling the burn surface
3. Providing pain relief and dressing the burn

All burning should be extinguished and clothing that is covered in hot water or burning should be removed. If clothing has melted and cannot be removed, cut around the most affected areas, leaving those bits of cloth adhering to the burn.

The burn surface should be cooled with water at 8 to 25 degrees Celsius (46-77 degrees Fahrenheit)—do not use ice. This reduces the area of the burn and provides pain relief. Flowing water is ideal, but spraying or sponging the wound or wrapping in cold, wet towels is acceptable. Cooling in this way should take place for 20 minutes. While this cooling is taking place, it is imperative to keep the rest of the victim warm. To be effective, cooling needs to take place within 3 hours of injury.

The burn should be dressed either in a clean gauze dressing, in cling film, or in proprietary burn dressings. Cling film stops air from coming into contact with the burn and will therefore reduce the amount of pain. Burned areas swell considerably within a few hours. For this reason, dressings should not be continuous around a limb or finger; overlapping layers are better. For a similar reason, all jewellery should be removed.

Dental Problems

Dental problems are common on protracted expeditions. It goes without saying that before any prolonged trip to a remote environment, team members should have routine dental checks and any dental work completed. Dental problems include loss of fillings, damage to teeth, or toothache due to abscess formation. Temporary tooth dressings can be purchased over the counter as premixed pastes along with first aid kits including a dental mirror and spatula. This temporary dressing can be used to fill a cavity if an old filling falls out or to dress a broken tooth. Toothache occurs because of a deep abscess within the jawbone. Treatment should be with painkillers and antibiotics, such as 375 mg of Augmentin three times daily. Painkillers and antibiotics will usually provide sufficient relief for a team member to carry on with an expedition. Mouthwash (e.g., Corsodyl) is useful for mouth ulcers and gum irritation.

Environmental Problems

Expeditions often take place in inhospitable environments with extreme temperatures (often both high and low during the course of one day) and a lack of fresh drinking water, or with torrential downpours of rain and wind dramatically lowering the effective temperature. The body's physiological processes are designed to work at the normal body temperature of 37 degrees Celsius (98.6 degrees Fahrenheit). This temperature is usually tightly controlled between 36.5 and 37.5 degrees Celsius (97.7-99.5 degrees Fahrenheit). For this reason, small differences in core body temperature have a significant impact on well-being.

Heat Illness

Heat illness is the name given to the body's inability to deal with heat production during exercise. It occurs infrequently in the United Kingdom and similar environments but often occurs in hotter climates. Some knowledge of the effects and signs of heat illness, as well as gradual acclimatisation to extreme temperatures, will ameliorate many problems.

Heat exhaustion may occur after a short exposure to heavy work in hot weather or after prolonged exposure to a hot environment. Symptoms include weakness, tiredness, dizziness, headaches, nausea and vomiting, cramps, flushing, and sweating. Treatment is aimed at reducing temperature and consists of removal to a cool place, fanning, spraying with water, and drinking water. Heat exhaustion needs to be taken seriously because it can lead to heatstroke, which is much more serious. If body temperature is measured, it should be less than 40 degrees Celsius (104 degrees Fahrenheit).

Heatstroke is a life-threatening condition where the body core temperature exceeds 40 degrees Celsius (104 degrees Fahrenheit). At this point the usual temperature-regulating mechanisms break down and the casualty may start to shiver or even feel cold to touch. Symptoms are the same as heat exhaustion but become more serious, including confusion, irritability, fitting (such as seizures or convulsions), and unconsciousness. Treatment is the same as for heatstroke, but other measures such as ice packs in the armpits and groin may be required. In extreme cases the ABCDE process must be followed.

Hypothermia

Hypothermia occurs when the core body temperature is less than 35 degrees Celsius (95 degrees Fahrenheit). This can occur acutely with falls into cold water or more commonly over several hours from exposure to the elements due to inadequate clothing. As with most situations, prevention through adequate preparation of equipment and clothing and attention to the weather forecast is better than providing treatment.

Hypothermia symptoms start with feelings of cold and loss of coordination and dexterity. As body temperature falls further, more severe symptoms ensue. These include deteriorating memory, loss of decision-making ability, and loss of volition. This leads to a cessation of shivering, and at about 28 degrees Celsius (82.4 degrees Fahrenheit), the heart is prone to arrhythmia, leading to coma and death.

Treatment is gradual rewarming. This involves removing wet clothing and putting on warm, dry clothes, taking care to cover the extremities and head; drinking warm, sweet fluids; and getting into shelter and into a sleeping bag (ideally with another person who has not got hypothermia). Hot-water bottles can be used (drinks bottles filled with hot water work well in this role), but they should be wrapped in clothing or towels, not placed directly next to the skin, and they should be held against the torso rather than limbs.

In severe cases, cardiac arrest will occur. This is predominantly due to the heart going into a rhythm called *ventricular fibrillation* (VF). Extreme care should be taken to move a severely hypothermic patient gently so as not to precipitate VF. When considering starting BLS, it is important to think about the fact that BLS may have to be continued for a long time (until the casualty is in a medical facility or has a normal temperature). This will exhaust a single rescuer. BLS should only be started if no pulse can be found in the neck after 1 minute (heart rate can be extremely slow in hypothermic patients).

Cold Injury

Cold injury encompasses both freezing cold injury (frostbite) and nonfreezing cold injury (trench foot). Frostbite occurs in temperatures lower than 0 degrees Celsius (32 degrees Fahrenheit). It is most common in the hands and feet, although any area can be affected. Damage occurs because of freezing within the tissues and subsequent death of the cells. The affected part becomes white and loses sensation. Recovery depends on how deeply and for how long an area is frozen.

Prevention is, once again, better than cure, and adequate footwear and gloves are essential. It is important to minimise contact with bare metal objects that conduct heat away from the body. Any state that decreases blood flow to the extremities will also increase the risk of frostbite, including dehydration, poorly fitting boots, and smoking.

Treatment consists of rewarming the affected part in water at 40 degrees Celsius (104 degrees Fahrenheit). This will be very painful and will require strong painkillers. After rewarming, the affected part should be dressed in sterile dressings to reduce the risk of infection. Rewarming should only occur when the risk of reexposure to freezing is minimal, such as in a hospital or at base camp. The casualty should be encouraged to move the affected part to increase blood flow.

Nonfreezing cold injury (trench foot) occurs with prolonged exposure to low temperatures and occurs without freezing. The affected area is white and numb. This continues after rewarming and may be permanent; however, usually a day or so after rewarming, sensation returns

Treatment for mild frostbite after reaching the summit of Kanchenjunga.

with a burning pain that persists until sensation returns to normal. At the same time the limb may develop more blood flow and become red in colour.

Prevention includes wearing adequate footwear with dry socks and regularly checking the feet, not sleeping in wet footwear, and being aware of any tingling or numbness as early signs of trench foot.

Sunburn

Sunburn is more likely to occur at high altitudes and in snowy environments due to the fact that at altitude there is less protective atmosphere and UV radiation is reflected from snowy surfaces. It does not have to be a cloud-free day for sunburn to occur; UV rays penetrate cloud, and cloud can provide an extra reflecting layer that bounces UV rays between snow and cloud.

Sunburn should be prevented by wearing high-factor sunblock (greater than factor 25), lip balm containing sunblock, and light clothing. The sun protection factor (SPF) reflects the amount of protection relative to unprotected skin (e.g., SPF 8 has eight times the protection of normal skin). Exposure to UV rays produces sunburn on unprotected skin with redness, blistering, and swelling. Symptomatic relief can be provided with proprietary creams or in severe cases, mild steroid creams (e.g., 0.1 percent hydrocortisone cream).

Snow Blindness

Snow blindness is caused by UV damage to the eyes in snow landscapes. The eyes become very painful and gritty. Prevention consists of wearing quality sunglasses with UV filters (a spare pair should always be carried). If no glasses are available, then a pair can be improvised from any piece of material that can be tied over the eyes with small slits or cross-shaped holes to reduce the entry of light into the eye. Treatment consists of padding the eye, administering antibiotic eye drops as a lubricant, and using drops to dilate the pupils (e.g., cycloplegics, such as atropine drops). In extreme cases, such as where painful eyes are limiting the ability to retreat down a mountain, local anaesthetic drops can be used; however, these are toxic to the eye and ideally should be avoided.

Ailments Relating to Foreign Travel

Traveller's diarrhoea is common when travelling in remote areas, affecting 20 to 50 percent of travellers. The condition is usually self-limiting and short lived; however, stomach cramps, diarrhoea, and vomiting can complicate mountain travel. Dehydration or illness may predispose one to the development of AMS, so the condition should be taken seriously. The cause is often bacteria that are not usually present in the traveller's home environment.

Prevention consists of good hygiene and not drinking untreated water. This includes toothbrushing and eating fruit or salads washed in untreated water. Treatment consists of maintaining hydration with electrolyte solutions (e.g., dioralyte if severe) and using antimotility agents to reduce the frequency of bowel motions (e.g., loperamide and antibiotics). Antimotility agents should not be used if the diarrhoea is bloody. Antibiotics (e.g., ciprofloxacin) shorten the episode of diarrhoea and can be effective as a single dose. In certain areas of the world there is antibiotic resistance amongst the bacteria commonly causing traveller's diarrhoea, and this information should be checked before departure.

Malaria is not a problem above 2,500 metres (8,200 ft) in any area of the world; however, malarial areas may be transited en route to remote areas. Obtain specialist advice regarding the area to be visited in terms of malaria prophylaxis and other vaccines against tropical diseases. Any illness, especially one with a fever, should be reported to a doctor, and details of foreign travel should be made known at an early stage.

Specific High-Altitude Problems

Altitude illness encompasses acute mountain sickness (AMS), high-altitude cerebral oedema (HACE), and high-altitude pulmonary oedema (HAPE). These illnesses can occur at any altitude above 1,500 metres (4,920 ft), although they are more common at very high altitude (>3,500 metres, or 11,485 ft). HACE probably represents a severe form of AMS (a common illness), whereas

HAPE may occur without AMS. HACE and HAPE can both be rapidly fatal, and anyone who travels to altitude must be familiar with the symptoms and signs of these conditions.

Acclimatisation to altitude begins immediately on attaining a new altitude and consists of several phases. Initially there is a rise in heart rate and breathing rate, which enables the body to increase the amount of oxygen entering the lungs for delivery to the tissues. To enable this increased rate of breathing, some hydrogen ions are excreted from the kidney. This can be recognised as an increased desire to pass urine. Over a longer length of time, the amount of haemoglobin in the blood increases.

Acute Mountain Sickness

The frequency at which AMS occurs changes with rapidity of ascent and the altitude reached. For example, 75 percent of those visiting Mount Rainier in the United States (4,394 m, or 14,415 ft) will experience symptoms of AMS. In many ways the symptoms of AMS are inevitable with gaining altitude, and gaining altitude can become a constant battle against AMS.

AMS typically occurs 6 to 12 hours after gaining altitude. Symptoms are headache, nausea or vomiting, fatigue at a greater level than expected for a given amount of exertion, loss of appetite, dizziness, and sleep disturbance. Presence of a headache is essential for the diagnosis of AMS. This helps differentiate AMS from other illnesses, such as traveller's diarrhoea.

Prevention of AMS principally involves a gradual ascent, allowing the body enough time to acclimatise. The recommended guidelines are that above 3,000 metres (9,845 ft), each night's sleep, or sleeping altitude, should be no more than 300 metres (985 ft) above the last, with a rest day every 1,000 metres (3,280 ft) climbed. Within these guidelines, more than 300 metres (985 ft) can be climbed in a day, providing a descent is then made to sleep (i.e., climb high, sleep low). On many occasions this guideline cannot be followed due to topography, in which case rest days should be added more frequently.

Drugs can be used to reduce the incidence of AMS. The only proven drug used for prophylaxis is acetazolamide (Diamox), which works by encouraging the excretion of hydrogen ions and speeding acclimatisation. The dosage is usually 250 milligrams twice daily, but other regimens, such as 500 milligrams at night or 125 milligrams twice daily, may be effective. It should be started 24 hours before ascent. There have been cases of AMS developing when the drug is stopped, so for this reason it may be best to continue until descent is made. Common side effects include pins and needles in the hands and feet, which can be severe (and necessitate stopping the drug), and fizzy drinks tasting flat.

Various strategies can be used to treat AMS. Mild AMS can be treated by halting the ascent, resting, and taking simple painkillers (e.g., paracetamol or ibuprofen). For more severe cases it is logical that since the condition occurs because of lack of oxygen, a reduction in altitude (hence increasing oxygen) is the mainstay of treatment. Wherever possible, the reduction in altitude should be to the point at which the climber last felt well. Alternative ways of increasing the oxygen are to use bottled oxygen (not practical in the long term) or a portable hyperbaric chamber (described later). Acetazolamide is useful for treatment (at a dose of 250 mg three times daily), and in severe cases, use dexamethasone (4 mg four times daily).

High-Altitude Cerebral Oedema

HACE is rare but potentially life threatening. It usually occurs above 3,500 metres (11,485 ft) but has been reported as low as 2,500 metres (8,200 ft). It represents the severe end of a spectrum from the onset of AMS through worsening AMS to HACE, and as such it is usually preceded by symptoms of AMS. The climber will have developed signs of AMS but then goes on to develop more serious features such as confusion, disorientation, hallucinations, loss of balance, and clumsiness. This will progress to lethargy, eventually leading to coma. The progression of these symptoms can be rapid (within 12 hours).

The treatment for anyone suspected of suffering from HACE is rapid descent. Dexamethasone (8 mg initially, followed by 4 mg every 6 hours) can be given (intravenously or through intramuscular injection in extreme cases), as well as oxygen. Acetazolamide has not been proven to be of use in treating HACE, but it can be added and will not cause any harm. Hyperbaric chambers are useful in the short term; their use is discussed later.

High-Altitude Pulmonary Oedema

HAPE is a condition that usually occurs above 2,500 metres (8,200 ft) and is often associated with strenuous exercise and significant height gains. The climber will be short of breath to a much greater degree relative to others and less able to exercise. This will progress to breathlessness at rest, especially at night and when laid flat, as well as a cough with bubbly, wet sputum, perhaps with blood staining. The severity of breathless distinguishes HAPE from high-altitude cough, which may produce blood-stained sputum due to trauma to the airways. As the condition worsens, it is associated with a high heart rate and temperature. If the chest is listened to with a stethoscope, there will be crackles in the lungs; however, these crackles also occur without HAPE.

Treatment consists of descent to lower altitude, preferably with minimal exertion. The patient will be more comfortable sitting upright and will gain dramatic improvement if bottled oxygen is available. Drug therapy with nifedipine (10 mg capsule broken under the tongue followed by 20 mg slow release every 6 hours) improves symptoms.

Treatment Using Portable Hyperbaric Chambers

AMS, HACE, and HAPE are brought about by a reduction in inspired oxygen due to low atmospheric pressure. Portable hyperbaric chambers are large pressure bags into which a patient can be placed. The pressure within the bag is then increased, and hence, an increased amount of oxygen is available. The bags are relatively lightweight and portable, and they rely on the use of bellows pumps to increase and maintain the pressure. By this means, a patient in a bag at 5,000 metres (16,405 ft) can be subjected to a higher pressure with the equivalent altitude (and therefore pressure of oxygen) of 2,500 metres (8,200 ft).

John Doyle and Leigh 'Woody' Woodhouse monitoring a member of the visiting team in the Gamow bag at Everest base camp, 2006. The Gamow bag, used for altitude-related illnesses, is pressurized and produces the same effects as a reduction in altitude.

Three manufacturers make these bags (PAC, Gamow, and Certec). The bags weigh around 5 kilograms (11 lb) and come with foot or hand pumps. The major advantage is that with no mechanical parts or reliance on bottled oxygen, they are reliable, portable, and easy to use. The drawbacks are claustrophobia for the casualty, heat build-up inside the bag, effort required to operate the pump, and the fact that the casualty has to be laid flat (although the head of the bag can be elevated).

With the rapid and significant descent that can be simulated with these bags, the casualty will often become significantly better and able to make a conventional descent down the mountain. However, the bags are not an alternative to descent.

EXPEDITION MEDICAL PLANNING

By considering the likely injuries and treatments outlined in the preceding part of this chapter, some elements of an expedition first aid kit should already be apparent. Before determining what drugs and equipment should be carried, consider the following questions:

1. What is the duration of the expedition and how many members are there? The likelihood of having to use drugs for minor ailments from an expedition first aid kit will increase with time, so for longer expeditions, more drugs will be required. Likewise, adequate stocks for a party of four will soon be depleted by a team of 12.

2. How quickly can an injured casualty be evacuated? This information will help determine the appropriate quantities of drugs to carry, such as antibiotic injections.

3. What altitude is the expedition climbing to? As stated previously, the risk of altitude-related illnesses (i.e., AMS, HACE, HAPE) increases with increasing altitude. The number of climbers exposed to risk and the length of time spent at altitude must be reflected in the quantity of drugs carried to treat these conditions. Bottled oxygen may be needed for climbing expe-

ditions to extreme altitude, whereas for treks to high altitude with easy descents and perhaps local medical facilities, it would be inappropriate for reasons of weight, expense, and risk.

4. Are there any specific environmental threats (e.g., heat, cold, venomous animals, malaria, vaccinations)? Although no specific medical kit is required for these conditions, knowledge of any threats to team members' health is an important part of the risk assessment and briefings prior to departure.

5. Are there any preexisting health problems amongst the team, and what are the team's expectations (e.g., is this a commercial expedition with a duty of care for its clients)? This will affect the range of drugs carried; for example, an elderly team with a history of heart problems may prompt the decision to carry specific treatments or even find an expedition doctor. This question will also affect the cost of any first aid kit.

6. What level of medical expertise is available within the team? Certain drugs will be appropriate depending on the skill of medical personnel on the expedition and their individual specialisation.

7. How portable does a medical kit need to be? This is a crucial point to address and is covered in the discussion of items for expedition medical kits.

The authors' practice is to split the medical kit so that each person has a first aid kit to provide for most minor eventualities and initial treatment. This kit needs to be comprehensive enough to deal with a wide range of events but small enough to be easily carried in the top pocket of a rucksack. Most expedition members will have favourite painkillers, throat lozenges, and antimotility drugs for diarrhoea. A few emergency dressings should also be carried. In addition, all team members are responsible for taking sufficient personal prescription drugs and keeping enough with them on a daily basis. An example of a personal first aid kit for a trek or walk to a remote area is given in table 5.2.

TABLE 5.2 Sample Personal First Aid Kit for a Trek to a Remote Area

Items	Examples	Number
Painkillers	Paracetamol, 500 mg	12 tablets
	Codeine phosphate, 30 mg	12 tablets
Antimotility drugs	Loperamide, 2 mg	12 tablets
Large absorbent dressing	First field dressing	1
Triangular bandage		1
Zinc oxide tape, 2.5 cm (1 in.)		1 roll
Assorted sticking plasters		6
Sunblock		1 tube
Throat lozenges		12
Survival bag		1

For trips to altitudes greater than 2,500 metres (8,200 ft), acetazolamide (250 mg × 4 tablets) and dexamethasone (4 mg × 2 tablets) should be added. Additionally, when climbing at higher altitudes, a pack containing injectable dexamethasone (4 mg in 2 ml), nifedipine (2 capsules), and a 2-millilitre syringe and needle is kept with each climbing group.

The main expedition medical equipment can be kept at base camp or with support teams to allow resupply for the individual kits as required or to treat more serious events. An example of an expedition medical kit is given in table 5.3. This is the equipment that was carried for a remote expedition to Kyrgyzstan, climbing at altitudes up to 6,000 metres (19,685 ft) with a team of 14, and at altitudes up to 6,900 metres (22,640 ft) in Argentina with a team of 16.

The merits and potential side effects of the various drugs carried are beyond the scope of this text. Clearly, the decision to take diagnostic medical equipment such as pulse oximeters relies on expedition members being able to interpret and act on the results. Pulse oximetry shows the percentage saturation of red blood cells with oxygen. The normal sea-level value is around 95 to 99 percent. This will fall with altitude and the absolute value is not necessarily an indication of acclimatisation, but the trend is a useful guide—percentage saturation will increase with acclimatisation. Additionally, patients with AMS or HAPE will have lower values than other expedition members.

Controlled drugs such as morphine can be carried across international borders with surprising ease. The expedition doctor (or doctor providing the drugs) should apply to the Home Office drugs branch for a permit to carry controlled drugs. In theory, this permit is only valid in the United Kingdom, but other countries are prepared to accept the licence. It is only sensible to carry evidence of any professional qualifications (e.g., a photocopy of General Medical Council registration for doctors) when carrying quantities of drugs, needles, and syringes.

Medicines can be obtained for expeditions by obtaining a private prescription from a doctor. This can become expensive because there will likely be a charge for the prescription and the cost of the drugs is paid rather than a one-size-fits-all prescription charge.

An expedition in a remote area may well be seen by the local population as bringing in considerable medical expertise and equipment that is poorly provided locally. This means local people may well present to the expedition requesting medical assistance. It is difficult for an expedition to provide any meaningful advice and treatment

TABLE 5.3 Sample Expedition Medical Kit

PAINKILLERS

Drug	Indication/dosage	No.
Paracetamol, 500 mg tablets	Mild-to moderate pain: Take 2 tablets every 4 hr.	200
Codeine phosphate, 30 mg tablets	Pain/diarrhoea: Take 2 tablets every 4 hr.	100
Ibuprofen, 600 mg tablets	Pain: Take 1 tablet 3 times daily.	100
Diclofenac, 50 mg tablets	Pain: Take 1 tablet 3 times daily.	50
Tramadol, 50 mg tablets	Severe pain: Take 1 tablet every 8 hr.	50
Ketamine injection, 10 ml (50 mg per ml)	Very severe pain: 0.5mg/kg for short term analgesia/sedation by suitably skilled doctor.	1

ALTITUDE SICKNESS

Drug	Dosage	No.
Acetazolamide, 250 mg tablets	Take 1 tablet twice daily.	30
Nifedipine, 20 mg slow-release tablets	Take 1 tablet 4 times daily.	20
Nifedipine, 10 mg capsules	Pierce 1 capsule and squeeze under tongue.	10
Dexamethasone, 2 mg tablets	Take 2 tablets 4 times daily.	20
Dexamethasone, 8 mg injection (2 ml vials)	Give 1 injection (4 mg) 4 times daily (i.e., 1 ml).	6

INFECTIONS

Drug	Indication/dosage	No.
Augmentin, 375 mg capsules	Antibiotic: Take 1 capsule 3 times daily.	60
Augmentin injection, 1.2 g	Antibiotic: Give 1 injection (1.2 g) every 8 hr.	2
Cefotaxime, 2 g injection	Antibiotic: Give 1 injection (2 g) 3 times daily.	2
Metronidazole, 400 mg tablets	Antibiotic: Take 1 tablet 3 times daily.	50
Ciprofloxacin, 500 mg tablets	Antibiotic: Take 1 tablet twice a day.	80

EYES, EARS, SKIN

Drug	Indication/dosage	No.
Chloramphenicol eye ointment, 4 g	Inflammation or foreign body: Apply 3 times daily.	3 tubes
Anusol cream	Piles: Apply 3 times daily.	1 tube
Hydrocortisone 0.1%	Severe sunburn: Apply twice only.	2 tubes
Piriton, 4 mg tablets	Itching: Take 1 tablet 3 times daily.	20
Various throat lozenges	Sore throat: Fisherman's Friend, Strepsils, Zubes, others	28 packets
Otosporin ear drops, 5 ml	Itchy ears: Take 3 times daily.	2 bottles
Calamine lotion	Skin lotion: Apply as necessary for relief of skin itching.	100 ml
Tincture of iodine	Antiseptic: 25 ml diluted to clean wounds.	Bottle

GASTROINTESTINAL

Drug	Indication/dosage	No.
Loperamide, 2 mg tablets	Diarrhoea: Take 2 tablets, then take 1 tablet 4 times daily.	100
Lansoprazole, 30 mg tablets	Indigestion: Take 1 daily.	20
Gaviscon tablets	Indigestion: Take 1-2 tablets every 4 hr.	40
Dioralyte tablets or similar electrolytes	Rehydration: Take 1 tablet in water as required.	20

MISCELLANEOUS

Stethoscope	1
Pulse oximeter	1
Aneroid sphygmomanometer	1
Syringes (2 ml, 5 ml, 10 ml, 20 ml)	10
Needles	15
Scalpel and blades	2
Scissors	2
Spencer Wells forceps	1
Tweezers	2
Potassium permanganate tablets	30
Lignocaine 1% injections, 5 ml (local anasthetic, short-acting)	10
Bupivacaine, 0.5% 10 ml (local anasthetic, long-acting)	2
Water for injection, 5 ml	20
Granuflex dressing	6
Triangular bandages	4
Elastoplast adhesive bandages, 5 and 8 cm (2 and 3 in.)	4 mixed
Opsite dressing, 10 cm $\times$ 10 cm (4 in. $\times$ 4 in.)	5
Zinc oxide tape, 8 cm (3 in.)	2 rolls
Melonin dressing, 10 cm $\times$ 10 cm (4 $\times$ 4 in.)	14
Elastoplasts, various	56
Steristrips, various	14
Sutures, various	4
Alcohol swabs	50
Cling film	1 roll
Small bags for dispensing drugs	20

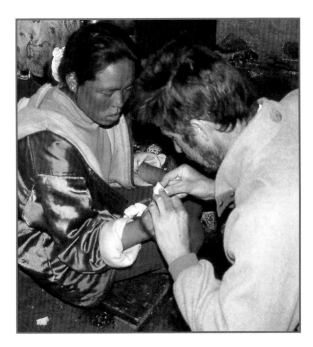

Helping out a local person in the Everest region, 2006.

for long-term health problems where follow-up of treatment is not practical. It is usually best to direct the patient to local services so as not to undermine what is available locally. Assistance to the injured should always be provided and care transferred to local facilities as soon as possible. An expedition has a responsibility to provide care to those in its employ (e.g., porters), which requires consideration when planning quantities for the medical kit.

Team doctor helping out a fellow trekker to the Everest region, 2006.

TRAVEL FATIGUE AND JET LAG

A significant amount of time and resources will be invested in your expedition. To get the most from all your hard work in training and preparation, you need to consider the effects that travelling to the destination may have on your body, as well as how you are going to cope with the new environment. Therefore, the following sections discuss travel fatigue and jet lag.

Carefully planning your expedition or trek-king itinerary is essential, and building in time to recover from travel fatigue and jet lag is necessary if you want succeed and enjoy your adventure. Some operators do not build in rest days following arrival. This may save money, but it does not allow you time to recover and cope with the fatigue of travelling and jet lag. Jet lag is of particular concern because your physical performance will be below par until you have adjusted to the new time zone (Reilly et al., 2007, Reilly, Atkinson, & Waterhouse, 1997). Arriving at your destination the night before and then starting your expedition the following morning is ill-advised, especially if you have been on a long flight.

Regardless of the mode of transport, travel-ling can cause discomfort and fatigue on any long journey, especially if you are travelling in cramped conditions. Signs of travel fatigue include disorientation, headaches, and weari-ness. These symptoms are typically caused or exacerbated by a combination of stressors asso-ciated with travelling. Sources of stress might include the disruption of normal routine; the hassle and aggravation of airport queues, waiting times, delays, changing arrangements, boarding, transferring, reclaiming baggage, etc. Addition-ally, dehydration and relative hypoxia can occur during long flights and contribute to fatigue (Reilly et al. 2007).

Travel fatigue can be easily reduced or pre-vented if certain guidelines and recommenda-tions are followed. As with all aspects of expedi-tions, planning is key. Address and prepare for the causes in advance so that you will be able to deal with the journey and any disruptions that might occur. For obvious reasons, get a good night's sleep. If you are going on a long journey, try to arrange for a stopover to break up the trip and allow recovery and relaxation between flights. Make sure your paperwork is in order, including visas if they are required, and that all members of the team have had their necessary injections and are carrying the necessary paperwork for the countries you will visit (including the stopover). It is best to sort this out well before departure day. Make sure all aspects of the journey, including transfers, accommodations, and an itinerary on arrival have been planned with your group and agreed on well before departure day. Ensure that team members take appropriate food and drink to cater to their specific dietary needs, likes, and dislikes (water and fruit are good things to carry in hand luggage—the former will need to be purchased after clearing security). On long flights, don't be afraid to ask for more water or juice if you know you need it—if you wait until you are thirsty you may get dehydrated. While some flights provide free alcohol, tea, and coffee, these are best avoided in excess because the effects of caffeine and alcohol can contribute to fatigue (Reilly et al. 2007).

When you arrive, take some time to relax, rehydrate, and take a bath or shower. If you are very tired, take a short nap—but resist the urge for a long sleep, as you'll need to try to get your overnight rest at the appropriate local time in order to adjust more quickly. Depending on time of arrival and time spent travelling, you may want to add some light exercise to your arrival itinerary, but only if you feel up to it (Reilly et al. 2007).

Jet lag is noticed during long flights, when travelling in an easterly or westerly direction, and when crossing at least three time zones rather than travelling directly north or south (e.g., from Europe to Asia along the same meridian). The crossing of time zones causes a discrepancy between your body clock and the new time zone at your destination. The symptoms of jet lag include the following (Reilly et al. 2007):

▸ Tiredness in the new daytime and yet unable to sleep at night

▸ Waking in the new night, unable to get back to sleep

▸ Less ability to concentrate or self-motivate

▸ Decreased psychological and physical performance

▸ Increased incidence of headaches and irritability

▸ Loss of appetite and general bowel irregularities

These symptoms are similar to those of travel fatigue, the difference being that these symptoms do not disappear overnight but may take several days because the ability to sleep is affected. It may take the number of days equal to two-thirds of the time zones crossed for your body clock to adjust to the new environment. So, for example, a long-haul flight from the United Kingdom to Nepal, travelling east crossing six time zones, may take at least 4 days for your body clock to adjust. The severity of jet lag increases with the number of time zones crossed (Waterhouse et al., 2007) and also depends on the direction of travel and individual body responses. Flights to the east are associated with more jet lag than flights to the west because they compress a 24-hour day, meaning you are likely to find it difficult to adjust to the new bedtime, whereas flights to the west tend to cause premature awakening (Waterhouse & Reilly, 1997). This lack of sleep will affect your physical performance, so time for adjustment should be considered before the start of your expedition. This is especially important because you are likely to be trekking or mountaineering in areas of the world that have other environmental stresses, such as altitude, that will only exaggerate these problems.

One strategy is to include a stopover, thus splitting your journey and the total time zone transition, which is likely to result in less severe jet lag (Tsai et al., 1988). However, you also need to consider the additional travel stresses of this strategy, as well as the extra cost, which may outweigh any benefits. There are other ways of coping with jet lag, including preflight, in-flight, and postflight strategies. Preflight strategies include planning to arrive a few days before starting your expedition and trying to schedule flights to arrive at your destination in the late afternoon or early evening. This will provide an opportunity for sleep in the new time zone sooner. Furthermore, you can start to adjust your sleep–wake cycle to the direction of travel. However, an adjustment in retiring to bed by more than 2 hours is likely to be counterproductive (Reilly et al., 2007) since this will affect your ability to maintain your daily routine and performance.

Once your flight has departed, it is worth altering your watch to the local time of your destination (Waterhouse, Reilly, & Edwards, 2004) and then living (eating and drinking) according to this new local time (Reilly et al., 2007), even if this means missing the odd in-flight meal. We know that meal times affect the body clock, and this strategy of altering your eating habits to the new time zone seems sensible. However, new research suggests that not eating on a long flight and then eating on arrival may allow people to recover more quickly from jet lag. Fuller, Lu, and Clifford (2008) discovered that a single period of starvation followed by a meal activates a food clock that adjusts the body clock much more quickly to a new time zone. Therefore, adapting your eating schedule on long flights by fasting for approximately 16 hours may be enough to engage this food clock, and eating as soon as you land in line with local mealtimes may help you to recover from jet lag more rapidly. However, this is a hypothesis that is based on running experiments with mice and is yet to be tested by research with humans.

Regardless of this food clock hypothesis, you should drink plenty of water during the flight, more than offered with your meal alone, because it is easy to dehydrate due to the dry air in the plane cabin. It is worth having a bottle of water with you throughout the flight. Avoid drinks such as coffee, tea, and alcohol because these act as diuretics, increasing urine output and dehydrating the body. In addition, certain fizzy drinks also act as diuretics. Some light exercise, such as stretching and walking up and down the aisles, is important to prevent stiffness and safeguard against deep vein thrombosis (House of Lords Select Committee, 2000). Sleeping and napping are only beneficial if it is nighttime at your destination (Reilly et al., 2007); otherwise you are counteracting any in-flight alterations in your body clock to the new time zone.

Once you have arrived at your destination, you can promote the adjustment of the body clock using light, which is probably the most effective way of alleviating jet lag (Waterhouse & Herxheimer, 2003). Exposure to bright light at certain times of day is of great importance in promoting the phase advance or phase delay of the body clock. Following an eastward flight (up to nine time zones to the east), you should try to advance your body clock by staying awake during the day, avoiding natural bright light in the morning, and staying outside as much as possible in the afternoon. When travelling east, it is likely that you will arrive at your destination in the morning; therefore it is recommended that you wear light shades on the plane and dark shades whilst travelling to your accommodation, and stay in dim indoor light on arrival to minimise exposure to the light (Waterhouse, Reilly, & Edwards, 2004). However, this is a hypothesis yet to be tested by proper research design, and how dim the indoor light needs to be is currently unknown (Waterhouse et al., 2007).

During a westward flight, try to phase delay your body clock by staying awake during the day and being exposed to natural bright light and then sleeping when it is dark. Bright light includes exposure to any natural light—even sitting in a room with windows will expose you to bright light (Reilly et al., 2007)—whereas avoiding bright light means being in a dimly lit room away from the windows. In eastward flights over nine time zones, adjust your body clock by phase delay rather phase advance (Waterhouse et al., 2002). For specific details of good and bad local times for exposure to natural bright light, which is dependent upon the number of times zones you have crossed in an eastward or westward direction, refer to table 5.4.

Trying to adjust the body clock by staying awake during the day at the new time zone may be difficult. The consumption of caffeine and exercise outside in bright light might assist in combating sleepiness. However, ensure that caffeine consumption does not affect your ability to sleep at night. Any exercise should fit in with the optimum timings for bright light exposure, and if you have travelled in an eastward direction, you should avoid morning exercise for the first few days because it could create a counterproductive phase-delay response (Edwards et al., 2002).

These strategies for adjusting the body clock to the new time zone should only be considered if your stay is longer than 3 days. Otherwise it is not possible to adjust your body clock, and these strategies should be avoided (Waterhouse & Reilly, 1997).

TABLE 5.4 Recommendations for Using Bright Light to Adjust the Body Clock After Time-Zone Transitions

	Bad local times for exposure to light	Good local times for exposure to light
Time zones to west		
3 h	0200-0800[a]	1800-2400[b]
4 h	0100-0700[a]	1700-2300[b]
5 h	2400-0600[a]	1600-2200[b]
6 h	2300-0500[a]	1500-2100[b]
7 h	2200-0400[a]	1400-2000[b]
8 h	2100-0300[a]	1300-1900[b]
9 h	2000-0200[a]	1200-1800[b]
10 h	1900-0100[a]	1100-1700[b]
11 h	1800-0000[a]	1000-1600[b]
12 h	1700-2300[a]	0900-1500[b]
13 h	1600-2200[a]	0800-1400[b]
14 h	1500-2100[a]	0700-1300[b]
15 h	1400-2000[a]	0600-1200[b]
16 h	1300-1900[a]	0500-1100[b]
Time zones to east		
3 h	2400-0600[b]	0800-1400[a]
4 h	0100-0700[b]	0900-1500[a]
5 h	0200-0800[b]	1000-1600[a]
6 h	0300-0900[b]	1100-1700[a]
7 h	0400-1000[b]	1200-1800[a]
8 h	0500-1100[b]	1300-1900[a]
9 h	0600-1200[b]	1400-2000[a]
10 h	Can be treated as 14 hours to west[c]	
11 h	can be treated as 13 hours to west[c]	
12 h	can be treated as 12 hours to west[c]	

a denotes promotion of a phase advance

b denotes a delay of the body clock

c reflects that the body adapts to large delays more easily than to large advances

Adapted from Reilly, Waterhouse, and Edwards 2005.

ACCLIMATISATION AND ASCENT STRATEGIES

As discussed earlier, AMS can develop into a life-threatening illness (HAPE or HACE), and if it is not dealt with appropriately, it will put an end to your expedition. The following section provides recommendations for acclimatising appropriately, which will hopefully minimise your chances of developing AMS and will enable you to have a safe and enjoyable expedition. These recommendations are based on the assumption that you have not adopted a preexpedition acclimatisation strategy (see chapter 3).

Travellers are unlikely to develop AMS at or below 2,500 metres (8,200 ft). In excess of 50 percent of travellers develop some form of AMS on direct ascent to 3,500 metres (11,485 ft), but virtually all will succumb on rapid ascent to 5,500 metres (18,045 ft) (Clarke, 2002; Deegans, 2002). Therefore, it is imperative that you avoid ascending rapidly to these altitudes.

However, there are occasions where this is not possible. Certain expeditions may approach Mount Everest Base Camp on the north side, via Lhasa in Tibet. This means flying directly into Lhasa, which is at 3,620 metres (11,875 ft), where many people may develop AMS symptoms, including vomiting. It is not unusual to hear people retching as the plane cabin is depressurised when going into Lhasa. It is also fairly typical for other symptoms of AMS to occur, such as headaches, nausea, fatigue or weakness, and dizziness, as well as difficulty sleeping for a couple of days. If you have to fly or drive into this sort of altitude (2,500-3,500 m, or 8,200-11,485 ft), it is imperative that you do not overexert yourself or move higher for at least the first 24 hours (Barry & Pollard, 2003). Several days at the landing altitude are advised to ensure affective acclimatisation. Overexerting yourself is easy to do, especially in a place like Lhasa, which has so much cultural history to explore. However, the main objective of any expedition is to summit your chosen mountain or complete your selected trek, which is what you should remind yourself to ensure you take adequate rest to enable more time to acclimatise.

To give yourself the best opportunity to acclimatise and succeed at your mountaineering challenge, the Expedition Advisory Centre (EAC) at the Royal Geographical Society recommends the following: At altitudes greater than 2,500 to 3,000 metres (8,200-9,845 ft), increase your sleeping altitude by no more 300 metres (985 ft) per day, with a rest day every third day or 1,000 metres (3,280 ft) of altitude gained. It is also recommend that you spend a week above 4,000 metres (13,125 ft) before sleeping at 5,000 metres (16,405 ft) (Clarke, 2002). This strategy should be adopted by climbers whether they are trekking or being driven into base camp. If you are being driven into base camp, you should take some exercise throughout your journey. On your rest days you should go trekking for a few hours, gain some altitude, and then return for rest. This ensures you are functionally acclimatising to the mode of exercise you are going to be undertaking later in the expedition.

The recommended strategy for ascent may seem extremely slow, but it is worth adopting if your expedition route allows for it. There are certain situations where this strategy may be impractical; for example, it would mean spending 10 or more days on Mount Kilimanjaro (inactive volcano in Northeast Tanzania) because of the relatively short distances. Therefore, the EAC suggests that in this type of situation, you should preacclimatise for several days on nearby peaks, such as Mount Meru (4,566 m, or 14,980 ft) or Mount Kenya (4,895 m, or 16,060 ft). However, do not let summit fever take over and push yourself too hard. The main aim is to use this time to preacclimatise, not to exhaust yourself before climbing Mount Kilimanjaro. Furthermore, if you do not summit, you are still likely to increase your likelihood of summiting Mount Kilimanjaro, as well as having a safer and far more enjoyable experience, than those travellers being pushed up the Marangu route on Mount Kilimanjaro in less than 4 days. This strategy may increase the financial burden of the expedition; however, this outlay is probably relatively small in comparison to the satisfaction of reaching the summit of Mount Kilimanjaro or the cost of a second attempt if you are unsuccessful the first time. This strategy of preacclimatising on other mountains is also used by high-altitude mountaineers, who may climb several 6,000-metre (19,685 ft) peaks before tackling their chosen 8,000-metre (26,245 ft) mountain.

Acclimatisation is best achieved by a slow ascent, allowing the body to adjust before going higher and reducing the chances of developing AMS. A large part of acclimatisation takes place over the first 1 to 3 days at a given altitude (Barry & Pollard, 2003). However, people vary in their rate of acclimatisation, with some able to ascend much faster than others. Women are less likely to suffer from AMS in comparison with men, with young men the most vulnerable, most likely due to their competitive streak. The fable of the tortoise and the hare is a suitable example of how to approach acclimatisation. Those who walk fast and are the first into camp every day due to the mistaken belief that greater fitness and strength will protect them against AMS are more likely to succumb to AMS in comparison to their slower counterparts. Be more like the tortoise, being last into camp and stopping frequently for rest breaks, thus ensuring affective acclimatisation. It is believed that the less fit you are, the slower you will want to walk, and thus the greater chance you have of acclimatising properly. Therefore, the best advice is to walk as slowly as possible, and if you are part of a large group, you should always walk at the pace of the slowest person in the group.

A flexible schedule with the inclusion of rest days is important. Rest days can be days of pure rest with no further ascent to provide your body with more time to acclimatise. Alternatively, they can be days where you climb to experience a higher altitude before returning to sleep low, another effective strategy adopted by mountaineers. In addition, AMS can be prevented by consuming an adequate amount of calories, including a high percentage of carbohydrate, as well as maintaining hydration (since dehydration can exacerbate AMS).

By the time you have arrived at your destination for your high-altitude expedition, it is likely that you have invested a lot of time and resource in your preparations—travel, equipment, clothing, nutrition, and training, to mention but a few. Cutting corners at this stage by trying to climb the mountain as quickly as possible is likely to be a false economy. Another way of ensuring effective acclimatisation is to adopt the preexpedition acclimatisation strategies discussed in chapter 3.

POSTEXPEDITION TRAINING AND RECOVERY

Depending on the length and intensity of the expedition, postexpedition recovery will vary in length and activity. The body and mind will need a greater amount of recovery after a long Himalayan expedition lasting 8 weeks or more than from a 1- to 2-week alpine trip. However, in both cases there are a few things to take into consideration.

After intense and prolonged effort, the body's reserves can become depleted, usually in the loss of fat and lean muscle mass, which needs to be recovered. In the case of fat mass, people may not want to replace all the fat lost if they started at a higher percentage of fat than required and feel fitter with a lower percentage of fat. Lance Armstrong performed more successfully in the Tour de France mountain stages after he had trimmed off a good percentage of his body mass (Armstrong & Carmichael, 2006). The same rationale may apply to a high-performing mountaineer.

Following an enforced assault on the body's reserves through the efforts of an expedition, the body's mechanisms go in to supercompensation mode wherein the body recovers the reserves (especially in the form of fat) and at every opportunity adds on a measure in preparation for the next assault (Stroud, 2004). Many athletes and mountaineers have succumbed to yo-yoing in weight gain and loss, which affects fitness. Therefore, it is probably not a good idea after an expedition or a phase of high-volume and high-intensity training to completely rest for more than 2 or 3 days without doing some complementary exercise. This is essential to control body mass. It should be complementary because the specific muscle groups and systems used on the expedition should not be taxed directly. Alternative exercises that you enjoy, such as swimming, skiing, and cycling, should be performed at low intensities and volumes. These should be done on a day-on, day-off basis to best maintain the fitness gained and facilitate adequate recovery.

Suggested Readings

The following texts expand the information provided in this chapter and can be used as background reading or reference material. There is value in including one or more of these texts in the first aid kit for an expedition depending on the group experience, location, and so on.

General First Aid

This is a useful resource for nondoctors covering all elements of BLS and first aid.

St. Andrew's Ambulance Association, St. John Ambulance, and the **British Red Cross**. (2006). *The authorised first aid manual of St. John Ambulance, St. Andrew's Ambulance Association, and the British Red Cross* (8th ed.). London: Dorling Kindersley.

High-Altitude and Expedition Medicine for Doctors

Pollard's book is very useful for medical knowledge pertaining to the high-altitude environment. It is available as a handy microedition, which is convenient to carry in a first aid kit. Ward's book is a very useful reference book that is the definitive text on the topic; this book contains in-depth physiology and medicine. Greaves is a comprehensive text covering all prehospital medicine, with useful chapters on trauma, acute medical and surgical problems, and a comprehensive formulary.

Pollard, A.J., & Murdoch, P.R. (2003). *The high altitude medicine handbook*. Oxford: Radcliffe Medical Text.

Ward, M.P., West, J.S., & Milledge, J.B. (2000). *High-altitude medicine and physiology* (3rd ed.). Arnold: London.

Greaves, I., & Porter, K. (2007). *Oxford handbook of pre-hospital care.* Oxford: Oxford University Press.

Useful Web Sites

www.expeditionmedicine.co.uk
　Discusses several topics related to mountain medicine, specifically the relative merits of various portable hyperbaric chambers and painkillers.

www.thebmc.co.uk
　Offers useful links to general mountaineering information, including links to International Mountaineering and Climbing Federation (UIAA) Mountain Medicine information sheets.

www.medex.org.uk
　Provides useful expedition medicine info and a free downloadable book, *Travel at High Altitude*.

www.fco.gov.uk
　Offers country-specific links with overall hazards and a detailed health section for vaccination requirements and current problems.

The length of active rest will differ depending on the timing of your next project and the volume and intensity of the previous one. However, a minimum of 2 to 3 weeks of active rest would be recommended for a three-season alpine climber and a maximum of 2 months for a Himalayan climber doing two projects a year.

KEY IDEAS

▸ Planning should take into account local infrastructure and the group's medical knowledge and ability.

▸ All expedition members have a responsibility to learn how to perform initial treatment for casualties.

▸ High altitude is associated with life-threatening medical emergencies, and all participants should be familiar with the prevention, recognition, and immediate treatment of these.

▸ First aid kits should be appropriate for the location and the skill levels of expedition members.

▸ The effects of travel fatigue and jet lag should be considered when planning expeditions abroad.

▸ All expedition members should be aware of the need to acclimatise to altitude and appropriate ascent strategies for doing so.

▸ Postexpedition training and recovery need to be built into planning and should be carefully implemented, especially on return from major expeditions.

CONDITIONING AND NUTRITION FOR EXPEDITIONS

CHAPTER

6

Fitness and Training

John O'Hara and Carlton Cooke

I f we all did the things we are capable of doing, we would literally astound ourselves.

Thomas Alva Edison

To keep safe and get the most enjoyment and achievement out of any mountaineering or climbing expedition, you must be fit enough to undertake the expedition you have selected as your objective. Thus, one component of preparation that is crucial in ensuring that you can achieve your objective is the physical training programme that you undertake to produce an appropriate level of fitness. When planning your training programme, you should aim to achieve a level of fitness that exceeds what you might expect to call upon to cope with the worst conditions you may experience on the expedition. This approach means that you should be able to begin your expedition confident that your physical training has provided you with a level of fitness that should be more than adequate to the task, with sufficient extra to cope with extreme conditions. It also underlines the importance of selecting an expedition that is within the level of physical fitness you can realistically expect to achieve with an appropriate training programme.

This chapter begins with an explanation of the components of fitness that are relevant to performance on both mountaineering and climbing expeditions. The principles of training that need to be applied in planning and implementing an appropriate training programme are then discussed, followed by the development of a

physiological profile that would provide the fitness suitable for mountaineering and climbing expeditions. Although we recommend working with professionally accredited sport and exercise scientists if you are undertaking a serious expedition to a remote, extreme environment, we have also provided some details of tests that can be performed without access to a laboratory.

COMPONENTS OF FITNESS

One of the benefits of regular participation in mountaineering or climbing, whether for recreational activity at weekends and during holidays or in preparation for high-performance expeditions, is that both your performance and health will benefit.

A number of definitions of physical fitness recognise components that are either health- or performance-related or both. We can therefore consider the fitness requirements for mountaineering and climbing in terms of those that are required for performance and that will benefit long-term health and well-being. Well-established health benefits to being fit and active include disease prevention and reduced incidence of diseases such as coronary heart disease, type 2 diabetes, many forms of cancer, and metabolic conditions.

Most organisations that promote the health benefits of physical fitness, as well as many sport and exercise scientists, consider health-related physical fitness to comprise five components. These components are also important in fitness for performance and are very relevant to mountaineering and climbing (each component will be outlined in more detail in the following sections):

▸ Endurance (cardiorespiratory fitness)
▸ Muscular strength and power
▸ Muscular endurance
▸ Flexibility
▸ Body composition

Endurance Endurance exercise is whole-body (large muscle mass), aerobic (with oxygen) activity, also referred to as cardiovascular endurance, cardiorespiratory endurance, or stamina. This aspect of fitness requires a well-developed heart able to pump large volumes of blood with each beat, lungs free from disease with airways that are clear, and large muscle masses with a good blood supply that are used to exercise. Endurance is an important component of fitness for performance in all forms of mountaineering and some forms of climbing, whether you are a recreational or high-performance participant. Not only will endurance training enhance your performance in the outdoors, but it will also make a significant contribution to your health and well-being. Endurance training for mountaineering and climbing is considered in detail in chapter 7.

Muscular Strength and Power This aspect of fitness relates most closely to the musculo-skeletal and nervous systems. Strength is the ability to exert force through your musculoskeletal system and power is the ability to exert force quickly. In extreme rock climbing, strength and power will be required to raise the whole body when only being able to grip with two fingers and a thumb. Strength and power are important in both climbing and mountaineering, especially on steep slopes when carrying loaded rucksacks. Lower-body strength and power are essential in both climbing and mountaineering. Upper-body strength and power are also critical for rock climbing, but they are not to be underestimated in importance for mountaineering and scrambling.

Just because you are relatively strong in one particular movement or muscle group, it does not mean you are a generally strong and powerful person. It is possible to have a strong lower body and weak upper body or one strong side and one relatively weak side. This has important implications for strength training, which is considered in detail in chapter 8.

Muscular Endurance This aspect of fitness is the ability to repeat a movement pattern for a certain amount of time without undue fatigue. Muscular endurance is an important element of fitness for both mountaineering and climbing because certain muscle groups are required to reproduce the same or similar movement patterns for prolonged amounts of time.

Flexibility Flexibility involves range of motion of the major joints. It is an important element of fitness for high-performance rock climbing—together with strength and power, it allows the climber to achieve the most technically demanding movements on rock faces or climbing walls. Good flexibility is also valuable for recreational climbers and in all aspects of mountaineering, from handling ropes and gear to progressing on technically difficult terrain.

Body Composition Contrary to what many people may think based on the global epidemic of obesity, having some body fat is vital to health and performance. Mountaineering and climbing also require well-developed muscles and strong bones. Some sports require high performers to have less than the normal levels of body fat, particularly where the sport involves transporting their own body mass, such as in endurance running. Generally speaking, low body fat is an advantage for both mountaineering and climbing, but as discussed later in this chapter, there are circumstances where starting an expedition with an increased percentage of body fat may be considered beneficial.

The five components of physical fitness just described are relevant for both performance and health. However, there are other components of fitness that relate more to the ability of the person to perform successfully in an activity or sport. These are commonly referred to as components of motor fitness, although it is generally acknowledged that there is some overlap between physical fitness and motor fitness (e.g., power is often considered under both categories). These components include speed, agility, balance, coordination, and reaction time.

Speed   Many sports require participants to be able to move all or part of their body quickly. The quickness of movement may be related to hand speed in sport climbing when completing a bold, dynamic move for a difficult hold. Absolute speed is not a central requirement for most mountaineering and climbing situations, although sustaining a critical speed can be important in lightweight alpine ascents, where little gear is carried and a slower speed could result in an unplanned night out with potentially disastrous consequences.

Agility   Agility is the ability to move quickly, change direction, and maintain balance. It is particularly important in climbing but is also valuable in mountaineering. It involves strength, speed, coordination, and sensory perception.

Balance   Balance is important in both climbing and mountaineering. It involves strength in the core muscles of the trunk and back, as well as the legs. The ability to shift body weight rapidly or make small adjustments is essential in climbing and important in many aspects of mountaineering.

Coordination   Coordination is the ability to perform smooth, accurate skills and techniques, combining sensory feedback with coordinated muscle contractions that affect both powerful whole-body movements and small, refined hand and foot movements. Coordination is essential in climbing and important in many aspects of mountaineering.

Reaction Time   Reaction time is the time taken to respond to a given stimulus. Visual reaction time is the slowest, whereas kinaesthetic response time, where feedback is from the proprioceptors in ligaments and tendons, is the fastest. Reaction time is generally not a major component of fitness for mountaineering and climbing, but a short reaction time can be useful in difficult circumstances that require a rapid response.

In terms of mountaineering and climbing, fitness may be described as the possession of attributes or characteristics that facilitate the performance of given tasks within these broad categories of activity. Though there are some common elements to rock climbing and moun-

taineering, there are also some specific requirements for high-performance rock climbing that have been mentioned in the list of fitness components described thus far. One common element is endurance fitness—the ability to keep going for prolonged lengths of time is a requirement for multiple-pitch climbing and more obviously for trekking and mountaineering, where expeditions can last from a few days to several months.

Both rock climbing and mountaineering require work against gravity, where participants are often carrying their body mass and equipment, food, drink, and clothes in a rucksack. This work against gravity and carrying loads requires extra energy expenditure that has to be delivered by the cardiorespiratory, energy, and musculoskeletal systems of the body. Load carriage is therefore a common requirement of both climbing and mountaineering and has to be factored into training and preparation.

Fitness is more than the physical, and a number of definitions recognise this. For example, fitness has been defined as 'a state of total well-being of the individual, physically, mentally, emotionally, spiritually and socially' (Fitness and Amateur Sport, 1992). For those who find enjoyment and satisfaction from spending time in the outdoors, including mountaineering and climbing, this holistic view of fitness is likely to resonate. This view certainly comes through in a number of the chapters of this book.

GENETICS AND TRAINING: NATURE VERSUS NURTURE

A common question asked by those with an interest in sport is whether high-performance athletes can be made through training or whether they are born to be champions—the nature-versus-nurture debate. The answer is that athletic achievement at the highest level requires a combination of both a good genetic blueprint and appropriate training.

Some sports require a particular body type for success. For example, front-row forwards in rugby union are not small and light, and Olympic gymnasts are not big and heavy. The best coaches cannot take front-row forwards and turn them into high-performance gymnasts, and vice versa. They need to have the right material to work with in the first place. In mountaineering there is not one body type associated with success; there are examples of both tall and short high-performance mountaineers. In rock climbing, there is also a range of body shapes and sizes, but the ability to handle your own body weight on tiny holds does define a key common attribute for success at the highest level. So, similar to most sports, there are key attributes in the genetic blueprint for success, though they are more strongly represented in the extremes of rock climbing than in mountaineering.

The good news is that whatever your size, shape, and potential defined by your genes, you can improve almost every component of fitness with appropriate training. The not-so-good news is that almost every component of fitness is affected by the ageing process. As is true in most sports, you do not have to possess the best genetic attributes to be able to enjoy mountaineering and climbing to a relatively high level of performance. Equally, it is good to know your limits.

PRINCIPLES OF TRAINING

The aim of training is to maintain or improve performance or health. In terms of exercise physiology, training for mountaineering and climbing is about stimulating structural and functional adaptations in the body so that you perform better in tasks associated with these forms of physical activity. At the same time, such training will maintain or improve health status as long as the training programme is appropriately designed and monitored. To stimulate the body to produce the required adaptations, a training programme is required that incorporates repeated bouts of planned exercise. If the training programme is appropriately planned and followed, it will result in chronic adaptations over time that will result in improved performance, be it in strength, speed, power, endurance, or other components of fitness, with the combination of adaptations dependent on the focus of the training programme.

Effective training programmes are based on the application of training principles. The primary principles are progressive overload, specificity, individuality, and reversibility.

Progressive Overload Progressive overload is a combination of two principles of training: overload and progression. The application of the overload principle in training is what stimulates an improvement in physiological function to produce a training response, which results in improved performance in one or more of the components of fitness (e.g., strength). Overload is achieved by manipulating intensity, frequency, and duration, most often with a focus on a particular type or mode of exercise. FITT (frequency, intensity, time, and type) is often used to summarise the principle of overload.

Manipulation of progression in the application of overload is a critical component of planning and delivering effective training programmes. The cycle of overload needs to be carefully manipulated through periodic training. Overload beyond the current capacity of the person will stimulate complex and integrated functional adaptations from the molecular to the systemic level of the body, which, linked with appropriate recovery, will result in an enhancement or supercompensation in performance. If progression is attempted through changes that are too large and the training is repeatedly and doggedly adhered to, the result will be a decrease in performance, along with an increased probability of injury, staleness, overreaching, and overtraining. This is why careful planning, monitoring, and evaluation are required to ensure effective training adaptations.

Specificity The specificity principle explains that adaptations to training are specific. Specificity of training applies to the mode or type of exercise, the muscles, the speed of movement, the range of motion, the intensity of the exercise, the energy systems used, and so on. Specificity therefore tells us that only the performance of the particular movements used in the chosen sport or exercise can be 100 percent applicable to training. Therefore, it is important to consider the extent of transfer from training to mountaineering or climbing.

For example, in strength training it is important to select appropriate exercises to target the particular muscle groups used in the movement patterns associated with mountaineering and climbing. However, it is also important to consider the timing, recruitment, and intensity of muscle contributions and try to mimic the specific movement patterns from the sport in order to maximise carryover. Strength development for climbers and mountaineers is not focussed on absolute strength but rather strength relative to weight and body composition. Specificity in training for rock climbing may suggest a need to focus on bouldering or climbing both indoors and outdoors to produce the relationship amongst relative strength, power, and flexibility that is required to improve rock climbing at the highest level of performance. However, for those who are progressing from hill walking and gentle scrambling to rock climbing and who cannot support their weight using only handholds, only a well-planned training programme that addresses their specific training needs will help them achieve success. For many people, this requires a change in diet and energy expenditure, as well as an appropriate resistance training programme in the gym.

Use of fingerboards and time on climbing walls and rock faces is specific to the needs of high-performance rock climbers. However, these specific forms of conditioning must be factored into an individualised training programme that is balanced by other forms of strength and conditioning together with adequate rest to avoid overtraining and injury.

Individuality   If two climbers or mountaineers subject themselves to exactly the same training programme, they will respond to it differently, which summarises the principle of individuality. A number of factors influence the individual nature of training response, including training history and state of fitness at the start of a training programme, genetic blueprint or predisposition, and other factors such as age and gender. Genetics defines the potential we each have for development in the various components of fitness, as well as the rate at which we will approach that potential. It is true that Olympic and world champions have chosen the right parents (i.e., they have a more optimal predisposition or blueprint), but without exposure to appropriate training programmes, they will not be able to reach their potential.

Individuality therefore explains why we have to plan, monitor, and evaluate training on an individual basis—copying better performers' training programmes may result in overtraining or injury. This is especially important for young mountaineers and climbers, who should not be encouraged to adopt the same training programmes and practices as adult high performers even though they may already be able to demonstrate excellence in their performance. Although there is only limited evidence from research with junior climbers, there is evidence from other sports that inappropriate training practices can lead to chronic injuries and conditions in young performers.

Related to individuality is the law of diminishing returns. This principle is based on the understanding that relatively inactive people beginning a training programme will show much larger improvements in a given time than high-performance mountaineers or climbers who have been training hard for many years. As years of training increase, the percentage of improvement in performance in a given time diminishes as we approach our genetic potential. High-performance athletes therefore do not expect to make large improvements in their performance; they accept that they have to work hard to see only small improvements.

Reversibility   If you stop training or reduce your training load considerably, your fitness and performance will decrease. In the same way that the molecules, tissues, organs, and systems of the human body adapt to the stimulus of training so that we become fitter, they will also adapt to the stimulus of detraining by reverting to pretraining status. The effects of detraining are significant after a couple of weeks of inactivity, which is associated with injury in sport. For example, decreases in muscle strength and cardiorespiratory fitness of about 3 and 5 percent have been shown after 2 weeks of inactivity. Interestingly, anaerobic performance seems to decline at a slower rate than strength and cardiorespiratory fitness. The rate and magnitude of the effects of detraining will vary from person to person and will also depend on the length of detraining, the training history, and the performance levels before detraining.

Reversibility and detraining should not be confused with tapering, where athletes cut down their training in preparation for a major championship or trial. Tapering allows performers to be at their best since they have decreased their training load in a controlled way so they are fresh and hungry for a particular challenge. In certain circumstances where peak performance is required for a particular challenge, performers will train through other challenges without tapering, working towards the main goals of their training programme. These goals are set so they can peak for their new Everest, whatever it may be.

Applying the principles of training to planning, monitoring, and evaluating training programmes is important so that realistic goals can be set and the best opportunity to achieve the desired performance improvements can be realised. So far this chapter has discussed the concept of fitness and training principles. The remainder of the chapter will consider various components of fitness and how they can be combined in an appropriate physiological profile, which can assist with the planning, monitoring, and evaluation of training programmes.

HOW TO MAKE A PHYSIOLOGICAL PROFILE

Obviously there are distinct differences in the level of physical fitness required to climb a small mountain in the United Kingdom in a single day (e.g., Scafell Pike, 978 m [3,210 ft], the highest point in England) versus tackling Mount Everest (8,848 m [29,029 ft]), which may take up to 50 days. Regardless of your starting point and your personal Everest, these challenges are based on endurance, or how long you can continue a sustained pace over a few hours, a few days, or a few months. Therefore, developing your endurance capabilities is essential whatever your goals are. Generally, if you are able to complete an Olympic-distance triathlon in a reasonable

time, then you will probably have the right physiological profile to climb Mount Everest. However, you will also need the ability to walk in the mountains for prolonged lengths of time (>12 hours) carrying up to 18 kilograms (40 lb). On the other hand, to climb Scafell Pike, you do not need to be able to complete a triathlon; being able to walk continuously and comfortably for a day with a small amount of weight in a day sack should ensure that you enjoy your walk and achieve your goal.

Comparing requirements of endurance fitness in various extremes of expedition illustrates the usefulness of considering your physiological profile, or your level in each element of fitness. You can then monitor the change in each fitness element as you implement your training, adjusting your programme as you adapt to the training stimulus. The following sections consider the important elements of a physiological profile for mountaineering and climbing expeditions. The main elements of physical fitness necessary for an appropriate physiological profile for mountaineering include body composition, aerobic endurance, maximal strength, and strength endurance.

Body Composition

Body composition is an important part of the profile because excess body fatness increases the energy demands placed upon the body, ultimately slowing a person down. Furthermore, someone who carries too much body fat may overheat and become dehydrated because considerable heat energy is produced by the body during exercise and fat is a good insulator. Norms of body-fat percentages for males and females range from 15 to 19 percent for men and 20 to 25 percent for women, whereas body-fat values observed for trained endurance athletes range from 3 to 8 percent for males and 8 to 12 percent for females. Essential fat constitutes about 3 percent of body mass in the reference man (McArdle, Katch, & Katch, 2007).

Because a high proportion of training for mountaineering is aerobic, the lower the body fat that can be achieved during the training phase, the better, as long as it is consistent with good health. This will reduce unproductive mass during the training phase. For example, when working with the 2006 Everest West Ridge team, we recommended that people with body-fat percentages above 12 percent should aim to reach this value, and those below this level should not make any dramatic changes. Even though a low body-fat percentage is recommended during the preparation phase of an extreme mountain challenge such as Everest, a small increase in body-fat percentage before departure may be appropriate, especially in people with low body-fat percentages (less than 10 percent). People with a high body surface area relative to their body mass will lose heat at a faster rate. Conversely, the thicker the layer of fat (adipose tissue) on the body, the better the body will be insulated, preserving core heat, as well as tolerating lower temperatures before shivering. Therefore mountaineers and climbers with extremely low body-fat percentages are more susceptible to the cold temperatures and burn more calories than their fatter counterparts in an attempt to keep warm. Thus, a small amount of insulation in such circumstances is beneficial.

Finally, you should maximise your lean mass (muscle tissue) before the expedition in order to combat the muscle degradation that occurs when spending longer amounts of time at altitude. This is another reason why strength training is important.

Aerobic Endurance

Mountain climbing at around sea level generally means that climbers are operating at 30 to 55 percent of their maximal oxygen uptake ($\dot{V}O_2max$) depending upon the terrain (Reilly & Waterhouse, 2005) for up to several hours a day. Therefore, it is a relatively low-intensity physical activity that is prolonged in nature, with a large emphasis placed on aerobic metabolism and endurance fitness. However, mountaineers do need an ability to tolerate high-intensity efforts, which make up a small proportion of the overall demands on a mountain day.

Mountaineering at extreme altitudes increases the physiological stress placed on the body for a given task compared with the same challenge at sea level. There is no precisely documented evidence of what physiological characteristics

are required to climb an 8,000-metre (26,245 ft) mountain. Nevertheless, no mountaineer will attempt to climb Mount Everest without a strong aerobic and endurance base. If the demands of the mountain are greater than your capability, then failure is inevitable. Therefore, developing your endurance fitness is essential for these types of challenges. Making improvements in all areas of an endurance profile is more important than a certain endpoint because the preparation and training required to make improvements will ensure that you are better able to cope with the challenge and the effects of altitude.

Several elements make up a good aerobic endurance profile. These include a relatively high $\dot{V}O_2max$, a lower heart rate response to a given submaximal exercise, and a delayed blood lactate increase in response to increased exercise intensity.

Maximal Oxygen Uptake

Maximal oxygen uptake, or $\dot{V}O_2max$, is a measure of cardiorespiratory function and an indicator of endurance performance potential, and it is therefore an important part of a mountaineer's physiological profile. $\dot{V}O_2max$ is the maximum rate at which a person can extract and utilise oxygen whilst breathing air at sea level (Astrand, Rodahl, Dahl, Sigmund, & Stromme, 2003). This component of fitness is an important prerequisite for high performance in UK endurance events such as the Bob Graham Round, a fell race over 42 Lakeland peaks in 24 hours covering 116 kilometres (72 mi), or the Original Mountain Marathon, a 2-day double-marathon mountain orienteering event. It is of lesser importance for those wanting to climb Scafell Pike in a day.

$\dot{V}O_2max$ is severely compromised with exposure to altitude, dramatically increasing the physiological stress of a given challenge in comparison to the same challenge at sea level, even in well-trained people. Due to a decrease in ambient pressure, $\dot{V}O_2max$ is reduced at altitudes between 1,500 metres (4,920 ft) and 6,100 metres (20,015 ft) at a rate of approximately 10 percent per 1,000-metre (3,280 ft) increase in altitude (McArdle et al., 2007). $\dot{V}O_2max$ is not a predictor of how well you are going to perform at altitude, and there is some evidence to suggest that the higher your $\dot{V}O_2max$, the greater the fractional decrease in comparison to less-trained people (Ogawa et al., 2007). However, endurance fitness is crucial in sustaining long, repeated days of effort in a mountain environment. Mean $\dot{V}O_2$max values of 61.3 millilitres per kilogram per minute have been observed in people from previous Everest expeditions (West et al., 1983), with ranges of 54 to 66 reported in the literature (Oelz et al., 1986). These numbers are similar to those shown by the Everest West Ridge team (45-66 ml per kg per min), the majority of whom were able to operate at 7,600 metres (24,935 ft), as well as those shown by a small group working at 8,000 metres (26,245 ft) without oxygen.

Submaximal Exercise Economy

In endurance sports such as running, it is advantageous to have a better economy of movement, and this is no different in mountaineering, where sustained effort is required on repeated long days on the mountain. Economy is defined as the submaximal oxygen consumption per unit body mass per minute ($\dot{V}O_2$, or ml per kg per min) for a given workload or power output, be this running speed for runners or load carriage with a heavy rucksack for mountaineers. Running economy has been shown to be superior (i.e., lower $\dot{V}O_2$) for high-performance endurance runners compared with club and recreational runners (Cooke, 2008), and there is no reason to believe that high-performance mountaineers will not have a better economy of effort than less experienced mountaineers. However, there is currently no research evidence to support this.

Given our discussion regarding the effective decrease in $\dot{V}O_2$max with increasing altitude, a better economy on the mountain would help counter the restrictive effects of altitude on $\dot{V}O_2$max. Irrespective of altitude, a better economy of effort on the mountain is also an advantage in terms of safety since economical mountaineers are able to sustain their efforts for a longer duration or at a higher intensity before compromising their safety on the mountain. Such economy in high performance is an application of the specificity principle of training. Though triathletes and marathon runners may have the aerobic fitness required for moun-

taineering, they will not all be able to transfer their fitness effectively to mountaineering. This explains why some successful mountaineers may not be as endurance fit as other athletes close to sea level but can perform better in a challenging mountain environment. The ability to cope or even thrive at high altitude in low temperatures and bad weather also adds to the specific fitness requirements of mountaineering.

It is therefore important to ensure that training for improved endurance performance specific to mountaineering and climbing incorporates sustained effort in an appropriate mountainous environment, using the skills and movement patterns that are essential to the mountaineer.

Oxygen-Carrying Capacity of Blood

Haematocrit represents the percentage of the blood occupied by the red blood cells; therefore, a low haematocrit value (<45 percent) indicates a decreased oxygen-carrying capacity. Haemoglobin is the oxygen-carrying component of red blood cells and thus is important for aerobic exercise. A low haemoglobin value will reflect a reduced oxygen-carrying capacity of the blood, which limits endurance performance. Furthermore, exposure to high altitude reduces the amount of oxygen carried by the haemoglobin; thus, it is beneficial to have normal levels before ascending to altitude. A typical range observed for males is 130 to 180 milligrams per litre, with females tending to have lower values. These variables are not trainable, but they do vary depending upon diet and training status, and it is important to maintain values in normal biological ranges.

Respiratory System

Breathing out (expiration) is largely a passive process, whereas breathing in (inspiration) is an active process relying on the inspiratory muscles (diaphragm and intercostals). Weak inspiratory muscles have been linked with the perception of breathlessness (Killian, 1988), which is related to respiratory fatigue. This impairment in lung function may limit endurance performance rather than superior lung function improving endurance performance. Therefore, normal lung function is an important part of the physiological profile. In the same way that resistance training can increase strength and endurance of specific muscles, breathing against an inspiratory load can enhance resistance to fatigue of the inspiratory muscles and reduce feelings of breathlessness. This can be achieved by training with a device called the *POWERbreathe*, which has been shown to increase maximum inspiratory pressure after 6 weeks, reduce inspiratory muscle fatigue, reduce respiratory effort sensations, and increase cycle time-trial performances by approximately 4 percent (Romer et al., 2002). The specifics of using the *POWERbreathe* are discussed in chapter 7.

Normal lung function and inspiratory muscle strength are even more important for people who are going to be exposed to altitude for short or long amounts of time. The reduced partial pressure of oxygen in the ambient air that is encountered at altitude increases the demands placed on the respiratory muscles. Even during light exercise at high altitude, respiratory rate and depth may match that observed during maximal exercise at sea level. This respiratory workload can only be sustained for a few minutes at a time. Sensible acclimatisation strategies during an expedition can aid the ability of the mountaineer to withstand these challenges. However, improvements in the strength and endurance of specific muscles that control respiration may also prove beneficial to maintenance of performance at high altitude.

Maximal Strength and Strength Endurance

Strength and power are important fitness components for both climbing and mountaineering. Relative strength and power are more important than absolute strength and power because in both mountaineering and climbing, you have to be able to handle your own body mass when moving against gravity. Lower-body strength and power are essential for all climbing and mountaineering skills and techniques. Upper-body strength and power are also critical for success in rock climbing, and they should not be underestimated in importance for mountaineering. Strength and power training are so important for improving performance in climbing and

mountaineering that they are considered in detail in chapter 8.

MONITORING AND EVALUATING CONDITIONING FOR EXPEDITIONS

A wide range of protocols and procedures for physical fitness assessment is available, but your selection will depend on the nature of your expedition, the areas of physical performance you want to improve, the resources you have to invest in this form of preparation, and the facilities you have access to.

The following list outlines some of the physiological variables you can have assessed as part of your preparations:

▶ Body composition (body mass [kg]; stature [m]; Body Mass Index; body-fat percentage via skinfold measurements, bioelectrical impedance, air-displacement plethysmography [Bod Pod], or dual energy X-ray absorptiometry [DXA] scan)

▶ Maximal oxygen uptake (ml per kg per min)

▶ Heart rate (beats per min) and blood lactate (mmol/L) responses during submaximal incremental exercise

▶ Lung function (inspiratory muscle strength, FVC, FEV_1)

▶ Blood haemoglobin (mg/L) and haematocrit (%) levels

▶ Arterial oxygen saturation (SaO_2) levels after acute exposure to altitude

▶ Maximal strength and strength endurance

For those who are preparing for an extreme challenge, we would recommend that you gain the support and services of a sport science laboratory, thus gaining access to state-of-the-art equipment and expertise. For climbing challenges in temperature extremes and altitude, we would recommend a sport science laboratory with an environmental chamber. To ensure quality service, you should employ the services of an accredited sport scientist and laboratory.

However, you can monitor your own progress using basic testing protocols and procedures, though they will not be as comprehensive or as accurate.

If you are an adult and you do not ordinarily take regular exercise—sustained vigorous physical training at least three times per week of more than half an hour with heart rate above 70 percent age-related maximum (estimated by (220 – age) × 0.7)—and you want to develop your fitness in preparation for a day in the hills or something more extreme, then you should have your health status assessed by your general practitioner before embarking on your physical preparations.

Body Composition

At a basic level, you can monitor your body mass (kg) using standard bathroom scales. You can then use your body mass with your height to calculate your BMI, which is an indirect estimate of body composition. Body mass should be measured on the same scales at the same time once every week, wearing minimal clothing. Ideally, stature should be measured with a stadiometer. For adults, this only needs to be done once a year. With shoes and socks removed, the subject stands on the stadiometer platform with feet together. The buttocks and shoulder blades should be in contact with the back of the stadiometer, and shoulders are relaxed with hands and arms hanging loosely at the sides. The head should be positioned into the Frankfort plane (a horizontal line from the ear opening to the lower border of the eye socket). The head board should be brought down to contact the vertex of the skull. The subject should keep the heels on the ground and, maintaining the Frankfort plane, stand as tall as possible. Gentle pressure should be applied by the observer beneath the mastoid processes (upwards under the end of the jaw) to stretch the subject upwards to the fullest extent. Stature is recorded to the nearest whole millimetre. If you do not have a stadiometer, the same procedure can be used standing against the wall whilst a friend uses a horizontal rule on top of your head to mark your stature on the wall with a piece of chalk. Then measure the height with a tape measure.

BMI is calculated by taking body mass and dividing it by stature in metres squared: 85 kilograms / (1.76 metres × 1.76 metres) = 27.5 kilograms per metre squared. The following BMI classifications are provided by NHS Direct:

▸ Underweight for height: < 18.5
▸ Ideal weight for height: 18.5 to 24.9
▸ Above ideal weight for height: 25 to 29.9
▸ Obese: 30 to 39.9
▸ Very obese: 39.9+

BMI is only an indication of whether you are classified as underweight, ideal, overweight, or obese. It does not take into account body type and shape, which will affect your score. It is only a simple tool used to track change in people who are starting an active lifestyle because it does not accurately apply to very muscular people (muscle is denser than fat, so BMI will overestimate fatness). Therefore, other methods of body composition analysis, such as establishing the amount of excess fat tissue, should be used wherever possible.

Measurement of skinfold thickness can be performed by a sport scientist and is a more accurate way of establishing whether you are carrying excess adipose tissue. The skinfold method measures a double fold of skin and subcutaneous adipose tissue by means of callipers, which apply a constant pressure over a range of thicknesses (Hawes & Martin, 2001). This is the most common method of establishing body-fat percentage. However, there is a complexity to establishing body-fat percentage from the sum of skinfolds. The selection of an appropriate equation to calculate body-fat percentage, which has been derived from a sample whose characteristics are similar to those of the subjects being measured, is required. Unfortunately, there is no specific equation for mountaineers. The use of an equation that is not specific to this population may over- or underestimate body-fat percentage.

However, there is merit in using the sum of skinfolds as an indicator of overall subcutaneous fatness. This measure avoids many of the untenable assumptions that are inherent in the use of a predictive equation for body-fat percentage. The method also provides specific information about increases or decreases in skin-fold thickness at various sites around the body. This is information that other methods cannot provide and that is easy to understand. More accurate and reliable measurements of body-fat percentage can be made using techniques such as air-displacement plethysmography or DXA scans. However, you will need access to a sport science facility for such techniques.

Submaximal and Maximal Assessment of Fitness

If you are preparing for an extreme challenge, you have access to a sport science laboratory, and you have the appropriate resources, then we recommend that you have your heart rate and blood lactate concentration responses to incremental exercise measured, as well as your $\dot{V}O_2$max. These tests can be performed either on a treadmill or a cycle ergometer. The preference would be to assess these physiological variables using a treadmill because it is more specific to mountaineering. However, if the majority of your training is going to be performed on a cycle ergometer, you may choose to use this mode of assessment. The protocol we recommend involves standard tests used to assess endurance performance (Jones, 2007).

Before the treadmill test, you should determine blood pressure, resting heart rate, body mass, stature, and resting blood lactate concentration in addition to completing a health screening questionnaire. A fingertip blood sample should then be taken and a telemetric heart rate monitor fitted, followed by your own warm-up and stretching regime.

The first part of the test is a discontinuous incremental protocol to establish your lactate threshold, lactate turnpoint, and heart rate responses. This information can then be used to establish individual training zones to structure your training. The starting running speed will vary depending upon your initial fitness level and should be negotiated with the sport scientist running your test. The treadmill gradient should be set at a 1 percent gradient to simulate normal running energetics (Jones & Doust, 1996).

You should complete five to nine 3-minute exercise stages with 30 seconds of rest between each stage, increasing running speed by 1 kilometre (.5 mi) per hour at the end of each stage. The number of stages will be dictated by your blood lactate concentrations and heart rate; once they reach approximately 4 millimoles per litre or 5 to 10 beats per minute of maximum, respectively, you have completed sufficient exercise stages. Heart rate will be recorded during the last 30 seconds of each stage, and fingertip blood samples will be collected at the end of each exercise stage.

You should be allowed up to 15 minutes of active recovery, or sufficient time to still feel warm and recovered before the second part of the test. This part of the test directly determines your $\dot{V}O_2$max. The running speed is continuous, being 2 kilometres (1.3 mi) per hour lower than the running speed during the last stage of the initial part of the test. However, the gradient is increased by 1 percent every minute from a starting gradient of 1 percent until volitional exhaustion, which is usually within 6 to 8 minutes. Expired air will be collected using Douglas bags or an online gas analysis system, with a fingertip blood sample at volitional exhaustion for blood lactate concentration. The same principles are also applied if a cycle ergometer is the preferred mode of exercise.

The technicalities involved in the direct assessment of fitness make this form of assessment unfeasible outside laboratory settings and therefore not accessible to everyone. However, there are alternatives, which will be discussed later in this section.

Progression is the key in developing your physiological profile in preparation for your challenge. Taking this into account, you can monitor your progression by designing your own simple but progressive exercise test with no need for fancy technologies, or you can use previously established field-based measures of fitness, such as the Rockport fitness walking test (Kline et al., 1987) or the maximal 12-minute Cooper test (Cooper, 1968).

A walking test is ideal for people who do not routinely take part in physical activity and are unable to run 1.6 kilometres (1 mi). A running test, on the other hand, is more suitable for those with a reasonable level of fitness, especially because the walking test will probably be too easy for them. However, a maximal exercise test may be inappropriate for many adults without medical clearance or where the testing environment does not have the necessary supervision and safeguards. Therefore, we strongly suggest that you have your general practitioner assess your health status before you embark on maximal exercise.

Here is an example of how to design your own fitness test. This test is based on walking, but similar principles can be used for running if you have a moderately active lifestyle.

If you do not have an active lifestyle but want to tackle a mountain in a day, you might start off by seeing how quickly you can walk a 1.6-kilometre (1 mi) route from and to your house without running out of steam on the flat. (You may find the following Web sites useful to plan your routes: http://walking.about.com/library/walk/blgooglemap1.htm; www.mapmyrun.com).

An ordinary person out for a walk should be able to complete 1.6 kilometres (1 mi) in 16 minutes, whereas someone with a good level of fitness should be able to complete the walk in less than 15 minutes. If you exceed 16 minutes for this distance, then you're not in the best of aerobic shape. The accuracy of this test depends on your pacing ability and motivation; therefore, it may take a couple of attempts to get your pacing accurate. With the introduction of an appropriate training programme, walking regularly will be a good start (see chapter 7 for further details) and you should start to bring your time down. Once you can complete 1.6 kilometres (1 mi) in less than 16 minutes, it is then time to extend your test route up to 3 kilometres (2 mi), aiming for less than 32 minutes, and then extend the test route to 5 kilometres (3 mi), aiming for less than 48 minutes. This pace is equivalent to 6 kilometres (3.75 mi) per hour.

Once you can walk 5 kilometres (3 mi) on the flat in under 48 minutes, start including a hill or two into your route. Then once this becomes easier (completed in less than 48 minutes), walk the route with a rucksack, carrying the weight and equipment you would normally take with you into the hills for a day, then start to increase the weight, and then start to progressively increase the duration and distance of your walks. Once you are able to walk continuously

with weight on your back for over an hour and a half, you should be ready to tackle something equivalent to one of the three Yorkshire peaks (Whernside, Pen-y-ghent, Ingleborough).

If you want to be a bit more scientific with your approach, then you can determine your estimated $\dot{V}O_2$max from a 1.6-kilometre (1 mi) walk using the Rockport fitness walking test (Kline et al., 1987). After a very gentle warm up for no more than 5 minutes walk a mile as fast as you can (do not run or race walk). Note the following variables to predict your estimated $\dot{V}O_2$max: Time to walk the mile in minutes and seconds, heart rate at the end of the walk (either from a heart rate monitor or by counting heart beats manually for 15 seconds and multiplying by 4), age (years) and body mass (pounds). You can then calculate your estimated $\dot{V}O_2$max using the following equation. Note that BM is your body mass in pounds; A is your age in years; G is your gender (female is 0 and male is 1); T is your time for 1-mile walk in minutes and hundredths of a minute; and HR is your heart rate taken at the end of the 1-mile walk in beats per minute.

$$\dot{V}O_2max \ (ml.kg^{-1}.min^{-1}) = 132.853 - (0.0769 \times BM) - (0.3877 \times A) + (6.315 \times G) - (3.2649 \times T) - (0.1565 \times HR)$$

You can see from the equation that your predicted estimate of $\dot{V}O_2$max will go down if you put on weight, take longer to walk, your heart rate is higher or you have a birthday. Therefore the key variables to monitor for your walk are heart rate, walking time and body mass, which you can compare with repeated tests every 3 months, before and after a focussed period of training, before and after an expedition, or before and after a period of time away from regular walking. That way you can compare changes in your own fitness and performance over time, which is the best use of such fitness tests.

The 12-minute Cooper test is a maximal running test, which may be more appropriate for people who are able to run 1.6 kilometres (1 mi) or more without difficulty. Instead of completing a set distance as fast as possible, the idea of this test is to cover as much distance as possible in 12 minutes, ideally running on a 400-metre (.25 mi) athletics track, although walking is allowed if necessary (Cooper,

1968). Then using the distance (D) covered in metres, $\dot{V}O_2$max can be calculated:

$$\text{Estimated } \dot{V}O_2\text{max} = (D - 504.9) / 44.73$$

As with the walking tests, practice and pacing are required to ensure the best prediction. This equation is much simpler and only uses distance covered, so in terms of monitoring your own fitness it basically comes down to distance covered in 12 minutes, which is easy. If you put on weight you will run a shorter distance and if you don't walk in the hills or train you will also cover a shorter distance. Conversely, as you train harder you will increase the distance covered in 12 minutes as you will be able to run faster.

The Rockport walking test and 12-minute Cooper test have been shown to be good predictors of cardiorespiratory fitness, but they are not as accurate as direct determination methods. Kline and colleagues (1987) reported a correlation of 0.93 between $\dot{V}O_2$max and time to complete 1.6 kilometres (1 mi), and Cooper (1968) reported a correlation of 0.90 between $\dot{V}O_2$max and the distance covered in a 12-minute walk–run. However, more important than accuracy is ensuring continued improvements in the variables tested.

Lung Function

Spirometry devices can be used to assess the condition of the airways. Forced vital capacity (FVC) can be measured, which is the amount of gas expelled when you have taken a deep breath and then forcefully exhaled maximally as fast as possible. Forced expiratory volume (FEV) can also be measured, which is the amount of gas that is exhaled during specific time intervals of the FVC test. Subjects with healthy lungs can exhale about 80 percent of the FVC within 1 second (FEV_1). The average healthy FVC is 5.0 litres and the average FEV_1 is 4.0 litres, or 80 percent.

Oxygen-Carrying Capacity of Blood

The sport science laboratory should also be able to measure your haemoglobin and haematocrit levels by taking a resting fingertip blood sample to assess the oxygen-carrying capacity of the blood, with typical values being 130 to 180 milligrams per litre and 45 percent, respectively. A low value will reflect a reduced oxygen-carrying capacity of the blood, which may limit endurance performance, especially at altitude. Improvements can be made in these variables by increasing consumption of foods rich in iron, such as red meats, fortified breakfast cereals, green leafy vegetables, dried fruits, pulses, nuts, and seeds. Iron absorption can be hindered by excessive intake of tea and coffee, which should be avoided at meal times. Iron absorption can be aided by the inclusion of vitamin C during each meal, such as a glass of orange or grapefruit juice or some broccoli, strawberries, or peppers. If these variables do not change after a period of dietary manipulation, then you should seek further advice from your sport scientist or general practitioner.

Arterial Oxygen Saturation Levels After Acute Exposure to Altitude

Using state-of-the-art expertise and equipment, certain sport science laboratories and hypoxic centres are able to predict your chances of developing AMS. They should be able to assess your arterial oxygen saturation (SaO_2) levels after acute exposure to altitude. This is important because low blood oxygen saturation has been highly associated with AMS. Furthermore, for certain mountain climbs, such as Aconcagua (Andes Mountains, Argentina), local authorities will not allow you on the mountain or beyond a certain point unless your blood oxygen saturation is above a certain level. They may use a protocol whereby they measure your SaO_2 via pulse oximetry from sea level up to 6,500 metres (21,325 ft). They then cross-reference your response with a scientific study by Burtscher, Flatz, and Faulhaber (2004), which has an 86 percent accuracy rate in predicting the likelihood of developing AMS on exposure to altitude (figure 6.1). This test will provide some basic information on how you might cope at altitude, and you can then prepare appropriately, spend longer

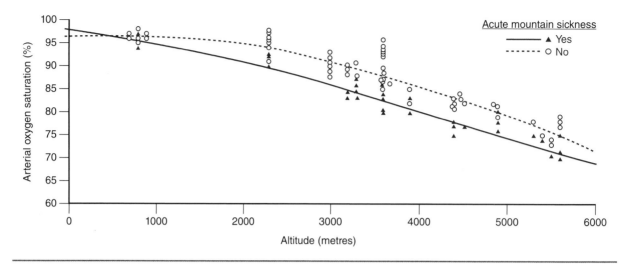

Figure 6.1 Prediction of susceptibility to AMS by SaO$_2$ values during short-term exposure to hypoxia.

Adapted, by permission, from Burtscher, Flatz, and Faulhaber 2004.

acclimatising in the country, or preacclimatise using a hypoxic chamber. The ideal preacclimatisation strategy would be to sleep in a hypoxic tent at home, steadily increasing altitudes 6 to 8 weeks before your departure.

INITIAL ASSESSMENT OF THE EXPEDITION TEAM

Regardless of your personal challenge, whether scaling the highest peak in the world, Mount Everest (8,848 m, or 29,029 ft), or the highest peak in Yorkshire, Whernside (736 m, or 2,415 ft), meticulous planning is essential. One part of being successful includes appropriate physical preparation relevant to the challenge you have set yourself.

The best way to plan your physical preparation is to assess your personal fitness and then to implement a training programme, the effectiveness of which should be evaluated and monitored regularly to ensure you are making improvements in all areas of your physical preparations. Your starting point and the physical demands of the challenge will guide the length of your preparation schedule. For example, if you do not undertake any physical

activity on a regular basis, then you may need at least 3 months of training to be able to climb Whernside safely. On the other hand, if you want to climb Mount Everest, regardless of your starting point you may need at least a year to get yourself in shape.

Within the Everest West Ridge team, there was a range of fitness levels, and a decision was made to have a long period of physical preparation to ensure that the entire team had the maximum amount of time to benefit. We had just over 12 months to assist in the team's physical preparations. We implemented four physical assessments every 4 months, and the information collected was analysed by the Leeds Met team. This analysis enabled the team and Chip Rafferty, its physical performance coach, to prescribe individualised training programmes in preparation for the expedition. The effects of these interventions were monitored and evaluated through follow-up tests and the submission and evaluation of training diaries. This schedule of testing and prescription ensured that the team members were in the best physical condition they could be prior to the expedition. The adoption of a similar testing, monitoring, and evaluation schedule would be recommended, especially for those who want to climb at altitude.

Physical Performance on the EWR 2006 Expedition

The Everest West Ridge team was put through the following physical assessments on each testing occasion: (1) the measurement of maximal oxygen uptake, heart rate, and blood lactate responses during maximal incremental exercise using a treadmill test; (2) the assessment of lung function (i.e., expiration and inspiration volume); (3) the assessment of blood haemoglobin and haematocrit levels; and (4) the assessment of body composition using body mass, stature, and estimation of body-fat percentage (skinfold measurements). The data collected from the initial set of physiological assessments were used as a baseline and to initiate individualised training interventions. The three follow-up assessments evaluated the effectiveness of the interventions and ensured that each team member progressed towards an optimal level of fitness prior to the expedition.

The information collected from each set of physical assessments was fed back to each team member via an individual report, as well as a team report for the expedition leader and the physical performance coach. Feedback meetings were held with the physical performance coach after each set of tests to discuss the details. Within each report, recommendations were made for improvements that were specific to each person. This enabled the physical performance coach to create specific training programmes based on the test results.

Table 6.1 shows the changes in certain physiological variables measured in one of the male team members over the duration of the intervention. This person started off with a high body-fat percentage and a relatively low maximal oxygen uptake. As previously stated, the aim of any intervention for this sort of challenge is to ensure improvement in all areas of the physiological profile, optimising each person's potential rather than everyone aiming for set end points. This climber was able to make

TABLE 6.1 Changes in physiological variables for one of the EWR 2006 team climbers.

	Test 1	Test 2	Change	Test 4	Change
Body mass (kg)	105.3	99.4	−5.9	97.5	−1.9
Sum of skinfolds (mm)	180.5	133.8	−46.7	127.6	−6.2
Body fat (%)	24.4	18.1	−6.3	17.6	−0.5
Maximal oxygen uptake: ml · kg^{-1} · min^{-1} (absolute – litres · min^{-1})	39.3 (4.14)	49.03 (4.88)	+9.7 (0.74)	46.7 (4.49)	−2.33 (0.39)

(continued)

EWR 2006 Expedition   *(continued)*

dramatic improvements in the initial 8 months of the intervention. He demonstrated a significant decrease in body mass and body-fat percentage and a significant increase in maximal oxygen uptake during this time. Within the last 4 months of the intervention, he was able to maintain his enhanced physiological profile with no real change except for a further reduction in body mass.

Even though this climber did not have the highest maximal oxygen uptake within the team, this did not seem to limit his performance. In fact, he was able to operate more effectively at 8,000 metres (26,245 ft) without oxygen than other climbers who had higher maximal oxygen uptakes. This underlines the fact that each person should focus on maximising individual potential rather than worrying about the values achieved. The verbal feedback from this climber was that without the training and the motivation of the fitness assessments, he would not have been able to contribute so successfully to the expedition.

KEY IDEAS

▸ Fitness will benefit from regular participation in training for mountaineering or climbing expeditions.

▸ Application of the principles of training to the planning, implementation, and monitoring of training programmes is important for achieving appropriate fitness in preparation for expeditions.

▸ Physiological profiling and access to accredited sport and exercise scientists is advisable for training programmes in preparation for extreme expeditions.

▸ Monitoring and evaluating training programmes through regular tests and measurements help ensure training is efficacious in improving fitness.

7

Endurance Training

Chip Rafferty, John O'Hara, and Carlton Cooke

Endurance is not just the ability to bear a hard thing, but to turn it into glory.

William Barclay

Numerous factors contribute to the development of a successful mountaineer, many of which are psychological, such as self-belief, motivation, accepting fear, and dealing with altitude. However, all these add up to very little without the physical ability to support them. Climbing mountains requires cardiorespiratory fitness, muscular endurance, strength, and power. It is a myth that psychological attributes can overcome limitations in physical fitness. A lack of cardiorespiratory and muscular endurance will prevent you from being able to sustain effort for a prolonged time, as is required in mountaineering. If the power and strength needed to overcome a climb aren't within your physical capacity, you will not succeed. Psychological resilience can get you started again, and that has often been the case in some heroic tales of mountaineering endurance. However, it can be argued that there are numerous failures and fatalities associated with the lack of physical endurance for the tasks being undertaken.

Apart from being genetically gifted with a predisposition for endurance, there is no other more important factor in developing physical ability for the mountain than a programme of balanced physical training. It is not by accident that many of the most successful mountaineers have used endurance training programmes before achieving their goals. Through appropriate training they prepare themselves for the debilitating effects of altitude, inadequate hydration and nutrition, intense heat and cold, and the many other factors that contribute to the potential for breakdown in performance. Improving endurance fitness to a level that will provide you with a reserve to deal with the most extreme conditions you may encounter, as well as helping you cope with the length of your journey, is therefore a key determinant of safety, enjoyment, and achievement in any climbing expedition.

This chapter provides the information required to help you set realistic goals and plan and implement your endurance training programme according to your individual needs, whether you are a high-performance mountaineer or a weekend warrior.

THE GOLDEN TRIANGLE

The starting point before embarking on any training regime is to consider the golden triangle, the components of which are the objective or goal, the individual, and the training programme (figure 7.1). Each of these must match up with the other components or the result will be a breakdown in performance. For example, if an individual chooses to climb a mountain that demands a level of fitness beyond her current capabilities and she does not have the physical ability or the time to train up to the required level, then she is set for failure. Again, an individual has a greater chance of failing before he starts if he chooses a training programme that is suited for short technical climbs, such as in the Alps, but has chosen to climb an endurance-sapping Himalayan giant.

Figure 7.1 Golden triangle.

The Goal

Your individual characteristics and subsequent development through a training programme must match the goal as closely as possible. Too many people fail in their mountaineering endeavours because of poorly thought-out and unrealistic goals. Those rose-tinted views of mountaineering gained from glossy pictures or extreme sport videos disguise the reality of being out in the cold, dehydrated, hungry, and lacking in both physical and psychological preparation for the enormity of the task in hand. You should focus your training so that you are more than prepared for your chosen mountaineering challenge, with something left in reserve. This allows for the many things that can and do go wrong in the mountains, such as suffering the effects of altitude, overcoming a crux on route, getting out of the way of falling debris, or helping a climbing partner in trouble.

It is also essential that you know your technical limitations. Climbing a relatively nontechnical mountain such as Aconcagua in Argentina (6,959 m, or 22,830 ft) is completely different to the physically draining alpine rock climb and experience of continually being exposed on a mountain such as Ama Dablam (6,865 m, or 22,525 ft) in the Himalayas. Selecting a goal that fits with your technical capacity as a

mountaineer or climber, as well as your capacity for fitness development and that of all team members, is therefore a crucial starting point for any expedition. Consider carefully your capacity for training and performance and the requirements of a training programme when deciding on your goal.

The Individual

A good investment before you ever think of embarking on a training programme is to perform a full physiological assessment at a sport science facility, similar to the ones used by the 2006 Everest West Ridge team (see chapter 6 for more details). Whether or not you have access to sport scientists and laboratory testing, the training history and physical profile questionnaire (figure 7.2) will provide a useful starting point for you to consider whether you have the endurance training and performance background to realistically undertake your goal through appropriate training. Writing down the information required to complete the questionnaire will get you thinking about whether the goal is a logical and achievable next step for you and is within reach in terms of the endurance training you will have to undertake. The data from the physiological assessments should be reviewed in conjunction with the information contained in the training history and physical profile questionnaire in assessing your readiness to undertake the training necessary to achieve your goal.

Consideration of the individual component of the golden triangle will help you bring clarity to what is realistic for you in terms of the selected goal and the training that is necessary to prepare for the goal. Do you have the endurance and performance training necessary to achieve the level of endurance fitness required by the goal? Do you have sufficient time, knowledge, understanding, and motivation to develop, implement, monitor, and evaluate the training programme that is necessary to achieve the goal?

Answering these questions in detail for each individual involved in the expedition will clarify whether or not the elements of the golden triangle fit with each person's capability and capacity for what is required in endurance fitness.

FIGURE 7.2
Physical Profile and Training History Questionnaire

Name: ______________________________ Preferred name: ____________________

DOB: ____ / ____ / ____

Address: ____

E-mail address: ________________________ Phone number: __________________

Employer: ____

Job title or description: ____

Physical Profile

Body mass: ____________________ Structure: ________________________

Resting heart rate (in bed in the morning): __________________

Present fitness level (1 to 10): __________

Training History

Time to train (daily): ________________________________

Preferred type of training: ____

Training locations (gym, outdoors, home, and so on): ____________________

1.5-mile run time: ____________________ 400-metre run time: ________________

Long run time (3-mile, 10k, other): ________________________

Longest endurance activity: ____

Endurance sports: ____

____

Notable endurance achievements: ____

____

Other sports: ____

____

Favourite sports: ____

____

Favourite leisure activities: ____

____

From C. Cooke, D. Bunting, and J. O'Hara, 2010. *Mountaineering: Training and preparation* (Champaign, IL: Human Kinetics).

Learning From My Experience

I spent 3 hard years training myself into a reasonable marathon runner (personal best: 2 hours, 19 minutes, and 35 seconds). However, those days, months, and years could have been a lot easier if I had trained smart. Training smart would have started by looking at the engine and then the chassis of my body. I would have undergone a series of physiological assessments to identify my strengths and weakness as an endurance athlete, which could have been used to develop a smart training programme. My early hit-and-miss approach to training relied on training in the discipline I enjoyed—long, slow distance training. Therefore, I became an efficient, steady plodder who broke down when the intensity of a race demanded a higher pace and the injection of explosive power. Though a large proportion of long, slow distance training should be performed to develop specific aspects of endurance, you also need the ability to perform high-intensity efforts that you can recover from (Twight & Martin, 1999).

My experience has taught me the importance of the golden triangle. If I had considered my goal in marathon running alongside my strengths, weaknesses, and training history as an individual, I would have formulated a different training strategy based on SMART principles (specific, measurable, achievable, recordable, and testable; see The Programme for details). Though the training I did was clearly beneficial to my performance, I believe that too much focus on long, slow endurance work and not enough on shorter, high-intensity work limited my performance improvement.

Learn from my lesson—consider the golden triangle carefully and apply SMART training principles, and your endurance training will be tailored well to your individual and expedition requirements.

—*Chip Rafferty*

The Programme

'Train hard, climb easy' is a mantra that underpins the methods illustrated in this chapter and chapter 3. The only caveat to that is training must be SMART:

Specific

Measurable

Achievable

Recordable

Testable

The type of training you undertake needs to be as specific to the mountaineering challenge as possible. For example, there are differences in the training required to summit a giant Himalayan mountain, an alpine-style route, or a Lakeland peak. The training needs to be measurable in relation to the training components of endurance, strength, and power. It should be achievable in relation to the time and effort you can put into the training, as well as your physical status and background as a mountaineer. The training should be tested with regular physiological assessments to ensure improvements in endurance and should balance volume, intensity, and frequency of training plus recovery. A record of these tests and any other training indicators should be kept in diary form to be reviewed and assessed before moving on to the next phase of training.

For example, referring to specificity, if training adaptation is to be useful, it must ultimately resemble the types of physical activity, recruitment patterns, and stresses required on the mountain. Although running, biking, and swimming have some great benefits for mountaineers in developing overall cardiorespiratory fitness and important supporting muscle groups, they do not mirror completely the specific stress of hard and sometimes fast mountain days, especially if there are specific technical sections. Therefore, these disciplines have to be trained specifically. With a bit of imagination and knowledge of anatomy and physiology, this can be done in training before getting to the mountain.

An example of how specific an exercise has to be can be illustrated in a cyclist changing body position only slightly on the bike by lowering the seat or altering the handlebars—a new pattern of recruitment of muscle groups needs to be trained to achieve the same performance as was previously trained through the original pattern of muscle activity. Another example is Lance Armstrong's cycling versus his running performance. At his peak in world-class cycling, he wouldn't have been in the first 10 percent of any top endurance running event because of the differences in neuromuscular coordination between cycling and running. The development of the correct neuromuscular coordination is important because it leads to the recruitment of specific muscle groups, thereby developing movement efficiency and economy for a specific activity.

The last example is from mountaineering, where an extremely talented climber and mountaineer in the armed services had a weakness in his cardiorespiratory endurance that was limiting his performance on longer routes. Once this weakness was addressed with an emphasis on longer, low-intensity exercise, his mountaineering potential developed in line with the effort he put in, resulting in him cruising sustained routes that had previously been difficult.

ENDURANCE TRAINING PRINCIPLES

This section applies principles of training from the perspective of endurance training for success in mountaineering and climbing expedi-

tions. You should be able to use the principles explained next together with the examples of training programmes and sessions discussed later in the chapter to plan and implement an individualised endurance training programme. This will be easier if you can also consult with a coach, conditioner, trainer, or sport scientist, but application of the information presented here to your individual circumstances will ensure you have the makings of a good endurance training programme.

Progressive Overload and Training Variety

Many people shy away from a structured training programme for good reasons. Often the structure and discipline in their working life are enough of a burden without adding them to their free time. Therefore, the first principle in designing any training programme is to make it as enjoyable as possible. However, in order to improve fitness and performance, the principle of progressive overload must also be applied. Progressive overload in training will incorporate the elements of the FITT principle (frequency, intensity, time, and type of endurance training) to progressively improve endurance fitness. An example of overload in endurance training is increasing the number of endurance sessions per week, which increases total training time and volume. The duration and intensity of each run can also be manipulated through changes in running speed.

An example of a programme Chip designed for British junior triathletes to ensure continued engagement in the sport is shown in figure 7.3. This is a long-term development plan lasting from their introduction to the sport at 12 years old to Olympic representation a decade later. The plan was based on a progressive system that started with playing at the sport with lots of complementary activities such as skateboarding, trampolining, and BMX riding—in other words, the games children play. As participants developed both physically and psychologically into all-rounders, complementary activities to the discipline of triathlon were introduced, including bodysurfing and surfboarding to develop them as swimmers; BMX and mountain biking

FIGURE 7.3
Long-Term Triathlon Development Plan by Paul (Chip) Rafferty

Stages	Biomotor development	Age	Events/ competition	Training (%)			Hours of training (per year)	Physiological key events
				Compli-mentary	General	Specific		
Initial (4 years)	Dexterity, co-ordination, Flexibility, speed, and agility	9-12	BTA Milk Race series	50%	45%	5%	100-250 (all years)	General growth
Basic (4 years)	Strength development, increased muscle profile, improved muscular coordination, interval training	13-16	BTA start races and Intro Sprint Youth and Junior Inter-national	35%	50%	15%	300-500 (all years)	Growth spurt at onset of puberty
Specific Aerobic Base (3 years)	Develop maxi-mum cardiac capacity, maxi-mum strength, maximum endurance	17-19	Youth and Junior In-ternational (sprint and distance); Intro Olympic distances	20%	40%	40%	600-800 (year 1) 600-800 (year 2) 900-1,000 (year 3)	Puberty; mus-culoskeletal and cardio vascular adap-tation
High-performance maximisation (2 years)	Consolidate all above in specific aerobic base	20-21	Elite domestic common-wealth games	15%	25%	60%	1,000-1,100 (year 1) 1,200-1,300 (year 2)	Musculoskel-etal, cardio vascular over-load, conver-sion of muscle fibre types
Maintenance (2 years)	Decrease vol-ume, increase specifics and intensity	22-24	International Olympics	10%	25%	65%	800-1,000 (all years)	Recovery and peak from previous High-performance maximisation and micro-physical adap-tations

to develop them as cyclists; and orienteering, football, and basketball to develop them as runners.

The next stage had 40 percent of the training and preparation specific to triathlon disciplines, but in a varied way: swimming galas and local swim competitions, athletic clubs and cross country, and local mountain bike and road racing clubs. However, during this time the competitive pressure was also deflected by not exposing participants to overcompeting. As they developed, the percentages of activities specific to the sport of triathlon progressed. However, complementary activities such as climbing, skiing, and skateboarding were maintained to add variety and enjoyment. Examples of progressive overload from figure 7.3 illustrate the progressive increase in hours of training per year, the shift to more training that is specifically focussed on triathlon, and the level of competition demands throughout the years. This long-term triathlon development plan was developed by Chip Rafferty, who once said, "I remember vividly back in the 1980s the last marathon I ever ran, standing on the elite start of the London marathon looking round at the other competitors, who in most cases could only be described as having lungs on legs. Many couldn't lift their own body weight and were plagued by overuse injury. I decided at that moment to train in a way that would give me all-round strength and endurance in a progressive and varied way that hopefully would be more enjoyable."

The lessons in progressive overload and variation from this example are transferable to developing yourself as a mountaineer. Although training for an expedition will be over a shorter time (which could vary from 3 months for weekend warriors preparing for their main annual holiday expedition to more than 2 years for Everest West Ridge 2006), the same principles apply in terms of progressive overload and variety. Plan to steadily increase your training load using the FITT principle and be prepared to adjust your programme based on how you are adapting. Do not increase too quickly, and if you feel tired all the time and performance is not getting better or is even getting worse, increase recovery because you are probably training too hard. Always allow a taper in training prior to your expedition where you maintain your endurance fitness but can then expect to start the expedition in great shape with lots of energy and enthusiasm to achieve your goal.

This approach is essential to all long-term and medium-term training no matter what your age because it provides all-round fitness and strength using many of the muscle groups and energy systems used in mountaineering. This enables the body to adapt and reduces the occurrence of overuse injuries, as well as developing specific muscle groups that will be used in later stages of training and in the arduous conditions encountered on the mountain.

For mountaineers, a wide variety of exercise is encouraged—unless you are lucky enough to be in the mountains every day, occasional visits will not provide enough stimulus to develop sufficient endurance capacity. Therefore, modes of exercise such as running, swimming, mountain biking, road cycling, spinning, swimming, stair-stepping, cross-country skiing, skiing, and snowshoeing are all relevant to improving your mountaineering endurance.

Road running or running on the flat has its place in a training programme, but trail running may be a more effective way of gaining mountain fitness. The irregular terrain in trail running makes it physically demanding and varies the loads on the joints and muscles, as well as being low impact in comparison to road running (Soles, 2006). The benefit of road cycling is that it provides a means of training for long durations, offering long, slow distance training. Due to the nature of the terrain, mountain biking, on the other hand, offers more interval-type sessions, with the chosen route dictating the type of training session.

Swimming has benefits such as developing respiratory capacity and working on alternative muscle groups, and open-water swimming helps develop a tolerance to cold environments (see chapter 3 for more details). A final example is cross-country skiing, which is an excellent whole-body aerobic workout, involving a pulling-down motion from the upper body that is suited to climbers (Soles, 2006). Even though this variety in training modes may be enjoyable, bear in mind that each session is a training session, not just a jolly, and there is a specific reason for the session that needs to be taken into account in the planning and execution of the training programme.

Training Intensity

Mountaineering is often regarded as a low-intensity activity in which demands on strength, power, and speed form only a small percentage of the overall demands on a mountain day. To an extent this could be true; many people with average fitness and a fairly sedentary background seem to be able to climb some of the world's highest mountains, including Mount

Everest. This may seem contradictory, but it is the paradox of Everest—it is a mountain often climbed by nonmountaineers, though generally supported by Sherpas.

Therefore, the question may be reasonably asked as to why you should go through all the pain of training in the first place. First, you will climb the mountain in much better style and with a lot less effort, therefore able to deal with the unexpected should the need arise. Furthermore, the more physically prepared you are for the mountain, the less likely you are to find yourself extremely fatigued, potentially avoiding the life-threatening situations that many climbers have found themselves in (Arnette, 2006). Next time you watch a mass marathon, look at the facial expressions of the leading 10 percent of the runners at the finish and then at the following 90 percent and you will see who is coping with the distance and physical effort.

Second, the adage 'Fail to prepare and prepare to fail' has serious implications for mountaineers. I have seen some top-class mountaineers return from the mountain both physically and psychologically shattered by the extreme effort required due to unexpected bad weather, altitude, or technicalities on the mountain that they had not factored into their preparation. Furthermore, certain routes, such as the more extreme alpine-style routes, require the climber to perform high-intensity efforts whilst recovering on the mountain. These are key reasons why you need to train beyond the capacity required before your mountaineering challenge.

Endurance training can be placed into three distinct zones, according to Shave and Franco (2006): long, slow, moderate-duration distance training; high-intensity training (HIT); and short-duration, very HIT. You cannot rely purely on your ability to perform at a long, slow pace if you want to be a successful mountaineer (Twight & Martin, 1999). The training programme needs to include the appropriate frequency and duration of each of these intensities to elicit the optimal improvements in endurance required for your chosen challenge.

The training intensities will develop specific components of endurance performance. For example, long, slow distance training will contribute to the ability to transport and utilise oxygen, thus improving the ability to burn fat,

the holy grail for endurance athletes. Moderate-duration HIT will predominately develop the lactate threshold. Short-duration, very HIT can be split into exercise intensities equivalent to or above the pace associated with your maximal oxygen uptake. Training at a pace equivalent to your maximal oxygen uptake will predominately develop maximal oxygen uptake and lactate tolerance. Untrained mountaineers may see increases of 20 to 30 percent in maximal oxygen uptake, whereas trained mountaineers may only see small increases of 2 to 3 percent, with variability over the training year. Training at a pace above your maximal oxygen uptake will predominately develop your neuromuscular patterns, speed, power, and local muscular endurance.

The identification of your lactate threshold (as described in chapter 6) is useful in identifying and regulating training intensities, as well as being an important predictor of endurance performance. The terms *lactate threshold* and *lactate turnpoint* were introduced in chapter 6 and will be referred to throughout the rest of this chapter. Lactate threshold is the first rise in blood lactate concentration above basal concentrations and lactate turnpoint is the exercise intensity that is associated with a substantial increase in blood lactate concentration during an incremental exercise test (Jones, 2007).

If you do not have access to a sport science laboratory that can provide your training intensities based on your blood lactate profile, an alternative approach is to use heart-rate training zones.

Long, slow, distance exercise should be equivalent to an exercise intensity around the lactate threshold but below the lactate turnpoint, where there is a lack of lactate accumulation since lactate utilisation and removal outstrips lactate production. It is somewhere between a marathon and half-marathon running pace. It is an exercise intensity that can be sustained for 60 to 120 minutes for running or 120 to 240 minutes for cycling.

To develop the lactate turnpoint workload, you should perform exercise sessions that produce the average heart rate or running speed or cycling power output associated with your lactate turnpoint (Keith, Jacobs, & McLellan, 1992). Your lactate turnpoint is approximately

Calculating Heart-Rate Training Zones

Using your heart rate to guide training intensities is not an exact science, but it is useful for mountaineers who do not have access to sport science facilities. Generally, there are four heart-rate training zones (Jeukendrup & Van Diemen, 1998):

Zone 1: Target heart rate of 60 to 70 percent (based on heart rate reserve as explained next)

Zone 2: Target heart rate of 70 to 80 percent

Zone 3: Target heart rate of 80 to 90 percent

Zone 4: Target heart rate of 90 to 100 percent

The best way to establish your target heart-rate training zones is based on the working range of your heart rate, termed the *heart-rate reserve* (HRR). The HRR can be calculated using the following equation proposed by Karvonen, Kentala, and Musta (1957):

HRR = maximum heart rate (MHR) – resting heart rate (RHR).

To calculate your target heart rate:

Target heart rate = (%HRR / 100) $\times$ (MHR – RHR) + RHR.

So if you want to exercise at 75% (zone 2) and you have a MHR of 200 beats per minute and a resting heart rate of 68 beats per minute, your target heart rate would be (75 / 100) $\times$ (200 – 68) + 68, giving you a target heart rate of 167 beats per minute.

This method requires the use of your RHR and MHR. RHR is best taken when you wake in the morning. There are two ways of determining MHR. You can simply subtract your age from 220 to estimate your MHR, though this method should be used with caution because it has been shown to have large standard deviations and can be out by 12 to 15 beats per minute (Wallace, 2006). The direct determination of MHR via a field-based test is more accurate. If you are a healthy athlete, you may choose to perform a series of 1-minute exercise bouts, increasing the exercise intensity at the end of each bout and taking a short rest between each bout until the last one is flat out, and note your MHR from your heart rate monitor. If you are not used to performing intense exercise and are over 40 years of age, it is recommend that you have your MHR assessed in a sport science facility with a doctor present.

MHR is variable depending upon the mode of exercise. The MHR you can achieve during various modes of exercise will be different due to differences in body position and the amount of muscle mass utilised. Therefore, it is worthwhile to establish your MHR for your training modes using the interval-based exercise test described previously. It is also important to be aware of cardiac drift when using target heart rates to monitor training intensity. In cardiac drift, over time your heart rate increases by as much as 20 beats per minute during exercise (Jeukendrup & van Diemen, 1998), which needs to be taken into account.

equivalent to your half-marathon or 16-kilometre (10 mi) running time (Jones, 2007) and is an exercise intensity that you should be able to maintain for 30 to 60 minutes at a maximum.

Short duration, very HIT exercise sessions are the icing on the cake. These sessions are high-intensity intervals that last between 1 and 5 minutes at a pace equivalent to your maximal oxygen uptake, interspersed with sufficient recovery of up to 2 minutes. A typical session may include four 1.6-kilometre (1 mi) runs at the running speed equivalent to maximal oxygen uptake. It is also useful to include sessions at an intensity above your maximal oxygen uptake that last up to 1 minute in order to further develop your speed and power. A typical session may include running 200-metre (656 ft) repetitions on an athletics track. These shorter interval sessions may also include hill sessions. These types of sessions develop strength, speed, and power without the stresses associated with high-intensity speed work. A good example is hills resistance training, where high intensities are reached through running or biking on steep hills, producing resistance without the impact associated with sprinting or peak efforts on the flat. Hill running sessions use the muscles in a more specific range of movements in a controlled and deliberate way.

Ultimately, as a mountaineer you are training to increase your muscles' contractility and therefore their ability to utilise oxygen at any pace required. Therefore, variety in training exercise intensities is key to developing the physiological variables associated with endurance training and in so doing your ability as a mountaineer.

Training Volume

It has been a long-held assumption that performance in endurance activities is directly linked to training volume. Back in the 1980s, long, slow distance running was regarded as the holy grail of all endurance athletes, with many runners covering 193 kilometres (120 mi) or more a week and professional bikers doing 966 kilometres (600 mi) or more a week, often totalling 9,656 kilometres (6,000 mi) of running and 48,280 kilometres (30,000 mi) of cycling a year. However, a new scientific approach took over in the 1990s amongst U.K. long-distance

runners and bikers. There was a shift away from the long, slow distance training towards more HIT, with a resulting dip in performance and medals at international level for over a decade. In more recent times, the high-volume approach has been adopted again, and it is paramount for success. There is no doubt that high-intensity workouts have their place in any endurance training programme, but you have to put in the distance to establish good endurance fitness.

To improve your endurance, as a starting point you should dedicate approximately 70 to 80 percent of your training time to long, slow distance training, although this may vary slightly depending upon the phase of training. (The phases of training will be discussed in more detail later in this chapter.) The physiological training effects of high-volume, long, slow distance training include an increased ability to transport and utilise oxygen through an increased capillary network, increased blood volume and mitochondrial size and density, improved fat oxidation, the development of neuromuscular patterns for this exercise intensity that leads to improved movement efficiency and economy, and greater muscular endurance (Shave & Franco, 2006). These training adaptations are essential for mountaineers, particularly at high altitudes.

Although we know the percentage of time you should be working towards at this long, slow training intensity, how much volume should it entail? Too little volume will not provide optimal improvements in endurance, but too much volume too soon would be foolish and result in overtraining and overuse injuries. The following formula is recommended for training volume, regardless of your training status. Calculate the average training volume over a given period of previous training and then at the most add 10 percent. If no previous training has been undertaken, an endurance athlete of average fitness should be able to tolerate around 6 hours of long, slow distance training a week. This is obviously split across a series of training sessions. Once the person has adapted to the volume of training, 10 percent can be added after a given period of not less than 1 month.

Ultimately, volumes at the long, slow distance training intensity should be taken as high as possible as long as they don't affect the high-intensity workouts, which are introduced following the base or initial training phase. Subsequently the volume of long, slow distance training should be reduced as you start to introduce and develop HIT sessions during the lactate turnpoint, power, and speed training phases. As a good starting point, these high-intensity sessions should constitute approximately 20 to 30 percent of your training time. Once the base training and high-volume, low-intensity work has been completed, the benefits gained need to be maintained by over-distance maintenance training performed once a week. This allows the overall weekly volume to be reduced whilst maintaining the benefits gained from the previous high weekly volume of training.

Frequency, intensity, and volume are closely interlinked, and a particular combination can have a positive or negative effect on different people. For example, some mountaineers may benefit from splitting a high-volume session into two sessions whereas others will not. The results are very much determined by the physiological and sometimes psychological characteristics of the person. However, the benefits of the depletion or over-distance training days cannot be gained by dividing the total volume. The extreme stimulus cannot be reproduced with the same cumulative cardiorespiratory, muscular, and skeletal demands on the body, even if the intensity is increased.

Recovery

Recovery is a crucial part of any training programme; without it, the body and mind will struggle to adapt and ultimately struggle to perform. Planning a good recovery programme is as important as planning the training programme. You need to include a session of complete rest in your weekly schedule, at least one day off from training whereby you do not undertake any demanding physical activity. Also, you should include recovery workouts in your training weeks. Some of your long, slow distance sessions, performed at below-marathon running pace (60 to 70 percent of your MHR), can be used as recovery sessions as long as they do not exceed 30 minutes. These recovery sessions are usually the first session of the day and are useful for increasing overall distance, helping the body recover from high-intensity sessions the day before, and preparing the body for training later the same day. These sessions place minimal stress on the neuromuscular system and should last no longer than 30 minutes for running but

Training With Depleted Energy Stores

By necessity and with some good luck, 20 years ago I came across the ultimate in high-volume training, which I call *over-distance* or *depletion days*, whereby in my job as an outdoor instructor I would train immediately after a day's caving or mountaineering activity, running back the 19 kilometres (12 mi) home or biking sometimes up to 160 kilometres (100 mi) after a day's work. This activity was done with low reserves of food and hydration, which had the effect of digging deeply into my physical reserves and developing an awareness of how my body might feel after a long mountain day. These sessions developed into the planned depletion days described in chapter 3. I would minimise my intake of food and water to simulate the effects of being thirsty and hungry on the mountain and allow my body and mind to gain an indelible imprint of that situation for future use.

—Chip Rafferty

longer for non-weight-bearing activities such as biking or swimming. Biking should normally last twice as long as the equivalent running sessions. Swimming is harder to quantify for time, and you should use your own judgement based on your swimming ability, but try to go for longer than 30 minutes if you can. If you are a good, relaxed swimmer, up to an hour is fine.

Sufficient recovery time is a key to good training so that you do not overreach or overtrain, which can be monitored through physiological or performance assessments. It is also important to understand reversibility, whereby too much rest and recovery can reverse the training-induced adaptations, be it planned or injury induced. Responses to recovery and the previously mentioned linked components are the areas where people differ the most. It is unlikely that any two mountaineers will recover from training at the same rate, which may result in one being undertrained and the other overtrained should they train together using exactly the same sessions. Note, too, that a good nutrition programme with appropriate supplementation is vital to recovery and general well-being (see chapter 9), as is the use of therapeutic methods such as massage, physiotherapy, yoga, and hydrotherapy pools, especially after hard training sessions.

Tapering and Peaking

As the expedition date nears, you need to consider reducing the training load. This is called *tapering*, the main aim of which is to reduce the accumulative fatigue associated with daily training, thereby improving your performance. There are four tapering strategies: linear taper, exponential taper (slow decay), exponential taper (fast decay), and step taper. The exponential tapers are more beneficial; see Mujika and Padilla (2003) for further details.

As suggested by the names the two exponential tapers describe the shape of the general curve representing the decrease in percentage of training over time. There is a steeper decline in percentage of normal training at the beginning of the taper phase (a decrease of the order of 20 to 30% of normal training in the first taper day for the slow and fast decay respectively) which

then flattens out with much smaller decreases as the taper phase progresses (from 30 to 25% of normal training for the slow decay and from 15 to 10% of normal training between the 10th and 14th day for the fast decay, respectively).

According to Mujika and Padilla (2003), the best way to taper is to maintain the training intensity but progressively reduce the volume of training by 60 to 90 percent and slightly decrease the training frequency by no more than 20 percent. Tapering your training will hopefully elicit improvements in your overall performance, bringing together and optimising all the physiological determinants required for your mountaineering performance, as well as ensuring you hit the mountain fresh but not detrained. This is called *peaking*, which needs to be planned to occur at the point of your expedition and is more of an art than a science. For short expeditions, aim to peak for the start. For longer expeditions involving overseas travel, a long walk in to the mountain and acclimatisation to altitude, you should try to peak for the critical period of your expedition, factoring in all the travel and acclimatisation to your training plan.

The tapering period is hard to specify and may vary from person to person, and it is dependent on the previous training load and the total length of training. The longer the overall training phase, the longer the tapering period that is required. However, if the tapering period is too long, then you may be susceptible to becoming detrained; on the other hand, if it is too short, then there is not enough time for sufficient recovery. The length of the expedition also needs to be taken into account; on a typical Himalayan expedition, the packing, the flight, the mountain walk in, and acclimatisation can sometimes take more than 2 weeks of virtual inactivity. On such expeditions, keep the training going more or less right up to the flight day and do not taper as significantly as if you were going on a shorter expedition or an expedition where you are on the mountain significantly sooner. In addition, you need to take into consideration long-haul travel during the tapering phase because travel fatigue and jet lag can adversely affect performance (see chapter 5). An example of a 21-day exponential taper (slow decay) can be seen in figure 7.4.

FIGURE 7.4
Sample 21-Day Exponential Taper (Slow Decay)

	Week 1	Week 2	Week 3
LONG SLOW DISTANCE TRAINING			
Number of sessions per week	8	6	4
Total duration per week	8 hours	4 hours	2 hours
HIGH-INTENSITY TRAINING			
Number of sessions per week	3	3	3
Total duration per week	2.5 hours	2 hours	1.5 hour
SHORT-DURATION, VERY HIGH-INTENSITY TRAINING			
Number of sessions per week	3	3	3
Total duration per week	2 hours	2 hours	1.5 hour
Total number of training sessions per week	14	12	10
Total training duration per week	12.5 hours	8 hours	5 hours

Putting the Principles Together

In summary, the main elements to any endurance training programme, if you discount tapering and peaking, are long, slow distance training; HIT; short-duration and very HIT. They are often named and sequenced in different ways. There are other elements of training that should be part of your programme, including strength training, flexibility, reactivity, balance, coordination, and agility, which are not covered in this chapter.

To achieve and adapt to the training set, the combination of the main components is important. One approach is sequencing, where the athlete initially develops a good cardiorespiratory foundation through long, slow distance training before moving on to the HIT sessions to develop the lactate turnpoint workload, power, and speed whilst still maintaining extensive endurance. A second approach is reverse sequencing, where the athlete increases the training volume by increasing the distance at an already improved speed.

You should consider including hill sessions within your training programme, often coupled with strength and conditioning training, after the development of a good cardiorespiratory foundation. An implication of this initial high-volume phase of training is a likely reduction in strength and power if it is not accompanied by compensatory strength and conditioning training, which needs to be included in preparation for the short-duration, very HIT sessions.

All the phases overlap and require careful placing of maintenance sessions outside the specific phase; otherwise detraining and reversibility may occur in the areas that are already trained.

The key to any successful endurance training programme for mountaineers is to match the components of the programme (progression, intensity, volume, frequency, and recovery), with the goal or mountain challenge—remember the golden triangle. Knowledge of your strengths and weaknesses using the physiological assessments on offer at many sport science facilities will help you and your coach develop the most appropriate training programme for you. Please see chapter 6 for details of the tests used with the Everest West Ridge team in 2006.

There is no quick fix, and reaching your maximum potential for performance is a long-term

Sample Training Programmes

We have included some weekly training programmes used to prepare the 2006 Everest West Ridge team, which you may want to use as a guide if your challenge is an energy-sapping Himalayan giant. We have also included a programme that is more appropriate for weekend warriors.

Weekend Warrior Sample Programme

The following is a typical weekly training programme that weekend warriors may want to use to develop cardiorespiratory endurance before engaging in any HIT training sessions (see figure 7.5). Note that everyone responds differently to training, and you should use the principles and explanations in this chapter to develop your own training programme. This specific phase of training should last a minimum of 6 weeks, depending upon the duration of time you have to prepare for your challenge, accumulating up to 6 hours per week of long, slow distance training.

Following the development of your cardiorespiratory foundation, you would start to increase the pace of some of your short training sessions (30 to 60 minutes) to an intensity equivalent to your half-marathon and 16-kilometre (10 mi) running pace, performing two of these sessions a week. Then after 4 weeks, you should include a hill training session once a week, which should be an additional session in preparation for short-duration, very HIT sessions. Once you have completed 4 weeks of integrating hill sessions into your training, you should then start to introduce the short-duration, very HIT sessions into your weekly schedule, building up to two sessions a week, whilst maintaining your extended endurance. These two sessions should replace existing sessions, such as the hill training session and one of your shorter long, slow distance training sessions. Examples of short-duration, very HIT sessions can be seen in the Everest programme.

Everest Sample Programme

The following is an example of a typical weekly training programme used by the Everest West Ridge team to develop cardiorespiratory endurance before engaging in any HIT sessions (figure 7.6). This was the first phase of training, and the key was for team members to enjoy the training, performing the activities they liked as long as they were at the specified intensities, and a good percentage of the training was weight bearing. They were told not to be obsessed with sticking directly to the programme. If they missed a day, they were to count this as their easy day or day off rather than doubling up the training the next day. It was also emphasised that each session was a training session, but they were not training to be elite competitive athletes; rather, they were training to reach their full physical potential as high-altitude mountaineers. Again, everyone responds differently to training, and you should use the principles in this chapter to develop your own training programme.

This specific phase of the training would last for a minimum of 6 weeks, depending upon the duration of time you have to prepare for your expedition, accumulating up to 10 hours per week of long, slow distance training. Following the development of your cardiorespiratory foundation, you would start to increase the pace of some of your shorter training sessions (30 to 60 minutes) to an intensity equivalent to your half-marathon or 16-kilometre (10 mi) running pace, performing two or three of these sessions a week. Then after 4 weeks, you would include hill training sessions every other day to develop your strength and power in preparation for the short-duration, very HIT sessions. Sample sessions may include the following:

Cycling: Hilly course (2 hours plus) or mountain bike course; four steep, hilly 30-minute repetitions.

Running: Hilly course (1 hour plus), mainly cross country trail running or hill repetitions: 10 minute warm-up, 100- to 200-metre (109-219 yd) repetitions, for approximately 20 minutes, followed by 5 minutes recovery, running up and down as follows: first repetition easy jog; second repetition high knee lift; third repetition jog but keep on balls of feet, letting heels drop but not touching ground. Then run downhill fast but with a relaxed, long stride. Take 5 to 10 minutes to cool down.

Once you have completed approximately 4 weeks of integrating hill sessions into your training, you then need to introduce the short-duration, very HIT sessions into your weekly schedule, building up to three sessions a week, whilst maintaining your extended endurance. Very HIT sessions may include intervals, which are between 1 and 5 minutes, at an exercise intensity equivalent to your maximal oxygen uptake, with up to 2 minutes recovery between repetitions.

Running: 4 × 1.6-kilometre (1 mi) runs

8 × 1-minute runs, on- or off-road terrain

Other examples of short-duration, very HIT sessions may include intervals, which are up to 1 minute in duration at an exercise intensity above your maximal oxygen uptake.

Running: 8 × 200 metres (219 yd) with 30 seconds recovery between each interval

12 × 150 metres (164 yd) with 30 seconds recovery between each interval

Cycling: 8 × 30-second repetitions on turbo trainer or on the road, with 30 seconds recovery between each interval

Swimming: 12 × 25-metre (27 yd) repetitions or 6 × 50-metre (55 yd) repetitions depending on ability, with 30 seconds recovery between each interval

Note that these are hard sessions at a pace above your maximal oxygen uptake and should only be performed once a week.

(continued)

FIGURE 7.5

Sample Week's Training Programme for a Weekend Warrior (Foundation Phase)

	Morning	Afternoon/evening	Recovery session
Sunday	Rest	Long, hilly walk over distance	Play, swim
Monday	20-minute run or swim or 40-minute bike at an intensity around the lactate threshold but below the lactate turnpoint	Rest	Climb wall (easy, introductory session); 30 minutes maximum or a strength and conditioning session in gym
Tuesday	Rest	Cross-country, hilly run 45-60 minutes or 90 minutes hilly bike at an exercise intensity around the lactate threshold but below the lactate turnpoint	Hydropool massage; yoga; swim
Wednesday	20-minute run or swim, or 40-minute bike at an intensity around the lactate threshold but below the lactate turnpoint	Rest	Rest
Thursday	Rest	Orienteering course point to point on mountain bike	Hydropool massage; yoga; swim
Friday	20-minute run or swim, or 40-minute bike at an intensity around the lactate threshold but below the lactate turnpoint	Rest	Rest
Saturday	Rest	Running session: 1.5-mile warm-up at an intensity below the lactate turnpoint; .5 mile at a pace averaging the lactate turnpoint .5 mile at a pace equivalent to maximal oxygen uptake; .5 mile at a pace below the lactate turnpoint (or do same on the bike, doubling distances)	Rest

FIGURE 7.6

Sample Week's Training Programme for an Everest West Ridge 2006 Team Member (Foundation Phase)

	Morning	Afternoon/evening	Recovery session
Sunday	Rest	Cross-country run up to 90 minutes or bike for up to 3 hours at an intensity around the lactate threshold but below the lactate turnpoint	30-minute swim at an intensity around the lactate threshold but below the lactate turnpoint, followed by a massage
Monday	Early morning 20-minute run or swim, or a 40-minute bike at an intensity around the lactate threshold but below the lactate turnpoint	45- to 60-minute run at an intensity averaging lactate turnpoint	Climbing wall (easy, introductory session) or strength and conditioning maintenance session in gym
Tuesday	Early morning 20-minute run or swim at an intensity around the lactate threshold but below the lactate turnpoint	Long mountain walk carrying a weighted rucksack or a 2- to 3-hour bike ride at an intensity around the lactate threshold but below the lactate turnpoint	30-minute swim at an intensity around the lactate threshold but below the lactate turnpoint or rest
Wednesday	Early morning 20-minute run or swim, or a 40-minute bike at an intensity around the lactate threshold but below the lactate turnpoint	Rest	Rest or hydropool massage
Thursday	Early morning 20-minute run or swim, or a 40-minute bike at an exercise intensity around the lactate threshold but below the lactate turnpoint	Cross-country hilly run for 60 to 75 minutes or 2-hour hilly bike at an intensity around the lactate threshold but below the lactate turnpoint	Climbing wall or strength and conditioning maintenance session in gym
Friday	Early morning 20-minute run or swim, or a 40-minute bike at an intensity around the lactate threshold but below the lactate turnpoint	Complementary training: skiing, hilly walk, open-water swim, or downhill mountain bike	30-minute swim at an intensity around the lactate threshold but below the lactate turnpoint or hydropool massage or yoga
Saturday	Rest	Running session: 1.5-mile warm-up at an exercise intensity below the lactate turnpoint; .5 mile at a pace averaging the lactate turnpoint; .5 mile at a pace equivalent to maximal oxygen uptake; .5 mile at a pace below the lactate turnpoint (or do same on the bike, doubling distances)	Rest

development. Therefore, don't expect instant results—improvements and adaptations can often take years. Very few Olympians have achieved gold-medal standard after the first year of training, so don't be disappointed if you don't achieve the levels you dream of in the early years. Be patient and remember the Guinness advert that says, 'Good things come to those who wait', which refers to the length of time it takes to produce the perfect pint of Guinness.

INSPIRATORY MUSCLE TRAINING

The majority of the specialist training and preparations for altitude and endurance are covered in other chapters of this book. However, there is one final training method that may benefit your endurance preparations, as well as assisting you in coping with the demands of altitude.

High-altitude mountaineering presents a significant physiological challenge. The low partial pressure of oxygen at altitude increases the demands placed upon the inspiratory muscles, making them more susceptible to fatigue. Sensible acclimatisation strategies during an expedition can aid the ability of the mountaineer to withstand these challenges. However, improvements in the strength and endurance of specific muscles that control respiration may also prove beneficial to performance at high-altitude. There is plenty of research evidence to suggest that the use of a pressure-threshold inspiratory muscle training (IMT) device called the *POWERbreathe* can improve the function of the thoracic inspiratory muscles with as little as 6 weeks of training (Romer, McConnell, & Jones, 2002). Strengthening these respiratory muscles before exposure to altitude may help reduce the perception of respiratory fatigue at altitude. However, there is limited evidence as to whether these adaptations are beneficial for exposure to hypobaric hypoxic conditions.

The use of IMT was something we introduced into the preparations of the 2006 Everest West Ridge team and subsequently the British Army's Shishapangma (Himalayas, South Central Tibet) 2007 team. Using some of these high-performance mountaineers, we compared individual perceptions of acclimatisation to high-altitude exposure after using IMT with previous acclimatisation experiences. Relative to previous high-altitude exposure and following 10 weeks of IMT, the mountaineers reported a reduction in the perception of respiratory demand and physical fatigue at altitude after IMT. This was previously reported by Romer, McConnell, and Jones (2002), who found a reduction in both respiratory and whole-body effort perceptions following 6 weeks of IMT, but only at sea level. Further research needs to be performed to quantitatively assess the effectiveness of IMT on helping to combat the challenges of altitude. However, integrating IMT into the preacclimatisation strategy of mountaineers may decrease their perceptions of effort during acclimatisation and subsequently improve their performance at altitude and therefore their enjoyment.

IMT requires you to inhale using a mouthpiece against a pressure load that is designed to be hard enough so that you are just able to overcome it. We recommend that you follow the standard IMT programme and instructions that come with the device. This should only take 10 minutes per day, whereby you aim to complete 30 inhalations twice a day (once in the morning and once in the evening; keep it by your toothbrush to remind yourself!) over a minimum of 10 weeks before your expedition. Your inhalation should be fast and forceful and your exhalation should be long and slow. Whilst you breathe out, you should slowly empty the lungs. Good breathing technique using the diaphragm is encouraged. It may take a little time to establish the resistance on the device that allows you to complete 30 inhalations; it may even take time to build up to this on the easiest tension setting. As with any training regime, progression is crucial, so once you are able to complete 30 inhalations with ease, increase the training load by increasing the tension on the IMT device. This may mean you can only achieve 26 inhalations during the next session, but within a few days you will be up to 30 again. Make sure you are standing in an upright and relaxed position when performing IMT.

Specificity is also an important training principle, and we recommend that you make the training specific to mountaineering after at least 5 weeks of IMT. This can be achieved by performing the IMT with a loaded rucksack on your back (the maximum weight you expect to carry regularly on your expedition) and a slight lean forward (the position you will be in when trekking).

IMT should be challenging, not painful, so if you feel any discomfort you should seek professional advice as soon as possible. Furthermore, you should discontinue IMT if you are suffering from a cold or other respiratory tract infection, and only resume once the symptoms have disappeared.

KEY IDEAS

▸ Mountaineering and climbing expeditions require endurance fitness appropriate to comfortably meet the challenge.

▸ The goal, the individual, and the training programme need to be considered together so you can select an expedition that you are capable of undertaking based on the necessary level of endurance fitness that you can achieve through training.

▸ Use SMART and FITT principles in planning and implementing your endurance training programme.

▸ Always build in adequate recovery, and increase your recovery if necessary due to cumulative fatigue or decrease in performance.

The authors would like to express their gratitude to Dr. Nick Monastiriotis (ASCC, UKA) for his valuable comments and suggestions.

8

Strength and Power Training

Theocharis Ispoglou, Christopher Low, and Carlton Cooke

When I dare to be powerful, to use my strength in the service of my vision, then it becomes less and less important whether I am afraid.

Audre Lorde

The purpose of this chapter is to provide anyone who has an interest in mountaineering and climbing with an understanding of the importance of strength and power in maximising performance either at a recreational or high-performance level. This chapter provides a useful guide that includes all the information required for designing resistance training programmes, as well as a range of exercise ideas.

IMPORTANCE OF STRENGTH AND POWER FOR MOUNTAINEERING AND CLIMBING

Strength and power are two vital factors for successful performance in activities such as mountaineering, climbing, and cross-country skiing. However, supporting evidence for the importance of strength and power in these activities is mainly anecdotal. To our knowledge, there are few, if any, well-designed training studies that have looked at the effects of training protocols on mountaineering and climbing. An overview of key findings in the following para-

graph provides support for the importance of strength (upper and lower body) in rock climbing, mountaineering, ski mountaineering, and cross-country skiing. (For definitions of terms, see the glossary on page 265).

Good muscular endurance and strength of the arms and shoulders are beneficial for climbing. Research has shown that success in climbing performance is best explained by trainable variables such as shoulder strength and endurance, forearm strength and endurance, and maximum grip strength, rather than anthropometric characteristics such as height and weight (Giles, Rhodes, & Taunton, 2006; Mermier, Janot, Parker, & Swan, 2000). Low body-fat percentage, low body mass, and a positive ape index traditionally have been perceived as beneficial in rock-climbing performance (Watts, Martin, & Durtschi, 1993). However, the majority of research suggests that low body mass, low body-fat percentage, and a positive ape index are not necessarily prerequisites for rock-climbing performance (Giles, Rhodes, & Taunton, 2006; Watts, 2004; Sheel, 2004). Mermier and colleagues (2000) in particular found that training variables such as knee extension and flexion, shoulder extension, and grip strength and endurance explain approximately 59 percent of the total variance in climbing, whereas anthropometric characteristics and flexibility explain 0.3 percent and 1.8 percent of the total variance.

In cross-country skiing, upper-body strength and quadriceps strength have been found to be good determinants of race performance, whereas strength of knee flexors has not (Ng et al., 1988). Upper-body strength in particular has been shown to improve performance in cross-country skiers mainly by improving work economy (Hoff, Gran, & Helgerud, 2002; Hoff, Helgerud & Wisloff, 1999). Ski mountaineering performance during uphill skiing seems to be highly correlated with the strength of knee flexors (Voutselas, Soulas, & Kritikos, 2005). The different findings between the studies by Ng et al. and Voutselas et al. are more likely attributable to the inclination of the ground. It seems that improved ski mountaineering uphill is directly linked with the strength of knee flexors. The latter finding emphasizes the importance of strengthening the knee flexors in order to maximize performance for this activity.

Another important finding is that absolute strength of elite climbers and the general population does not differ, but relative strength is better in climbers than nonclimbers (Giles, Rhodes, & Taunton, 2006). Thus, it has been suggested that low body mass might improve rock-climbing performance. Similarly, during ski mountaineering, low body mass index (BMI) is highly correlated with performance (Voutselas, Soulas, & Kritikos, 2005). Maintaining a low body mass in order to improve relative strength and performance might not necessarily be the best option for mountaineers and climbers. Also, the fact that mountaineers who attempt to climb mountains such as Everest tend to lose up to 7 percent of their body weight during an expedition suggests that weight loss before an expedition might not be desirable (Wiseman, Freer, & Hung, 2006). A better alternative to increase relative strength and thus performance might be an increase in maximum strength rather than a decrease in body mass. Gains in maximum strength would in turn increase relative strength, provided the gains in muscle hypertrophy are minimal or of smaller magnitude compared with strength gains.

Anecdotal evidence and climbing literature suggest that climbers in particular believe that a decrease in body mass and a specific training regime that imitates climbing activities are the best ways to improve performance in rock climbing. Even though the importance of technique-specific training and low body mass should not be underestimated, the traditional belief that specific training and a decrease in body mass are the best ways to improve performance can be challenged. Regardless of the fact that rock climbing is a highly technical event, if athletes are not strong enough, they will not be able to hold a particular position for the same length of time as athletes who have equally good technique but are stronger.

Technique is just one part of the equation for improved performance. We would also argue that excessive use of weighted jackets or extra weights whilst climbing not only compromises technique but also is time consuming. Instead, as explored in following sections, an appropriate strength and conditioning programme will create greater physiological adaptations more conducive to strength gains than use of extra weights whilst climbing. Even though they emphasise the importance of climbing, elite climbers also incorporate resistance training in their sessions, as the following quotes from rock climber Ben Moon (www.climbandmore.com/climbing,431,0,1,training.html) show:

> In an ideal world I'd like to do weights twice a week.

> I think that young people worry too much about training and don't climb enough. . . . In the early days I'd climb, climb, climb.

Such training does not seem to be the case with the majority of climbers, who seem to be narrowly focussed on technique and using extra weights whilst climbing. Imagine a coach who coaches athletes in pole vault and asks them to wear weighted jackets in order to improve strength, power, and potentially jumping performance. Sole use of such a method would be questioned by high-performance coaches, and they would not adopt it for important reasons: There are better ways to improve relative strength and power than body weight and addition of weight during an activity and the risk of injury and accident would greatly increase, particularly for athletes who are weaker and inexperienced.

We propose that alongside improvement in climbing technique, a strength and conditioning programme is important to improve rock-climbing performance at all levels. We do not seek to undermine the importance of climbing technique that should be taught from the initial stages of training, but we believe that the gains associated with a structured strength and conditioning programme are too often overlooked. Even for the experienced climber, a strength and conditioning programme would be beneficial. Climbers who have previously used more specific training activities, such as campus boards and fingerboards, but have found performance plateauing can use weight training to shock the system and help break that performance ceiling. A cycle of strength training can also provide the key to a climber who, for example, may simply lack the physical strength to perform the crux move on a route but has sufficient endurance to get to the crux every time.

The relationship between strength and muscular endurance is demonstrated with an example comparing the strength and muscular endurance of twins. Identical twins both have a mass of 80 kilograms (176 lb). However, one of the twins (A) can lift 160 kilograms (353 lb) during 1-repetition maximum (1RM) strength testing of the bench press whereas the other twin (B) can lift 70 kilograms (154 lb). Which one can do the most press-ups? See table 8.1 for the mathematical solution using the estimated number of repetitions based on 1RM strength. From an energy expenditure perspective, when twin B is doing the press-ups at 100 percent effort, twin A is doing the press-ups at 50 percent maximal effort.

The stronger twin would be able to lift his body weight 44 times more than the weaker twin. The estimated number of repetitions was worked out using prediction tables (Baechle, Earle, & Wathen, 2000). This relationship is equally important for several strength exercises in the gym (see sample programmes later in the chapter), which can increase the capacity to perform more repetitions in climbing-specific movements. Increase in maximal strength (or increase in capacity to produce force) means that submaximal efforts become more efficient (i.e., less energy cost for the same amount of work). Becoming more efficient helps climbers and mountaineers not only by conserving energy, which is vital in extreme conditions, but also by decreasing the risk associated with mountaineering and climbing activities. Safety is of paramount importance in extreme conditions. People who use a higher percentage of their maximum strength at high altitude are not only likely to lose balance and coordination but are also more likely to be fatigued as a result of excess energy consumption. As well as increased safety at altitude, the greater efficiency in energy consumption would mean a greater reserve for the traditional climber pushing for the on-sight flash at a new grade or reducing the risk factor when the climbing is loose or bold. For the sport climber or boulderer, it would mean more attempts at the route in a single session. Regardless of the types of activities that take place during a mountain expedition (figure 8.1)

TABLE 8.1 Estimated Number of Repetitions Performed at Various 1RM Loads

Twin A	Twin B
160 × 1 = 160	70 × 1 = 70
150 × 2 = 300	67 × 2 = 134
140 × 5 =700	60 × 5 = 300
130 × 8 = 1,040	55 × 8 = 440
120 × 10 = 1,200	50 × 10 = 500
110 × 12 = 1,320	47 × 12 = 564
100 × 15 = 1,500	46 × 15 = 690
Sum: 6,220 / 80 kg = 78 times	Sum: 2,698 / 80 kg = 34 times

Adapted from Baechle, Earle, and Wathen 2000.

Figure 8.1 Mountain expedition.

or a rock-climbing expedition (figure 8.2), the evidence clearly suggests that strength gains can improve performance.

The strength and conditioning programme should not be viewed as a replacement for climbing but rather as supplementary. It is possible to do a weight training session after climbing, provided that the climbing was more finger orientated and not overhanging (Gresham, 2004). Maintaining a climbing programme during the strength programme is important for transferring the increased levels of strength and power into greater climbing performance. Unless you're an experienced climber, the best way of converting the pure strength gains into climbing gains is through bouldering (figure 8.3). By combining bouldering sessions with a weight training programme, technique and strength can develop together. Experienced climbers may wish to combine a strength and conditioning programme with system boards and system training, along with campus boards and fingerboards. However, care is necessary to avoid overloading the body during this phase of training. It is not in the scope of this chapter to discuss implementation of system training and

Figure 8.2 Rock-climbing expedition.

Figure 8.3 Bouldering on the gritstone.

Figure 8.4 Skinning in the mountains.

the detailed use of campus boards, but excellent online articles are available that give advice on these training activities (for example, see www.moonclimbing.com, www.davemacleod.com, and www.planetfear.com).

Mountaineers and ice climbers would benefit greatly by adopting a strength and conditioning programme as part of their preparation for the winter season or an expedition. In particular, the development of strength and power in the legs is useful for activities such as skinning (figure 8.4).

The strength of knee flexors and extensors, shoulder girdle, and grip are considered important for successful performance in mountaineering and climbing activities. The proposed resistance training programme presented in a subsequent section will therefore primarily focus on developing the strength of muscles involved in these movements.

RESISTANCE TRAINING PROTOCOLS

Strength can be increased using a variety of resistance training protocols (Carpinelli & Otto, 1998; Coleman, 1977; Pollock et al., 1993; Stadler, Stubbs, & Vucovich, 1997). Two to three training sessions per week for 4 to 16 weeks is usually adequate to increase strength (Carpinelli & Otto, 1998). The magnitude of strength gains usually ranges from 10 to 40 percent and depends on many factors, including the intensity and frequency of the training sessions, the training status of the participants, the mode of exercise (e.g., isokinetic or isoinertial dynamometry), and the duration of the training programme (Braith et al., 1989; Carpinelli & Otto, 1998; Pollock et al., 1993). The American College of Sports Medicine (ACSM) has suggested typical ranges in magnitude of strength gains from approximately 40 percent in those who are untrained, 20 percent in those who are moderately trained, 16 percent in those who are trained, 10 percent in those who are advanced, and 2 percent in those who are elite over durations ranging from 4 weeks to 2 years (Kraemer et al., 2002).

According to the position stand of the ACSM (Kraemer et al., 2002), the initial resistance for novice subjects should be in the range of 8RM to 12RM, and as they progress they can move to heavy loading in the range of 1RM to 6RM using at least 3-minute rests between sets at a moderate contraction velocity of 1 to 2 seconds for lifting the weight and 1 to 2 seconds for lowering it (Kraemer et al., 2002). In addition, a training frequency of 2 to 3 days per week is recommended for novice and intermediate training and 4 to 5 days for advanced training (split routines). The initial position stand recommended 8 to 12 repetitions for 8 to 10 exercises (ACSM, 1998), which was found to be effective in improving strength in previously untrained subjects (Coleman, 1977; Feigenbaum & Pollock, 1999). This was further developed and now includes progression models for people who want to progress in their training regime.

A variety of loading also seems to be most effective for long-term improvements in muscular strength (Fleck, 1999). The findings of a meta-analysis by Rhea, Alvar, Burkett, and Ball (2003) to determine the dose response for optimal strength development supports the position stand by ACSM (Kraemer et al., 2002). The findings of Rhea and colleagues showed that in order to elicit maximal gains in strength, untrained people should perform 4 sets per muscle group three times a week at a mean intensity of 60 percent of 1RM, whereas trained people should perform 4 sets per muscle group two times a week at a mean intensity of 80 percent. In a more recent meta-analysis, Peterson, Rhea, and Alvar (2004) showed that the mean intensity and training volume for athletes is even higher (85 percent of 1RM and 8 sets per muscle group) than for trained people and the training frequency is the same (twice a week), thus supporting the progression model outlined by the ACSM (Kraemer et al., 2002). Do not confuse

training frequency (twice a week) with number of training sessions per week, which might be up to six (split routines); training frequency refers to the number of training sessions for a particular muscle group.

Periodisation (planned variation in training programme variables such as volume, intensity, and choice of exercise) is recommended for optimal strength gains. The training phases are usually planned in blocks of 2 to 6 weeks, with a full training cycle lasting approximately 12 to 24 weeks.

Typical training frequencies range between two and four times per week depending on variables such as training intensity and volume, training phase, and choice of exercise. Training more frequently allows split routines such as upper and lower body or specific muscle-training routines. The optimal training frequency seems to be three times a week (4 sets per muscle group) at lower intensities of 1RM (approximately 60 percent) for untrained and intermediate people. For the more advanced, optimal training frequency seems to be 2 days per week and 4 to 8 sets per muscle group at 80 to 85 percent of 1RM. Training twice a week would allow more advanced people to further increase the training volume and intensity during a training session and also allow them to fully recover before the next training session.

Strength and power are only two of the main factors that can lead to improved performance, so every effort should be made for participants to fully recover before subsequent sessions. Ideally, a resistance training session should be followed by a rest day or low-intensity training day. A resistance training session might take place the same day as an endurance or speed workout (usually following the end of the speed or endurance workout), thus allowing more time for recovery.

During the initial training phases, usually the volume is high and the intensity low. In the first 2 to 4 weeks of training, emphasis should be on technique, improving any imbalances between muscle groups, strengthening tendons and ligaments, and improving muscular endurance; the number of repetitions per exercise should be high and the intensity low. The second phase should focus on improving strength by some degree of muscle hypertrophy; the number of repetitions should be medium and the volume high. A typical third phase would focus on improvement of maximum strength and power; the number of repetitions should be low and the intensity high.

A strength and power workout typically involves high intensities (80-100 percent of 1RM), few repetitions (1-6), and full recovery between sets (3-6 minutes). A hypertrophy workout involves medium intensities (less than 85 percent of 1RM), relatively high number of repetitions (8-12), and short recovery between sets (approximately 1 minute). A muscular endurance workout typically involves a high number of repetitions (above 12), low intensity (less than 70 percent of 1RM), and short recovery between sets (less than 30 seconds). From a mountaineering and climbing perspective, muscle hypertrophy might sound undesirable. However, some degree of hypertrophy will lead to gains in maximum strength. As a result, relative strength gains would be expected to be greater as well.

Measurement of 1RM strength and then use of prediction tables and prediction equations is one way to estimate submaximal training loads. The drawbacks accompanied by this method are that it puts people with less-than-perfect technique at risk of injury and may inaccurately estimate the training load; as the training loads increases, the deviation of the estimated load from the actual load increases.

The alternative we propose in this section is to use an estimated load initially and then work out the exact training load within a training session by making adjustments. For example, if the target is 3 sets of 10 repetitions with 1 minute of rest between the sets, the athlete needs to estimate a load based on 1RM or any other multiples of RM. If the athlete cannot perform 10 repetitions during the last set, the load needs to be adjusted so that in a following session the athlete will be able to perform the 3 sets.

When gym equipment is not available, several exercises can be performed using body weight, elastic bands, and dumbbells. Dumbbells and elastic bands can be carried easily and can be purchased from many commercial stores or online (e.g., www.bodycare.co.uk, www.skf-services.com) at a low cost. The training load and intensity can be increased to some extent by using elastic bands of greater resistance, increasing the number of repetitions, modifying the time of muscle activation (slow and fast muscular actions), and choosing a technically more difficult exercise.

This chapter does not allow for all the detail that is involved in designing a resistance training programme. Two recommended books on all aspects of resistance training are *Designing Resistance Training Programs* by Fleck and Kraemer (2004) and *Essentials of Strength Training and Conditioning* by Baechle and Earle (2000).

STRENGTH TRAINING EXERCISES

The following section provides illustrations and explanations of coaching points for key exercises that may be incorporated in a resistance training programme for mountaineers and climbers. Examples will also be given as to how the muscle groups used in the exercises relate to various climbing situations.

The proposed training exercises were chosen using the following criteria.

Specificity Leg, forearm, and shoulder strength are beneficial for performance in mountaineering and climbing activities. The majority of the exercises presented in the following pages activate muscle groups important for mountaineering and climbing.

Multimuscle, Multijoint, and Single-Joint Exercises Multimuscle, multijoint exercises are effective in creating an anabolic environment favourable to muscle hypertrophy and gains in strength. Single-joint exercises have their own place in a strength conditioning programme, especially during the initial stages of training. However, multimuscle, multijoint exercises not only cause a greater number of adaptations, they are also more time efficient. Primary use of single-joint exercises would require the inclusion of many exercises within a training programme in order to train all muscle groups. On the other hand, inclusion of multimuscle, multijoint exercises allows the exercising of many muscle groups at the same time, thus saving time.

KEY MULTIMUSCLE, MULTIJOINT EXERCISES

The following multimuscle, multijoint exercises may produce greater physiological adaptations than single-joint exercises and are therefore recommended for resistance training programmes. Two or three of these exercises should be part of each resistance training session. Inclusion of more than two exercises is likely to cause excess fatigue and potential injury. Training twice a week would allow the incorporation of almost all of the exercises. For example, the squat, deadlift, and push press can be performed in session 1 and the front squat, overhead squat, and sumo deadlift in session 2.

Normally, multimuscle, multijoint exercises are placed at the beginning of a resistance training programme and are followed by single-joint exercises. Some of the exercises described in following pages activate groups of muscles rather than single muscles and should also be performed early in a training programme. In addition, to allow for adequate recovery during the session, lower-body exercises may be followed by upper-body exercises (e.g., squat by bench press) and exercises that activate extensor muscles may be followed by exercises that activate flexor muscles (e.g., triceps extensions followed by biceps curls).

In any vertical or slab environments, the role of the legs is to support the body weight whilst the arms maintain balance (Quaine, Martin, & Blanchi, 1997). Leg strength is therefore important, but it is an area that is often ignored. Climbers often move into deep squats in either one or both legs, either to place protection or to rest and analyse the next route section (figure 8.5). When climbing moves become more dynamic, then lower-leg strength, along with musculature of the arms and back, becomes increasingly important. For full-blown dynos, such as the Buckstone Dyno at Stanage Edge, the leg extensors generate the required momentum for flight.

The deadlift exercise activates almost all muscle groups. The sumo deadlift activates the quadriceps and adductor muscles to a greater extent and the back muscles to a lesser extent than the deadlift. Deadlifts have the added advantage of isometrically strengthening the forearm muscles without the risk of injury to the fingers.

Inappropriate technique in the following exercises will not only minimise the potential benefits of training, it will also increase the risk of injury. An ideal situation would involve supervision by an experienced strength and conditioning coach. If that is not possible, use lighter weights until technique is perfected, and training with a partner should always be a priority. For increased safety, when lifting heavy weights it is vital to always take a deep breath, contract the abdominal muscles, and arch the lower back.

Figure 8.5 Climber in a deep squat, analysing the rock for the next move.

Squat

1. Stand with feet shoulder width apart and toes pointing slightly out.

2. Take a deep breath and press chest up and out, flexing hips first and then knees. Back should remain tight throughout the movement. Lower until thighs are parallel with the floor, keep knees aligned over feet, and keep looking straight ahead.

3. Extend hips and knees at the same time with chest up and lower back tight and slightly curved.

Front Squat

1. Stand with feet shoulder width apart and toes pointing slightly out, bar resting on shoulders with elbows up.

2. Flex hips first and then knees. Back should remain tight throughout the movement. Lower until thighs are parallel with the floor, keeping knees aligned over feet and looking straight ahead.

3. Extend hips and knees at the same time, with chest up and lower back tight and slightly curved.

Overhead Squat

1. Stand with bar overhead with arms straight and wide grip, feet shoulder width apart, and toes pointing slightly out.

2. Flex hips first and then knees, keeping chest up and out and knees aligned over feet. Lower until thighs are parallel with the floor, keeping bar overhead.

3. Extend hips and knees at the same time. Bar remains overhead, with chest up and lower back tight and slightly curved.

Push Press

1. Stand with feet shoulder width apart and toes pointing slightly out, bar resting on shoulders with elbows up.

2. Flex knees and keep the body in an upright position, knees aligned over feet.

3. Drop elbows slightly and extend knees explosively, knees remaining aligned over feet. Push bar above head.

Deadlift

1. Stand with feet hip width apart and toes pointing slightly out, bar over the balls of feet and close to shins, shoulder width grip, shoulders slightly over and in front of bar, and chest up and out. The angle of the torso to the floor should be approximately 45 degrees.

2. Maintaining torso angle constant to the floor, push with feet (do not use back and arms during the first pull). As bar moves towards knees, push knees backwards, and when it reaches knees,

straighten torso whilst at the same time straightening legs. Note that by using a reverse hand grip, you can lift much heavier weights.

Sumo Deadlift

The sumo deadlift does not put as much pressure on the lower back compared with the classic deadlift.

1. Stand with feet wider than shoulder width apart and toes pointing slightly out and aligned with knees, bar over balls of feet and close to shins, chest up and out, and thighs parallel with the floor (note grip in photos).

2. Extend knees and hips at the same time, bringing torso in an upright position and pulling shoulders back.

3. Lower bar to the floor whilst holding your breath, keeping the back slightly curved.

UPPER-BODY EXERCISES

Up to four exercises from the following two sets of exercises can be used within a training session. The reasons for separating exercises into two groups are to ensure a more complete and effective training programme. The two sets of exercises ensure that training of major muscle groups occurs at least twice per week, but selection from the two groups ensures that the same major and smaller muscles are activated in slightly different ways. Altering patterns of activation through variations in loading and angles of movement is more likely to result in better all round training adaptations for the varied and complex movement patterns involved in climbing and mountaineering. Variation through selection from the two groups also helps avoid boredom and a plateau in performance, which is more likely to occur if the same exercises are used all the time.

The bench press and incline press work muscles such as the front deltoids, helping to balance the back muscles predominantly used for climbing and mountaineering. Of these, the main climbing muscle is the latissimus dorsi (Gresham, 2004). The lats are important for pulling-down actions by the arm, as demonstrated by the right arm of the climber in figure 8.6.

The seated row and barbell row work the muscles of the upper back. This will not only help in the maintenance of good posture by preventing forward chin posture or belay neck (www.bodyresults.com/E2UpperStrengthRock.asp) but also in training the muscles used on steep faces and roofs (Gresham, 2004).

Figure 8.6   A climber using the lats to stabilise the arms whilst placing the left foot.

Exercises for the biceps (e.g., hammer curls, concentration curls) clearly benefit pulling down on holds, but they are also helpful for climbing that involves undercutting (figure 8.7). Exercises that strengthen the triceps (e.g., triceps extensions) are useful for top-outs, mantelshelfs, pressing moves (figure 8.8), and chimneying. Muscles used in chimneying, which involves pressing-type actions, can be strengthened using front and lateral arm raises. Performing the arm raises whilst leaning over will change the emphasis and work shoulder muscles more commonly used for the majority of climbing (Gresham, 2004).

Figure 8.7 A climber using the biceps during an undercut move with the right hand.

Figure 8.8 A climber using the triceps in a press move.

SET A

Bench Press

1. Lie on a bench with feet flat on either the floor or bench, eyes same level with bar, overhand grip slightly wider than shoulder width. Lift bar and stabilise above chest.
2. Breathe in and lower bar to middle or lower part of chest, keeping elbows and hands beneath the bar.
3. Extend arms, progressively exhaling towards the end of the effort.

Lat Pull-Down

1. Grip bar with wide overhand grip, keeping lower back slightly arched.
2. Take a deep breath and pull bar until hands are almost aligned with shoulders. Push chest out and pull elbows back.
3. Return bar slowly to initial position.

Hammer Curl

1. This exercise can be performed standing or sitting. Hold dumbbells and make sure palms face each other whilst arms are fully extended.
2. Take a deep breath and raise forearms either together or one at a time.
3. Lower until arms are fully straightened.

Reverse Wrist Curl

1. Sit on a bench or kneel and rest forearms on the bench. Hold bar with overhand grip and lower hands as far as they can go.
2. Raise bar as far as you can by extension at the wrist.
3. Lower to initial position.

Machine Triceps Extension

1. In a standing position, hold the handles, making sure palms are facing back. Keep upper arms firm to the body and push elbows back, trying to keep torso in an upright position.
2. Take a deep breath and fully extend forearms.
3. Return to initial position by slowly flexing elbows.

Front Arm Raise

1. Stand with feet shoulder width apart and knees slightly bent, push chest out, and hold dumbbells with an overhand grip, resting dumbbells on front of thighs with palms facing back.
2. Take a deep breath and raise dumbbells alternately to eye level, keeping arms straight.
3. Lower slowly to initial position.

Lateral Dumbbell Raise

1. Stand with feet shoulder width apart and knees slightly bent, push chest out, and hold dumbbells with overhand grip, arms hanging next to body and palms facing towards centre of the body.
2. Take a deep breath and raise arms out from sides of the body until horizontal. Elbows should be slightly bent and hands slightly more forward than elbows.
3. Lower slowly to initial position.

One-Arm Dumbbell Row

1. Hold dumbbell with one hand and place opposite hand and knee on the bench to support body, torso parallel with bench. Move hand slightly in front of head, palm facing in.
2. Take a deep breath, pull with arm, and lift elbow as high as possible by bending it. Push chest out and pull shoulder blades together, trying to maintain torso parallel with the bench.
3. Lower slowly to initial position.

SET B

Incline Bench Press

The bench is approximately 45 to 55 degrees.

1. Sit on a bench, feet flat on the floor, eyes same level with bar, using overhand grip slightly wider than shoulder width. Lift bar and stabilise above head and chest.
2. Breathe in and lower bar to middle and upper part of chest, keeping elbows and hands beneath the bar.
3. Extend arms by lifting bar above head and progressively exhaling towards end of effort.

Seated Row

1. Sitting with feet flat on foot pads, lean torso forward and fully extend arms, palms facing each other.
2. Bend elbows and pull them back using arms and back. Keep chest up and out; lower back should be arched.
3. Return slowly to initial position.

Concentration Curl

1. Sit on a bench with feet flat on floor and dumbbell in hand. Place elbow against inner thigh, palm facing diagonally forward. Fully extend arm.
2. Take a deep breath and raise forearm as high as possible, by flexing at the elbow.
3. Lower slowly until arm is fully straightened.

Wrist Curl

1. Sit on a bench or kneel and rest forearms on the bench. Hold bar with underhand grip and lower hands as far as you can.
2. Raise bar as far as you can, by flexion at the wrist.
3. Lower to initial position.

Dumbbell Triceps Extension

1. Hold dumbbell with one hand and place opposite hand and knee on the bench to support your body, torso parallel with bench. Raise elbow by keeping it bent, palm facing in.
2. Fully extend forearm.
3. Lower slowly to initial position.

Bent-Over Lateral Raise

1. Hold dumbbells with both hands, feet hip width apart, knees bent, torso leaning forward 60 degrees (aim to reach an almost horizontal position), arms fully extended in hanging position, and palms facing each other.
2. Move arms from hanging position to horizontal position out to the sides, elbows slightly bent.
3. Return slowly to initial position.

Upright Row

Use either a bar or dumbbells.

1. Stand with feet shoulder width apart and knees slightly bent, push chest out, and hold dumbbells or bar with overhand grip slightly wider than shoulder width.

2. Take a deep breath and raise elbows as high as possible, keeping the dumbbells or bar as close as possible to the body throughout the movement.

3. Lower slowly to initial position.

Bent Row

1. Hold bar with overhand grip. From a standing position and with feet hip width apart, lean forward (torso should be angled 45 degrees to floor) until bar is just below knees (knees bent). Push chest out and keep a lordotic curve in lower back, arms fully extended.

2. Take a deep breath and pull bar up to chest.

3. Breathe out slowly and lower bar slowly to initial position.

LOWER-BODY EXERCISES

Choose up to four exercises from the following two sets to use within a training session, as explained previously. Some practical benefits of increased lower-leg strength were highlighted in the section on multimuscle, multijoint exercises. Further examples include rockover moves, which require knee extensor power, and squat positions even in overhanging terrain.

Calf raises have a clear benefit to climbers pushing up on and applying forces to foot-holds, but leg curls can also be extremely useful for overhanging terrain, such as heel-hooking manoeuvres (figure 8.9). This photo demonstrates why climbers need good all-round strength and power training for the lower body, using a variety of exercises. Bouldering requires strength and power to be exerted with the points of contact in an infinite combination of positions. As shown in figure 8.9, this is why it is important to develop and maintain a high degree of flexibility, as well as appropriate lower-body strength and power.

Figure 8.9 A climber using the heel to progress up a boulder.

SET A

Leg Press

1. Place feet shoulder width apart with legs straight.
2. Bend knees until thighs are parallel with footplate, knees aligned with feet. (The higher the feet are placed on the footplate, the greater the activation of gluteal muscles and hamstrings.)
3. Straighten legs and return to initial position.

Lying Leg Curl

1. Lay facedown with ankles positioned under pad.
2. Bend legs at the same time by trying to bring heels as close as possible to gluteal muscles.
3. Uncurl legs and return to start position.

Dumbbell Lunge

1. From standing position, feet shoulder width apart, hold dumbbells with both hands and arms fully relaxed at sides.
2. Take a step forward whilst keeping torso straight. Bend at one knee until thigh is parallel with the floor.
3. Return to initial position and repeat with other leg.

One-Legged Standing Calf Raise Using Dumbbell

To make the exercise more advanced, use a footplate so the gastrocnemius muscle is slightly stretched before raising the heel.

1. Stand on one foot and keep the body in a vertical position. Hold dumbbell with one hand and maintain balance using other hand.
2. Raise heel and briefly balance on ball of foot.
3. Return to initial position.

Stiff-Legged Deadlift

1. From standing position, hold a bar with overhand grip, feet and hands shoulder width apart.
2. Lean forward, trying to maintain straight back and legs. Lower back should be slightly arched and knees aligned.
3. If you cannot maintain a straight back, return to initial position and then repeat.

SET B

Dumbbell Squat

1. From standing position, hold dumbbells with both hands and arms fully relaxed at sides, feet shoulder width apart.
2. Bend first at hips and then at knees to lower the body until thighs are parallel with floor. Keep chest up and out, lower back slightly arched, and knees aligned with feet.
3. Straighten legs and return to initial position.

Seated Leg Curl

1. Position thighs between pads, with legs extended and feet dorsiflexed.
2. Bend knees.
3. Return to initial position.

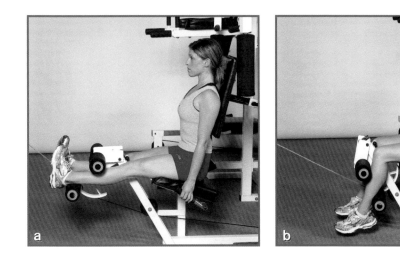

Barbell Lunge

1. Stand with feet shoulder width apart. Place bar across upper back.
2. Take a step forward and try to keep torso straight. Bend at one knee until thigh is parallel with floor.
3. Return to initial position and repeat with other leg.

One-Legged Seated Calf Raise Using Weight Plate

To make the exercise more advanced, use a footplate so the soleus muscle is slightly stretched before raising the heel.

1. Sit on a bench with a 90-degree angle at knee joint and place a weight plate on one or both thighs (directly above knees).
2. Raise heels.
3. Return to initial position.

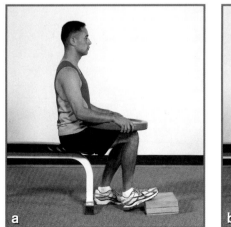
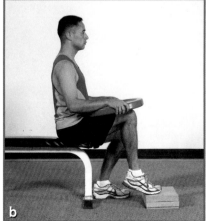

ABDOMINAL EXERCISES

Abdominal strength is extremely important in rock climbing, particularly when the terrain becomes overhanging. Good body tension is vital for the arms and legs to not only work effectively in a coordinated way but also to ensure that handholds and footholds can be used appropriately. When there is a full rack of gear to be carried, abdominal strength becomes even more important (figure 8.10). Exercises such as hanging leg raises can be made more climbing specific by using a fingerboard to simultaneously develop endurance in the forearms and fingers.

A select number of back and abdominal exercises follow. Strengthening of these muscle groups should take place from the initial stages of training. The exercises can either be incorporated within a resistance training programme or within another type of training programme. These exercises might include dumbbell side bends, hanging leg raises, sit-ups with feet on a bench or standard sit-ups and crunches.

Figure 8.10 A climber showing good abdominal strength to move through the roof whilst carrying a full rack of gear.

Side Bends

1. Stand with feet shoulder-width apart and hold a dumbbell with one hand. The other hand is at your waist (or as alternatives, it can be straight to your side or behind your head).

2. Bend the torso to the opposite side of the dumbbell.

3. Return slowly to the starting position and then bend the torso to the same side of the dumbbell before returning to the initial position. You should try to bend from the lower thoracic region of the spine rather than the lumbar region.

Hanging Leg Raises

1. Use a leg raise station or hang from a fixed bar (weaker individuals should use wrist straps for greater stability) with arms and legs fully extended.

2. Inhale and start lifting your legs by contracting your abdominal muscles and not by momentum (e.g. by swinging your legs) until your legs are parallel to the floor.

3. Exhale whilst returning slowly to the initial position. You should not relax the abdominal muscles at any point throughout the movement.

Sit-Ups With Feet on a Bench

1. Lie on the floor and place your feet and/or calves on a bench. The angle between your thighs and the calves should be approximately 90 degrees.
2. Place your hands behind your head and push your elbows back. Do not push your head with your hands. Take a deep breath and exhale whilst lifting your shoulders off the floor.
3. Exhale when returning to the starting position. Try to maintain the abdominal muscles contracted throughout the full range of motion.

BODY-WEIGHT AND OTHER EXERCISES

If training equipment is not available, body weight, elastic bands of varying strengths, and a few dumbbells might be used for resistance training. These exercises can easily translate to a wall environment and could be performed immediately after a climbing session, provided that the climbing session was primarily a finger-focussed type of climbing on terrain that was not mainly overhanging. The majority of exercises recommended in the previous sections can be easily performed using dumbbells or elastic bands. Following are some exercises that may be included.

These exercises can be useful for individuals who are preparing for mountaineering or other forms of expedition, but are spending time away from home and their normal training environments. For example, team members preparing for the EWR expedition, who were stationed abroad with the military on active service, used body-weight exercises. The flexibility of being able to substitute these training exercises with your strength and conditioning programme allows you to maintain a regular training programme even if you are not able to generate the same training effects you can get with access to free weights.

Push-Up

1. Lie on the floor facedown with hands at shoulder level. Keep feet together, fingers pointing forward and elbows out.
2. Fully extend arms by keeping upper and lower body aligned.
3. Return slowly to initial position.

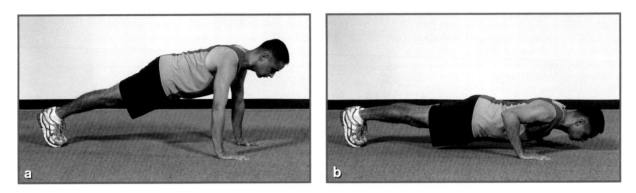

Chin-Up With Overhand Grip

1. Hang from fixed bar, arms fully extended, holding bar in overhand wide grip.
2. Fully flex arms by bringing chest to the same level as bar.
3. Return slowly to initial position.

Reverse Chin-Up

1. Hang from fixed bar, arms fully extended, holding bar in underhand narrow grip.
2. Fully flex arms by bringing chest to the same level as bar.
3. Return slowly to initial position.

Triceps Dip

1. Place hands on bench, making sure palms are securely on the bench and fingers facing forward. Keep upper arms firm to the body and fully extended.
2. Take a deep breath and start bending elbows slowly. Push elbows back by keeping torso in an upright position (you may lean slightly forward).
3. Return to initial position by fully extending arms.

Squat Against a Wall

1. Stand with back flat against a wall, feet shoulder width apart, and toes pointing straight ahead or slightly out. Knees should be bent and thighs parallel with the floor, knees aligned over feet.
2. Maintain position for 20 to 30 seconds.

Floor Hip Extension

1. Lean on elbows and kneel on one knee whilst bringing other knee close to chest.
2. Extend hip fully; ankle, hip, and shoulder joints should be completely aligned.
3. Lower leg slowly to initial position.

Leg Abduction

1. Lie on side, supporting head with hand. Legs are straight and parallel.
2. Raise leg, keeping knees straight and legs parallel.
3. Lower leg slowly to initial position.

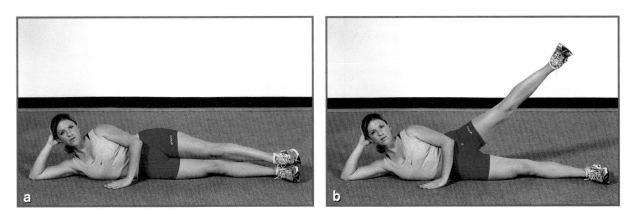

Biceps Curl

1. Standing with feet on elastic band, hold both handles and make sure palms face each other whilst arms are fully extended.
2. Raise and rotate forearms upwards, either together or one at a time. Keep upper arms fixed to body. At the end of the pull, palms should face up.
3. Lower until arms return to initial position.

Hammer Curl

1. Standing with feet on elastic band, hold both handles and make sure palms face each other whilst arms are fully extended.
2. Take a deep breath and raise forearms either together or one at a time.
3. Lower until arms are fully straightened.

Lateral Arm Raise

1. Standing with feet shoulder width apart on elastic band and knees slightly bent, push chest out and hold handles with overhand grip, arms hanging with palms facing the body.
2. Take a deep breath and raise arms until horizontal. Elbows should be slightly bent and hands slightly more forward than elbows.
3. Lower slowly to initial position.

Upright Row

1. Standing with feet shoulder width apart on elastic band and knees slightly bent, push chest out and hold handles with overhand grip slightly wider than shoulder width.

2. Take a deep breath and raise elbows as high as possible, keeping handles as close as possible to the body throughout the movement.

3. Lower slowly to initial position.

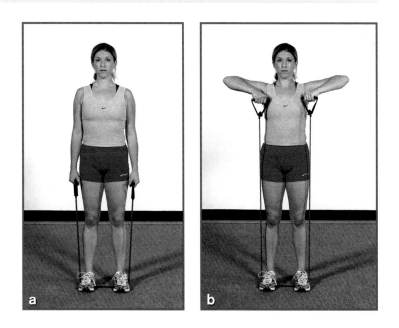

SAMPLE RESISTANCE TRAINING PROGRAMMES

Based on the information presented previously and key resistance training variables, the proposed training programmes that follow are guidelines for mountaineers and climbers. Table 8.2 provides an overview of factors to consider when designing a resistance training programme. It demonstrates the relationships between phases of training with different emphases, number of repetitions and sets, exercises, and rest periods. Phase 1 focuses on the development of muscular endurance, with a shift in Phase 2 to a focus on hypertrophy and strength, finishing with Phase 3 where the emphasis is on strength and power. Note the contrasting patterns of change across these phases, with number of repetitions per set

and number of exercises decreasing from phase 1 to 3 and number of sets and time for recovery increasing from phase 1 to 3. Figures 8.11 and 8.12 provide examples of resistance training programmes, applying the principles set out in table 8.2 for someone training two or four times per week. It is important that you are realistic about what you can manage in terms of your resistance training programme, as it must fit in with your other training commitments and work/life. It is important to use more time building up over a period of weeks with slower achievable progressions that maintain your enthusiasm and energy levels, rather than committing to a programme you cannot really manage effectively. If you start a programme that is not manageable you will become stale and your performance will plateau and training will not be enjoyable.

TABLE 8.2 Variables to Consider When Designing Resistance Training Programmes

	Emphasis	Repetitions	Sets	Rest between sets	Number of exercises	Exercises
Phase I (2-4 weeks)	Muscular endurance	Above 12	2-3	Less than 30 seconds	12-15	WB: 2-3 UB: 4 LB: 4 AB: 2-4
Phase II (4-6 weeks)	Hypertrophy and strength	8-12	3-5	Approximately 1 min	6-12	WB: 1-3 UB: 0-5 LB: 0-4 AB: 2-3
Phase III (4-6 weeks)	Strength and power	1-6	3-5	Full recovery (3-6 min)	4-8	WB: 1-2 UB: 0-3 LB: 0-3 AB: 0-2

WB = whole-body exercises; UB = upper-body exercises; LB = lower-body exercises; AB = abdominal exercises.

Note: The number of exercises per session will vary depending on the intensity and frequency of the training programme. During high-intensity workouts such as those during phase III, the total number of exercises should be smaller than the number of exercises in phases I and II.

FIGURE 8.11
Sample Resistance Training Programme

	Monday	Tuesday	Wednesday	Thursday	Friday	Saturday	Sunday
Training frequency	Two times a week (hypertrophy phase) for 4-6 weeks using 8 exercises which can be varied						
Whole-body exercises		Squat; Deadlift			Front squat; Sumo deadlift		
Upper-body exercises		Bench press; Reverse wrist curl			Incline bench press; Seated row		
Lower-body exercises		Leg press; Stiff-legged deadlift			Seated leg curl		
Abdominal exercises		Side bends in hanging position; Side leg raises in hanging position			Sit-ups with feet on a bench; Hanging leg raises		

FIGURE 8.12
Sample Resistance Training Programme

	Monday	Tuesday	Wednesday	Thursday	Friday	Saturday	Sunday
Training frequency	4 times a week (hypertrophy phase) for 4-6 weeks using selected exercises which can be varied						
Whole-body exercises	Squat; Deadlift	Push press		Front squat; Overhead squat	Sumo deadlift		
Upper-body exercises		Bench press; Lat pull-down; Reverse wrist curls; Machine triceps extension			Incline bench press; Seated row; Wrist curl; Upright row		
Lower-body exercises	Leg press; Lying leg curl; One-legged standing calf raise using dumbbell; Stiff-legged deadlift			Dumbbell squat; Seated leg curl; Barbell lunge; One-legged seated calf raise using weight plate			
Abdominal exercises		Side bends; Hanging leg raises; Sit-ups with feet on a bench			Sit-ups with feet on a bench; Hanging leg raises		

KEY IDEAS

▶ Gains in strength and power through an appropriately designed resistance training programme may be accompanied by performance gains in mountaineering and climbing.

▶ Muscle growth will not necessarily have a negative impact on mountaineering and climbing activities as long as it is accompanied by gains in relative strength and power.

▶ A medium number of repetitions (8-12) with short recovery is likely to enhance strength as a result of muscle hypertrophy, whereas a low number of repetitions (<6) with long recovery is more likely to increase strength with minimal hypertrophy.

▶ Multimuscle, multijoint exercises may cause greater physiological adaptations than single-joint exercises.

▶ Get the technique right before you start increasing the load.

▶ Try to train each muscle group at least twice a week.

▶ Resistance training may take place at the end of a climbing session or any other training session.

▶ The day following a resistance training session should be a recovery day or an easy training session (e.g., low-intensity runs, core stability exercises).

Nutrition for Training

Louise Sutton, Roderick King, and John O'Hara

Nutrition can be defined as the sum of the processes involved in the intake and utilisation of food, including ingestion, digestion, absorption, transport and metabolism of nutrients found in food and their assimilation into body tissues. This definition focusses on the biochemical and physiological functions of the food we eat but nutritional intake can also be affected by a range of psychological, sociological and ecomonic factors.

Jeukendrup and Gleeson (2004)

The nutritional requirements of hill walkers and mountaineers have received limited attention from researchers despite physiological and psychological consequences of sustained walking over prolonged amounts of time, sometimes in adverse weather conditions. This chapter introduces the links amongst nutrition, health, and performance. It addresses the fundamentals of a healthy diet and the influence of nutrition on exercise performance, along with a solid foundation of knowledge on which to develop good eating practices to support training for both the occasional day out in the hills and extended expeditions. It considers factors that affect food intake and choice, as well as methods of collecting and analysing dietary information to assess nutritional needs for training. Research has shown that nutritional strategies based on carbohydrate and fluid intakes can help endurance athletes improve their performance. Much of this research has concentrated on endurance runners and cyclists, but as a recreational hill walker or an extreme mountaineer you can apply similar principles to your own endurance activities. The chapter ends with a brief look at the value of nutritional supplements in the training diet.

The prolonged duration of hill walking and mountaineering can place exceptional demands on participants, making training for such endeavours desirable. Whether planning a day's walk in the Dales or an expedition to Everest, good nutrition is essential to maintain your training schedule. Your training schedule also provides the opportunity to practise and evaluate nutritional strategies. Nourishing food and fluids will provide energy and nutrients to support effective training and recovery.

Whatever your chosen challenge, the training diet bears many similarities to nutritional guidelines for long-term health. In addition to general health and well-being, particularly the ability to defend against and recover from disease, the right balance of nutrition is essential to both physical and mental growth, as well as performance and productivity in daily living. In regards to hill walking and mountaineering, the longer your sorjourn into the hills or mountains, the more important training and nutritional planning and preparation become.

NUTRITION FOR HEALTH AND PERFORMANCE

Whatever your hill walking or mountaineering goals, diet can play an enormous part in improving performance. Foods contain six major nutrients: carbohydrate, protein, fat, vitamins, minerals, and water. Fat and carbohydrate are the two main energy sources for exercising muscles. Energy is supplied by carbohydrate, protein, and fat in differing amounts. Recommendations on the correct mix of macronutrients for those undertaking regular physical training are 55 to 60 percent carbohydrate, 20 to 30 percent fat, and 15 to 20 percent protein.

Carbohydrate   The main function of carbohydrate in the diet is to supply energy. Eating a diet adequate in carbohydrate is essential for restoring muscle and liver glycogen on a daily basis. Failure to restore will result in diminished capacity for training and performance. These foods can be filling, though. Starchy foods, especially those that are unrefined, provide a steady supply of energy. To achieve optimal carbohydrate stores during training, however, you may need to top up with sugary foods that are more rapidly absorbed, such as sweets, dried fruit, fruit juice, and sugary drinks, particularly during intense periods of training when you may be spending long days out in the hills or mountains. See figure 9.1 for examples of simple (sugar) and complex (starch) carbohydrate.

The best approach is to base all your meals and snacks on starchy complex carbohydrate foods and eat at regular intervals. Some athletes will be able to enjoy a substantial meal or snack 2 to 4 hours before training, but others might suffer severe gastrointestinal distress. You will need to experiment to find out what works best for you at different exercise intensities, remembering that on the hill you are likely to eat and be on the move again quickly. It is also important that you consume sufficient levels of carbohydrate every day. Table 9.1 shows how to estimate your daily carbohydrate needs.

A conscious effort to increase carbohydrate intake in the final 1 to 3 days before your hill walk or mountaineering challenge is a useful strategy. To achieve this, eat plenty of complex carbohydrate, such as whole-grain breads and cereals, pasta, rice, and potatoes.

FIGURE 9.1
High-Carbohydrate Foods

Simple Carbohydrate (Sugars)

Sugar	Jam
Honey	Marmalade
Sugary carbonated beverages	Fruit squashes
Boiled and jelly sweets	Fudge
Dried fruit	Fruit bars
Fruit juice	Sport drinks, gels, and bars

Complex Carbohydrates (Starches)

Bread	Bagels
Crisp bread	Crackers
Rice	Pasta and noodles
Polenta	Potatoes
Breakfast cereals	Pulses
Root vegetables	

TABLE 9.1 Estimated Carbohydrate Requirements Based on Daily Activity Levels

Level of daily activity	Grams of carbohydrate per kilogram of body weight
1 hour	4-5 g
1 hour	5-6 g
1-2 hours	6-7 g
2-3 hours	7-8 g
4 hours plus	8-10 g

Protein Protein is essential for growth and repair of body tissues, and it can be used as an energy source in situations of negative energy balance. In most cases, if you are eating a normal varied and balanced diet and meeting your energy requirements, you should automatically be eating enough protein. Normal protein requirements are in the range of 0.75 to 1.0 gram per kilogram of body weight per day. Those undertaking regular programmes of intense physical training do require greater intakes of protein per kilogram of body weight in order to promote tissue growth and repair. The Lausanne consensus conference (2003) on sports nutrition recommended an intake of 1.2 to 1.7 grams per kilogram of body weight per day.

Training should not result in a loss of lean body mass through inadequate energy balance. Susceptibility to this is more likely in the immediate lead-up to an extended expedition when greater demands may be placed on training and expedition planning for departure.

Fat Fat is a concentrated source of energy that supplies the predominant fuel for low-intensity activity. Those engaging in regular intense training programmes should aim for 20 to 25 percent contribution to total intake to achieve recommended carbohydrate intakes, but in absolute terms (grams) may consume similar or slightly greater quantities, depending on training volume compared to fat intakes recommended for the sedentary population.

Vitamins and Minerals Micronutrients occur naturally in a wide variety of foods. Any increase in requirements as a result of training should naturally be met by increased food consumption. Vitamin and mineral supplements will not improve performance, especially in those already well nourished and consuming a varied diet and sufficient calories. For recommendations on vitamin and mineral intake, see Department of Health COMA 41 (1991).

Fluid To maintain fluid balance, you need to drink approximately 30 to 35 millilitres per kilogram of body weight per day, although greater volumes will be needed to cover the demands of training. Inadequate fluid intakes can lead to dehydration. Hill walkers and mountaineers are particularly prone to dehydration because of a combination of factors such as high fluid requirements, increased diuresis, poor availability of fluids, increased insulation of clothing, and intense heat generated by reflected ultraviolet sun rays on snow. The section in chapter 3 on training for dehydration highlights the implications of inadequate hydration and the difficulties in measuring hydration status; it also challenges conventional thinking on hydration strategies but concludes that drinking sufficient quantities to avoid the development of thirst may be the key. The thirst mechanism is slow to respond to the body's need for fluids (i.e., if you are thirsty, it is too late!). Therefore, to ensure adequate hydration, drink before you feel thirsty. You should normally begin training sessions fully hydrated with 400 to 600 millilitres 2 to 4 hours before exercise.

If training sessions are short (less than 30 minutes), fluid ingested during the session will not benefit performance. However, to optimise hydration during longer training sessions, you should consume 200 to 250 millilitres of fluid every 15 to 20 minutes during exercise, although this may not always be practical.

After training it can be useful to check your body weight. As a guide, a 1-kilogram weight loss during a training session has been shown to equate to a 1-litre fluid loss. Practical recommendations suggest replacing this loss 1.5 times (i.e., 1.5 L). You can easily monitor the status of your hydration by checking your urine colour. A pale colour indicates you are well hydrated; dark yellow indicates severe dehydration. Accustom your body to increased fluid intakes during training. Start rehydration immediately after training, and always rehydrate before drinking alcohol.

Sports drinks are an option for carbohydrate and water ingestion during and after activity. There are three types of sports drinks (hypertonic, isotonic, and hypotonic); their absorption by the body is dependent on their concentration of certain fluids. Added carbohydrate in a sports drink boosts energy supplies, and added sodium aids water uptake and stimulates carbohydrate absorption.

Hypertonic drinks contain the most carbohydrate (greater than 10 g per 100 ml) in the form of sugar or glucose polymers and are useful for the repletion of glycogen stores. These drinks are less quickly absorbed and are not the best choice if fluid replacement is the priority. They may be useful if training at a high intensity for long periods and are best used after exercise.

Isotonic drinks are designed to be in balance with the body's own fluids to provide fast fluid absorption and a boost to carbohydrate supplies. They contain approximately 5 to 7 grams of carbohydrate per 100 milliliters and are suitable for use before, during, and after training.

Hypotonic drinks are less concentrated than your body fluids (2 to 3 grams carbohydrate per 100 ml) and are designed to be absorbed quickly. Hypotonic drinks emphasize fluid replacement, not energy. These drinks are suitable for use before, during, and after training.

Your choice of drink will depend on whether you need to replace fluid quickly or whether your priority is to replace fuel, or both. One of the most important considerations in choice of drink is taste. If you choose a palatable drink, you are much more likely to drink it! You should try out products during training and not assume that what tastes fine when consumed at rest in the home will taste good on the hill during an expedition.

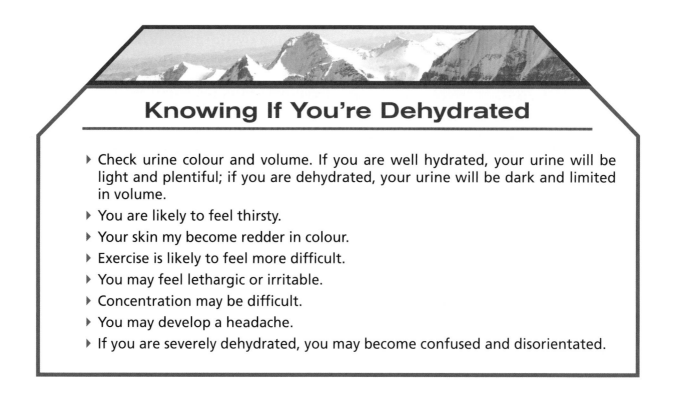

Knowing If You're Dehydrated

▸ Check urine colour and volume. If you are well hydrated, your urine will be light and plentiful; if you are dehydrated, your urine will be dark and limited in volume.
▸ You are likely to feel thirsty.
▸ Your skin my become redder in colour.
▸ Exercise is likely to feel more difficult.
▸ You may feel lethargic or irritable.
▸ Concentration may be difficult.
▸ You may develop a headache.
▸ If you are severely dehydrated, you may become confused and disorientated.

ESTIMATING INDIVIDUAL ENERGY REQUIREMENTS

Regarding diet, you need to take into account the extent of your hill walking or mountaineering challenge. In simple terms, longer duration and higher altitude will place greater demands on nutritional planning and preparation. The amount of energy required in your diet is dependent on several factors: body mass, age, sex, distance to be covered on the hill or mountains, total altitude gained, and backpack weight carried during your walk or expedition. (Note that mass and weight are synonymous for the purpose of this chapter and hence are used interchangeably.) Exercise intensity in hill walking tends to be light to moderate but prolonged and often over varied terrain, imposing high overall demands on energy; ascents to high altitude incur additional energy requirements.

Energy requirement can be estimated by multiplying basal metabolic rate (BMR, the energy required to maintain basic functions) by a physical activity level (PAL, an estimate in physical activity based on occupational and leisure-time activity).

To estimate energy requirements, you first need to calculate basal metabolic rate in kilocalories per day by using the equation in table 9.2 where W is weight in kilograms.

Total energy requirement (TER) is estimated by applying PALs (physical activity levels) to BMR (TER = BMR × PAL). PALs require you to make an assumption about the energy demands of both occupational and non-occupational activity levels (see table 9.3). Athletes in normal training have been shown to have PALs of 2.0 to 2.5. Athletes in rigorous training have levels of 2.5 to 4.0. Values greater than 4.0 have been reported during periods of extreme physical endurance.

TABLE 9.2   Calculating Basal Metabolic Rate in Kilocalories per Day

Males	18-29 years	$BMR = 15.1 \times W + 692$
	30-59 years	$BMR = 11.5 \times W + 873$
	60-74 years	$BMR = 11.9 \times W + 700$
Females	18-29 years	$BMR = 14.8 \times W + 487$
	30-59 years	$BMR = 8.3 \times W + 846$
	60-74 years	$BMR = 9.2 \times W + 687$

Reprinted, by permission, from Committee on Medical Aspects of Food and Nutrition Policy (COMA) 1991. Data for 60-74 year olds from Thomas and Bishop 2007.

TABLE 9.3   PALs for Adults at Three Levels of Occupational and Non-Occupational Activity

NON-OCCUPATIONAL ACTIVITY	OCCUPATIONAL ACTIVITY					
	Light		Moderate		Heavy	
	M	F	M	F	M	F
Non-Active	1.4	1.4	1.6	1.5	1.2	1.5
Moderately Active	1.5	1.5	1.7	1.6	1.8	1.6
Very Active	1.6	1.6	1.8	1.7	1.9	1.7

M = male, F = female.

Reprinted, by permission, from Committee on Medical Aspects of Food and Nutrition Policy (COMA) 1991.

As an example of this equation, the BMR for a 26-year-old male with a body weight of 70 kilograms is 1749 kilocalories (7321 kJ).

$$BMR = 15.1 \times W + 692$$
$$= (15.1 \times 70) + 692$$
$$= 1057 + 692$$
$$= 1749 \text{ kcals}$$

Estimated total energy requirements, assuming he has a sedentary office job (light) and a heavy training programme (very active), are 2798 kilocalories (11712 kJ).

$$TER = 1749 \times 1.6$$
$$= 2,798 \text{ kcals}$$

Estimated total energy requirements, assuming he has a manual job and a heavy training programme (very active), are 3323 kilocalories (13910 kJ).

$$TER = 1749 \times 1.9$$
$$= 3,323 \text{ kcals}$$

TRAINING DIET RECOMMENDATIONS

When developing sound eating habits and nutritional strategies to support training for hill walking, climbing, and mountaineering, the following need consideration:

- The types of food eaten to support training
- The timing of meals and snacks around training
- Ensuring a balanced diet of all nutrients
- Maintaining sufficient fluid intake and hydration status
- Promoting long-term health and reducing the risk of chronic disease
- Minimising the risk of injury and illness

Your nutritional requirements will vary according to the following:

- Type of training
- Intensity of training
- Duration of training
- Frequency of training
- Age and training status
- Fitness level

As discussed, whether training for the occasional day out in the hills, a multiday climbing trip, or an expedition of several weeks, good nutrition will make its greatest contribution by allowing you to train consistently and effectively to meet the demands of your training programme. Your diet must meet the demands that training places on your body, particularly when you are training for a multiday trip or longer expedition. To achieve this, adhere to the following recommendations:

- Start refuelling as soon as possible after training, when muscle capacity to refuel is greatest.
- Organise yourself by carrying snacks and fluid in your kit bag or backpack.
- Avoid restricting eating to traditional mealtimes. Try smaller, more frequent meals and snacks to fit eating around training.
- Rest days are important. Use the extra time to eat sensibly and make up for hurried mealtimes, particularly during intense training sessions.
- Use the eatwell plate to plan meals and snacks (Food Standards Agency 2007):
  - Base meals and snacks on starchy carbohydrate foods.
  - Try to have five or more servings of fruits and vegetables each day.
  - Remember to include dairy foods.
  - Include meat or fish in your diet, and try alternatives such as peas, beans, lentils, and eggs.
  - Limit foods high in fat.
  - Remember, sugary foods can aid refuelling.
- Aim to consume a carbohydrate snack as soon as possible after training, when glycogen resynthesis in most efficient. Choose a snack with high or moderate glycaemic index because it will be absorbed more quickly (see figure 9.2).

FIGURE 9.2
Glycaemic Index of Various Foods

Glycaemic index expresses the effects of carbohydrate foods on the rate and amount of increase in blood glucose levels after ingestion.

High Glycaemic	Moderate Glycaemic	Low Glycaemic
Sugar	Pasta	Lentils
Honey	Instant noodles	Soya beans
Bread	Porridge oats	Milk
White rice	Grapes	Plain yougurt
Baked potato	Orange	Ice cream
Weetabix	Potato crisps	Grapefruit
Corn flakes	Milk chocolate	Apple
Lucozade	Orange juice	Peanuts
Mars bar	Rye bread	Dried apricots
Ryvita	Baked beans	
Shortbread biscuits	Banana	

▸ Maintain an adequate fluid status.

▸ If consuming alcohol after training, rehydrate fully beforehand.

▸ Take care in planning, choosing, and cooking food; these are good habits to establish in preparation for an extended expedition.

▸ Enjoy your food and don't become too obsessed with your training diet!

ASSESSMENT OF NUTRITIONAL NEEDS AND ENERGY BALANCE FOR TRAINING

To assess your nutritional intake, keep a record of all food and drink you consume for at least 3 days, including 1 weekend day. For a more detailed evaluation, record your intake for a full week (see figure 9.3). Record everything you eat and drink. Be as accurate as possible and do not modify your dietary intake at this stage; otherwise you will not be evaluating your typical diet. Carry the record with you at all times to record food and drink as they are consumed so you don't foget any items. Record as much information as possible, including the following:

▸ The type of food and drink consumed and how much, either as an estimation of portion size using standard household measures, such as slices of bread, cups of vegetables, and so on, or as an actual weight, either weighed or recorded from the packaging. (Note: Weighing all foods is likely to result in unnessary burden and choices of foods that are easy to weigh, thus providing an unrepresentative record of usual intake.)

▸ The time the food and drink was consumed and where you were when you consumed it. These points are often useful to consider when assessing external factors that affect your dietary intake.

▸ Any activity or training you undertake, including duration and intensity (i.e., light, moderate, or hard).

Once complete, compare your record with the guidelines of the eatwell plate (Food Standards Agency 2007). For example, do you base your

FIGURE 9.3
Food Record

	Monday	Tuesday	Wednesday	Thursday	Friday	Saturday	Sunday
Breakfast							
Midmorning snacks							
Lunch							
Midafternoon snacks							
Evening							
Supper snacks							

meals around starchy foods, do you include five or more servings of fruits and vegetables each day, do you include at least three servings of dairy, and so on? In addition to the types and amounts of food you eat, this record may give you an idea about how your daily life and training patterns dictate what, when, where, and why you eat. This dietary analysis will provide you with a useful index of the strengths and limitations of your dietary intake and allow you to address any deficiencies in your taining diet. For a more detailed analysis of your intake, consult a registered dietitian or sports nutritionist.

USE OF DIETARY SUPPLEMENTS

The attraction of supplementation is no less relevant to hill walkers or mountaineers than it is to the public at large. Supplements usually come in the form of specific, combined, and variable concentrations of substances, taken from either natural or manufactured sources, that have been identified as potentially beneficial to the diet. It should not be necessary to take supplements in the form of specific natural, organic, specialist, or manufactured tablets, capsules, or foods if adherence to the recommended healthy, balanced, and varied diet is observed. This statement is based upon the Department of Health COMA 41 (1991) and Food Standards Agency (2007) guidelines that cover requirements for the broadest population possible.

A potential limitation of this approach is immediately apparent in that there is great diversity of intake within the average population due to food preferences and the fact that the requirements of those who engage in nonnormal lifestyles differ greatly from the average requirement. Those who engage in training may have a special set of circumstances that nessecitates greater attention to meeting nutritional requirements. This is especially true when the nature of the activity, in this instance training for either casual or serious hill walking, climbing, and mountaineering, precludes the use of a decent kitchen and store. The fact that intake, frequency, and amount of a healthy, well-balanced, and varied diet may be compromised by participation in such activities means that considerable effort should be made to balance food supplies by adding specific nutrient needs that have the best evidence base.

Imbalance may occur due to nutrient exclusion or restriction. Though there is now evidence that supplementation may be beneficial in such circumstances, this is largely when demonstrated deficiencies occur and is by no means universal for all macro- and micronutrients. In this situation, additional intake of convenient food from an appropriate source or from specific supplementation may be invaluable. In such instances, it would be necessary to restrict supplementation to an amount appropriate to fulfil the needs identified from imbalance due to actual or projected dietary intake or mismatch of needs during training.

Nutritional supplements used to compensate for an inadequate diet or to meet the demands of training might take the form of multivitamin and mineral supplements or sport drinks, gels, bars, powders, or meal replacements. Sport drinks are a good way to replace fluid and provide energy before, during, and after training. Energy bars may provide a convenient source of energy during prolonged training. Vegetarians, people with food intolerances, and erratic eaters may benefit from vitamin and mineral supplementation.

Nutritional supplements that may be useful, including vitamins, minerals, carbohydrate, and protein, and those contained in herbs or similar nutritional substances are different from drugs (substances not normally contemporary with physiological or biochemical processes and metabolism). It is especially important to delineate the types of evidence-based claims because these range from natural structure–function relationships (e.g., glucose structure and metabolism within the body) to more extensive claims that should be substantiated by safety studies (e.g., hazard and toxicity) and where possible, strict clinical trials based on the gold standard of randomised, double-blind, placebo-controlled crossover in human participants.

Consumers should ask questions about the structure, function, dose, mechanism, efficacy, and research trials of supplements. This is especially important to those who are training for serious mountaineering because the cost–benefit analysis of the whole endeavour should not be compromised by inclusion of nonworthwhile activities or practises. This applies to nutrition and supplements as it does to any other aspect of an expedition. Here are some suggested questions:

▸ Is the dietary supplement recognised by science, in particular the fields of nutrition, physiology, and biochemistry?

▸ Have ethically approved and peer-reviewed trials been conducted?

▸ Has the supplement a robust scientific evidence base for its use?

▸ Is there documented evidence in humans for use in the intended situations?

▸ Were double-blind, randomised, and placebo-controlled trials used to obtain the evidence base?

▸ Were appropriate methods used to evaluate changes in performance, body composition, or desired effect of the supplement?

▸ Were valid and reliable methods and protocols used to evaluate supplement efficacy?

▸ Were confounding factors and variables controlled during the data collection for the evidence base?

▸ Were data pertaining to the acceptability and legitimate use of the supplement properly analysed, interpreted, and presented?

Those embarking on intense training programmes for extended expeditions may benefit from a full nutritional assessment undertaken by an accredited sport nutritionist to identify energy and nutrient intake goals and the benefits of preexpedition supplementation.

PUTTING IT INTO PRACTICE

Whether you are planning to undertake a day's walk in the Dales or an expedition to Everest, it is hoped that the guidelines in this chapter will help you establish sound nutritional strategies to support your endeavours. The following scenarios provide some context in which to apply these guidelines.

Scenario 1: You're a recreational hill walker undertaking the occasional weekend walk to the Peak or Lake District, maintaining your fitness by daily walks of 3 to 5 kilometres (2-3 mi).

The healthy eating recommendations for the general population will be sufficient to support your level of training. Calorie intakes should be based on 35 calories per kilogram (2.2 lb) of body weight. You should aim to achieve at least 50 percent of calorie (energy) intake from carbohydrate, no more than 30 to 35 percent from fat, 15 to 20 percent from protein, and no more than 6 percent from alcohol. Aim for 4 to 5 grams of carbohydrate per kilogram of body weight, a protein intake between 0.75 and 1.0 gram per kilogram, and a fat intake around 70 grams per day for women and 90 grams a day for men.

To ensure adequate intakes of vitamins and minerals, opt for unrefined carbohydrate sources and at least five servings of fruits and vegetables each day. If training is well spaced, you have adequate time to replenish muscle glycogen stores.

On a day trip, you will want foods that are reasonably light to carry and energy dense to avoid fatigue due to lack of energy. Foods high in carbohydate should form the majority of your provisions for the day and are ideally consumed in frequent, small amounts. A carbohydrate-rich meal before you start and at the end of your walk should allow for adequate preparation and recovery.

A sample lunch for a day's steady walk lasting 5 to 6 hours could include the following:

▸ Two rolls or sandwiches
▸ Dried fruit or cereal bar
▸ Bar, chocolate, or small bag of peanuts
▸ At least 2 litres of water
▸ Sweets for emergency use

Add another sandwich or snack for each additional 2 hours of walking.

Scenario 2: You've decided to undertake a 10-day walking holiday, and in preparation you are increasing the duration of your daily walks and heading for the hills most weekends.

You'll require more energy, and to ensure that energy stores are maintained, increase the percentage of calories consumed from carbohydrate to 60 percent and drop fat to 25 percent. Aim for a carbohydrate intake equivalent to 5 to 6 grams per kilogram (2.2 lb) of body weight, a protein intake in the region of 1.2 to 1.4 grams per kilogram of body weight, and a fat intake around 70 grams per day for women and 90 grams per day for men. Base all your meals around starchy carbohydrate foods, with protein portions around 75 to 100 grams and at least three servings from the dairy food group each day. Greater intakes of carbohydrate will also result in greater intakes of protein.

Increased frequency and duration of training will incur greater fluid losses from the body. For training sessions less than 30 minutes, it is not usually necessary to drink during training, but for prolonged walks, start with the maximum amount of fluid you can tolerate in your stomach and aim to stay ahead of the sensation of thirst by sipping fluids at regular intervals.

Scenario 3: You're now training for an extended expedition where rough terrain and altitude will be encoutered. You may have added other endurance activities to your training programe such as running or cycling.

Carbohydrate requirements will increase further to 7 to 8 grams per kilogram (2.2 lb) of body weight per day, protein intake will remain between 1.2 and 1.4 grams per kilogram of body weight, and fat intake will remain around 70 grams for a female and 90 grams for a male.

Evidence suggests that hard exercise depletes the body of antioxidant vitamins, so take care to achieve adequate intakes of fruits and vegetables. As training frequency and intensity increase, the timing and content of meals and snacks become important to facilitate glycogen refuelling.

Consume a carbohydrate snack as soon as possible after training, when glycogen resynthesis is most efficient. Remember to opt for carbohydrate with a high or moderate glycaemic index since these will be absorbed more quickly (figure 9.2). Good choices include bananas, dried fruit, a chocolate bar, or jam sandwiches. During exercise, an isotonic sport drink may help to delay fatigue and maintain training intensity by providing a source of carbohydrate and fluid.

Scenario 4: You are training more than once a day for an ascent on Everest.

The general recommendation for those engaging in heavy endurance training is to achieve a carbohydrate intake of 65 to 70 percent of calorie intake, equivalent to 8 to 10 grams per kilogram (2.2 lb) of body weight per day. To achieve this, you will need to increase your reliance on carbohydrate from sugary sources. Protein requirements should not exceed 1.7 grams per kilogram of body weight, and fat intake will probably not exceed the values previously stated. Timing of meals and snacks becomes increasingly important to maintaining glycogen stores. Menu planning will require greater attention, and it would be useful to carry high-carbohydrate snacks at all times, especially for use immediately after training.

It is important to minimise the risks of dehydration. As mentioned, fluid losses can be up to 1 litre per hour in endurance exercise, and this can be higher if exercising in hot, humid conditions. As a rough guide, aim to consume 5 to 7 millilitres of fluid per kilogram (2.2 lb) of body weight before exercise, or as much as can be tolerated, and the equivalent of 2 millilitres per kilogram of body weight every 15 minutes, or 200 to 300 millilitres every 15 to 20 minutes. Fluid replacement can be facilitated by drinking still, less-concentrated, cool drinks of a reasonable volume, but higher exercise intensities will slow fluid absorption.

Weight and urine checks provide a useful way of monitoring fluid status. A weight reduction of 1 kilogram (2.2 lb) during a training session is roughly equivalent to a 1-litre fluid loss. These simple weight checks before and after exercise can help determine your fluid requirements postexercise. In general, frequent trips to the toilet to pass plentiful quantities of pale-coloured urine are an indicator of good hydration, whereas small volumes of dark-coloured urine indicate poor hydration. After training, aim to replace fluid losses one and a half times to ensure adequate rehydration.

KEY IDEAS

▸ Diet plays an important part in training for and completing mountaineering and climbing expeditions.

▸ A balanced, varied, and healthy diet is good for training, performance on expeditions, and health, but quantities will need to be adjusted to meet the extra energy demands.

▸ Do not try new diets or supplements on an expedition; always try both in training under realistic conditions.

▸ Ensure good hydration in training and on expedtions.

▸ Start refuelling as soon as possible after training, and carry adequate food and fluid on mountain days, with some extra rations for emergencies or contingencies.

▸ Consider using supplements for hard training and long mountain days, but always trial them before use on expeditions.

10

Nutrition for Expeditions

Louise Sutton, Roderick King, and John O'Hara

> To eat is a necessity, but to eat intelligently is an art.
>
> *Francois de La Rochefoucauld*

Preexpedition training can place a great deal of stress on the mountaineer's body. Chapter 9 dealt with the links amongst nutrition, health, and performance and took a practical look at nutritional requirements and strategies to support training for hill walking and mountaineering. This chapter focuses on expedition nutrition, particularly for high-altitude mountaineering, and considers planning and preparation for maintaining energy balance on expeditions, practical nutrition when mountaineering, food safety and the effects of foreign foods, monitoring of nutritional intake, and the use of specialist products and dietary supplements.

Evidence suggests there is a need for practical advice to translate general sport nutrition recommendations into practice to help mountaineers increase their energy and nutrient intake sufficiently to meet the energy demands of expeditions. In extreme environments, this practical advice will be to maximise energy and nutrient intake. Requirements for expedition food are not the same as those for a healthy, balanced everyday diet. On expedition, it is appropriate to follow the healthy-eating messages identified in chapter 9 where possible, but meeting energy requirements for the enforced circumstances of the expedition may compromise this.

PLANNING FOR AND MAINTAINING ENERGY BALANCE DURING EXPEDITIONS

Food satisfies both physiological and psychological requirements. These factors become more significant in a high-altitude environment. Planning for adequate nutritional intake improves the ability to operate safely in a mountainous environment and decreases the risk of injury and fatigue.

Challenges of Nutrition at Altitude

The fundamental challenge of nutrition at high altitude is to maintain energy intake when normal eating patterns are seriously compromised, appetite has changed, energy demands are high and variable, and food provision is affected by climate and location. Although studies have reported that the combined effects of altitude, cold temperature, and the performance of physical activities over rugged terrain combine to increase energy expenditure, energy intake has been observed to decrease as a result of anorexia (loss of appetite), limited food availability, and difficulty of food preparation (Butterfield, 1999). This is particularly problematic during initial exposure to high altitude when the symptoms of AMS interfere with food and fluid intake.

Increased altitude also has the potential to suppress appetite and alter taste sensation, all conspiring to make meeting nutritional requirements a difficult task.

To compound matters, increased altitude also brings about a greater risk of dehydration due to diuresis, water lost in breath and sweat, as well as difficulty maintaining an adequate intake of water. Fluid requirements may exceed 5 to 6 litres per day when physically active at altitude.

If energy balance is not maintained, several physical and psychological consequences are commonly observed along with the symptoms of AMS. These include fatigue, exhaustion, lethargic behaviour, loss of strength, and weight loss (as much as 15 to 20 percent of total body mass, according to some accounts).

Importance of Nutritional Balance

Diet is paramount in maintaining body mass, nutritional status, and physical and mental well-being whilst at extreme altitude (Reynolds et al.,1999). Diet is the only practical method to preserve lean body mass, replenish glycogen stores, maintain body weight, and sustain mental ability, physical fitness, and endurance. Careful consideration of nutrient choice and timing of provision can minimise depletion of energy reserves and erosion of physical and psychological capacities. When undertaking nutritional planning and preparation for mountainous environments, consider the following general recommendations:

▸ Energy requirements may be more than double normal amounts, which requires the provision of more foods and fluids with a high energy content.

▸ Consuming regular carbohydrate-rich snacks and sport drinks may assist in achieving increased energy and carbohydrate requirements.

▸ There is a high probability of dehydration, but easily accessible hydration systems that allow the consumption of fluid without the need to stop will be beneficial.

▸ Food provision for unexpected delays and prolonged duration should be factored in.

▸ Anticipate likely energy and fluid deficits during active phases and aim to restore these as soon as practical, usually at the start and end of the day.

General recommendations for nutrient requirements at high altitude stress the need for a balanced provision of macronutrients together with minerals, vitamins, and sufficient water, especially in situations of prolonged exposure that may last from days to weeks (Butterfield, 1999).

Following are nutritional considerations at high altitude:

▸ Energy intake—potential for a two- to threefold increase in basal energy requirements

▸ Energy composition—approximately 60 to 70 percent carbohydrate, 25 to 30 percent fat, and 15 percent protein

▸ Fluid intake—approximately 4 to 6 litres per day

▸ Vitamin and mineral intake—dietary reference values used as a target

There is an obvious potential for long periods of energy imbalance during extended continuous climbing, with only late-evening and early-morning opportunities for sufficient food intake. Despite the difficulty of assessing daily food intake at high altitude, there is little doubt on the need to increase energy intake up to two to three times greater than sea-level resting values. Energy requirements are reported to be in the range of 4,500 to 6,000 calories per day.

Prolonged hypoxia has been associated with a reduction in carbohydrate preference (Rose et al., 1988), but there is evidence that increased carbohydrate intake at first exposure to high altitude is of benefit. Carbohydrate is a more efficient fuel source than either fat or protein for meeting energy demands. Additionally, the main fuel for the brain is glucose, and mental performance relies upon an adequate blood glucose concentration. If blood glucose concentration falls below the normal range of 4.5 to 5.5 millimoles per litre, cognitive function may be impaired, especially if frank hypoglycaemia occurs (<3.0 mmol/L), resulting in problems with attention, memory, vigilance, self-regulation, and decision making. This places an even greater importance on adequate carbohydrate consumption, preferably 60 to 70 percent of total energy intake.

Early accounts from Himalayan expeditions (Pugh, 1954) recognised the importance of basic nutrition, such as increased sugar intake either in combination with other foods or as a sweetener for hot drinks. Other practical measures include frequent (almost hourly) carbohydrate intake throughout the day, which is important for maintaining blood glucose at altitude.

If expeditions to high altitude are to succeed, then nutritional strategies that address the energy demands of climbing and recovery are paramount. Previous studies report losses of body mass up to 20 percent, with significant contributions made by losses in lean body mass. Lean body mass is lost due to energy demands exceeding conventional energy supply from reserves of fat and glycogen at critical points during the climb. During such times, shortfall will be made up from protein from lean tissue. This sacrificial loss of protein will also occur if daily energy intake and nitrogen balance are not maintained during rest, especially after each climbing session, when recovery for the next climbing session ought to be the sole focus.

The goal of sustained energy provision without loss of body mass has been unattainable in many expeditions. However, weight loss at

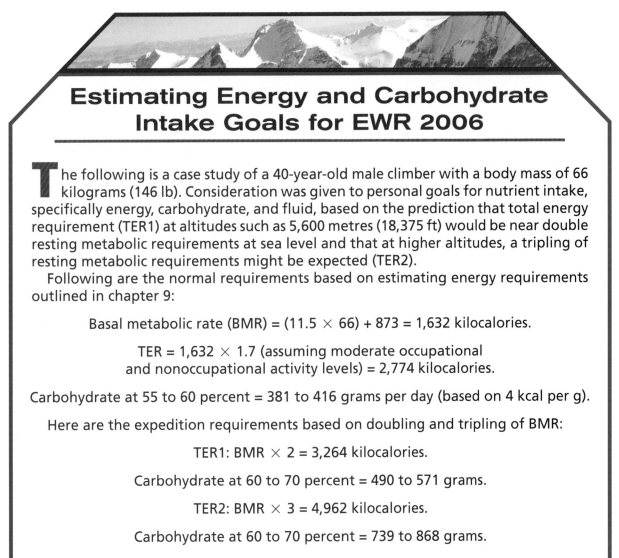

Estimating Energy and Carbohydrate Intake Goals for EWR 2006

The following is a case study of a 40-year-old male climber with a body mass of 66 kilograms (146 lb). Consideration was given to personal goals for nutrient intake, specifically energy, carbohydrate, and fluid, based on the prediction that total energy requirement (TER1) at altitudes such as 5,600 metres (18,375 ft) would be near double resting metabolic requirements at sea level and that at higher altitudes, a tripling of resting metabolic requirements might be expected (TER2).

Following are the normal requirements based on estimating energy requirements outlined in chapter 9:

Basal metabolic rate (BMR) = (11.5 × 66) + 873 = 1,632 kilocalories.

TER = 1,632 × 1.7 (assuming moderate occupational
and nonoccupational activity levels) = 2,774 kilocalories.

Carbohydrate at 55 to 60 percent = 381 to 416 grams per day (based on 4 kcal per g).

Here are the expedition requirements based on doubling and tripling of BMR:

TER1: BMR × 2 = 3,264 kilocalories.

Carbohydrate at 60 to 70 percent = 490 to 571 grams.

TER2: BMR × 3 = 4,962 kilocalories.

Carbohydrate at 60 to 70 percent = 739 to 868 grams.

(continued)

Estimating Energy and Carbohydrate Intake Goals for EWR 2006 *(continued)*

As a rough guide, 1 millilitre of fluid per kilocalorie of energy requirement can be used to predict fluid requirements.

Table 10.1 is a sample menu from the 2006 Everest West Ridge expedition that would meet the needs of this climber at higher altitudes.

TABLE 10.1 Sample Everest West Ridge 2006 Menu

Food item	Kcal	Carbohydrate (g)
1 Complan and Oats	250	30
1 freeze-dried breakfast	600	125
1 freeze-dried main meal	700	65
1 Complan drink	250	35
1 Boost bar	310	35
1 bag Jelly Babies	600	145
2 muesli bars or flapjack bars	350	55
1 50 g (1.8 oz) bag of peanuts	300	5
1 tuna sachet	135	0
2 energy gels	180	40
1 All the Way multipack	425	60
2 normal tea bags	0	0
2 herbal tea bags	0	0
1 coffee latte sachet	110	10
1 hot chocolate sachet	120	20
2 Cup-a-Soups	80	15
2 L energy drinks	540	135
Totals	4,950	775

Calories are approximations to the nearest 5 kcals; carbohydrate values are approximations to the nearest 5 g.

altitude can be minimised by increased energy intake (Butterfield et al., 1992). Careful consideration of nutrient choice and timing of nutrient provision during all stages of an expedition is a practical way to limit erosion of the human body and depletion of energy reserves sufficiently to attain the goals of the expedition without irreversible damage to health.

Nutrition and Morale

Getting nutrition right is important on any expedition, but food should not be viewed simply as fuel. Adequate nutrition also helps to maintain social interaction, morale, and task motivation, particularly for long expeditions. Unappetising food will have a negative impact on any expedition team no matter how energy-providing and nutritious the food is. Inadequate, repetitive, and plain nutritional diets have been associated with negative experiences when living at altitude. Alongside energy and nutritional content, important factors in food selection include weight, bulk, durability, ease of preparation, and special dietary requirements.

Expedition meals should aim to be the following:

▸ Energy dense—Needs enough energy to meet increased requirements.

▶ Lightweight—An important consideration if carrying food supplies, paying for porters, or travelling by plane.

▶ Varied and appetising—Energy-dense meals and snacks have no value if not consumed.

▶ Easily prepared—Preparation time should be kept to a minimum.

▶ Durable and easily stored—If food perishes, it is wasteful of effort and funds spent in transport.

Nutritious meals and snacks are required, taking into account the likelihood of menu fatigue, and where possible, individual preferences. Meals and snacks may be supplemented by energy bars, drinks, or gels. Meal-replacement products such as Complan or Build-Up not only provide additional calories but also protein and micronutrients during long expeditions. Table 10.2 shows the nutritional composition of Complan Original. This was used on the Everest West Ridge 2006 expedition because a daily two-sachet serving met reference nutrient intakes

TABLE 10.2 Complan Original Nutritional Composition

	TYPICAL VALUES PER 100 G (3.5 OZ) POWDER	TYPICAL VALUES PER 57 G (2 OZ) POWDER
Energy	1,848 kJ / 439 kcal	1,053 kJ / 250 kcal
Protein	15.4 g	8.8 g
Carbohydrate	61.1 g	34.8 g
Carbohydrate (of which sugars)	40.1 g	22.9 g
Fat	14.8 g	8.4 g
Fat (of which saturates)	6.6 g	3.8 g
Sodium	0.23 g	0.13 g
Vitamin A	350 mg	200 mg
Vitamin D	4.4 mg	2.5 mg
Vitamin E	8.8 mg	5.0 mg
Vitamin C	53 mg	30 mg
Thiamin	1.2 mg	0.7 mg
Riboflavin	1.4 mg	0.8 mg
Niacin	16 mg	9.0 mg
Vitamin B_6	1.8 mg	1.0 mg
Folic acid	180 mg	100 mg
Vitamin B_{12}	0.9 mg	0.5 mg
Biotin	0.13 mg	0.075 mg
Pantothenic acid	5.3 mg	3.0 mg
Calcium	570 mg	320 mg
Phosphorus	470 mg	270 mg
Iron	6.7 mg	3.8 mg
Magnesium	79 mg	45 mg
Zinc	4.2 mg	2.4 mg
Iodine	61 mg	35 mg

A daily two-sachet serving meets reference nutrient intakes for a number of micronutrients and makes a valuable contribution to protein, carbohydrate, and fat intake.

Source: http://www.complanfoods.com/nutrition_complan_original.php.

for a number of micronutrients in addition to making a valuable contribution to protein, carbohydrate, and fat intake.

Hydration

Hydration is one aspect of nutrition that many climbers and mountaineers neglect. Factors that increase fluid requirements at high altitude include the following:

▸ Increased ventilation

▸ Increased urinary losses due to the diuretic effect of altitude and cold

▸ Sweating related to physical exertion (further magnified at high altitude or in hot climates)

▸ Vomiting associated with AMS

▸ Diarrhoeal losses

Small amounts of liquid should be consumed consistently throughout the day. Mountaineers and climbers should develop a programme of regularly scheduled drinking. Hydration bladders allow for frequent drinking on the move, and insulated bladders and hoses should prevent freezing during cold-climate mountaineering, especially if hot water is poured in and sealed.

Mountaineers should carry a stove and boil up 3 litres of water every 8 to 10 hours to refill the bladder system. The time spent melting snow and boiling water is offset by enhanced performance and mental alertness from maintained hydration. The practical aspect of when and where to stop for food and fluid intake should be factored in during the planning phase. Finally, it is vital to rehydrate before you go to sleep.

USE OF DIETARY SUPPLEMENTS

People who engage in extreme activities have special dietary requirements, especially when the activity is mountaineering, where the typical fallback of a decent kitchen and local store is not available. It is intuitive that dietary imbalance may occur due to nutrient exclusion or restriction whilst on expedition. As discussed, an expedition that might be days to months away from the nearest food supply requires careful planning to maintain an adequate nutritional intake. The very fact that intake, frequency, and amount of nutrition may be compromised means that there should be a greater drive to balance food supplies through planning. Although there is now evidence that supplementation may be beneficial in such circumstances, this is largely when demonstrated deficiencies occur and is by no means universal for all macro- or micronutrients. In mountaineering, additional intake of convenient food from an appropriate source or from supplementation may be valuable. In such cases, it would be necessary to restrict additional supplementation to an amount appropriate to fulfil the needs identified from any imbalance due to actual or projected dietary intake or mismatch of requirements.

The temptation of using a supplement is that it is presented as an essential component of the diet that you may be short of and it would be better if you took more to ensure success. The attraction of supplements is related to both perceived and actual ergogenic benefits, including enhanced performance, desirable body composition, or both.

Sound nutritional intake maintains good health that in turn provides stable body composition, and this should be the primary prerequisite for mountaineering success. However, supplements can help to optimise body composition for a desired outcome, be it additional body fat for prolonged expeditions or improvements in power-to-weight ratio. Supplements in this situation could be prescribed quantities of the core macronutrients (fat, protein, and carbohydrate) in amounts that differ from the simple position stand for the balance of good health and dietary reference values. An example would be an increase in supplemental protein to maintain nitrogen balance during energy deficit, as experienced during extreme climbing with low energy intake and high energy expenditure. Another example would be the use of carbohydrate to improve glycogen stores before or after key climbing sessions.

These are examples of acute use of macronutrients as supplements superimposed on the requirements for a simple balance of good health. The specific properties of macronutrients can be exploited because there is good evidence

Supplementary Energy Bars
and Powders for EWR 2006

Preexpedition research for the Everest West Ridge 2006 expedition indicated the need for a solid as well as a liquid product to assist in meeting overall energy demands. The primary aim was the development of products that addressed the need to maintain energy balance and preserve lean body mass. One product was formulated as a cereal bar, the other as an energy powder to mix with water for drinking.

Cadbury Schweppes has a history of providing adventurers with nutrition solutions. In 1911, the company provided Robert F. Scott with cocoa for his expedition to the South Pole. Researchers at the Cadbury Schweppes Global Science Centre developed two pioneering cereal bars and an energy drink to support the British Army on the EWR expedition.

As discussed, one of the greatest challenges of mountaineers is maintaining energy balance where malnutrition is the main contributor to negative energy balance at high altitude (Westerterp, Kayser, Wouters, Le Trong, & Richalet, 1994; Pulfrey & Jones, 1996). Evidence suggests that the decline in energy consumption at increasing altitude is not accompanied by shifts in the distribution of macronutrient intake (Reynolds et al., 1998) or energy digestibility (Kayser, Acheson, Decombaz, Fern, & Cerretelli, 1992). Despite the difficulty of accurately assessing daily food intake at high altitude, when mountaineering there is an increased energy expenditure two to three times that of sea-level resting values (Reynolds, Lickteig, Howard, & Deuster, 1999).

High-Altitude Energy Bars

The cereal bar underwent development for two requirements—cold-temperature consumer use and nutritional composition. It was possible to provide two varieties: Enhanced bars, with low glycaemic index but with full macronutrient combination of fat, protein, and carbohydrate for use at altitudes up to 6,000 metres (19,685 ft), and All the Way bars, with higher glycaemic index and additional features specifically for high, cold altitudes beyond 6,000 metres by virtue of a low glass point of –19 degrees Celsius (–2 degrees Fahrenheit). These bars could be eaten at cold temperatures without biting and chewing difficulty, and they were designed and tested for use at extreme altitude to provide wholesome nutrition whilst actively climbing. They came as multipack minibars, as well as 75-gram (2.7 oz) bars for specific types of active climbing. The 75-gram Enhanced bars were designed and tested for use at lower altitudes and less extreme temperatures, especially as a supplement to be consumed at Base Camp, lower intermediate camps, and the end of climbing sessions.

Enhanced bars were designed to deliver slow-release energy when consumed at rest. These bars contained more fat, protein, and fibre to slow digestion, as well as complex carbohydrate to maintain glycogen stores and blood glucose availability. The binding syrup contained sugars with a low glycaemic index and soluble fibres. The

(continued)

target macronutrient balance was 60 to 75 percent carbohydrate, 15 to 25 percent protein, and 15 percent fat.

All the Way bars were designed to deliver fast-release energy when consumed on the move. These energy bars were formulated with higher levels of refined carbohydrate, and the binding syrup was glucose based for rapid absorption. The macronutrient balance was 75 to 80 percent carbohydrate, 10 to 15 percent protein, and 10 percent fat.

The packaging featured easy-open flow wrap so that it could be removed with a gloved hand, which was important for climbers on the move in extreme conditions.

High-Altitude Energy Powders

The energy powder underwent development for two requirements—ease of preparation with hot water from melted snow and a balanced macronutrient blend of protein and carbohydrate with specified vitamins and minerals. The powder was formulated both as a recovery preparation mixed at full strength and as an active-use preparation mixed at half strength. The powder was designed to formulate into a solution without congealing when mixed with water between 70 and 80 degrees Celsius (158 and 175 degrees Fahrenheit).

The energy powder used as a recovery preparation was designed to deliver both slow-release and fast-release energy when consumed at rest. This powder contained more protein and carbohydrate to replete both muscle and liver glycogen stores and maintain blood glucose availability. Whey protein provided an easily digested but balanced source of essential and nonessential amino acids to support nitrogen balance. The target macronutrient balance was 70 to 80 percent carbohydrate and 20 to 30 percent protein. The energy content was 360 kilocalories per 100 grams. When used at full strength as a recovery solution, each litre supplied 360 kilocalories and 100 grams of carbohydrate–protein mix.

The energy powder for active-use preparation was designed to deliver significant fast-release energy when consumed on the move. When used at half strength as an active-use solution, each litre supplied 180 kilocalories and 50 grams of carbohydrate–protein mix.

The basic formulation of the powder contained minerals and vitamins necessary to support needs in a high-altitude environment. Supplementation levels were designed to be major fractional parts of reference nutrient intake, assuming consumption of 1 to 2 litres of recovery strength or 2 to 4 litres of active-use strength per day.

Field Results

The bar products provided significant nutritional support in a compact form. Package design facilitated use at altitude whilst climbing or camping and was space efficient for ease of transport. Field use showed that the products were advantageous during both climbing situations when energy demands were high and recovery when camped. The powder products were of use not only as energy and protein liquid supplements at camps but also whilst climbing.

for using certain combinations of amino acids in protein (e.g., casein and whey), the glycaemic index for carbohydrate (high for immediate energy and low for sustained energy release), and saturation balance in fats (proportions of monounsaturated and polyunsaturated fatty acids). Macronutrient intake can be altered to achieve desired body composition targets both before and during an expedition.

As highlighted, energy demands whilst climbing can be considerable, yet the provision of adequate nutrition to meet energy and nitrogen balance is difficult for several reasons, including the logistics of supply, lack of opportunity to eat regularly, environmental extremes, and physiological responses to the situation. Energy imbalance is almost inevitable, but supplementation whilst climbing can be beneficial if it is in the form of easily ingested and digested substances. Table 10.3 lists the calorie and carbohydrate content of Everest West Ridge 2006 food supplements and meals. This nutrition resource was displayed in the mess tent at Base Camp for team members to monitor progress towards daily intake goals.

MEETING NUTRITIONAL REQUIREMENTS WHEN MOUNTAINEERING

Preexpedition identification, acquisition, and supply of nutrients can allow for tailor-made ration packs for all stages of an expedition, from the journey to base camp to the summit bid. Evaluation of likely energy and macronutrient needs for your team is a key in food trial and selection. Well-chosen products based on sound scientific platforms should underpin dietary provision. Careful attention to meeting basic nutritional requirements is important, as are catering for taste preferences and menu fatigue and making sure sufficient food supplies are available.

At many of the stages identified in this section, moderate- to high-intensity physical work sustained for long amounts of time will benefit from high carbohydrate intakes. In addition, adequate hydration should not be overlooked. This section discusses nutritional requirements throughout the following stages:

▸ Two to 3 weeks before departure
▸ One week before departure
▸ Departure
▸ Journey to base camp
▸ Base camp
▸ Beyond base camp

Two to Three Weeks Before Departure

At this stage, there should be no conflict between eating for health and eating for performance. Sound nutritional strategies have a great part to play in optimising intake and allowing you to train consistently and effectively in the final weeks before departure. If training intensity remains high, energy requirements will remain high. It is important to meet requirements through the correct mix of macronutrients (approximately 60 percent carbohydrate, 25 percent fat, and 15 percent protein).

Diet must meet the demands that training places on the body; see the basic training diet recommendations in chapter 9 for more details. Additional energy and carbohydrate may be required to support increased training, body composition, and maintenance of lean body mass. These requirements may be met by consuming supplements in the form of snacks. Carbohydrate snacks are especially important for the resynthesis of glycogen during this time. See figure 10.1 for a list of snacks that are rich in carbohydrate, provide approximately 250 calories, and can easily be incorporated into your usual diet.

One Week Before Departure

In the final week before departure for an expedition, you should attempt to increase your carbohydrate intake beyond that consumed to support your training. This is especially important if you have been undertaking hypoxic training as part of your preacclimatisation strategy. It is also advisable to pay close attention to your fluid intake. Simple urine colour and volume checks are advised; you should look for pale and plentiful urine.

TABLE 10.3 Calorie and Carbohydrate Content of Everest West Ridge 2006 Food Supplements and Meals

Product	Weight in g (oz)	Calories/portion	Carbohydrate/ portion (g)
Babybel cheese	25 (.9)	75	0
Bassett's Fruity Babies	165 (5.8)	510	120
Bassett's Fruit Allsorts	180 (6.3)	575	140
Bassett's Jelly Babies	180 (6.3)	600	145
Bassett's Liquorice Allsorts	105 (3.7)	370	80
Complan drink	57 (2.0)	250	35
Complan and Oats	60 (2.1)	250	30
Ainsley Harriott couscous	100 (3.5)	370	80
Brunch bar	35 (1.2)	160	20
Cadbury Schweppes energy drink	150 (5.3)	540	135
Cadbury milk chocolate biscuit bar	49 (1.7)	255	30
Cadbury milk chocolate bar	49 (1.7)	255	30
Cadbury fruit and nut bar	49 (1.7)	240	30
Cadbury Boost bar	60 (2.1)	310	35
Cadbury Crunchie bar	50 (1.8)	240	35
Coffee sachet—latte	22 (.8)	110	10
Coffee sachet—mocha	22 (.8)	90	15
Dorset flapjack	85 (3.0)	350	55
Dried meat pepperoni	10 (.4)	50	0
Hammer energy drink sachets	29 (1.0)	100	25
Hammer energy gel	36 (1.3)	90	20
Hot chocolate sachets	28 (1.0)	120	20
Mother Earth muesli bar	32.5 (1.1)	130	20
Mother Earth Baked Oaty Slice	50 (1.8)	190	25
Super Noodles	100 (3.5)	175	25
KP peanuts	50 (1.8)	300	5
Hammer Recoverite sachet	30 (1.1)	160	30
Real Field Meal breakfast	185 (6.5)	600	124
Real Field Meal main meal	151 (5.3)	700	65
Ainsley Harriott risotto	140 (4.9)	550	95
Tinned sardines	125 (4.4)	230	0
Soup sachet (slim)	20 (.7)	45	10
Soup sachet	20 (.7)	50-80	10-15
John West tuna sachet	85 (3.0)	135	0

Calories are approximations to the nearest 5 kcal; carbohydrate values are approximations to the nearest 5 g.

FIGURE 10.1
Carbohydrate-Rich Snacks

5 Jaffa Cakes

1 Complan drink made with water

1 Complan and Oats made with water

1 Complan chocolate bar

1 low-fat yoghurt with a digestive biscuit

2 large bananas

1 litre of isotonic sport drink

75 grams (2.7 oz) of wine gums or similar fruit sweets

1 small tin of rice pudding

1 fruit scone with jam

75 grams (2.7 oz) of dried fruit

.5 litre of semi-skimmed milk

1 fruit smoothie (4 oz)

1 Cadbury Crunchie bar

2 slices Soreen malt loaf

2 Weetabix with 158 millilitres of semi-skimmed milk

1 small bowl of flaked cereal with 158 millilitres of semi-skimmed milk

1 toasted bagel with jam

2 thick slices of toast with jam

1 large currant tea cake

1 small bowl of vegetable soup with a slice of bread

Departure and Travel

When your travel arrangements involve air travel, start preparing the body for expedition at least 3 days before departure. Concentrate on optimising carbohydrate and fluid intakes.

Before departure, try to get lots of sleep to compensate for any sleep you might lose during the flight and to help minimise the effects of jet lag. Try to avoid or limit alcohol consumption the day before departure and then during the flight. Alcohol is a potent diuretic and is likely to increase urine output and dehydrate the body during the flight. Also, limit caffeine-rich drinks, such as coffee and cola. These can have a mild diuretic effect that can exacerbate fluid loss and contribute to dehydration. During the flight, carry a bottle of water and drink plenty.

Pack portable carbohydrate-rich snacks for your flight to assist in maintaining a high carbohydrate intake. The calorie content of these nutrition travel packs should be 500 to 1,000 kilocalories. Maintaining a high-carbohydrate diet may help to lessen the effects of altitude sickness during initial altitude exposure. Try to adopt a meal pattern in line with your new time zone once your flight has departed; it is likely that the airline will have considered this in their in-flight service schedule.

On arrival, adopt a regular meal pattern in line with your new time zone as soon as is practical and sustain a high fluid intake until you are well hydrated. Check urine colour and volume; your urine should be pale and plentiful.

Journey Into Base Camp

If your journey is to altitude, you may experience unhelpful appetite and thirst responses if food and fluid intakes are neglected. High carbohydrate and fluid intakes should be maintained at all times. Dehydration can intensify the symptoms of altitude sickness, which will result in reduced food intake. Anticipating the consequences of altitude that cause impaired appetite and enforced feeding may minimise secondary consequences of altitude sickness, such as depleted muscle glycogen and loss of lean body mass. In addition, exposure to altitude increases carbohydrate usage at rest and during exercise. Carbohydrate intake can be supplemented with sport drinks. If you are reliant on a trekking company to supply main meals for the expedition, supplement with carbohydrate-rich snack foods such as chocolate bars, cereal bars, and energy drinks.

Base Camp

As discussed, eating enough food is the major nutritional priority at altitude. Weight loss is almost inevitable. Changes in body composition such as losses in body fat and lean tissue can be incapacitating, and loss of insulating fat can decrease tolerance to cold temperatures. Nutritional menus should be conceived in an attempt to mitigate this, but vigilance is required to make sure you consume enough food and fluids.

At base camp, you may be fed by a cook provided by a trekking company; however, due to the potential monotony of local cuisine for long expeditions, it is essential to add variety to the menu. To ensure that food never becomes a chore, include menu items in the food plan that will boost spirits. These could be classed as the magic menu items, which proved popular with the Everest West Ridge 2006 team.

Beyond Base Camp

During the climbing phases of an expedition, food packs can be divided into two categories: low-mountain rations (LMR) and high-mountain rations (HMR). A key difference in the composition of LMR and HMR is the snack items. HMR packs, where weight is likely to be of concern, should contain energy gels, drinks, and bars, whereas LMR packs may contain more conventional snacks. Do not pack foods that you do not find appetising. If you do not consume them, you have wasted the energy required to carry them. If foods are not palatable at sea level, there is a high probability that they will not be consumed at altitude. Food caches at strategic points along the route can be used to hold additional food and as dumps for food that has not been consumed.

Table 10.4 lists typical daily food items, with magic menu items in bold. Snack items to be consumed on the move should be high in carbohydrate, easy to access, palatable, easy to digest, and worth their weight and pack space to carry. The following foods fit this profile: jelly beans, fruit gums, liquorice, fudge, dried fruit, sport gels, and bite-sized cereal or flapjack bars.

Food Safety and the Effects of Foreign Foods

Hygienic food practices are essential on expedition. Ingestion of contaminated water or food

can result in mild to disabling diarrhoea. To minimise the risk of diarrhoea, clean hands thoroughly before eating, do not eat exterior surfaces of fruit and vegetables, and avoid eating meat unless you are sure it has been properly refrigerated. In addition, the high magnesium content of glacial water can have a laxative effect on the bowel.

Constipation is another common complaint on expedition. It is more prevalent at high altitude, where excessive fluid losses rob water from the large bowel and reduced oxygen availability slows down the intestines. Excessive intestinal gas is another common complaint. Some find relief by limiting consumption of dehydrated high-carbohydrate foods.

KEY IDEAS

Following are do and do-not checklists of high-altitude nutrition strategies.

Do

Establish a food plan.

Emphasise a high carbohydrate intake.

Try to consume at least one hot meal a day.

Provide a variety of main meals and snacks.

Schedule and enforce eating and drinking.

Flavour water to increase consumption.

Discourage alcohol consumption.

Monitor colour and volume of urine.

Test foods before your expedition.

Remove any unnecessary packaging.

Monitor weight loss (if practical).

Monitor food and fluid intake (if practical).

Do Not

Skip meals and snacks.

Force-feed when nauseous or vomiting (but do encourage drinking).

Drink unpurified water.

Restrict water intake to avoid having to urinate.

View the expedition as a deliberate opportunity to lose weight.

TABLE 10.4 Typical Daily Food Items

Type of meal	Food item
BASE CAMP	
Breakfast	Porridge, cereals, eggs, beans, bread, chapattis, jams and spreads, dried fruit and seeds, **tinned grapefruit, mandarins**
Lunch	Tinned fish, pulses, soup, chapattis or tortillas, **hot-dog sausages, tinned meats, bread,** crackers with pâté
Dinner	Soup, rice, pasta, potatoes, sauce (with lentils, beans, meat, or vegetables), **tinned fruit, cake, custard, jelly**
Snacks	Biscuits, crackers, dried fruits, nuts, seeds, **Pringles,** salted nuts, sweets, chocolate bars, **cakes, pretzels,** cereal bars
Drinks	Tea, coffee, hot chocolate, Horlicks, fruit-flavoured powder mixes, energy drinks, herbal teas
LMR	
Breakfast	Porridge or muesli mixed with skimmed milk powder, cereal bars, hot drinks
Lunch	Noodle soup, tuna or mackerel cold pasta mix, Ryvita with Primula cheese or pâté, flapjack, chocolate bar, energy drinks
Dinner	Soup, boil-in-the-bag meal, pudding, hot drinks
Snacks	Jelly sweets, cereal bars, chocolate, energy bars, peanuts, dried fruit, nuts, seeds
Drinks	Tea, coffee, hot chocolate, skimmed milk powder, sugar sachets
HMR	
Breakfast	Porridge or muesli mixed with skimmed milk powder, Complan and Oats, dehydrated breakfast, cereal bars, hot drinks
Lunch	Noodle soup, Ryvita with Primula cheese or pâté, flapjack, chocolate bar, energy drinks
Dinner	Soup, dehydrated meal, dessert
Snacks	Jelly sweets, cereal bars, chocolate, energy bars and gels, peanuts, dried fruit

Food and Nutrients at All Stages of the Expedition

Preexpedition identification, acquisition, and supply of food and nutrients enabled shipment of ration packs tailored for all stages of the expedition, from the journey into Base Camp to the summit bid. Evaluation of likely energy and macronutrient needs for the team and its members was a key driver for selection, trial, and prescribed use of the provisions. Local Nepalese and Tibetan food provided the bulk of meals at Base Camp, supplemented by familiar products (chocolate and cereal bars, sweets, and Complan meal-replacement drinks) shipped from the United Kingdom specifically for ease of consumption and contribution to carbohydrate intake.

▶ Composition of Camp Packs

Absolute weight of camp packs is an important consideration since food has to be carried by the mountaineer. As discussed earlier, food packs were divided into two categories during the climbing phases: LMR and HMR. The HMR packs contained energy gels, drinks, and bars, whereas the LMR packs contained more conventional snacks. All camp packs were analysed for their nutritional composition and provided approximately 60 to 65 percent of calories from carbohydrate, 20 to 25 percent of calories from fat, and 10 to 15 percent of calories from protein. Both packs were supplemented with additional snack items according to personal preference.

LMR Camp Pack

- 1 boil-in-the-bag breakfast
- 1 boil-in-the-bag main meal
- 1 boil-in-the-bag dessert
- 1 Complan drink
- 1 Enhanced bar
- 1 50-gram (1.8 oz) chocolate bar
- 1 muesli bar
- 1 Mother Earth Baked Oaty Slice
- 1 fruit bar
- .5 packet Ryvita crackers
- 1 pâté portion
- 1 50-gram (1.8 oz) bag of peanuts
- 2 black tea bags
- 2 herbal tea bags
- 2 coffee sachets
- 1 hot chocolate sachet
- 2 soup sachets

HMR Camp Pack

- 1 Complan and Oats
- 1 freeze-dried breakfast meal
- 1 freeze-dried main meal
- 1 Complan drink
- 1 Enhanced bar
- 2 muesli bars or flapjack bars
- 1 50-gram (1.8 oz) bag of peanuts
- 1 tuna sachet
- 2 energy gels
- 1 All the Way bar
- 2 black tea bags
- 2 herbal tea bags
- 2 coffee sachets
- 1 hot chocolate
- 2 Cup-a-Soups
- 2 litre energy drinks

Monitoring and Maximising Nutritional Intake at Altitude

Short-lived exposure to altitude does not require significant increases in nutrients, with the exception of increased fluid. If intended exposure is no more than 2 or 3 days, any deficit can be regained on return. However, the duration of the 2006 Everest West Ridge expedition made careful planning and monitoring important for maximising nutritional intake.

The limited evidence to date suggests that group and self-regulation of performance, including nutrition and hydration monitoring, are imperative for successful adaptation and functioning at altitude. Diet monitoring and a conscious effort to maintain energy intake and dietary intake goals (energy, carbohydrate, and fluid) may help replenish glycogen stores, maintain endurance, preserve physical fitness, and sustain mental ability by minimising losses in body mass. Table 10.5 shows an example of a completed daily food and fluid record from the 2006 expedition. Note this is not a specific recommendation for food or supplement intake.

TABLE 10.5 Sample Daily Food and Fluid Record

Time	Food or fluid consumed	Portion size
0600	Orange drink powder with water	30 ml (2 tbsp)—large mug
	Oatmeal block	75 g (2.6 oz) dry weight
	Hot water	74 ml (5 tbsp)
	White sugar	2 sachets
	Semi-skimmed milk (dried)	10 ml (2 tsp)
	Dried raisins	30 ml (2 tbsp)
0700	Supplement (multivitamin)	1 tablet
0830	Tea with sugar	1 L
	Chocolate bar (Mars)	50 g (1.8 oz)
1030	Beef jerky	1 packet (50 g [1.8 oz])
	Oat slice	50 g (1.8 oz)
	Energy drink	1 L
	Instant hot chocolate mix	30 ml (2 tbsp)
	Hot water	Small mug
1300	Instant chicken soup	1 sachet
	Hot water	Large mug
	Real Field Meal (freeze-dried meatballs and pasta in tomato sauce)	1 packet
	Orange drink powder with water	30 ml (2 tbsp)—large mug

(continued)

TABLE 10.5   *(continued)*

Time	Food or fluid consumed	Portion size
	Dried fruit and nuts	Large handful
1520	Instant coffee powder	5 ml (1 tsp)
	Hot water	Large mug
	White sugar	10 ml (2 tsp)
	Fruit and nut chocolate bar	49 g (1.7 oz)
1700	Tea	1 L
	Fruit gum sweets	.5 packet
1930	Real Field Meal (freeze-dried chilli con carne)	1 packet
	Real Field Meal (freeze-dried chocolate pudding with chocolate sauce)	1 packet
	Instant coffee powder	5 ml (1 tsp)
	Hot water	Large mug
	White sugar	10 ml (2 tsp)
	Energy drink	1 L

EXPEDITION LEADERSHIP AND PSYCHOLOGY

Psychological Skills in the Outdoors

John Allan and Jim McKenna

Only those who will risk going too far can possibly find out how far one can go.

T. S. Eliot

Adventure represents a willingness to take risks and learn through uncertainty. The unpredictable and dynamic nature of the outdoors helps to facilitate this capacity for change. Although the challenges of adventure education may differ in terms of difficulty, adventure is created by appropriately matching skills to emerging risks. This concept applies across the range of participants and skill sets, from the use of rudimentary navigation by novices on low-level terrain to the complex planning and technical expertise required by mountaineers undertaking a full-scale ascent of Mount Everest in the West Ridge.

In chapter 12, we identify the development-by-challenge philosophy and the components that interconnect to determine the impact of adventure education. These elements include the physical or natural setting, participants, type of activities, group dynamics, and facilitation or leadership of experiences. When these factors are interwoven effectively, they initiate whole-person challenges because they concurrently test physical, psychological, and social capabilities. In this chapter, we will look at a range of psychological skills relating to these areas. We argue that appropriate adventure education enhances individual and collective outcomes. Our thinking relates to the two main

aspirations within preparation. The first is to reduce the likelihood of unwanted but predictable responses and outcomes. The second is to ensure adaptive responses to extraordinary, often unpredictable, challenges. In the first part of the chapter, we identify psychological issues raised in modern adventure education. In the latter sections, we consider the application of sport psychology techniques.

PSYCHOLOGY IN ADVENTURE EDUCATION

Psychological skills in the outdoors, as in life, do not operate in isolation. Although we are unique individuals, we are all composed of physical actions, thinking capacity, feelings, instincts, and moral core. These areas develop through maturation and experience, so expansion can occur in all of them. Deeply satisfying adventurous experiences, especially those placing balanced demands on these facets of human development, create a broader repertoire of skills that can help manage future challenges. This positive psychological thinking is consistent with modern adventure philosophy in which growth and change is best achieved when participants feel challenged and supported yet are still free to make informed choices.

Thoughts and emotions stimulate action in challenging situations. Therefore, these psychological elements underpin the capacity to interact with any adventure education environment that offers realistic consequences for actions. For instance, making an incorrect navigational decision can automatically create a longer distance to travel; there is no choice. Deciding to press on when the demands outweigh individual or group capacity can produce more hazardous consequences than just extending travel time. Thus, psychological fitness is a key component in acquiring and using the skills necessary in adventure activities. More specifically, these skills include the following:

▸ Technical competence (efficient movement and use of equipment)

▸ Physical fitness (activity-specific conditioning, general endurance, perseverance)

▸ Humanistic skills (self-determination, concentration, management of fear, appreciation of others)

▸ Environmental awareness and respect (being in tune with changeable demands, appreciation of aesthetic and ethical issues)

Personal development through adventure education begins with attaining an ideal psychological state for growth. Aligning thought processes (cognition) and emotions (affect) within a moral framework enables people to interact flexibly and reciprocally within the changing environment (setting). Because adventure education can be a social endeavour and a medium for teaching, group processes (social) also help to determine effective psychological functioning. An adventurous experience exposes the need to be psychologically flexible in all of these areas, which makes it an ideal learning environment for refining these skills; management training groups justify their adventure education using precisely this argument. For instance, the need for effective decision making (cognitive skill), unselfishness (emotional skill), and cooperation (social skill) are all imperative in mountain-based expeditions. The key to developing psychological fitness is to progressively overload capability in all these areas by practicing and receiving feedback on that practice. We look at each of these areas in turn throughout the first section of this chapter and consider how the underpinning skill areas can be refined.

CLEAR THINKING (COGNITION) IN ADVENTURE EDUCATION

We all differ in how we think, feel, and behave. This in turn influences how we face challenges. Thinking stimulates responses in line with emotional states and inner value systems. Learning to maintain a balance of these areas, especially in tough circumstances, creates an important pathway for human growth. The thinking, or cognitive, component of our being also relies on balance; too much concentration on reasoning alone may inhibit decision making and resultant action. Consider how decision-making capability in adventure education can be affected by too much thinking (paralysis by analysis); for example, it can lead to hesitation about making a tough call, such as when pressure is exerted by changeable weather conditions or alterations in the needs of group members.

Wisdom and intelligent thinking are not fixed qualities. Each needs to adapt to the changing forces of nature, so each change in external circumstances can create a new learning opportunity. The aim of intelligent decision making is not to show cleverness; it is to consider the prominent facets of any situation and weigh each in the light of experience in order to create a judgement. Nowhere is this more important in adventure education than when safety may be compromised or when enjoyment and learning are impeded. Being vigilant to, but humble about, the capacity of humans to influence nature is another facet of thinking that can help prevent complacent decision making.

A measure of the courage needed to deal with uncertainty in adventure education is not dominance over the environment; this would be futile and foolhardy. Authentic courage relates to how well people flow in response to each new challenge. Egotistical desire, on the other hand, often impedes experiencing beautiful and powerful natural settings. In moments of adventure, humility often reflects intelligent thinking and a deep awareness of risk. High-altitude mountaineers comment that they can summit over 8,000 metres (26,245 ft) only when the weather allows it. It takes real courage to recognise personal limitations and make the appropriate decision to either push on or retreat with dignity when all the risks have been evaluated. Bravery does not develop by simply overcoming fear but through managing it intelligently to direct behaviour towards achieving goals and aspirations.

Thinking skills, similar to other psychological skills, can be taught. Cognitive intelligence does not just relate to fixed intellectual abilities. It encapsulates a range of qualities and activities—scholarly or otherwise—that are developed by the cooperative links forged between personal attributes and the environment. The capacity to think effectively can be trained through deliberate practice in adventure education. *A Review of Research on Outdoor Learning* (Rickinson et al., 2004) states that adventure education enhances problem-solving competencies, academic performance, and environmental knowledge and understanding through positive effects on long-term memory.

When interacting with unforgiving environments, as in high-altitude mountaineering, the information that is processed reflects immediate assessments based on previous experience and expertise. The achievements we experience—and part of what makes us smart—come from combining effort with the expertise acquired over time. Mental skills that underpin effective operation in the outdoors encompass many of the less obvious elements of cognitive intelligence. These range from problem solving and maintaining focus to inquisitiveness and creativity.

In the context of adventure education, many of these thinking skills are essential. Renowned Stanford University psychologist Carol Dweck (2007) promotes the concept of a *growth mindset* and has completed extensive research showing that the psychological environment contributes to this productive and adaptive pattern of development. According to her work, holding the belief that intelligence is learned allows humans to embrace challenges, persist in the face of setbacks, and perceive effort as the pathway to mastery. It may even be that holding this belief system supports our own contention that adventure education can create personal growth.

Problem Solving and Foresight

Problem solving and foresight, or realistic prediction making, are strongly associated with adventure education. They are considered the most complex of intellectual functions and they are central to effective decision making. Each involves weighing options, even in the face of deep uncertainty, analysing and then summarising situations to provide realistic solutions. Such skills need to be based on reality, not on blind ideas inspired simply by hope or faith. They comprise a blend of systematic thinking, common sense, and intuition.

Anticipation of problems can avert the need to make rash decisions. Solving problems in a fluid environment is influenced by available time—a subjective notion—and this can lead to making decisions too early or too late. For example, consider the implications of getting timing just right whilst attempting a push for the summit in high-altitude conditions. Withdrawing from an outdoor activity early on (say, when weather conditions deteriorate) risks denying valuable opportunities for learning and achievement. However, being blasé about the worsening circumstances might not only compromise safety but also alienate participants from future endeavours.

In *Outdoor Leadership*, John Graham (2003) states that systematic time management overcomes many of the problems that emerge in volatile external circumstances. In timing a decision, the best course of action is to begin by considering the overall schedule of the activity, in particular the latest hour of the day at which you must end the session (for example, the completion of a mountain walk). Once this is established, determine the time needed to implement activity options (long or short route) and subtract the time needed to implement the slowest option (longer route) before making the decision. Using this process, rational choices displace reactive decision making based on guesswork.

Problem solving in adventure education also needs to be logical and progressive. In conditions of anxiety, this involves an initial calming phase—taking a deep breath, or creating a moment of psychological silence—followed by a preliminary scan of available options. This initial calming is important because anxiety is known for creating tunnel vision, which may narrow the range of what can be attended to. To widen the search for possible options, look for unconventional alternatives. For group activities, this may involve short all-in meetings. Once the best information is gathered within the available time, a risk-versus-benefit exercise can be employed for each option, and the option where benefits best outweigh risks can be implemented. As circumstances change, this course of action can be refined.

Concentration

Concentration involves directing thinking to intended targets. With variable channel capacity, people have a limited capacity to concentrate for long amounts of time, intermittently, or with competing demands. The ability to concentrate in an uncertain environment will depend on factors such as emotional and physical state (the need to feel rested and calm), effort, enthusiasm, and confidence in skills (the more we know what to do in variable circumstances, the less anxiety affects focus). Therefore, learning and practicing concentration skills and strate-

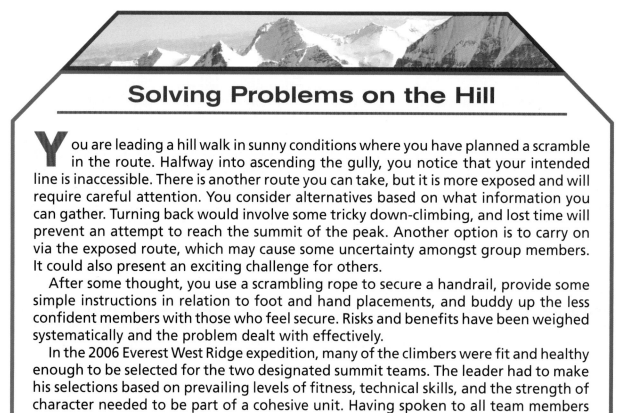

Solving Problems on the Hill

You are leading a hill walk in sunny conditions where you have planned a scramble in the route. Halfway into ascending the gully, you notice that your intended line is inaccessible. There is another route you can take, but it is more exposed and will require careful attention. You consider alternatives based on what information you can gather. Turning back would involve some tricky down-climbing, and lost time will prevent an attempt to reach the summit of the peak. Another option is to carry on via the exposed route, which may cause some uncertainty amongst group members. It could also present an exciting challenge for others.

After some thought, you use a scrambling rope to secure a handrail, provide some simple instructions in relation to foot and hand placements, and buddy up the less confident members with those who feel secure. Risks and benefits have been weighed systematically and the problem dealt with effectively.

In the 2006 Everest West Ridge expedition, many of the climbers were fit and healthy enough to be selected for the two designated summit teams. The leader had to make his selections based on prevailing levels of fitness, technical skills, and the strength of character needed to be part of a cohesive unit. Having spoken to all team members about their preferred options, climbers were selected using systematic thinking to assemble and then assess the options, risks, and benefits. Common sense and intuitive thinking aimed at predicting possible performance outcomes also guided the decision-making process. By allowing team members access to the overall process, emotional highs and lows were channelled into a collective force that added momentum for the climbers and the squad. This process demonstrated the high value that was attributed to every team member and to every role within the team.

gies enables people to successfully direct their attention. Improved concentration also helps to overcome the negative effects of arousal, which range from boredom and daydreaming to high levels of worry and fear.

In adventure education, participants may be required to keep focussed for extended times (such as on long multipitch climbs). Where events are changing, concentration can be consciously regulated by adjusting your focus up (or down) as situations demand (e.g., skiing on variable terrain). Such regulation involves selectively attending to priorities; in mountain guiding, this may include attending to navigational waypoints, weather, and group needs.

Maintaining ideal levels of physical and psychological freshness not only minimises environmental noise but also helps support concentration. Making the effort to say 'Stop!' when the mind is wandering is one simple way of restoring lost focus. Intentionally resorting to tunnel vision by attending only to one source can be refined through sustained practice. To displace the anxieties that might emerge from feeling overwhelmed by a large task (for example, an elongated, complicated climb), it may be helpful to cognitively break down that task into smaller, discrete chunks. This can restore the sense of control and mastery that characterises the growth mindset.

Another approach is to park, or banish, specific worries and address them in downtimes (times when you can relax). Setting a time to return to negative thoughts can help to displace those concerns in favour of more pressing issues. Knowing how people best learn and receive information—through observing, writing, listening, or practical methods—can also optimise their capacity to concentrate. Staying mentally active within any learning opportunity, which might include regularly asking searching questions of ourselves, others, and other options, can prevent boredom and allow new material to merge into what is already known. Importantly, lack of knowledge or understanding is often a cause of poor concentration. Between bouts of concentration, changing physical and psychological states (moving around, thinking about other things) can also help to rekindle interest and renew focus.

Staying Power and Effort

Endurance and tolerance within an unpredictable setting are abilities that draw on cognitive, emotional, and social skill sets. Patience and perseverance in the face of delay or provocation are helpful in remaining calm and mentally alert, especially in long-term adventures. Thinking rationally and empathetically is especially relevant in laborious endeavours where comfort may be hard to find. This quality was abundantly demonstrated by the Everest West Ridge climbers when they carried heavy loads for up to 8 hours without complaint in hostile, lonely conditions. Most already knew that they were undertaking this task without having any chance of being selected to make a summit attempt.

Hard work and persistence bring rewards in relation to personal development. New competencies are realised through dedicated practice, so despite setbacks and plateaus in learning, learning still takes place. For example, the learner who falls most during initial climbing sessions may well go on to become the better climber.

Attention to Detail

To minimise danger, precision and accuracy are requirements of adventure education. These include correct use of technical equipment and knowledge, leaving as little possible to chance. Luck always has a role to play in adventure education due to the fluidity of the environment. Still, this has to be balanced with the requirement for exact preparation and making in-field judgements. Methodological protocols for equipment use (so they become habits) and for monitoring changes in circumstance all help to minimise errors and promote safe practice, especially where stress might prevail (e.g., belaying and rope work, whiteout navigational conditions). Being precise in areas of personal responsibility (e.g., camping skills, personal accountability for kit) also protects against overburdening others.

Creative Thinking and Intuition

Adventure requires inventiveness and resourcefulness to prevail in times where there is no clear rationale for action. Common examples include the need to build a shelter from sparse materials or to find creative uses of available resources. Therefore, imagination must combine with analytical, logical thinking. Intuition has been described as a different way of knowing; it is not reliant on articulate fluency, but involves a holistic appreciation of a given situation (Claxton, 2000). Staying connected to use creative insight and spontaneity is essential in adventure education. Sometimes it is possible to know something without understanding why or how. Although there is a strong requirement for rationality and intentionality in adventure education, the freedom to develop intuitive thinking should be encouraged. Guided experimentation within activities and exploratory reflective practice both help to develop intuition.

Inquisitiveness and Curiosity

The celebrated outdoor educationalist Colin Mortlock (1984) regards inquisitiveness as the single most important aspect of intelligence in adventure education. He has referred to it as a prerequisite for adventure. It not only involves the acceptance of uncertainty but a willingness to explore unknown territory in the quest for challenge. This stimulus for the acquisition of knowledge and new experiences relates to both journeys to physical destinations and inner journeys of self-discovery. When people seek adventure, they typically embrace uncertainty whilst seeking to broaden horizons. This approach requires a curious mind and a desire to engage in unaccustomed behaviour to convert future possibilities into distinct probabilities. Inquisitiveness and asking questions of ourselves develops the capability to cope with a range of situations and contexts.

EMOTIONS (AFFECTIVE DOMAIN)

Feelings portray the immediate state of mind. They are entirely personal and link to innermost values. As with thinking, emotions need to be balanced—every positive emotion has a direct opposite. Emotions fluctuate with experiences and can influence the quality of further endeav-

ours. Experiencing a range of emotions (positive and negative) is necessary to expand the capacity to deal with the unpredictable challenges of mountaineering. Much adventure philosophy emphasises the human need to encounter the edges of individual psychological possibility, which involves feeling destabilised and emotionally disoriented. Personal development through adventure education involves appreciating the value of emotional ups and downs and accepting that learning emerges as much from mistakes as from success.

Learning to create positive emotions whilst facing a tough challenge is important for forward momentum. Today's theorists, such as Barbara Fredrickson (Fredrickson, Tugade, Waugh, & Larkin, 2003), take the view that positive emotions widen the array of cognitive and behavioural tendencies that people can deploy in a given situation. Building positive emotional skills (or intelligence) through progressive training can help people become more resilient in their learned attributes, social bonds, and abilities. By living in this way, and through regular involvement in challenging circumstances, these emotions can come to characterise individuals.

Consider the following example: A novice is grasping the fundamental techniques of rock climbing in a disused quarry. Her underlying tension about falling is inhibiting progress, even though she helped set up the safety system and is proficient on indoor climbing walls. She becomes increasingly reactive rather than coordinated and proactive. To help her, the facilitator aims to draw the negative emotions from her interpretations of these concerns. For example, he allows her to feel the protective quality of the harness, fall at will, take rests, and not be overly concerned about displaying precise technical skills. This allows the novice to adapt to the variations in the conditions (e.g., feel and condition of the rock, use of foot- and handholds, exposure to the elements). Eventually, a calmer approach develops and confidence grows—a better balance becomes established between current and evolving skills and the effort needed for success.

This measured approach builds positive emotions and self-belief by reducing the perceived risks and by supporting the courage needed to deal with them. The authenticity of the experience also provides the opportunity to develop new competencies.

Developing positive emotional skills allows people to feel confident in their capacity for success. An increase in perceived competence also heightens self-regulatory behaviour, where achievement is attributed to persistence and self-mastery over the task at hand. Figure 11.1, adapted from Bandura's self-efficacy theory (Bandura, 1997), shows how the development of confidence affects immediate and future learning. Providing climbing challenges matched to individual skill develops self-belief. This enables people to control perceived risks. Peer approval and encouragement from leaders inspires an even stronger sense of competence, which leads to self-fulfilment.

From such processes, it seems that adventure education can have a positive impact on attitudes and self-perceptions. It demonstrably improves

independence, confidence, self-esteem, feelings of control, self-efficacy, and coping strategies (Hattie et al., 1997). However, these positive developments hinge on effective facilitation. If a significant mismatch occurs and there is no support and encouragement, then the picture could be painted very differently. Panic (a negative emotion) can replace feelings of control, leading to feelings of inadequacy or even shame (more negative emotions). In contrast, when a challenge appears beyond the reach of a person, any sustained efforts to achieve it should be recognised and applauded. Positive feedback about improvement, wherever it can be found, refocuses attention on the task at hand. When dealing with anxiety, fear, or even panic, help the person to become calm, and be honest—frightened people are more scared of the unknown than the known. When appropriate, injection of humour can also lighten the moment.

Perceived competence = success

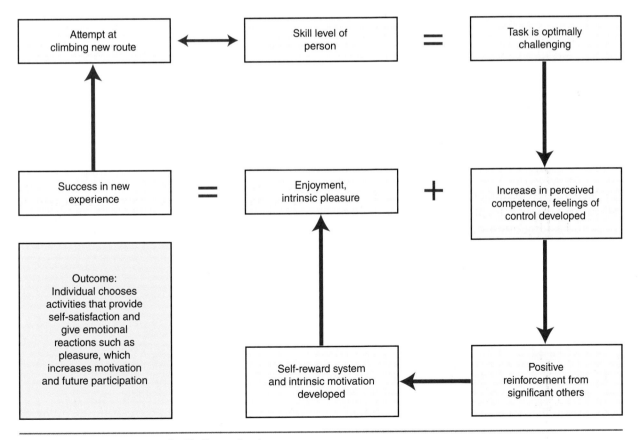

Figure 11.1 Competence and self-efficacy development.

One feature that seems central to developing emotional capability is courage. Using courage to manage fears involves resolving the cognitive, social, and emotional risks associated with a given scenario. These tests can include trying something new and persevering despite the fear of failure to forming relationships, showing humility, dealing with conflict calmly and with compassion, admitting error and learning from mistakes, maintaining integrity in the face of opposition, and so on. Overcoming such emotionally destabilising experiences creates an array of emotional intelligences that are not only beneficial in themselves but also build capacity for subsequent growth. Here are some other important emotional qualities associated with development through adventure education.

Vigour Vigour relates to the possession of vitality and energy. It may manifest itself in various forms, such as enthusiasm for challenges, dealing with disappointment, and optimism when things look bleak. Vitality in the face of fear may mask the inner struggle that eventually gives rise to constructive solutions.

Honesty in Yourself Honest personal evaluations provide an important safeguard for both individuals and groups. However, when people adopt egocentric evaluations, they can signal a loss of confidence in the value of decision making. Further, egocentric evaluations can lead to deception, cheating, and taking shortcuts on routine tasks. This threatens safety on any expedition, not least when any such behaviour creates problems for others. In this moment, trust in others can become compromised. Consider the implications of a social climate where trust is declining—put yourself in the position of a mountaineer beginning to experience the symptoms of altitude sickness on an 8,000-metre (26,245 ft) peak when others in the expedition seem driven by personal glory.

Empathy and Altruism Empathy is about appreciating another's need, and altruism involves providing assistance without expecting any reciprocal gesture. These qualities are socially derived and contain a strong emotional dimension. Based on compassion and cooperation, empathy and altruism represent the social

glue that binds people together. Such bonding and emotional displays develop trust. Sharing a rope or the hardship of expeditions helps to generate an appreciation of others' needs.

GROUP PROCESSES (SOCIAL SKILLS)

Humans are social creatures. The development of harmonious relationships in adventure education is necessary to succeed in complex tasks requiring coordinated effort. This even relates to a day's hill walk with unknown walking partners. Though some might like to believe that the creation of mountaineering teams is a magical process, it is better undertaken with clear thinking, common sense, and care for others. For the whole to be more effective than the sum of its parts, good leadership and interpersonal skill development are warranted. Such skills include good decision making and planning, ownership and sharing of responsibility, providing clear messages within equally clear channels of communication, commitment to team goals, trust building, and willingness to deal with unrest.

Research from the team event that was the 2006 Everest West Ridge expedition is helpful here. The approach to team selection was based on more than a combination of team members' knowledge and technical competence. We interviewed the mountaineers throughout their 2-year preparation and at Base Camp, and it became clear how the selection of team members and continual focus of squad activities were instrumental in maintaining harmony. In order of importance, the selection criteria included social compatibility, total commitment to the task, tolerance and support of others (especially regarding mistakes and shortcomings), loyalty, and communication in teamwork. Technical capability was lower on the list of priorities, especially for initial selection.

These priorities highlight the importance of developing a social network characterised by connectivity, emotional competence, trust, and dependency on others, since these are all qualities that will be sorely tested in prolonged exposure to extreme conditions. By prioritising these features, the expedition leaders were aiming to minimise the likelihood that unwanted developments might occur, such as individual isolation, hostility, and lost team cohesion. The sheer scale of what these climbers faced signifies the need for social connectivity. Imagine these experiences and compare them with your daily life: Prepare for 3 years; be away from home for an 80-day event that may not succeed just because of the weather; accept that a day's progress might move you forward 35 metres (115 ft) for 8 hours of work; and cope with continually losing your footing and winds that freeze and knock you over. Dressing will require 2 hours in –20 degrees Celsius (–4 degrees Fahrenheit), every step takes 10 breaths, and all you are aware of is your fatigue, your breathing, and your heartbeat.

Although these are extreme endeavours, the messages remain clear about the need for cohesion even in smaller adventure initiatives. Principles formulated by the leader and adopted by the group set the tone for the purpose and direction of the activity. This ethos should be agreed upon and made explicit to create and reinforce a clear philosophy of engagement in adventure education. It seems that certain qualities are required if people are to work well together in adventure education. Many of these qualities are related to the ability to act in personally responsible ways and in collectively responsible ways.

SPORT PSYCHOLOGY

How would you characterise the needs of a mountaineer who might be expected to successfully climb Everest? Burke and Orlick (2004) have identified seven core features: focus (especially in descents), mental toughness, setting short-term goals, drawing on past experiences, connecting to bodily sensations, feeling supported by other climbers, and believing you have the personal capability to complete the climb.

These features match well with the verbs and nouns that preface any reputable sport psychology text, including *Advances in Sports Psychology* (Horn, 2008). These labels all detail the concerns of sport psychology and include *behaviour, variations, group, leader, anxiety, motivation, traits, dispositions, orientation, skill, ability, understand, modify, explain, predict,* and *environment*.

They underline the range of issues that form the central business of sport psychology and therefore how it might be adopted to help mountaineers at the various stages of their careers.

Although *change* is not in the list, it is implicit to these concepts. A central feature of what sport psychologists do is manage change to optimise athletic performance, whether judged by a single event, a prolonged amount of time (such as on an expedition), or a lifetime. However, sport psychology is a relatively new science, and coherent relationships amongst the key variables remain elusive. Researchers and theoreticians continue to develop appropriate research paradigms and theoretical bases, and practitioners continue to adopt do-best approaches to help themselves or their charges.

Sport psychology moves beyond immediate responses to given events. Instead, attention is paid to recalling, practicing, and then refining appropriate behaviours through regular exercises to prepare for events that may arise. This not only refines technique, which makes outcomes more predictable, but also helps people to resort into their adaptive responses, whether the problem they foresee is physical or mental. Since some of what happens in mountaineering might be reasonably predicted in terms of fatigue, discomfort, risk of injury, and so on, this approach has considerable value. These issues also recur across the profile of experience, not least because experience often brings the pursuit of more demanding challenges. For example, Burke, Sparkes, and Allen-Collinson (2008) identified how climbers attempting to summit Everest recurrently experienced self-doubts about continuing their attempt and were regularly challenged by their own thoughts about quitting.

There is clear evidence in the published literature that athletes generate specific mental states, with and without training in sport psychology. Though athletes may behave in systematic ways to control their mental activity, even in the late 1990s sport psychologists reported that they could still learn new things about top athletes' psychology. For example, 24 U.S. psychologists reported four surprising facts that they had discovered about elite athletes: They were the same as other people, they were sometimes fragile with low self-confidence, they had self-control concerns, and they sometimes didn't work hard but still performed well (Sullivan & Nashman, 1998). That psychologists found these facts surprising underlines the need for interventions that are athlete and evidence based. What has not been shown is the extent of athletes' natural use of mental skills and their impact on areas such as performance, reaction to performance, or recovery from injury.

Sport psychology is an influential factor in achieving positive change in all these areas, yet sophisticated advocates recognise the need to more closely examine how change takes place, how it is best facilitated, and to what effect. Different approaches to sport psychology can regard mental activity as an antecedent, a mediator, or a consequence of sport-related behaviour. Further, prediction is often central to the business, such as how athletes will react whilst playing away from home in front of a hostile crowd and carrying an injury. In the context of mountaineering, selection of partners may involve how we predict the performance and behaviour of others during the tough times that we can anticipate.

MENTAL TRAINING

There has been a long tradition of seeking the appropriate cognitive set for levels of achievement within specific sports. It remains difficult to establish cause and effect between naturally occurring success and use of higher forms of cognition (such as metacognition, which is the act of thinking about thinking). However, what distinguishes novice from expert performers is the cognitive advantage of the elites, which develops through years in the sport. This may relate to winning medals, achievement of high performance standards, satisfaction with one's performance, and the length of the athletic career.

In mental training, or psychological skills training (PST), the sport psychologist's aim is to help athletes develop mental control, thought control, or concentration, which are all concepts that nonspecialists might regard as the same thing. The core PST skills, or the practices that develop mental control, are often grouped under

the term *mental exercises* or *mental skills exercises* (MSEs). Although there are unique features about mountaineering that contribute to its challenge and appeal, one of the reasons why a sport psychology approach may be helpful to participants relates to what we already know about how humans think when faced with risk.

Humans adopt two main types of thinking. System 1 thinking is characterised by limited thinking, risk aversion, automaticity, and simplicity. This type of thinking can be triggered by events or situations considered threatening or frightening. Inexperienced or novice participants may most readily adopt this approach, although we should not imagine that even experienced people are inured to fear in the mountains. In contrast, system 2 thinking is analytical, complex, rule-based, and less emotional. Grasping these distinctive thinking styles helps to explain why we believe personal growth emerges through systematic exposure to the demands of mountaineering. Having the skills that allow clear thinking in the face of risk enhances the chances of realistic prediction making. This is a core feature in ensuring safe and enjoyable sport involvement.

One characteristic that shows the shift from system 1 to system 2 thinking is that the current circumstances are no longer understood in terms of other people, systems, bad luck, or the sheer impossibility of existing tasks. System 1 thinking often is the result of preconscious or automatic mental processing, whereas system 2 thinking requires people to counter any individual preference to externalise and instead consider what they need to do to resolve the issues. Further, when resources are limited, priority is placed on what most effectively generates system 2 thinking and then identifying the smallest changes that bring about the most profound improvement. As part of intensive preparation for mountaineering, therefore, sport psychologists would encourage the development of psychological skills that can be deployed for any situation.

The many skills espoused by traditional sport psychology include goal setting, imagery, self-talk, and reinforcement. Although they each can be understood in isolation, they also can be used concurrently and to greater effect.

Goal Setting

Goal setting describes the planning associated with having clear outcomes for judging performance, supported by clear pathways (process goals) towards those outcomes. Goal setting can be distinguished from do-besting, which is an instinctive, unplanned, and less formalised way to do what is thought best in any given moment. Writing personal goals helps to develop and refine them whilst also heightening individual commitment and accountability to the goals. Empirically, the impact of goal setting is often compared with do-besting and is found to be far more effective. After completing a successful climb, a traditional do-best approach to get back safely can be compared with setting specific safety goals for the stages of the descent. Goals might include setting arrival times for the stages of the descent, directing attention to specific descent practices, or planning refuelling stops. The flexibility of goal setting means that it can be widely applied across a range of behaviours. Although there are limitations, adoption of the SMART acronym (specific, measureable, achievable, realistic, and time based) is widely supported not only for creating but also for judging the completion of goals.

Though there are strong, intuitively appealing reasons for setting group goals in group-based mountaineering, there is a lack of empirical evidence supporting the benefits of this. However, there may be advantages to group-based approaches. For example, they help make goals obvious, which brings accountability (answering the questions of who, how, and when). Discussions can also adjust unrealistic goals and add stretch to goals that are too easy.

For goal setting, Weinberg and colleagues (1993) reported that females set goals most frequently, team sport athletes set more goals for winning, and a majority of athletes (60 percent) preferred moderately difficult goals. Perhaps for this reason more than any other, many sport psychologists recommend an individualised approach to PST. In this way, PST can build on preexisting self-confidence and strengths.

Goal setting has a long history of effectiveness, but it is not universally effective. Even amongst athletes who report their best and worst sporting experiences, there are clear differences in goal-setting styles. In best experiences, 66 percent used performance goals (focusing on things to do). In worst experiences, 88 percent set goals relating to the result of the performance, or what it means to win or to lose (Jackson & Roberts, 1992). This highlights the need for developing and refining goals though several rounds of goal setting.

Coaching relationships also influence goal setting. For example, in set-up-to-fail syndrome, the idea of needing help (such judgements are often based on below-expected performance) simply emphasises low self-esteem. The extra attention that this often generates, albeit with the best of intentions, then confirms what athletes already know—that this response is reserved for underperforming people. The athlete's sense of competence, control, and motivation is reduced and worsens with every further misguided intervention. We sink into low expectations and are boxed in a trap of our own creation. Ironically, given the positive effects of goal setting, when people are trapped inside the set-up-to-fail syndrome, one unwanted response is taking misguided risks in an attempt to reestablish lost reputation.

More effective approaches may begin with an open exchange of views on what contributes to low-level performance. This progresses to describing how low performance was established, including the role of both parties. It concludes with everyone involved planning remedial actions to help solve the problem. Both parties then pay close attention to managing relapses from the new plan, which creates positive cycles but requires superiors to take a low-control approach.

Imagery

Imagery, as the word suggests, involves creating mental pictures relating to performance; the notion of the mind's eye captures what imagery is all about. Images may involve athletes seeing themselves negotiating difficult tasks or completing a highly technical skill. Recent studies suggest that the greater the detail that accompanies the mental images, the stronger will be the performance effect. Aspects such as specific physical movements, environmental factors (e.g., wind, isolation, cold), task, timing, learning history (i.e., experience), emotion, and perspective (i.e., implications of the event being imaged) should be considered in developing adaptive images. Some athletes need to imagine the timing or pattern of their movement at the appropriate speed because mistimed imagery can impair performance in highly technical activities. Athletes need to link to what they know of the performance context (mountaineers would need to connect to ambient temperature, hydration, fatigue states, and strong features of living circumstances) to optimise the value of imagery exercises.

One crucial understanding about imagery is that it is the controlled re-creation of beneficial images of the athlete performing. This is one way of increasing so-called time on task, even when physical training is not possible or is unwise (e.g., when fatigued, when access to physical practice is impossible, when the physical environment is unduly hazardous). Climbers who are preparing for big expeditions often report reading all available accounts of previous climbs and consulting widely with others who have made those climbs, both of which may enhance imagery. Whatever the situation for adopting imagery, we recommend considerable practice to heighten the vividness and controllability of the images, positive attitudes and expectations regarding imagery effects, skills in achieving relaxation at will, and capacity for internal focus.

Outdoor athletes have long reported using imagery to improve their performance by controlling either their cognition or motivation (Salmon, Hall, & Haslam, 1994). For example, amongst 28 New Zealand Olympic-class sailors, 17 (61 percent) practiced visualisation exercises (Legg et al., 1997). Almost all U.S. athletes (99 percent) have reported using imagery, and over 90 percent of U.S. coaches have reported working to develop this skill in athletes (Murphy, 1994).

Self-Talk

Self-talk exercises aim to control the ways in which we talk to ourselves. Given that there are so many occasions when mountaineers might be isolated, this may be an important skill for sustaining quality performance. Although mental chatter seems universal (try to stay mentally silent for 30 seconds and you will see what we mean), the way in which people go about it can be distinctive. In everyday life, negative self-talk is often at the root of avoiding important tasks, which may make it problematic in demanding mountaineering scenarios. This underlines the need for preplanning and practicing adaptive coping approaches. Positive self-talk may relate to emotional-based coaching (e.g., 'I can cope with this,' 'This is what I planned for') or coaching- or problem-based coping (e.g., 'Move your right hand, then with your left foot . . .', 'To handle this we need to . . .').

Obviously, the various forms of self-talk can be combined, but they are most effective when they are planned and repeated. Preplanning on challenging routes may help mountaineers establish their private patter for different parts of a climb. Leaders may also provide moments of quiet so that team members can withdraw from group activities to get their minds right. In this moment, they are adopting choice points, which are known to enhance the use of preplanned self-talk. Experience may help some people develop a set of self-talk statements that manage most expectable issues, whereas unexpected events may create more problems. Establishing strong routines may be one way to ensure a predictable self-talk response. For extended high-altitude expeditions where long amounts of downtime can be spent in tents and where winds are so strong that they prevent conversation, self-talk may be central to maintaining morale.

Planning the script for self-talk may be as important for coping with the inevitable hardships associated with performance as it is for handling high levels of success. Other forms of self-talk include the repetition of positive, preplanned affirmations (e.g., 'Love steep climbing') triggered by common daily events (such as the telephone ringing). Mountaineers might adopt this approach by repeating specific affirmations at regular points in the day, such as when they first handle a specific item of equipment or every time they pick up their rucksack. The positive effects of self-talk may be as much to do with displacing negative notions (e.g., 'Don't let me fall') with action-oriented expressions. Although self-talk is usually unheard, promoting its private use may be one way to create a positive spoken environment.

Reinforcement

Reinforcement is central to motivation and sustained involvement, especially in challenging circumstances. Anything that increases the likelihood of repeating a specific behaviour is a reinforcement agent. Therefore, at an interpersonal level, we need to think beyond obvious material rewards to attention, praise, and the provision of even modest resources (such as a square of chocolate). There are positive and negative rewards, or rewards that are either broadly pleasurable or punishing. Others consider rewards as either primary (where the reward meets a basic need such as food or water) or secondary (where the reward is a consequence of something else, such as a pat on the back for doing something well).

In high-altitude mountaineering, it may be important that climbers find value in undertaking the dog work so that others may succeed. Another intrapersonal reinforcement for international mountaineering may be the desire to interact with other cultures or with transcendental experiences of just being in the mountains. Time should be allocated for these factors so that motivation is sustained. Clearly, then, an understanding of reinforcement is crucial for leaders and can guide how leaders orient group members to the interpersonal behaviours they wish to see on expeditions.

Another approach recognises two other rewards: intrinsic (where the pleasure associated with the reward has no obvious external value but satisfies some covert need or desire) and extrinsic (where the reward meets an externally validated standard, such as money or recognition). Although it may seem counterintuitive, providing rewards at the wrong times or in the wrong ways can undermine motivation. Central to these unwanted outcomes is anything that leads to participants feeling manipulated or where the rewards undermine the intrinsic pleasure associated with an activity.

The use of punishment is an example where responses can be delayed but subversive, not least because the relationship between the punisher and the punished may become strongly altered. Equally, providing substantial positive rewards for modest behaviour change or success can undermine the effects of subsequent praise. Rewards can also be undermining after success has been achieved; some rewards (such as too much beer) may undo months, and possibly years, of training and preparation. It may be wise to include any such rewards within normal preparation routines so that when success does come along, these behaviours are not so destructive.

The reward system employed by a coach or leader creates a motivational climate that athletes quickly learn to understand. Leaders determine the reward system through the ways in which they most consistently reward group members; therefore, leader behaviour sets the tone. Depending on how interactions develop, there are two main pathways for the resulting motivational climate. In the first, leaders can create a particularly adaptive environment by offering rewards to group members (or units) according to their effort, persistence, and strategy. This becomes the currency by which further rewards are earned. In the second approach, rewards centre on judgements of outcome quality and on personalisation. Problematically, this second approach encourages favouritism, undermines effort-based approaches, and may undermine some group members to the extent that they engage with self-handicapping and sabotage of group attempts. Clearly, the first approach seems most suited to groups where hardship and setbacks will be relatively commonplace.

Arousal (or Emotional) Management

Arousal describes the all-inclusive range of factors that switch on when the idea of an athletic challenge comes to mind. For this reason, arousal has both physical and psychological components and can be used to gauge how appropriately aroused a person is for that task. Overarousal is associated with anxiety, and it is debilitating because it is characterised by internal discomfort and nervousness. The tension it produces especially impairs decision-making and fine-motor skills, not least because of the effort needed to reregulate the imbalanced state. In relation to group-based activities, the emotional regulation associated with arousal is also important.

Given our human proclivity to respond to the emotions around us, it is clear that over- and underaroused people will influence others. Attention, therefore, may need to be paid to establishing how camp talk influences morale (in much the same way as corridor conversations influence the workplace). In Burke and Orlick's (2004) accounts of climbers who successfully ascended Everest, feeling the support of other climbers was an important factor. This type of support has a powerful effect on the emotional climate for mountaineers. Burke and Orlick's sample comprised mostly men, demonstrating that it is unwise to dismiss this subject as unmasculine.

Within positive psychology, positive emotions are seen as a direct antidote to negative emotions, not least because they signal safety and freedom from fear. Positive emotions actively displace negative emotions and require little mental effort for their effects to become obvious. This contrasts with the impact of negative emotions, which often preclude accurate prediction making and consideration of possibilities. For this reason, emotional regulation may offer a gateway to improved openness, learning, and creativity. Cognitive psychologists suggest that this may be, in part, due to improved working memory and verbal fluency.

Positive psychology is also appealing to so-called ordinary people because the behaviours leading to positive emotions are accessible to, and easily practiced by, most people. Positive psychology is rooted in people's actions as they overcome the daily hassles and anxieties that pepper even the most normal of lives. It is great to know that we can think and act ourselves into positive emotions.

This relationship supports the adoption of the Big Mac attack in working with others. The Big Mac attack roughly describes, in diagram form, how much reward and correction coaches and mentors should use to facilitate athletes' learning. For bun, read *praise*, and for burger, read

correction. However, just as buns and burgers come in different sizes, so too does our capacity to handle correction (which is often experienced as criticism) and our need for support. These issues have been expressed arithmetically in the positivity-to-negativity ratio. Importantly, the idea of a ratio suggests trading off behaviours and interactions.

The positivity-to-negativity ratio suggests that every negative emotional experience must be countered by a minimum of three positive emotional experiences. In this understanding, the creation of positive social environments is more than a luxury; it is an absolute necessity for high-level human functioning. Environments that produce the greatest positivity typically involve appropriate levels of challenge, generating positive social interactions with both friends and unfamiliar others. Given that 80 percent of adults are in the counterpart state to flourishing—that is, languishing—preferences for criticism sit uncomfortably alongside the positivity of the newly revised Big Mac attack. Perhaps counting daily instances of how often we praise others would be a good starting point.

Given the lack of obvious examples for mountaineering, it may be instructive to follow the six principles proposed by Freudenberg and colleagues (1995) for guiding effective interventions. These include (1) tailoring to the specific population and its setting; (2) involving participants in planning, implementation, and evaluation; (3) integrating efforts to change people, social and physical environments, communities, and policies; (4) linking participants' concerns to broader life concerns and to a vision of a better society, (5) using existing resources within the environment; and (6) building on the strengths of participants and their communities.

CONCLUSION

We have aimed to present a comprehensive evaluation of psychological skills that can be adopted within adventure education, and mountaineering in particular. The first section considered a humanistic appreciation for psychological functioning that can be developed through experiential learning in adventure education. The second section looked at psychological strategies that can enhance specific performance outcomes.

It is clear that, despite differences in focus, application, and terminology, both the humanistic and psychological approaches attend to adaptable aspects of human behaviour, whether from cognitive, emotional, or social perspectives. Each has something to offer mountaineers at the different levels of performance. Both approaches show that for human potential to be realised, there is a need to blend systematic, philosophical, and creative skill learning. This is achieved through effective practice in realistic environments with supportive mechanisms. Both approaches also advocate holistic, longitudinal development of the intuitive, automatic, or self-regulated strategies that direct behaviour.

KEY IDEAS

▸ Adventure is a relative concept that can facilitate personal growth within a broad range of participants.

▸ Psychological fitness is a key element in the acquisition and performance of adventure-based skills such as technical proficiency, social competence, and environmental awareness.

▸ An ideal psychological state is achieved through the optimal alignment of thoughts, feelings, and physical capability with challenges presented.

▸ Cognitive skills in adventurous activities involve more than decision making or problem solving. Other skills include mental sustainability, tolerance, effort, precision, creativity, and curiosity.

▸ Broadening of emotional capacity (intelligence) through adventure heightens self-regulatory behaviour and helps develop new competencies.

▸ Social connectivity and compatibility, as opposed to combined technical proficiency, can be more important in adventure endeavours with shared objectives.

▸ Sport psychologists help manage systematic change to optimise athletic performance in preparation for and within singular or prolonged events.

▸ The range of issues that underline sport psychology can also be adapted in a performance context within adventure activities such as mountaineering.

▸ An array of psychological skills can be used in adventure settings, such as goal setting, imagery, self-talk, reinforcement, and arousal (emotional) control.

▸ Using such skills, mountaineers can purposefully adopt analytical system 2 thinking rather than emotionally reactive system 1 approaches in situations of risk.

▸ Effective interventions bring tailored-made programmes of positive skill practices into the performance environment and broader life contexts.

CHAPTER

12

Resilience

Jim McKenna, John Allan, Steve Cobley, and Mark Robinson

That wonderful world of high mountains, dazzling in their rock and ice, acts as a catalyst. In the extreme tension of the struggle, on the frontier of death, the universe disappears and drops away beneath us. Space, time, fear, suffering no longer exist. Everything then becomes quite simple. As on the crest of a wave, or in the heart of a cyclone, we are strangely calm—not the calm of emptiness, but the heart of action itself.

Maurice Herzog, from Annapurna: The First Conquest of an 8,000-Metre Peak

In this chapter we describe the broad range of factors that make up psychological resilience. We also provide a rationale for why we need to build resilience across societies. Using a blend of theory and practical application, we demonstrate how resilience can be developed through adventure education. Notwithstanding the semantic debates about what distinguishes adventure education from outdoor education and so on, we explain how the broad spectrum of adventure can be used in helping people to become resilient, from junior school children to youths, parents, teachers, students, and captains of industry.

WHAT IS RESILIENCE?

Look at the statements in the following list. As you read through this chapter, try to keep at least some of the items in mind because we will also refer to them. Give yourself a score for each item using a scale from 1 (not very good at this) to 10 (very good at this). Be honest.

Score (1-10)

____ I am compassionate and contribute to society.

____ I am empathetic.

____ I am stress hardy.

____ I establish realistic goals and expectations.

____ I feel in control of my life.

____ I feel special (not self-centred) and I help others to feel the same.

____ I learn from both success and failure.

____ I live responsibly based on considered values.

____ I use effective communication and interpersonal skills.

____ I use solid problem-solving and decision-making skills.

If you had to provide a label that defines the items in this table, what would it be? We suggest an appropriate collective term for these 10 questions might be *resilience*, which has strong relevance for notions of personal growth. Resilience is commonly associated with the ability to bounce back from situations that test our resolve. Despite its rarity in the tightest of times, it is a remarkably common feature. Resilience links to personal growth through the deployment of strategies learned through previous experiences with adversity. This form of growth allows us to bounce beyond our original position to face future testing circumstances with greater capacity.

Though resilience seems to have everyday relevance, its universal meaning remains difficult to establish. Psychologists continue to debate whether resilience is an instinctive, underlying psychological quality that underpins human development or a series of related yet distinctive qualities. Here we use the term to describe the beliefs people hold about themselves and others. These beliefs and other qualities make up the mindset that helps people deal with daily and prolonged hassles. Three core features provide the essential scaffolding of a resilient life: the capacity to face and then face down hardship, the ability to find meaning in life, and the ability to improvise (Coutu, 2009).

One recent review by Joseph and Linley (2006) asserted that a slightly different range of strategies allows us to adjust our behaviour in difficult situations. These strategies include building and nurturing relationships, staying positive, achieving life balance, and becoming more reflective. Although some of these options may seem beyond us, when they result from intentional acts they place us at the heart of creating a resilient mindset. Resilience, therefore, can be learned. Having the capacity to share positive resilience experiences with others also suggests that resilience may be catching. Providing opportunities to share these experiences may be a first step in helping it grow in others. Adventure education that is properly conceived, planned, and facilitated can offer the opportunity to develop not only the knowledge but also the skills that lead to personal growth.

Resilience is not a new concept. Life is harsh and resilience may have been expected of people in order to survive. Monty Python's 'Four Yorkshiremen' recounts progressively more absurd stories of harsh upbringings, the sketch illustrating that each person or subsequent generation claims to have endured the greatest suffering. Contrary to the notion of the youth of today not knowing they're born, the complex interactions of stressors that we each face make it impossible to directly understand another person's hardships. What we do know, though, is that modern society is just as full of incidents of triumph over adversity as history is replete with survival stories from horrendous conditions that can teach

and inspire us. Many best-selling adventure books reflect stories of breathtaking courage and determination in seemingly impossible circumstances and environments—think of Joe Simpson and Tony Bullimore in recent times and the extraordinary Ernest Shackleton in the last century. However, most of our struggles relate to daily life—job uncertainty, local environmental problems (such as flooding), relationship disturbances, domestic or residential instability, ill health—and these can appear mundane by comparison with the great adventurers' experiences. However, all of these experiences can create not only an isolated burden but also an accumulating load that causes people to malfunction in some way.

Although we can label people as resilient, they may be just as likely as anyone else to experience the shock, anger, grief, or sadness of any given event. Our interest lies not in fixed labelling but how we can help people build and maintain personal growth by learning to adapt to their circumstances. What marks the resilient mindset is its ability to take control and restore functioning rather than accepting a disturbed state as normal. For this reason, the resilient mindset parallels with early ideas relating to intelligence (Piaget, 1963). In a rejection of narrow definitions of intelligence it has been defined as knowing what to do when you don't know what to do, which is something that is central to our thinking about resilience. In relation to adventure education, many educators believe such a definition of intelligence is also appropriate given the speed with which environmental conditions can change and the importance of knowing how to respond to unfolding circumstances.

In exceptional human endeavours, such as high-altitude mountaineering, where situations change rapidly and demands and risks are high, resilience is needed to sustain both performance and performers. In 2004, British military climbers preparing to climb Everest in 2006 by arguably its most difficult route—the West Ridge—collectively penned a list of 10 expectations for each team member. Their democratically devised list was indicative of their need for interpersonal compatibility. Expedition members, and especially the expedition leaders, vigorously pursued these features during preparations. This all helped to establish the ethos of the expedition, which was to provide personal growth for expedition members. Each climber also carried a credit-card-sized list of these expectations throughout the 3 years of preparation to reinforce the agreed-upon principles. Additionally, the cards were intended to generate a sense of collective responsibility and social connection. These were all factors that the expedition leaders saw as important for building the conviction needed to complete the challenge. The list was compiled in no particular order and is detailed here:

> Honesty in yourself
>
> Tolerance of others
>
> Loyalty
>
> Teamwork
>
> Communication
>
> Mental robustness
>
> Attention to detail
>
> Sense of humour
>
> Total commitment to the task
>
> Physical fitness

This range of qualities has considerable resonance with our initial list of statements. They also can be grouped in other ways, such as according to other accepted hallmarks of resilience, namely emotional competency (learned awareness, control, management of one's own and others' emotional states), cognitive competence (positive thinking, decision-making capability), and social connectedness (skills required to communicate effectively, including asking for assistance). We will revisit these qualities later when we discuss group resilience.

The responses of high-altitude climbers to unpredictable conditions or accidents, sometimes involving the death of teammates, is similar to reactions of people to natural disasters, such as Hurricane Katrina or England's 2007 floods. Such events become catastrophic when their negative emotional effects impede the capacity to think and respond. Alternatively, positive handling of negative events can invigorate people to persevere in adversity and attain unexpectedly high levels of achievement. Rather than focusing on negative features of human development, positive psychology embraces the notion that growth occurs when positive factors enhance personal strengths and mental health. Focusing on growth and the capacity to learn new skills can build resilience to the most arduous of circumstances.

In preparing for the Everest West Ridge expedition, climbers learned to become resilient by recognising, building, and then reliving their personal strengths. These signature strengths might include strong emotional regulation, which is often the precursor to imaginative problem solving and decision making. In any unexpected adventure education environment, it is wise to extend personal and group boundaries by establishing a group culture that celebrates unified strength. The overall effect of such a climate is that people foresee more options in any given situation and look for solutions rather than focusing on problems. Therefore, this apparently unimportant issue of atmosphere is central to knowing what to do when you don't know what to do. We will show how adventure education can help build resilience in positive ways with an aim of transferring such learning to other contexts. We begin by providing a rationale for resilience building based on the fundamental relationship of resilience to health.

RESILIENCE HAS HEALTH-GIVING PROPERTIES

Growing evidence supports the need to build resilience within our so-called advanced societies. Change is happening faster than we can understand or manage, from our ecological concern for the planet to financial collapse, from education to welfare. To survive and even prosper in potentially destructive times, people rely on the flexibility and self-awareness that resilience provides. The connections between negative experiences and ill health make this clear. Research continually shows that feeling bad about something is more meaningful than feeling it is just a passing experience. The fields of social epidemiology (how social conditions influence health) and psychoneuroimmunology (how psychological processes interact with our nervous and immune systems) show that what we think about our circumstances will predict short-, mid-, and long-term health. Emotional dysfunction resulting from ordinary stressors such as relationship problems or poor working conditions can bring a cascade of harmful health effects such as immune deficiency and clinical depression. Even where people appear to suffer no apparent ill effects, they may be adopting coping strategies that only repress the true impact, which emerges later. Adventure education may provide an important antidote to such pervasive life conditions.

Where stress is intensive and perhaps prolonged, such as in war or civil disturbance, the end result may be post-traumatic stress disorder (PTSD), a nervous breakdown or a combination of harmful diseases. For example, recent data from the Iraq War suggest that there may be more damage done to U.S. veterans through PTSD than through battlefront attacks. These may appear to be adult-only concerns, but in recent years the prominence of PTSD amongst young people has begun to be recognised. Thirty-three years after the Aberfan disaster (where 144 people, 116 of them children, were killed when coal waste slid onto a mining village), symptoms of PTSD were still found in almost one in three survivors. Other recent events and trends, such as the rise in attacks on schoolchildren (e.g., Columbine), exposure to problematic parenting, drug abuse, and low educational attainment have led the American Psychological Association to identify resilience as one of the three revised Rs of education (the others being responsibility and reasoning). These events refute, at least in part, the oft-quoted aphorism, 'What doesn't kill you only makes you stronger.'

Resilience helps protect against stress and ill health. Numerous case studies have shown that positive adaptation to distressing situations helps to sustain both health and healing. These stressors might include chronic illness or injury, poverty, sequential failures, relationship breakdown, unemployment, or bereavement. Paradoxically, the intentional development of resilience involves deliberate exposure to a harmful or unpleasant experience. Just as immunity to infections is gained through the controlled exposure to a harmful agent, overcoming challenges provides a form of psychological inoculation where further equivalent harmful experiences create no harm. Additionally, more positive responses can emerge in the absence of harm. Other understandings see resilience as reducing the scale of immediate damage whilst also quickening a return to normal functioning, or recovery.

Building resilience systematically involves first developing and then refining the capacity to repel negativity, which then creates the possibility for expanding the problem-solving repertoire. In another psychological domain, flourishing, researchers emphasise the importance of having three positive experiences for each negative experience to ensure high-level functioning in daily life. For this reason we broadly reject the wilful creation of harmful biological states, some of which may create irreversible biological effects, and we advocate a focus on authentic, positive developmental programmes. We recommend carefully scaled and progressively weighted challenges. This weighting involves individualised perceptions of reality and what would represent a demand beyond established capacity. Sufficient time and support should then be provided to optimise adjustment and development. Systematic adventure education generates challenges that require people to seek—and find—something extra within themselves.

Meeting a challenge often initiates positive feelings (confidence and excitement) that quickly replace initial anxiety, fear, and self-doubt. To demonstrate the practicalities of building resilience, we now identify how the major characteristics of adventure education interact to facilitate personal growth. These interconnected components include the physical environment, participants, challenges or activities, group dynamics, and the facilitation of experiences that people benefit from and can take away into other elements of daily life.

ADVENTURE EDUCATION CAN BUILD RESILIENCE

Adventures obviously include elements of uncertainty. This uncertainty is created by combining unfamiliar environments with unknown outcomes. The combined effects of a novel physical and social environment plus a culture of perceived risk taking can provide an ideal breeding ground for resilience. In essence, carefully nurtured adventure education takes people back to their basic elements in ways of thinking and responding to adversity. Carefully handled, these experiences can generate new perspectives on daily circumstances.

The ability to improvise in difficult situations is a core feature of resilience. The unknowingness, potential adversity, and need to improvise add a unique dimension to the ways in which resilience might be tested and developed. Recognising this link, the maxim 'Improvise, adapt, and overcome' seems appropriate. Consider the following scenario as a relatively common form of unknowingness in the outdoors:

> You are out walking on a broad, flat, undistinguished, and boggy moor. You are with two colleagues. Without warning, a dense mist descends, reducing visibility to less than 10 metres (33 ft). You cannot see the broader landscape or physical markers to help identify where you are. You decide to keep walking, but after 20 more minutes, you realise you are utterly lost.

What aspects of resilience would be best deployed here? What elements should you use to assist a fearful colleague? How can you use this experience to help develop your colleague's resilience?

Many people report that adventure education creates a new sense of freedom and identity. Further, group activities challenge people to interact with others and learn to value their contributions. This understanding sustains our view that authentic adventure education acts as a motivator for positive behaviours and the development of those protective qualities contained in our original list.

Research suggests that a range of activities can have a positive impact on participants' attitudes, beliefs, and self-perceptions. Land- and water-based pursuits are used as vehicles within a natural context to engender personal growth. It is not so much the activities themselves that bring about these outcomes but a combination of inherent holistic challenges (with distinctive emotional, physical, and cognitive features) interacting with the environment.

In support of this contention, we offer this line of evidence. In a recent study of over 1,500 university students attending a 1-week adventure education programme, we tried to identify any unique characteristics of the low-resilience students. Comparing their responses to a range of attitudes, values, and adventure education experiences, the only difference amongst low-resilient students was that they were less frequently inspired by the countryside. No differences in exposure to eight elements of programme content could distinguish the levels of resilience. These results point to the importance of mindset for determining how people respond to experiences. For guides and leaders, it also emphasises the importance of making time to appreciate the splendour of the environment. Equally, it underlines the need to be sensitive and respond to any growing negativity or anxiety that may close the mind to such beauty.

This interconnectivity between the recipient and the environment provides a context that may result in a revised sense of wholeness. The solitude of the wide ocean and the beauty of the snow-topped peak contribute to moments of affirmation, and they can exist despite living a quite different life away from adventure education. There is little doubt that the inspiring effects of being in a natural setting can create a sense of appreciation, belonging, unity, and tranquillity. The quote introducing this chapter and the following scenarios exemplify the significance of this flowlike immersion of integrated activity within a stimulating environment.

> Eight hours into a summit attempt, a climber is perched on the North Face of Everest above 8,000 metres (26,245 ft). He is in the death zone where bodily functions are rapidly decreasing. In between taking 10 breaths for every step of a traverse, he records the sunrise on a small camera, thinking, 'Just look at that sunrise—who else is going to see this?'

> A senior member of the expedition team records that 'coming back morally intact' is the foremost purpose, even at the expense of not summiting following 3 years of methodical preparation.

> —*2006 Everest West Ridge expedition*

Dawn rises in the Spanish Pyrenees and even though it is a summer month, it is bitterly cold at this hour. Three climbers ascend 1,000 metres (3,280 ft) from their camp in a secluded col before it becomes unbearably hot. They are traversing the high-level route of the whole mountain range in 50 days and are behind schedule. Still, they devote time to observe the majestic sight of griffon vultures rising on a whirlpool of invisible warm air until the birds are almost in touching distance on the knife edge of the ridge. This is not a moment to be missed. The moment lasts over an hour.

—*John Allan, Pyrenees Traverse expedition, 1993*

People with resilient mindsets demonstrate self-awareness and interdependency with others, as well as what can be deemed *spirituality*. This brings to surface a feature of Coutu's (2009) recent characterisation of resilience, drawn from the accounts of Holocaust survivors, who survived within unspeakable environments. These people held a deep belief that life, no matter the circumstances, is meaningful. For some, personal survival was connected to their wish to stay alive to tell others about what happened. The similarity with items from our initial list, such as 'I live responsibly based on considered values,' 'I feel in control of my life,' and 'I feel special (not self-centred),' suggests that these may all be interconnected, existential issues. These perceptions and experiences are associated with increased coping skills, greater resistance to stress, greater optimism about life, greater levels of social support, and lowered levels of anxiety.

An ecological appreciation of the natural environment states that human existence equates with that of all other species and that we must protect the environment that sustains these species. In his pioneering book *Adventure Alternative*, Colin Mortlock (1984) describes peak experiences in adventure education and how people experience a respect and fusion with different cultures (whether from different layers of our own society or from others) and natural settings. These have been described as going through a door into another world and living on the edge of life—in essence, coming to understand how engagement with the outdoors holds clues to some of the riddles of human existence. It also seems that even in the most arduous of circumstances in adventure education, a timeless appreciation of beauty and moral philosophical positions can occur. This may also underline why adventure education is valuable for generating self-autonomy and ideals for collective community.

CAN ADVENTURE EDUCATION BUILD RESILIENCE FOR ALL PARTICIPANTS?

Studies suggest that age, gender, background, and expectations of participants may influence the benefits of adventure education. Adults who are participating voluntarily may benefit due to high motivation from the outset. Likewise, people expecting to gain from a programme may be motivated to achieve more than those with lower expectations.

Adventure, however, is a relative concept—what is perceived as challenging and high risk for one person will be seen differently by others. People have different levels of competence, and because environments and situations possess variable levels of risk, adventures will differ by person, place, and context. Adventure education is known for its inclusive appeal and for flexibility in meeting the needs of distinctive groups. This ranges from children with learning disabilities aiming to become more independent to executives striving to become more effective leaders. Resilience is the element that houses much of the potential for behavioural change. It is how we construct and modify adventure education that releases this potential. Age, gender, and ability should not be a limiting factor for such achievement—challenging competence whilst also offering support is what will ignite capability and transform it into achievement.

Consider this example: On a perfect October day, a diverse group is being led on a hill walk to ascend Tryfan in North Wales. There are male and female students, a young boy of 10, and a middle-aged woman. Some are experienced walkers, others complete novices. All have different expectations and do not know what they will encounter. Techniques are progressively introduced in relation to safe movement and group management. The route is exposed and seems beyond the participants' technical capacity, yet all achieve the goal of reaching the summit and returning safely.

On reflection, all the participants learned from their involvement. The range of challenges presented was as diverse as the group. At certain stages some operated below their existing competency, and still they experienced fun activities where little concentration was required. Others, despite operating near their personal limitations, felt their control increasing as the end of the walk neared, building their confidence for hill walking. Others may have been generally fearful, and for them the walk represented the unknown and untested. For some, their uncertainties were linked to the group or having to exert unfamiliar levels of effort. Consider the wide-ranging nature of resilience-building qualities from our original list that have been promoted within these few hours. Which of them could now be transferred to similar contexts?

ADVENTURE EDUCATION BUILDS COLLECTIVE RESILIENCE

Adventure education often generates group situations that depend on social integration and responsibility. This collective dependency, as might be seen in everyday interactions on an expedition, can be used to shape individual or group characteristics. The reciprocity that evolves within groups also provides participants with a sense of being valued and supported. These subjective experiences create bonds that not only help the group to function but also support individuals through testing moments. Such mutual reliance may also require that group members learn to balance the needs of the group with their own. Altruistic behaviour and the ability to gain the support of others are attributes associated with relational competence, another component of resilient behaviour.

Resilience literature stresses the importance of peer relationships for learning about shar-

ing, taking turns, patience, empathy, and communication. In adventure education, this is never more important than when planning, preparing, and executing long-term expeditions, which involves many people in multiple tasks and roles. How well these individuals interact, coordinate, and connect will affect the quality of the required outcomes. Earlier we considered the 10 principles that denoted the ethos of the 2006 Everest West Ridge expedition and that house many features of resilience. In this context, feelings of mutual dependence focussed on common objectives that helped to bond team members—the atmosphere was strongly kinlike. This created and sustained honest emotional expression and sharing. Though these qualities are generic and broad, they provided the context within which particular values, thoughts, attitudes, and behaviours were supported. Leaders had determined that these qualities and behaviours were central to developing individual and social qualities whilst also helping to build the social health of the group. These leaders had wisely appreciated that elements of social connectedness and relationships have as much to say about health as they do about interpersonal behaviour, effectiveness, or productivity.

Loyalty was another of the 10 attributes listed for the expedition, and synonymous with loyalty is trust. Trust is a key feature in maintaining group resilience, and it comes in at least three forms: organisational, strategic, and personal. Leaders, coworkers, and group members all play a role in building or undermining trust, which influences understandings of cause and effect and, therefore, the predictions people make about impending actions or events. Where trust is low, so too is predictability. Low trust profoundly limits the potential for planning and committing to any plans that need to be made in anticipation of future events.

The immediate implications for outdoor events are obvious. High trust is necessary for successful management of environments that have low predictability—that is, we already know what we should do in difficult moments where direct assistance and communication may not be possible. However, these conditions have added subtlety, such as when groups include people from backgrounds where trust was uncommon or where interpersonal relationships and behaviour continually erode levels of trust. This highlights the importance of trust building and considerate care for others, as reflected in our scale item, 'I feel special (not self-centred) and I help others to feel the same.'

A further example may be helpful. It highlights the social skills needed to manage events in hazardous adventure education conditions.

Imagine a strong, healthy climber who feels ready for an impending adventure education challenge, having trained hard for a weeklong trip in the mountains with two friends and one friend of a friend. At about 3 p.m. on the last day of their expedition in late October, heavy rain starts. Equipment is lost and all four members of the group are hungry, wet, and cold. Within minutes, low cloud descends, minimising visibility and bringing biting cold air. Just as two of the members fall out, another trips and breaks an ankle.

Which elements of resilience are most likely to break down in the least resilient member of your group? What behaviours or responses may result?

As we considered our response to this unexpected challenge of lost kit and injury in hazardous conditions, we identified an ongoing need within groups to detect the factors that can cause one person to react badly in a given moment and another to accept the events and continue towards a positive resolution. Calhoun and Tedeschi (2004) describe this as shifting from surviving to thriving. Clearly, our hypothetical situation implicates thinking, feeling, and behaviour and has relevance to skill development, group selection, and group behaviour and conduct. For all these layers and considerations, resilience seems an appropriate concept on which to focus when preparing to be in the outdoors either for prolonged amounts of time or when personal or collective resources are being stretched.

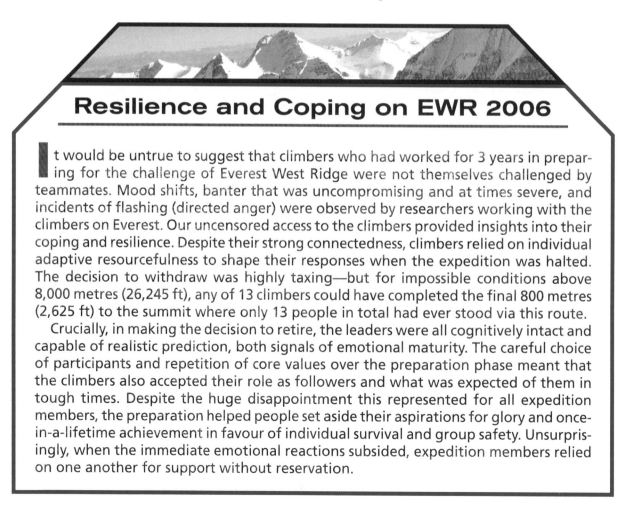

Resilience and Coping on EWR 2006

It would be untrue to suggest that climbers who had worked for 3 years in preparing for the challenge of Everest West Ridge were not themselves challenged by teammates. Mood shifts, banter that was uncompromising and at times severe, and incidents of flashing (directed anger) were observed by researchers working with the climbers on Everest. Our uncensored access to the climbers provided insights into their coping and resilience. Despite their strong connectedness, climbers relied on individual adaptive resourcefulness to shape their responses when the expedition was halted. The decision to withdraw was highly taxing—but for impossible conditions above 8,000 metres (26,245 ft), any of 13 climbers could have completed the final 800 metres (2,625 ft) to the summit where only 13 people in total had ever stood via this route.

Crucially, in making the decision to retire, the leaders were all cognitively intact and capable of realistic prediction, both signals of emotional maturity. The careful choice of participants and repetition of core values over the preparation phase meant that the climbers also accepted their role as followers and what was expected of them in tough times. Despite the huge disappointment this represented for all expedition members, the preparation helped people set aside their aspirations for glory and once-in-a-lifetime achievement in favour of individual survival and group safety. Unsurprisingly, when the immediate emotional reactions subsided, expedition members relied on one another for support without reservation.

CREATING A HEALTHY ADVENTURE EDUCATION ENVIRONMENT

In adventure education, learning often comes from facing the consequences of actions; authentic experiences can heighten the engagement of people who ordinarily are disengaged. Learning from mistakes signifies that achievement comes as a result of stretching oneself by applying continued effort and working collaboratively. Adventure education helps people create a resilient mindset where the fixed, ego-driven perspective of can't-do is replaced by flexible, task-focussed, can-do persistence. This process can be facilitated by providing immediate and accurate feedback on the effort and strategies employed by individuals, subgroups, and whole groups.

Lessons must be real and natural (e.g., getting wet and cold through lack of planning and kit selection, hiking extra distances due to navigational error), as must be rewards (e.g., witnessing sunsets over the ocean and mountaintops, enjoying feelings of self-fulfilment and accomplishment). To reinforce the value of such experiential learning, feedback from facilitators should not define success or failure through reward or punishment, but should allow the natural environment and the support of others to show the way in overcoming challenges. This creates a path to sustainable resilience. Here are a few practical tips:

▸ Only provide solutions when managing the immediate dangers is beyond the capabilities of the participants.

▸ Continue to ask questions when difficult issues arise. This promotes self-discovery and a sense of control over outcomes. By learning in uncertain environments, whether through success or failure, participants learn about themselves and others. They also acquire knowledge that they have generated and feel they own. Learning to extend comfort boundaries relies on time, effort, and persistence—often the process is more important than the product. Accomplishment results from stretching oneself and is not a fixed asset; it is achieved through perseverance.

▸ Allow the natural environment to impose standards for performance. The dramatic consequences that people anticipate whilst mountaineering often regulates how much effort they expend in seeking specific outcomes. Facilitators should complement the realism of the natural environment by encouraging self-assessment in participants rather than overpraising them when they are successful. Artificial or imagined experiences with low standards will not create personal growth that can be transferred to other life settings.

Being inspired to achieve within adventure education comes from participants mastering the skills that overcome uncertainty in spite of the dangers and risks they may perceive. Establishing mastery in such circumstances comes from a need to challenge self-perceptions and insecurities. Initially, these challenges often seem overwhelming, and they are often individualised. Effective responses rely on active control over mental, emotional, and physical resources. For example, when experiences are facilitated appropriately, learning in one session can progress from the need to ask for help in using equipment to eventually acquiring the skills to help others stay safe and secure as environmental conditions worsen.

Providing the means to be successful also involves careful distancing by instructors, even when real dangers are present. For this reason, knowing how long to wait before intervening represents one of the biggest challenges for optimising personal growth. Leaders may wish to profile particular group members according to specific resilience items and intervene in those areas with those individuals.

Providing a range of options and giving the freedom to make important choices empowers people by helping them to realise not only their personal impact but also their interdependency with others. Retreating with dignity from an activity and making a reasoned choice to pursue a challenge are equal antecedents of adventure. Removing the power for people to decide for themselves means that they typically attribute successes or failures not to themselves but to the decision makers. Achieving a balance between self-determination and recognition of contributing qualities are both important in determining success. Resilience building, then, is about changing beliefs in one's ability to cope in uncertainty.

FACILITATING RESILIENCE IN ADVENTURE EDUCATION

We have already noted that resilient mindsets can be established, and we also recognise that behaviour adaptation and potential for growth are based on the complex interactions of pre-dispositions, experiences, and opportunities. It is these complex interactions that develop new competencies within changing tasks and contexts. We have also recognised that adventure education can provide a valuable context in which to develop resilience. These factors are dynamic and are not uniformly applicable across tasks and contexts.

Because the response to any given adventure education event is highly subjective, it is crucial to appreciate the value of an instructor who can positively influence what is learned and taken away. Crucial to positive experiential learning is constructive sharing of information. Through the facilitation of the instructor, this new understanding may then transfer to other contexts or tasks.

One way to consider how aspects of resilience can be made applicable to other tasks and contexts is to consider the principle of transfer. Three types of transfer can help explain how adventure education can be linked to personal mindsets and behaviour adopted in completing others tasks or in different contexts. *Nonspecific transfer* of principles, values, and attitudes such as caring for others or issues of morality can occur. *Specific transfer* considers how specific skills, such as technical proficiency, leadership, or effective communication, have strong similarities to requirements in other life domains. For example, businesses often value adventure education because the leadership it reveals can relate directly to the demands of leadership in daily work. This type of transfer needs to be refined so that the specific leadership qualities are not only clarified but also developed and then transferred via specialised delivery and feedback processes. Finally, *metaphoric transfer* takes place in situations with symbolically identical interactions, such as group cooperation. Effective adventure practitioners systematically vary the context, roles, and the nature of adventure education challenges to facilitate these types of transfer. The attention placed on resilience for meeting life challenges shows the relevance of practical work relating to coping.

In sport psychology literature, coping has traditionally focussed on emotional and problem-based coping rather than on personal estimates of what needs to be managed, avoided, or diffused. Facilitated review and reflection needs to be immediate, meaningful, and capable of meeting the evolving needs of the person based on individual coping competencies; otherwise, associated growth is restricted. The messages that are transmitted through reflective practice need to emphasise personal and group strengths, especially those based on effort, strategy, and persistence. Success and failure have to be assessed in the same manner—the journey in addressing challenges is often more important than the outcome. The following are practical tips for reviewing experiences with messages of strength.

▸ Send messages that encourage effort, persistence, and strategy rather than emphasising winning and losing—participants should not be labelled in either way.

▸ Ask participants to explore the effort and tenacity they demonstrated whilst challenging themselves emotionally, cognitively, physically, and socially. Ask them to provide examples of displays of strength in these areas.

▸ Help participants understand the need to stretch into areas of uncertainty. Provide reminders that undertaking new challenges requires using the mind as a muscle—this muscle, like most others, can grow through training (which is when people practise and learn). Meeting new challenges creates new brain connections.

▸ Emphasise that learning is progressive and takes time. Even the most accomplished people once started as beginners. Ask questions such as the following: What elements have you learned today that you can use for next time? What constructive criticism would you give yourself to enable you to improve? Wait for the answers and respect what is said.

▸ Praise the growth that results from practice, choices, and using specific strategies. Even when outcomes are less than desired, praise efforts and achievements thus far.

The following capturing-the-moment prompts can be used for ongoing reviewing:

▸ Imagine that you can make a wish come true. Your wish is for something that is missing right now. When you have this thing, the situation will go better. How can you make the situation go in this direction using what you already have?

▸ What made you smile today?

▸ If this were a game of snakes and ladders, where were the ladders, what were they like, and where have they taken you?

▸ What issues have shifted down or off the agenda because you have already dealt with them?

▸ What did you do that contributed to today's successes?

▸ What are the strengths of your team? What can you share? What are you proud of from today?

RESILIENCE AS *THE* SURVIVAL SKILL?

The unique influence of the outdoors, as detailed within the components of adventure education, contrasts strongly with the normality of daily life. Spending any amount of time in the outdoors is likely to represent some challenge to most sedentary, urban-dwelling people. Even when people are more experienced in the out-

doors, different elements and their associated climatic conditions can offer challenges beyond normal expectations. Extreme environments may generate extreme physical, social, and psychological challenges. This adds to their appeal in the pursuit of ever-challenging experiences.

Given the understanding that adventure education provides an environment that can foster personal growth, it is hardly surprising that militaries find such value in exposing recruits to adventure education as part of their development and preparation for duty. In the British Army, an expressive phrase underlines the obvious parallels between adventure education and battle: No plan survives contact with the enemy. The flexibility demanded by the outdoor environment is seen as a relevant, if not direct, simulation for learning to survive and respond to difficult moments associated with both warfare and peacekeeping. Learning drawn from adventure education has transferability to situations associated with military service. Positive adventure education may well contribute to new self-perceptions ('I am calm in the face of danger'), enhanced relationships ('I can trust these people'), and changed life philosophy ('I work hard to make a difference, but what will be, will be'). These are characterisations of personal growth that indicate profound changes, and they can be distinguished from fleeting yet pleasurable behavioural episodes. Many would suggest that both the physical and the adventure education training in the military focus on changing the person. Implicitly this is about building resilience, which increases what a person can do in body and mind during difficult events.

Consider the following: Which of the resilience factors in our scale would you use to survive for over 24 hours in the open sea? This happened to a couple who were scuba diving on the Great Barrier Reef in June 2008. They surfaced from diving to find that the company vessel that had provided their passage was gone. Would you use the same features to maintain your grip on a stretcher handle whilst carrying an injured colleague in temperatures of 37 degrees Celsius (98 degrees Fahrenheit) and humidity of 94 percent within a tropical forest?

Adapting to Challenges on Expeditions

Within the 2006 expedition, we had the unusual opportunity to explore resilience and survival issues amongst a group of new army recruits who were selected to shadow the main team of climbers, climbing a much lower peak. The members of this group were unaccustomed to high altitude and therefore required a higher degree of protection and reliance on their strengths. Our interview questions focussed on how the recruits saw themselves changing as a result of their engagement in the expedition, as well as how intermediate and novice climbers protected themselves and adapted to the challenges posed by preparing and climbing in the Himalayas whilst also navigating their new life within the army. Here is an example of an exchange within one of these interviews, this time with one of the expedition instructors.

Q: Do you think through adventure training, whether civilian led or in the military, there is a spillover effect into people's personal lives?

A: Oh yeah, without a doubt. I mean, yes it does, because you have confidence in your ability to cope with something and on a mountain. You know, if you're on dodgy ground or if the weather's poor you can spend quite a long time in pretty bad conditions, let's say, coping with high anxiety. You spend quite a lot of time not only coping with high anxiety but actually having to sometimes make decisions and do things correctly under that strain. Now if you think about it, you are in risk of life and limb, especially if you've got a lot of rockfall or whatever. Now actually if you can go through that, you know, what in a day-to-day life is, you know, so you've done something wrong or the boss is losing his rag, it's like—yeah, you know, you're not gonna kill me. I mean, it's accepting and dealing with levels of punishment or levels of poor outcomes that tells you something about yourself.

—Adventure training instructor, Everest West Ridge, 2006

It seems that—possibly contrary to the stereotypical boot-camp idea for preparing battle-hardy recruits—the generic adventure training philosophy has evolved into a measured approach to promoting personal growth. It emphasises that the feeling of competence can indicate that a challenge can be met, often based on facilitated support and team building. Another instructor from the 2006 expedition explained it like this:

Good instruction is vital and also at the right level of activity for the person. If you throw someone in the deep end, they just spend their whole time being petrified, or if you make something so arduous that they are uncomfortable and feel bad about themselves all the time it won't be . . . they won't draw the things out of them, whereas if it's done at the right level then they will get masses out of it. It is about not learning to teach but understanding how to help people learn.

—Senior officer and adventure training instructor, Everest West Ridge, 2006

CONCLUSION

This chapter investigated the notion of resilience and its use within society, with special emphasis on the role of adventure education in bringing about personal growth. Resilience is a multidimensional construct that can be expressed uniquely in individuals, as well as be developed for infinite uses. It possesses common properties that can be transferred across a range of contexts and prevailing conditions. It can signify emotional and cognitive intactness, even when surrounded by others who are demonstrating poor judgement or detrimental actions. Resilience promotes continuity, adaptability, and optimism in unfavourable, against-the-odds situations. On the one hand, resilience can be reactionary (e.g., maintaining self-discipline), but on the other it becomes embedded within the forces that help bind groups.

Within our increasingly risk-averse society, adventure education can be cherished, whether it helps people enjoy the activity for its own sake or is used as a vehicle for personal growth. Learning to manage unpredictability allows us not only to spring back from potential adversity but also to spring forward with added vigour and confidence when confronted by fresh challenges. Through such processes, we may no longer see subsequent events as threatening and compromising, instead welcoming them as positive opportunities for growth that will enhance quality of life and general health. The spirit of adventure encapsulates a sense of timeless purpose and freedom to change that can be realised by many. This can be accomplished by undertaking historical feats of endurance or through the growing self-realisation of what you can achieve when you believe you can grow. Quotes collected by the authors from first-year university students after a 1-week residential adventure education experience in the Lake District in 2007 illustrate this:

> I would be prepared to try any activity no matter how scared. I would feel confident and optimistic doing it because you feel a real sense of achievement in the outdoors.

> We eventually arrived back from the mountain day—and I remember standing squelching in my dripping waterproofs, complete with wet hat and hair—perhaps more significantly I had a huge smile on my face. I had truly achieved something. An experience like this is as rewarding as the amount of effort you put into it; abnormal conditions can be used to your advantage in the creation of life's lessons—as long as you add enthusiasm and positivity to your list of ingredients.

KEY IDEAS

▸ Resilience is developed through outdoor activities and adventure education.

▸ Resilience is multidimensional, is expressed through individual growth, and can be applied in everyday life.

▸ Resilience results in emotional and cognitive judgement that leads to calm and positive action, even in the face of extreme adversity.

▸ Resilience can be manifest in individuals and as a sign of group cohesion.

C H A P T E R
13

Leadership

Dave Bunting

The task of leadership is not to put greatness into people, but to elicit it, for the greatness is there already.

John Buchan

Leadership is a role that we all have to take on during our lives in one shape or another. Due to its inevitability, it's something that is better faced early on in life in order to learn how to cope with it rather than avoiding the responsibility and falling flat when the moment arrives.

At a young age, I found it invaluable to challenge myself, and as a teenager I found I was more often taking a committed step forward than a shy step back. The earliest influence for taking this approach was my grandfather, who had served for 19 years in the army, including with the elite Chindits in Burma. I hugely admired his calm but confident manner with a hint of humour that commanded respect from all.

If you have aspirations to lead, it's likely you will have role models to compare yourself with. Observing those leaders you admire most and trying to take the best of what you witness will help you to cope with a variety of situations you may find yourself leading in.

I often hear the phrases *born leader* or *natural leader*, but I am not sure whether such people exist, especially in terms of leading in every conceivable situation. I have witnessed some superb leaders who have been outstanding in certain situations and yet they have been appalling when the environment changes, completely unable to adapt to the new challenges. To help you adapt to a variety of leadership roles, it's important to recognise where your strengths and weaknesses lie in leadership and accept that you can't master everything. During expeditions, a leader will be tested in a wide variety of situations, many of which will be difficult to foresee even with the best preparation. However, it is still important to question, research, and practise expected scenarios to ensure your strategies will deal with them in the best manner. Though shorter expeditions can get away with a democratic decision-making process, lengthier challenges will require direction and a watchful eye most of the time.

This chapter explores the elements of leadership that I have observed throughout my life, both in the military and on a variety of expeditions. It includes gaining experience, learning from early expeditions, and developing your own style of leadership to suit future challenges. Finally, it explores turning your vision into a reality, first gaining the support to make it happen and then leading your team to meet the requirements for the expedition.

GAINING EXPEDITION EXPERIENCE

To gather the experience to lead your own expedition, it is important to either take lesser roles or commit to easier adventures to gather the knowledge, skills, and attitude that are required. Your first expedition experience should be thought through carefully, because many people have been put off by the harsh nature of the initial experience. A relatively tame but progressive adventure is the ideal first step and will encourage you to go further rather than giving in before you really get started. Expeditions bring together a multitude of skills that can be difficult in isolation, and it's easy to become overwhelmed by biting off too much in the beginning. Familiarity with various roles will always be valuable once you start to lead your own expeditions.

My first expedition, relatively short in time but certainly not in distance, was to Britain's classic Pennine Way, where I developed many planning, preparation, training, and decision-making skills that gave me a quality grounding for future expeditions and leadership. Methodical by nature, I found this first experience of expeditions and leadership to be invaluable because it allowed me to build each step of knowledge in a situation where if things went wrong, I would not have to fall back too far to find familiar ground. I loved the simplicity of

being on this long-distance path with just my rucksack and teammate to think about, and this carefree lifestyle captured my imagination even then. Although there were only two of us, I may have even started to take a leadership role on this first venture, probably because my outdoor experience was slightly more than that of my companion. The Pennine Way was a fabulous trial and taught me a number of key skills and simple lessons, many of which can be useful in any expedition.

Plan Ahead   When planning an expedition, give yourself considerably more time than is required. Many unexpected issues can arise, especially during large-scale ventures. By putting the time in beforehand, you will allow the expedition to run smoothly and give yourself and your team both the best experience and the highest chance of success. You will be surprised by how many unexpected difficulties can arise, especially for adventures to undiscovered, remote, and foreign regions.

Preexpedition planning.

Remain Flexible and Be Willing to Change Plans Your first idea, no matter how bright or experienced you are, will never be perfect. During the preparation and planning stages, the expedition leader must be flexible to new ideas that will help shape the initial vision and turn it into something special. Being a good listener is one of the greatest qualities of a leader, and absorbing new slants on your vision can help make it even better. The expedition environment itself is ever changing, and it's not just the weather, climbing conditions, or foreign bureaucracy, it's also your team—humans can act irrationally once they face the realities of the expedition environment. A flexible approach and willingness to change as a leader are crucial in such situations.

FIRST BIG EXPEDITION

After the Pennine Way, I was lucky enough to experience numerous smaller trips around various climbing venues and to go the Alps, but my first big expedition was to the greater mountain ranges. In my early 20s, I was given the opportunity to head out to the Nepalese Himalayas and tackle the Annapurna Circuit and 6,000-metre (19,685 ft) Pisang Peak. In many ways the expedition was a big step up for me, but I had many of the skills already in place, including physical fitness, climbing ability, and knowledge of how to look after myself in the hills. However, the one thing I was not prepared for was the environment, in particular the extreme effect that the altitude can have. No one in the team, including the leader, knew how to handle the dangers of altitude. The totally wrong approach and pace were set, and we carried far too much equipment in the early stages. Some harsh lessons were quickly learned, but I believe if we had just had one person who had been to altitude in a remote environment before, we could have overcome a lot of misery. For future leadership situations, I learned three key lessons from this expedition.

Team planning meet at Base Camp Everest.

Use Local Support The local people, particularly in poorer countries where many expeditions take place, earn their highest possible income by carrying equipment for foreign expeditions, so most are only too willing to do so. By gaining support from the local porters, you will give yourself the chance to slowly adapt to the difficult terrain and ascents whilst enjoying your surroundings and minimising risk of injury. Also, at the higher levels of challenge you will not succeed if you don't employ the unmatchable abilities of the indigenous people, such as the Sherpas in Nepal. As a leader, you should always consider employing the best support to achieve your goal, and porters and Sherpas can add a special element to your team.

Set the Pace The pace and tone of an expedition should be set by the leader, ensuring that a relaxed and sensible working atmosphere is adopted from the beginning. This is not to say that you are in the front of your team all the way, but by educating your members to the dangers of competiveness and environmental risks such as altitude, the right tone and pace for the expedition will be established early on. During my first trip, I behaved as if I were in a low-altitude environment in the United Kingdom where I could pace out and test my personal fitness on a daily basis against the constantly steep terrain experienced in Nepal. This was a big mistake, and once on Pisang Peak I suffered so badly that I still look back and think it was one of the worst physical experiences of my life. I succumbed to terrible AMS and at 5,000 metres (16,405 ft), I had the worst night possible. I now endeavour to be the last to the daily camp and stop to enjoy drinks and rest stops regularly. If I am the leader of an expedition with novices, then I personally set the pace and insist that no one overtakes me

Our Sherpas on the Everest West Ridge Expedition.

on the first few days. This both acclimatises team members to the new altitude and gets rid of the U.K. mentality of testing your fitness against fellow team members on a daily basis.

Employ the Right Knowledge My last key lesson from this early expedition is the importance of taking someone, even one person, who knows what to do. If we had invited someone along who could advise us on coping with altitude, it would have been a much more rewarding trip. It is the harsher environments where the biggest lessons are learned and the damaging effects of mistakes can be greater. I remember landing in Lukla in the Everest region and meeting with a group of climbers from the elite Parachute Regiment who were just finishing their expedition. Their 4 weeks had been out-and-out torture because they had adopted their usual competitive marching ethos, and they were lucky no one had died as a consequence. I admired the young officer who had gone out of his way to give this opportunity to his men, but if he had just employed someone who knew the ins and outs, the whole experience would have provided a lasting positive memory that could have inspired new mountaineers rather than the nightmare that they never wanted to experience again. The leader does not need to have all of the answers for every situation; however, it is the leader's responsibility to gather a wide range of knowledge, skills, and talent in the team to help overcome whatever you may face.

DEVELOPING LEADERSHIP

When undergoing your apprenticeship, make sure you have each stage right before advancing to the next; otherwise you can be overwhelmed. I prefer to take a building-blocks approach, making sure the team's skills and my own are learned and reinforced before going on to the next stage. Finally, those who don't learn from their mistakes will inevitably not return from an expedition one day.

Once the foundations of your personal skills are in place, expeditions offer a fabulous environment to learn and test new skills, and team responsibilities in particular provide the oppor-

tunity to challenge yourself as a team player, organiser, and leader. On each of my expedition experiences, I have made every effort to take on a new role within the team. Several of these roles have been alien to me, but they have all taken me out of my comfort zone and forced me to learn new skills in challenging real-life situations. With each expedition, I was selected for a new role, and eventually I began to be chosen for leadership roles such as deputy leader and climbing leader. I quickly built a varied portfolio of leadership experiences that prepared me for bigger things to come, ultimately leading to leadership of a big trip of my own. The expeditions where I took a bigger role in the decision making became hugely rewarding, and I enjoyed analysing situations and being involved in the movements of equipment and team members in order to take things forward. But at the same time, the energy and time required to make things come together can place heavy pressures on your life, so support from those close to you is vital. You cannot lead successfully in isolation.

After a number of experiences, expeditions started to take over my life. One of my biggest motivations became the joy of introducing others to the life-changing opportunities that can be discovered through these journeys.

Make sure you have the right skills to take on a leadership role, and make sure your previous experience is appropriate to prepare you for the next step. You may be a good leader on a weekend camping in the Peak District in Derbyshire (U.K.), but that doesn't mean you will be the same on a 3-month expedition in some far-flung corner of the earth. As I have already mentioned, I prefer the methodical approach to expeditions and building experience slowly. Before jumping into the hot seat as the expedition leader, it pays to fulfil an organising role as a deputy leader or climbing leader, where you have leadership responsibilities and the opportunity to make hard decisions but don't hold the ultimate responsibility. This can give you a feel for the pressures of real-life situations, trial your ability to analyse risks and rewards, and gain confidence in yourself to make the right choices.

I was lucky enough to be climbing leader and deputy leader on five Himalayan expeditions before I became the overall expedition leader, and these experiences allowed me to discover my own strengths and weaknesses, which has proved invaluable in creating the right team around me. I now tend to build a leadership team that complements my abilities rather than overshadows them, one where decisions can be reached through careful consideration by a number of people. Being climbing leader of my first expedition to Nepal was far too much responsibility for someone of my experience at the time. I learned some harsh lessons and it could have put me off for life. Now that I have had several good experiences in a leadership team, I relish the challenge.

MAKING YOUR VISION A REALITY

We all have dreams of what we would like to achieve in life, and for most of us they remain a dream unless we take action. Throughout life I have had many ideas that came to nothing. To have a vision that is going to come to fruition, a methodical, progressive, and well-thought-out path should be taken. If you are going to take on a leadership challenge, you must think things through carefully and consider every conceivable alternative and escape plan in case you need to opt for a change of direction. As a leader, you should establish a clear vision of what you are trying to achieve, and starting with the end in mind is always a good way to approach this. For me, the journey is more vital than the actual goal, and if that journey has developed the team, lessons have been learned, fun has been had, and everyone has returned in one piece, then it's likely to have been an educational, rewarding experience for everyone involved.

The great thing about having a vision and taking on your own challenge is you can shape the project exactly how you want. However, as a leader you must be open to new ideas. This may change elements of your vision, but it means you oversee the big picture and maintain the overall shape of the project, giving great satisfaction as you see your idea become reality.

Once your vision has been established, it's important to consider the details. This is only achieved through careful reflection and research, which takes valuable time, but it can be helped along by delegation to appropriate members of your team. The Internet and guidebooks are an incredible help, and much can be gleaned from route maps. Personal accounts and photos also give fabulous information about a particular area. As a team leader, you should use all the information you can find from reliable sources to help in your planning. However, nothing beats the input of people who have been there and are able to give you their firsthand view of what to expect. Whenever possible, I go out of my way to contact people who have visited the places that are the focus of my next expedition.

However, what makes an expedition much more exciting is going where no one (or very few people) has ever been before. A new leadership and planning approach is needed for this style of expedition, and it needs plenty of support in place to allow for the unexpected, such as extra equipment and a daring team.

Finally, an important part of a leadership vision is having the ability to communicate it to your team. You can come up with an idea and take your vision forward, shaping its progression as you go, but then it's important to drive the vision and make sure your team members understand and agree with what you are trying to achieve. This support and understanding can be gained through good communication and involving every team member in open dialogue for new ideas, giving them ownership and loyalty to you and the cause. Clearly it's impossible to think of everything and a flexible approach is essential, but don't become so flexible that your vision loses direction and you lose control of your plan.

GAINING SUPPORT

Gaining support is crucial, and the key is being a good salesperson. You need to map out your vision clearly and gain the confidence of those whose support you want. When trying to gain this support, remember that you don't get a second chance to make a first impression. If you don't get your sales pitch right, that support could be lost forever. If you come up with a well-thought-out expedition that contains groundbreaking aspects, then there is a good chance that everyone will want to be involved and get a piece of the action. It is important to weed out people who may not be helpful, and you must recruit quality, knowledgeable, and enthusiastic support that will help you move forward.

The Team

At the early stages of leading an expedition, you must carefully consider whom you want in the core of your team to help push forward your idea. This includes not just technical performers but a loyal, hardworking, and effective group whom you can always rely on to support you and take your vision to reality. The people in this small group need to share your vision and values, and you need to know them well and trust them implicitly. It helps if you have already shared an experience similar to the expedition you are about to undertake and thus you have seen them under similar pressures. If you haven't had these shared experiences, then you risk being surprised when, under new strains and in alien environments, you both react differently to what is ahead. By employing the right people with the right qualities, you will quickly gain the necessary momentum and they will help you to inspire supporters and other team members alike.

Supporting Each Other

The core of the team in my most recent expedition, Everest West Ridge, consisted of people I knew I could work with throughout the whole 3.5-year challenge. They would encourage me to keep going, help me with the workload, and drive me when times got tough.

▸ My lifetime best friend, Leigh Woodhouse, could be trusted to unwaveringly support me in every situation and to develop key tasks without me having to continuously watch over his shoulder.

Leigh 'Woody' Woodhouse at 7,800 metres (25,590 ft) on the North Face of Everest approaching Camp 5.

(continued)

▸ John Doyle, climbing leader, is an inspirational performer with whom I had already worked and who I had been on two expeditions with to challenging peaks. Super focussed and capable, he would influence external support and inspire people to achieve their very best.

John Doyle and Dave Bunting discussing tactics and organising teams.

▸ Dave Wilson, deputy leader, was someone with whom I had already shared a leadership experience. I knew we would be able to take the plan forward shoulder to shoulder, and if there was any form of disagreement it would be handled in a sensible and supporting manner. Although we would now swap roles for this challenge, I knew that, similar to our previous trip, we would make things happen together.

Dave Wilson leading a group in the Alps in preparation for Everest.

Family and Friends

Volunteering for a big project that is going to take years to plan can result in a single-minded and selfish time in your life, and unless you have no family and friends, you are signing up more people than yourself to the forthcoming project. If you don't have the absolute support of your family and close friends, then it will be a difficult time for you, and it may be too demanding to overcome the stresses and strains placed upon you. I have always thought that when you are single it's much easier because you can be relatively selfish and use your free time to totally immerse yourself in the planning process, but the understanding and support of those close to you can help you achieve so much more. The time required for planning a big project should not be underestimated.

Family and friends should be informed and encouraged to get involved. Organise team meets aimed at gathering families and friends so that they become involved in at least the social network associated with the expedition. They can put names to faces and get to know the people with whom you are working so closely and in whom you are investing your trust for extreme undertakings. This widens the expedition family-and-friends network. Some family and friends can also help organise social and fund-raising events, relieving pressure from the leaders in delivering these important activities. The information you give your family and friends about the expedition should be thought out carefully. Too much detail, particularly if they are not experienced or knowledgeable about the activity, could make them unnecessarily worried.

Patrons

The importance of a quality core team and support from your family and close friends cannot be underestimated, but the power of influential supporters who are well positioned to gain sponsorship or cut through red tape is also crucial. Expedition patrons have long offered support and guidance for bigger expeditions, and their contacts and knowhow can prove crucial if finances are not going as planned or an in-country embassy is being difficult. It is, however, a balancing act because you require people who are powerful and carry influence but at the same time are not so busy that they can't offer you their time.

Retired members of the House of Lords or retired mountaineers are often signed up to these roles, and from my experience, they are worth their weight in gold. In addition, a guiding and advisory committee can be invaluable when developing big projects.

Sponsors or Partners

I have been involved in a number of expeditions where gaining sponsorship was critical to getting sufficient finances and logistical support to make the project happen. To gain support, you need to consider what companies and organisations are looking for. Here are a few ideas.

Achieving a First   Being able to suggest that your project is a first and also is high risk is very attractive to companies. Many British companies still have great pride in supporting exciting ventures that may see their flag planted alongside the Union Flag in some untrodden ground, thus producing media attention. In addition, there is a big adrenaline junkie culture that captures the eye of the media, so if you can suggest that the risks are high and the chances of success are slim but you have the right team to do it, often you can gain support. Aiming to succeed in the face of adversity will also gain media attention.

Development   Undertaking a high-level, high-risk venture requires top performers who know what they are doing and are able to deal with the difficulties that will be faced. Always opting for a team of out-and-out gladiators is not a good idea, however. Taking along some relative novices and intermediates will also attract support, and it will help develop the next generation of high-performance mountaineers. Given enough time to train and prepare, people with the right attitude will soon pick up the skills. I have seen many people quickly advance to the required level when they have the right physical attributes, mindset, and guidance.

Inclusivity   Similar to encouraging an ethos of development, it is also important to step back and look at the combination of people in your team. Diverse teams are much more attractive to

Staying Connected

When I was preparing for my leadership of the Everest West Ridge attempt, my young nephew was convinced I was a computer attachment, not a mountaineer—from the time he was born I had spent so much time e-mailing and creating important documents that he knew no different! Throughout my expedition planning phases, I have been incredibly fortunate to have the most supportive family, and the selfless support of my parents has been amazing. My dad, however, would always mock about the waiter service he provided, bringing me drinks and meals whilst I was hard at work!

sponsors and supporters because they generate more interest from outside parties and give the project more angles and stories to tell. Young and old, male and female, novice and advanced—all have their benefits when selling your vision. However, as a leader it is important to maintain the balance between inclusivity and the values, beliefs, and attitudes of the team as a whole.

Whomever you get on board, the important thing is that you don't just want a sponsor; you want an expedition partner. This means a much bigger buy-in, including attendance at training meets and social events. If you have pulled together a good team, the partners will become so engrossed in the project that they will end up supporting you above and beyond what you ever thought possible.

Media

The media are not that straightforward in terms of support because they have a job to do, and that is to find out information and sell stories. The best stories are exciting, death defying, and controversial, so the media will always be looking for a slant and may sometimes put you under pressure that you don't need. On the positive side, having a national newspaper or TV channel on board can attract huge sponsorship if pitched right. The expedition leader therefore needs to

be clear in defining the shared expectations for media participation in a large-scale expedition. Clarification of responsibility for resources for camera crews and other media team members is important for planning and logistics, but the overall responsibility for the expedition in terms of the nature of the team, journey, objectives, and ethos must remain with the leader.

Smaller expeditions can also benefit from engagement with the media. Local newspapers and regional television are often looking for local stories on people and teams that are undertaking challenges such as expeditions. Contacts made through working with local media can also increase local support and sponsorship, and stories can focus on aspects of development and the journey rather than just headlines about summiting.

LEADERSHIP IN TRAINING AND PREPARING YOUR TEAM

This section covers a vital part of the expedition. As the leader, you must set the standards for your expedition, give advice, and carry out detailed preparation and planning to ensure every chance of success.

Dave Bunting talking live to Sky News on EWR 2006 for a TV documentary on the expedition and for the Army.

Select Your Team Because this subject is covered elsewhere in this book, I won't go into too much detail. However, the selection of a suitable team has major implications for your style of leadership. It is crucial to select a team that shares your values and has certain skills. Some larger projects have been known to select a team based on climbing CVs and interviews; however, I strongly advise against this because it undervalues the importance of people skills and having complementary team members. I begin with inviting applications and carrying out interviews, which leaves me with a squad of people that allows for reserves. This squad can then enter a selection phase of training where a person's true colours can be tested and uncovered, allowing the opportunity to choose the very best team for the venture. Careful selection of your team will help you throughout the venture and will make your job more straightforward in the long run.

Although smaller expeditions do not need to be too concerned with large and structured leadership teams, the coherence and integrity of the team are still critical in the need to share responsibilities and support the leader. On bigger expeditions, a deputy leader and technical climbing leader are essential for the following reasons:

▸ *Sounding board*—Often when you are in difficult decision-making situations, if you are experienced enough you will know the answer, but it's good to be able to bounce your ideas off someone else to give you the confidence to make an announcement and know you have others' support.

▸ *Support*—When involved in a complex project with daily movements and decisions that are taxing, having support to lean on and encourage you can help immensely and boost your confidence.

Team members training for Everest in poor conditions in the Alps.

▸ *Cover*—During long expeditions, you will do well to be on top form day in day out, and it will be impossible to be everywhere at once. When you are feeling low from illness or recovering from exhausting physical exertion, having a good deputy to fill in for you keeps the situation under control and maintains the direction and focus rather than just letting the team drift. Additionally, I have been on expeditions where the leaders are performing so well on the climbing front that they find themselves deep in the weeds, immersed in their activity and unable to see the big picture. Cover from a good deputy leader in such situations will again ensure that direction is maintained.

Delegate Team Responsibilities Any expedition, no matter how small, is best conducted with responsibilities shared amongst the team. This not only allows people to take on new roles and develop themselves, but it also makes it much more likely that the job will get done. Most important, it allows the expedition leader to step back, take a strategic view, and move the project ahead by exploring ideas and chasing leads.

Identify What's Important It is necessary to decide exactly what is required to get your team ready for the upcoming challenge. The best way to start is with the end in mind, and if you study exactly what is needed to succeed, then you won't waste time messing around with pointless training and preparation. Use past experiences and talk to those who have been where you are going in order to learn about techniques and skills that are crucial to overcoming the particular challenge. It's no good honing rock-climbing skills for a route that is mainly snow and ice.

Pay Attention to Detail It is your job as expedition leader to always think of the big picture but also regularly observe the detail without becoming a micromanager. 'Leave no stone unturned' was the motto we used on my last expedition to Everest West Ridge. We took all past experiences and information and turned them upside down and inside out to ensure the most thorough preparation. If we ran into something we did not know about, then we would have already trained for sufficient flexibility to overcome it. A useful military strapline comes to mind—'Train hard, fight easy.'

Keep It Interesting and Diverse Most expeditions of any reasonable scale require a long lead in time, and it is important to make sure your team maintains focus and doesn't become bored and complacent. It is the expedition leader's responsibility to inspire and lead the way. A key component in my leadership strategy is setting a training programme that is exciting and focussed on achievement of the goal but is also diverse, containing team-building aspects as opposed to just specific activities. I have always found it useful to have someone in charge of training who can oversee planning and progression, as well as search out and employ experts in particular fields.

Maintain Focus Maintaining focus comes back to identifying what is important. Though you may be creating a project that is interesting and exciting as a journey, don't forget that you are trying to achieve a particular goal. It would be a real shame to have lots of fun-oriented training meets and forget to prepare for the real situations you may face. I remember once going on an expedition to a high-altitude peak and although the training had been rewarding and regular, it was not until we were over 6,000 metres (19,685 ft) on the side of a Himalayan giant that the other lead climber and myself discovered our fixed-rope techniques were different. It only required a 10-minute discussion to agree how we would proceed, but it could have resulted in a nightmare of wasted time.

During our 2 years of training for the ascent of Everest, the leadership team drew up a contract that was gathered from the team members to define our values and help maintain focus. These shared values guided our attitudes and behaviour towards each other and our shared goal, significantly shaping what became an

The Everest West Ridge 2006 team.

incredibly strong team. Team members carried a list of the values with them at all times, ensuring everyone kept focus:

- ▸ Total commitment to the task
- ▸ Honesty in yourself
- ▸ Tolerance of others
- ▸ Loyalty
- ▸ Teamwork
- ▸ Communication
- ▸ Physical fitness
- ▸ Mental robustness
- ▸ Attention to detail
- ▸ Sense of humour

Manage Your Team From Within Managing your team on a complex project means you need to adopt a number of styles to fit the moment. You will most certainly have to employ a variety of skills to overcome problems, and a single leadership style will not work for all people in all situations. I find that a flat hierar-

Dave Bunting load carrying to camp 2 on Everest, 2006.

chy works well on expeditions where the leader is one of the team and decisions are openly talked about and resolved. Placing yourself on a pedestal is only lining yourself up for a big fall when you make a wrong judgement. If you have placed yourself amongst your team in a friendly and down-to-earth manner, there is a good chance many will come to your aid when the moment comes.

Adapt to the Situation As a leader, you need to be able to gather information effectively to quickly determine the best course of action for the given situation. If you don't collect all of the data required, then you risk making the wrong decision. Although quick decisions need to be made occasionally, try to think things through if you get the time. Every team and project are unique, so you must adjust your style to fit what's required or create a project from scratch and shape it fully. The styles I adopt differ completely when I am taking an experienced team of climbers versus a group of novices, and for the latter much more care and energy are required to ensure a quality, safe experience.

Learn From Experience If you are fortunate enough to have past experiences on expeditions, then it is worth observing the leadership and what worked and what didn't. I was lucky enough to have been on two large-scale expeditions prior to my leadership on Everest, and the lessons I learned were invaluable. Both expeditions were led with different styles and each had ups and downs, allowing me to pick the best aspects of leadership from each and adapt them to my style. Interestingly, the two leaders, for whom I have the greatest of respect, were very different characters, had considerably different technical abilities, and led quite different teams, which meant they had to adopt different styles of leadership even though the mountains were equally challenging.

One leader led mainly from base camp, directing a high-performance team to achieve his vision. Due to his knowledge and judgement and the high motivation levels of the team, his strategic view of what was happening facilitated huge success on the mountain, although I believe this style could not be adopted with a lesser team. The second leader was a physically strong climber and was able to be amongst the climbers forcing the route up the mountain. His team members were less experienced on the whole, and so his lead-by-example style was required to inspire his team to keep going. Sadly, the second expedition did not reach the summit, but the route was incredibly challenging and the weather was unfriendly.

Having witnessed the two styles, I attempted to fall somewhere in between the two, and I wanted to be amongst the climbing to help with forward movement but also able to step out of the weeds and see what was happening as required. Later in my Everest expedition, I was able to choose myself to be in one of the summit parties, but only because I had a strong deputy leader who could take over in terms of viewing the big picture. There is rarely a clearly right or wrong style, but different situations call for different styles. Each will have advantages and disadvantages; the key is identifying what will be best for a given expedition and having the flexibility to adapt to each situation, phase, and challenge.

KEY IDEAS

▸ *Know your strengths and weaknesses.* The advantage of gaining experience and testing yourself is that you get to know your strengths and weaknesses. Understanding yourself helps you plan strategies that suit your style and create situations that will move the plans forward.

▸ *Clearly communicate your vision.* We all have dreams, and they will remain dreams if we don't take action to turn them into reality. Once you have decided what you want to aim for, research it thoroughly and clearly communicate it to your team and supporters.

▸ *Gain the right support.* Ineffective support is a drain on your valuable energy and time. Make sure you carefully consider whom you invite to be involved, or they won't help but will hinder you.

▸ *Select a capable team.* As with gaining support, it's important to carefully consider whom you select; otherwise your project will suffer.

▸ *Challenge your team to achieve the vision.* Merely presenting an idea to your team is not good enough to take the project forward in a dynamic way. If you are hoping to develop your team as well as achieve your goal, you must regularly lay down challenges that stretch your team members and make them rise to the challenge.

▸ *Support your team throughout.* If you take on a daunting objective, then your team will be under similar pressure, particularly if you have chosen to take along novices and intermediates. They will need extra guidance and support to build confidence alongside their responsibilities.

▸ *Trust your team to get on with the job.* Micromanagement will not work in a large-scale expedition; there are too many facets to control and they all advance at a rapid rate. Trusting your team during the planning stages is important because once you are on the expedition itself, you will need to trust them, potentially with your life. On bigger mountains the team can be spread out over large distances, and the need for trust in handing over a level of responsibility is unavoidable. This is partly why team selection is so important.

▸ *Delegate.* Trying to stay on top of too many tasks will place unneeded pressure on you when you could be taking the project forward elsewhere. It is essential to share the work. Team members will not thank you if you take on so much that the important things don't happen and the expedition fails to even launch.

▸ *Step back and see the big picture.* It is important to take a strategic step back to review progress on a regular basis to ensure everything is on track. This can only happen if the rest of the key points have been achieved.

Glossary

absolute strength—The ability to exert maximum force independently of body weight (Bompa, 1999). Absolute strength can be a reliable way to make comparisons within the same group or between matched groups; however, it is not recommended when there are differences in body size.

acute mountain sickness (AMS)—Associated with high altitude, the occurrence of AMS depends on elevation, rate of ascent, and individual susceptibility. Symptoms include headaches, nausea, fatigue, and vomiting.

adaptation—Adjustment to environmental conditions or a new stimulus (such as training) involving adjustment of an organism to the intensity or quality of stimulation; modification of an organism or its parts that make it fitter for existence under the conditions of its environment.

ambient air—The air in the surrounding environment.

ape index—A comparison of arm span to height. A positive ape index can be established when arm span is greater than height (Giles et al., 2006). On average, elite climbers have a 2.5-centimetre (1 in.) ape index, which does not differ from the general population (Mermier et al., 2000).

apnea—Transient cessation of respiration.

body mass index—BMI is the most widely used weight-for-stature index and is calculated as weight divided by height squared (kg/m^2); may be used as a marker of adiposity (Heymsfield, 2005).

cardiorespiratory adaptations—Any stimulus that results in an increased ability of the cardiorespiratory system (hearts, lungs, blood) to pump oxygen and nutrient-rich blood to body tissues.

central adaptations—Primarily refers to the central nervous system and a training stimulus that allows for increased motivation or increased subconscious neuromuscular firing that results in increased performance.

Cheyne-Stokes respiration (periodic breathing)—An abnormal pattern of breathing categorised by periods of breathing with gradually increasing and decreasing tidal volume interspersed with periods of apnea.

dehydration—The removal of water from an object.

electrolytes—Minerals in blood and other bodily fluids that carry an electrical charge. They affect the amount of water in the body, blood acidity (pH), muscle action, and other important processes.

erythropoiesis—The process of red blood cell formation or production. In humans, erythropoiesis occurs almost exclusively in the red bone marrow. From erythro ('red blood cells') and poiesis ('to make').

erythropoietin (EPO)—A protein hormone produced by the kidney. After being released into the bloodstream, it binds with receptors in the bone marrow, where it stimulates the production of red blood cells (erythrocytes).

force—Davies, Heiderscheit, and Brinks (2000) define force as a push or pull exerted by one material object or substance on another. See also torque.

gastric emptying—The process of emptying food from the stomach.

glycogen—The storage form of glucose in animals and humans. It is synthesised and stored mainly in the liver and muscles.

haematocrit—The proportion of blood volume that is occupied by red blood cells.

haematological—Involving blood and blood-producing organs.

haemoglobin—A component of red blood cells, the main task of which is the transport of oxygen in the blood.

hypertrophy—An increase in muscle size by the addition of myofibrils. The cross-sectional area (diameter) of a muscle fibre increases as additional myofilaments of myosin and actin are added to each myofibril, leading to splitting and increased number of myofibrils (Goldspink et al., 1992; Kraemer, Fleck, & Evans, 1996).

hyponatraemia—An electrolyte disturbance as a result of a sodium concentration in the plasma below 135 millimoles per litre.

hypoxia—A deficiency of oxygen that normally reaches the tissues of the body, such as at altitude (generally considered less than 21 percent oxygen).

hypoxic living—The chronic adaptations and acclimation that occur when one spends a majority of time in hypoxic conditions (either consistently living at altitude or spending a significant amount of time in a simulated altitude environment such as a tent).

hypoxic training—The acute adaptations that occur when training in a hypoxic environment.

hypoxic ventilatory response (HVR)—Hyperventilation due to a reduction in arterial partial pressure of oxygen.

intermittent hypoxic training (IHT)—Situation where one lives at sea level but undertakes intermittent hypoxic training.

lactate threshold—The exercise intensity at which lactic acid production is greater than removal, resulting in the accumulation of lactic acid in the bloodstream.

live high, train low—Situation where one primarily lives in a hypoxic state but trains in normoxic conditions (for example, someone who lives at altitude but drives down the mountain to lower altitudes to train, or someone who sleeps in a tent to simulate hypoxia but does all training at sea level).

maximal oxygen uptake—The maximum amount of oxygen that can be taken up and used whilst operating at sea level.

maximum strength—The highest force that can be generated during a maximum voluntary contraction, or MVC (Bompa,1999). MVC refers to a condition in which a person attempts to recruit as many fibres in a muscle as possible in order to produce force (Knuttgen & Kraemer, 1987).

metabolism—Refers to the breakdown of food and its transformation into energy. It consists of both anabolism and catabolism (the build-up and breakdown of substances).

muscular endurance—The ability of muscles to maintain work for a prolonged time (Bompa, 1999), or the ability of a certain muscle or muscle group to perform repeated contractions against a submaximal resistance (Harman, Garhammer, & Pandorf, 2000).

normobaric—A barometric pressure equivalent to sea-level pressure.

normoxia—The normal oxygen content reaching tissues and organs at sea level (with 21 percent oxygen in the air and a sea-level atmospheric pressure of 760 mmHg).

one-repetition maximum strength (1RM)—The maximum isoinertial strength for a specific exercise; resistance at which a subject can perform only one attempt (Knuttgen & Kraemer, 1987). Similarly, 10RM indicates that a subject can perform 10 repetitions at a given resistance. Repetition maximum is the highest number of repetitions that can be performed at a given resistance and with proper lifting technique (Fleck & Kraemer, 2004). This system is widely used for assessing strength and power.

oxidation—The loss of electrons by a molecule, atom, or ion.

oxygen saturation—The percentage of haemoglobin binding sites in the bloodstream that are occupied by oxygen.

oxygen-saturation oximeter—A device that monitors the amount of oxygen carried by the haemoglobin in red blood cells.

partial pressure of oxygen—According to Dalton's law, this is the pressure exerted by oxygen in a mixture of gases.

peripheral adaptations—Any stimulus that causes adaptation in any organ or tissue that is away from the core of the body (e.g., training that increases mitochondria in the leg muscles).

power—The ability to perform an explosive movement in the shortest time possible (Bompa, 1999). Power (P) can also be defined as the rate at which mechanical work (W) is performed with respect to time (P = W / T) or as the product of force (F) and velocity (V) (P = F × V) (Sale, 1991).

pulse oximeter—See *oxygen-saturation oximeter*.

relative strength—The ratio between absolute strength and body weight (Bompa, 1999). Relative strength has been used as a measure of normalised strength, which would allow for comparisons between studies.

strength—The ability to exert force. Sale (1991) defined strength as the peak force or torque developed during an MVC under a given set of conditions. Another definition, provided by Knuttgen and Kraemer (1987), is that strength is the maximal force that a muscle or muscle group can generate at a specified velocity.

torque—A force that produces rotation about a point or axis.

vasoconstriction—The narrowing of the blood vessels resulting from contraction of the muscular wall of the vessels, restricting blood flow.

vasodilation—The widening of the blood vessels resulting from the relaxation of the muscular wall of the vessels, increasing blood flow.

References

American College of Sports Medicine (ACSM). (1998). American College of Sports Medicine position stand: The recommended quantity and quality of exercise for developing and maintaining cardiorespiratory and muscular fitness and flexibility in healthy adults. *Medicine and Science in Sports and Exercise, 30* (6), 975-991.

Armstrong, L., & Carmichael C. (2006). *The Lance Armstrong Performance Program—7 weeks to the perfect ride.* London: Pan Macmillan.

Armstrong, L.E., Hubbard, R.W., Szlyk, P.C., Mathew, W.T., & Sils, I.V. (1985). Voluntary dehydration and electrolyte losses during prolonged exercise in the heat. *Aviation Space and Environmental Medicine, 56,* 765-770.

Arnette, A. (2006). Everest 2006 season coverage. www.alanarnette.com/alan/everest2006.php.

Astrand, P.O., Rodahl, K., Dahl, H.A., Sigmund, M.D., & Stromme, B. (2003). *Textbook of work physiology: Physiological bases of exercise* (4th ed). Champaign, IL: Human Kinetics.

Baechle, T.R., & Earle, R.W. (2000). *Essentials of strength training and conditioning* (2nd ed.). Champaign, IL: Human Kinetics.

Bandura, A. (1997). *Self-efficacy: The exercise of control.* New York: W.H. Freeman.

Barry, P. & Pollard, A. (2003) *Altitude Illness.* British Medical Journal. 326, pp 915-919.

Bergman, B., & Brooks, G. (1999). Respiratory gas-exchange ratios during graded exercise in fed and fasted trained and untrained men. *Journal of Applied Physiology, 86* (2), 479-487.

Bernardi, L., Schneider, A., Pomidori, L., Paolucci, E., & Cogo, A. (2006). Hypoxic ventilatory response in successful extreme altitude climbers. *European Respiratory Journal, 27* (1), 165-171.

Bompa, T.O. (1999). *Periodization: Theory and methodology of training* (4th ed.). Champaign, IL: Human Kinetics.

Bonington, C. (1985). *I chose to climb.* Leicester: Ulverscroft.

Braith, R.W., Graves, J.E., Pollock, M.L., Leggett, S.L., Carpenter, D.M., & Colvin, A.B. (1989). Comparison of 2 vs. 3 days/week of variable resistance training during 10- and 18-week programs. *International Journal of Sports Medicine, 10* (6), 450-454.

Burke, S., & Orlick, T. (2004). Mental strategies of elite high altitude climbers: Overcoming adversity on Mount Everest. *Journal of Human Performance in Extreme Environments, 7,* 15-22.

Burke, S., Sparkes, A.C., & Allen-Collinson, J. (2008). High altitude climbers as ethnomethodologists making sense of cognitive dissonance: Ethnographic insights from an attempt to scale Mt. Everest. *Sport Psychologist, 22,* 336-355.

Burtscher, M., Flatz, M., & Faulhaber, M. (2004). Prediction of acute mountain sickness by SaO_2 values during short-term exposure to hypoxia. *High Altitude Medicine and Biology, 5* (3), 340-350.

Butterfield, G.E. (1999). Nutrient requirements at high altitude. *Clinics in Sports Medicine, 18* (3), 607-621.

Butterfield, G.E., Gates, J., Fleming, S., Brooks, G.A., Sutton, J.R., & Reeves, J.T. (1992). Increased energy intake minimises weight loss in men at high altitude. *Journal of Applied Physiology, 72* (5), 1,741-1,748.

Calhoun, L.G., & Tedeschi, R.G. (2004). Authors' response: "The foundations of posttraumatic growth: New considerations." *Psychological Inquiry, 15* (1), 93-102.

Carpinelli, R.N., & Otto, R.M. (1998). Strength training: Single versus multiple sets. *Sports Medicine, 26* (2), 73-84.

Cheuvront, S., Carter, R., & Sawka, M. (2003). Fluid balance and endurance exercise performance. *Current Sports Medicine Reports, 2* (4), 202-208.

Clarke, C. (2002) *High Altitude and Mountaineering Expeditions.* In The RGS-IBG Expedition Medicine Manual, Profile Books.

Claxton, G. (2000). The anatomy of intuition. In T. Atkinson & G. Claxton, G. (Eds.), *The intuitive practitioner: On the value of not always knowing what one is doing* (pp. 32-52). Buckingham: Open University Press.

Coleman, A.E. (1977). Nautilus vs. universal gym strength training in adult males. *American Corrective Therapy Journal, 31* (4), 103-107.

Cooke, C.B. (2008). Maximal oxygen uptake, economy and efficiency. In R. Eston & T. Reilly (Eds.), *Kinanthropometry and exercise physiology laboratory manual: Tests, procedures and data* (3rd ed., vol. 2, pp. 174-212). London: Routledge.

Cooper, K.H. (1968). A means of assessing maximal oxygen uptake: Correlation between field and treadmill testing. *Journal of the American Medical Association, 203*(3), 201-204.

Coutu, D.L. (2009). How resilience works. In *Harvard Business Review on managing through a downturn* (pp. 1-18). Cambridge, MA: Harvard Business School Press.

Coyle, E. (2004). Fluid and fuel intake during exercise. *Journal of Sports Sciences, 22*, 39-55.

Davies, G.J., Heiderscheit, B., & Brinks, K. (2000). Test interpretation. In L.E. Brown (Ed.), *Isokinetics in human performance* (pp. 3-21). Champaign, IL: Human Kinetics.

De Bock, K., Derave, W., Eijnde, B.O., Hesselink, M.K.C., Koninckx, E, Rose, A.J., Schrauwen, P., Bonen, A., Richter, E.A., & Hespel, P.J. (2008). Effect of training in the fasted state on metabolic responses during exercise with carbohydrate intake. *Journal Applied Physiology*, April 2008; 104: 1,045-1,055.

Deegans, P. (2002) *The Mountain Travellers Handbook*, UK, BMC.

Dweck, C. (2006). *Mindset: The new psychology of success*. New York: Random House.

Edwards, D., Waterhouse, J., Atkinson, G. &Reilly, T. (2002) *Exercise does not necessarily influence the phase of the circadian rhythm in temperature in healthy humans*. Journal of Sport Sciences 20, pp 725-732.

Feigenbaum, M.S., & Pollock, M.L. (1999). Prescription of resistance training for health and disease. *Medicine and Science in Sports and Exercise, 31* (1), 38-45.

Ferretti, G., & Costa, M. (2003). Diversity in and adaptation to breath-hold diving in humans. *Comparative Biochemistry and Physiology—Part A: Molecular & Integrative Physiology, 136* (1), 205-213.

Fitness and Amateur Sport. (1992). *ActiveLiving: A conceptual overview*. Ottawa: Government of Canada.

Fleck, S.J.(1999). Periodized strength training: A critical review. *Journal of Strength and Conditioning Research, 13*, 82-89.

Fleck, S.J., & Kraemer, W.J. (2004). *Designing resistance training programmes* (3rd ed.). Champaign, IL: Human Kinetics.

Food Standards Agency (FSA). (2002b). *McCance & Widdowson's The composition of foods* (6th ed.). London: Royal Society of Chemistry.

Food Standards Agency (FSA). (2007). Eatwell plate. London, www.eatwell.gov.uk/healthydiet/eatwellplate.

Fredrickson, B.L, Tugade, M.M, Waugh, C.E., & Larkin, G.R. (2003). What good are positive emotions in crisis? A prospective study of resilience and emotion following the terrorist attacks on the United States on September 11th, 2001. *Journal of Personality and Social Psychology, 84*, 365-376.

Freudenberg, N., Eng, E., Flay, B., Parcel, G., Rogers, T., & Wallerstein, N. (1995). Strengthening individual and community capacity to prevent disease and promote health: In search of relevant theories and principles. *Health Education Quarterly, 22*, 290-306.

Fuller, P.M., Lu, J. & Saper, C. B. (2008) *Differential Rescue of Light and Food Entrainable Circadian Rhythms*. Science. 320 (5,879), pp 1,074-1,077.

Giles, L.V., Rhodes, E.C., & Taunton, J.E. (2006). The physiology of rock climbing. *Sports Medicine, 36* (6), 529-545.

Goldspink, G., Scutt, A., Loughna, P.T., Wells, D.J., Jaenicke, T., & Gerlach, G.F. (1992). Gene expression in skeletal muscle in response to stretch and force generation. *American Journal of Physiology, 262* (3, Pt. 2), R356-R363.

Graham, J. (2003). *Outdoor leadership technique, common sense & self-confidence*. Seattle: The Mountaineers.

Gresham, N. (2004). Neil Gresham's guide to weight training. www.planetfear.com/articles/Neil_Gresham_Guide_to_Weight_Training_203.html.

Harman, E., Garhammer, J., & Pandorf, C. (2000). Administration, scoring, and interpretation of selected tests. In T.R. Baechle & R.W. Earle (Eds.), *Essentials of strength training and conditioning* (pp. 287-317). Champaign, IL: Human Kinetics.

Hattie, J., Marsh, H.W., Neill, J.T., Richards, G.E. (1997) Adventure Education and Outward Bound: Out-of-class experiences that make a lasting difference. *Review of Educational Research, 67*(1), 43-87.

Havryk, K., Gilbert, M., & Burgess, K. (2002). Spirometry values in Himalayan high altitude residents (Sherpas). *Respiratory Physiology and Neurobiology, 132* (2), 223-232.

Hawes, M.R., & Martin, A.D. (2001). Human body composition. In R. Eston & T. Reilly (Eds.), *Kinanthropometry and exercise physiology laboratory manual: Tests, procedures and data* (2nd ed., vol. 1, pp. 7-46). London: Routledge.

Hawley, J., Brouns, F., & Jeukendrup, A. (1998). Strategies to enhance fat utilisation during exercise. *Sports Medicine, 25*, 241-257.

Heymsfield, S.(2005). *Human body composition* (2nd ed). Champaign, IL: Human Kinetics.

Hinckson, E.A., Hopkins, W.G, Edwards, J. S., Pfitzinger, P., & Hellemans J. (2005). Sea-level performance in runners using altitude tents: A field study. *Journal of Science and Medicine in Sport, 8* (4), 451-457.

Hoff, J., Gran, A., & Helgerud, J. (2002). Maximal strength training improves aerobic endurance performance. *Scandinavian Journal of Medicine and Science in Sports, 12* (5), 288-295.

Hoff, J., Helgerud, J., & Wisloff, U. (1999). Maximal strength training improves work economy in trained female cross-country skiers. *Medicine and Science in Sports and Exercise, 31* (6), 870-877.

House of Lords Select Committee on Science and Technology (2000) *Air Travel and Health* London, The Stationery Office.

Jackson, S.A. & Roberts, G.C. (1992) Positive performance states of athletes: Toward a conceptual understanding of peak performance. *The Sports Psychologist.* 6: 156-171.

Jeukendrup, A. and Van Diemen, A. (1998) Heart rate monitoring during training and competition in cyclists. *Journal of Sports Sciences,*16(3), Supplement 1, 91-99.

Jeukendrup, A. (2004). Carbohydrate intake during exercise and performance. *Nutrition, 20* (7-8), 669-677.

Jones, A.M. (2007). Middle and long distance running. In E.M. Winter, A.M. Jones, R.R.C. Davison, P.D. Bromley, & T.H. Mercer (Eds.), *Sport and exercise physiology testing guidelines* (pp. 147-154). Routledge: London.

Jones, A.M., & Doust, J.H. (1996). A 1% treadmill grade most accurately reflects the energetic costs of outdoor running. *Journal of Sport Sciences, 14,* 321-327.

Joseph, S. & Linley, A. (2006) *Positive Therapy: A meta-Theory for Positive Psychological Practice,* Hove, Routledge.

Karvonen, M. J., Kentala, E. and Musta, O. (1957) The effects of training on heart rate; a longitudinal study. Annales medicinae experimentalis et biologiae Fenniae 35(3): 307-315.

Kayser, B., Acheson, K., Decombaz, E., Fern, J., & Cerretelli, P. (1992). Protein absorption and energy digestibility at high altitude. *Journal of Applied Physiology, 73* (6), 2,425-2,431.

Keith, S., Jacobs, I., & McLellan, T. (1992). Adaptations to training at the individual anaerobic threshold. *European Journal of Applied Physiology and Occupational Physiology, 65,* 316-323.

Killian, K.J. (1988). Assessment of dyspnoea. *European Respiratory Journal, 1,* 195-197.

King, R.F.G.J., Cooke, C., Carroll, S., & O'Hara, J. (2008). Estimating changes in hydration status from changes in body mass: considerations regarding metabolic water and glycogen storage. *Journal of Sport Sciences, 26* (12), 1,361-1,363.

Kline, G., Porcari, J.P., Hintermeister, R., Freedson, P.S., Ward, A., McCarron, R.F., Ross, J., & Rippe, J.M. (1987). Estimation of V̇O₂max from a one-mile track walk, gender, age and body weight. *Medicine & Science in Sports & Exercise, 19*(3), 253-259.

Knuttgen, G.H., & Kraemer, W.J. (1987). Terminology and measurement in exercise performance. *Journal of Applied Sport Science Research, 1* (1), 1-10.

Kraemer, W.J., Adams, K., Cafarelli, E., Dudley, G.A., Dooly, C., Feigenbaum, M.S., Fleck, S.J., Franklin, B., Fry, A.C., Hoffman, J.R., Newton, R.U., Potteiger, J., Stone, M.H., Ratamess, N.A., & Triplett-McBride, T. (2002). American College of Sports Medicine position stand: Progression models in resistance training for healthy adults. *Medicine and Science in Sports and Exercise, 34* (2), 364-380.

Kraemer, W.J., Fleck, S.J., & Evans, W.J. (1996). Strength and power training: Physiological mechanisms of adaptation. *Exercise and Sport Sciences Reviews, 24,* 363-97.

Legg, S.J., Smith, P., Slyfield, D., Miller, A.B., Wilcox, H., & Gilberd, C. (1997). Knowledge and reported use of sports science by elite New Zealand Olympic Class sailors. *Journal of Sports Medicine and Physical Fitness, 37,* 213-217.

Levine, B., & Stray-Gunderson, J. (1997). Living high, training low: The effect of high altitude acclimatization with low-altitude training on sea level performance. *Journal of Applied Physiology, 82,* 102-112.

McArdle, W.D., Katch, F.I., & Katch, V.L. (2007). *Exercise physiology: Energy, nutrition, and human performance.* Baltamore: Lippincott, Williams & Wilkins.

Mermier, C.M., Janot, J.M., Parker, D.L., & Swan, J.G. (2000). Physiological and anthropometric determinants of sport climbing performance. *British Journal of Sports Medicine, 34* (5), 359-366.

Mortlock, C. (1984). *The adventure alternative.* Cumbria: Cicerone Press.

Morris, T. (1997). *Psychological skills training in sport* (2nd ed.). Leeds: National Coaching Foundation.

Mujika, I., & Padilla, S. (2003). Scientific bases for precompetition tapering strategies. *Medicine and Science in Sports and Exercise, 35* (7), 1,182-1,187.

Murphy, S.M. (1994) Imagery interventions in sport. *Medicine and Science in Sports and Exercise.* 26(4), 486-494.

Ng, A.V., Demment, R.B., Bassett, D.R., Bussan, M.J., Clark, R.R., Kuta, J.M., & Schauer, J.E. (1988). Characteristics and performance of male citizen cross-country ski racers. *International Journal of Sports Medicine, 9* (3), 205-209.

Noakes, T. (2007). Drinking guidelines for exercise: What evidence is there that athletes should drink "as much as tolerable", "to replace the weight lost during exercise" or "ad libitum". *Journal of Sports Sciences, 25* (7), 781-796.

Oelz, O., Howald, H., Di Prampero, P.E., Hoppeler, H., Claassen, H., Jenni, R., Buhlmann, A., Ferretti, G., Bruckner, J.C., Veicsteinas, A., et al. (1986). Physiological profile of world-class high-altitude climbers. *Journal of Applied Physiology, 60,* 1,734-1,742.

Ogawa, T., Hayashi, K., Ichinose, M., & Nishiyasu, T. (2007). Relationship between resting ventilatory chemosensitivity and maximal oxygen uptake in moderate hypobaric hypoxia. *Journal of Applied Physiology, 103,* 1,221-1,226.

Peterson, M.D., Rhea, M.R., & Alvar, B.A. (2004). Maximizing strength development in athletes: A meta-analysis to determine the dose-response relationship. *Journal of Strength and Conditioning Research, 18* (2): 377-382.

Piaget, J. (1963). *The psychology of intelligence.* New York: Routledge.

Pollock, M.L., Graves, J. E., Bamman, M.M., Leggett, S.H., Carpenter, D.M., Carr, C., Cirulli, J., Matkozich, J., & Fulton, M. (1993). Frequency and volume of resistance training: Effect on cervical extension strength. *Archives of Physical Medicine and Rehabilitation, 74* (10), 1,080-1,086.

Pugh, L.G.C.E. (1954) Scientific aspects of the expedition to mount everest, 1953. *The Geographical Journal,* Vol. 120, No. 2, pp. 183-192.

Pulfrey, S.M., & Jones P.J.H. (1996). Energy expenditure and requirement while climbing above 6000m. *Journal of Applied Physiology, 81* (3): 1,306-1,311.

Quaine, F., Martin, L., & Blanchi, J. (1997). The effect of body position and number of supports on wall reaction forces in rock climbing. *Journal of Applied Biomechanics, 13,* 14-23.

Rebuffat, G. (2005). *The Mont Blanc Massif: The hundred finest routes.* London: Bâton Wicks.

Reilly, T., Atkinson, G. & Waterhouse, J. (1997) *Travel Fatigue and Jet Lag.* Journal of Sport Sciences. 15, pp 365-369.

Reilly, T., Atkinson, G., Edwards, B., Waterhouse, J., Torbjorn, A., Davenne, D., Lemmer, B. & Wirz-Justice, A. (2007) *Coping with jet-lag:* A position statement for the European College of Sport Science. European Journal of Sport Sciences. 7(1) pp 1-7.

Reilly, T., & Waterhouse, J. M. (2005). *Sport, exercise, & environmental physiology.* Edinburgh: Elsevier Churchill Livingstone.

Reynolds, R.D., Lickteig, J.A., Deuster, P.A., Howard, M.P., Conway, J.M., Pietersma, A., deStoppelaar, J., & Deurenberg, P. (1999). Energy metabolism increases and regional body fat decreases while regional muscle mass is spared in humans climbing Mount Everest. *Journal of Nutrition, 129,* 1,307-1,314.

Reynolds, R.D., Lickteig, J.A., Howard, M.P., & Deuster, P.A. (1998). Intakes of high fat and high carbohydrate foods by humans increased with exposure to increasing altitude during an expedition to Mount Everest. *Journal of Nutrition, 128,* 50-55.

Rhea, M.R., Alvar, B.A. Burkett, L.N., & Ball, S.D. (2003). A meta-analysis to determine the dose response for strength development. *Medicine and Science in Sports and Exercise, 35* (3), 456-464.

Robach, P., Schmitt, L., Brugniaux J.V., Roels, B., Millet, G., Hellard, P., Nicolet, G., Duvallet, A., Fouillot, J.P., Moutereau, S., Lasne, F., Pialoux, V., Olsen, N.V., & Richalet, J.P. (2006). Living high, training low: Effect on erythropoiesis and aerobic performance in highly trained swimmers. *European Journal of Applied. Physiology, 96* (4), 423-433.

Romer, L.M., McConnell, A.K., & Jones, D.A. (2002). Effects of inspiratory muscle training on time-trial performance in trained cyclists. *Journal of Sports Sciences, 20,* 547-562.

Rose, M.S., Houston, C.S., Fulco, C.S., Coates, G., Sutton, J.R., & Cymerman, A. (1988). Operation Everest II: Nutrition and body composition. *Journal of Applied Physiology, 65* (6), 2,545-2,551.

Sale, D.G. (1991). Testing strength and power. In J.D. MacDougal, H.A. Wenger, & H.J. Green (Eds.), *Physiological testing of the high-performance athlete* (pp. 21-97). Champaign, IL: Human Kinetics.

Salmon, J., Hall, C. & Haslam, I. (1994) The use of imagery by soccer players. *Journal of Applied Sport Psychology.* 6: 116-133.

Saltin, B., & Costill, D. (1988). Fluid and electrolyte balance during prolonged exercise. In E.S. Horton and R.L. Terjung (Eds.), *Exercise, nutrition, and energy metabolism* (pp. 150-158). New York: Macmillan.

Sharwood, K., Collins, M., Goedecke, J., Wilson, G., & Noakes, T. (2002). Weight changes, sodium levels and performance in the South African Ironman triathlon. *Clinical Journal of Sports Medicine, 12,* 391-399.

Sharwood, K., Collins, M., Goedecke, J., Wilson, G., & Noakes, T. (2004). Weight changes, medical implications, and performance during Ironman Triathlon. *British Journal of Sports Medicine, 38,* 718-724.

Shave, R., & Franco, A. (2006). The physiology of endurance training. In G. Whyte (ed.), *The physiology of endurance training.* London: Churchill Livingstone, Elsevier.

Sheel, A.W. (2004). Physiology of sport rock climbing. *British Journal of Sports Medicine, 38* (3), 355-359.

Soles, C. (2006). *Climbing: Training for peak performance.* Seattle: The Mountaineers.

Stadler, L.V., Stubbs, N.B., & Vucovich, M.D. (1997). A comparison of 2-day and 3-day per week resistance training program on strength gains in older adults. *Medicine and Science in Sports and Exercise, 20* (5 Suppl.), S254.

Stroud, M. (2004). *Survival of the fittest: Understanding health and peak physical performance.* London: Yellow Jersey Press.

Sullivan, P.A., & Nahman, H.N. (1998). Self-perceptions of the role of USOC sport psychologists working with Olympic athletes. *Sports Psychologist, 12,* 95-103.

Townsend, N., Gore, C., Hahn, A., McKenna, M., Aughey, R., Clark, S., Kinsman, T., Hawley, J., & Chow, C. (2002). Living high, training low increases hypoxic ventilatory response of well-trained endurance athletes. *Journal of Applied Physiology, 93,* 1,498-1,505.

Tsai, T.H., Okumura, M., Yamasaki, M. & Sasaki, T. (1988) *Simulation of jet lag following a trip with stopovers by intermittent schedule shifts.* Journal of Interdisciplinary Cycle Research. 19, pp 89-96.

Twight, M., & Martin, J. (1999). *Extreme alpinism: Climbing light, fast, and high.* Seattle: The Mountaineers.

Voutselas, V., Soulas, D., & Kritikos, A. (2005). Physiological predictors of performance in mountaineering ski. *Inquiries in Sport and Physical Education, 3* (3), 277-282.

Wallace, J. (2006). Principles of cardiorespiratory endurance programming. In *ACSM's resource manual for guidelines for exercise testing and prescription* (5th ed.). Philadelphia: Lippincott Williams & Wilkins.

Waterhouse, J. & Reilly, T. (1997) *Jet-Lag.* The Lancet. 350 (9091), pp 1,611-1,617.

Waterhouse, J., Edwards, B., Nevill, A., Carvalho, S., Atkinson, G., Buckley, P., Reilly, T., Godfrey, R. & Ramsay, R. (2002) *Identifying some determinants of 'jet lag' and it symptoms: A study of athletes and other travellers.* British Journal of Sports Medicine. 36, pp 54-60.

Waterhouse, J. & Herxheimer, A. (2003) *The prevention and treatment of jet lag: It has been ignored but much can be done.* British Medical Journal. 326, pp 296-297.

Waterhouse, J., Reilly, T. & Edwards, B. (2004) *The stress of travel.* Journal of Sport Sciences. 22 (10), pp 946-966.

Waterhouse, J., Reilly, T., Atkinson, G. & Edwards, B. (2007) *Jet Lag: Trends and Coping Strategies.* The Lancet. 369, pp 1,117-1,129.

Watts, P.B. (2004). Physiology of difficult rock climbing. *European Journal of Applied Physiology, 91* (4), 361-372.

Watts, P.B., Martin, D.T., & Durtschi, S. (1993). Anthropometric profiles of elite male and female competitive sport rock climbers. *Journal of Sports Sciences, 11* (2), 113-117.

Weinberg, R.S., Burton, D., Yukelson, D. & Weigland, D.A. (1993) Goal setting in competitive sport; An Exploratory investigation of practices of collegiate. *The Sports Psychologist.* 7(3); 275-289.

West, J.B., Boyer, S.J., Graber, D.J., Hackett, P.H., Maret, K.H., Milledge, J.S., Peters, R.M. Jr., Pizzo, C.J., Samaja, M., Sarnquist, F.H., Schone, R.B., & Winslow, R.M. (1983). Maximal exercise at extreme altitudes on Mount Everest. *Journal of Applied Physiology, 55,* 688-698.

Westerterp, K.R., Kayser, B., Wouters, L., Le Trong J.L., & Richalet, J.P. (1994). Energy balance at high altitude of 6542m. *Journal of Applied Physiology, 77* (2), 862-866.

Wiseman, C., Freer, L., & Hung. E. (2006). Physical and medical characteristics of successful and unsuccessful summiteers of Mount Everest in 2003. *Wilderness and Environmental Medicine, 17* (2), 103-108.

About the Editors

Carlton Cooke is the Director of University Research, Carnegie Professor of Sport & Exercise Science and Head of the Carnegie Research Centre for Performance Sport at Leeds Metropolitan University.

Carlton has presented and published extensively on aspects of sports performance and physical activity, exercise and health, principally in the areas of exercise physiology and biomechanics. He has worked with a range of partners in high performance sport in facilitating, developing or delivering sports science support and research. He worked in support of the British Army expedition to Everest West Ridge in 2006, together with a team of sport & exercise scientists from Leeds Metropolitan University. The University continues to support preparations for Army expeditions and support other expeditions in the outdoors alongside a commitment to optimizing the role of the outdoors in Higher Education through the Carnegie Great Outdoors. Carlton has participated and competed in a range of outdoor sports and activities and continues to enjoy the outdoors both professionally and recreationally.

Dave Bunting is director of training and cofounder of My Peak Potential, an experiential learning and development centre in the Bavarian Alps of Southern Germany. He served 24 years in the British Army, predominantly within the Army Physical Training Corps, where he became a specialist in mountain leadership training. He has instructed in mountain training centres in Wales, Norway, Canada, and Bavaria. In Bavaria, he undertook the arduous year-long German Army Mountain Guide's (Heeresbergfuhrer) course, becoming one of only a few British soldiers to have gained this prestigious qualification. Dave has a passion for mountaineering and has been involved in the organisation and execution of numerous expeditions, including 10 to the Himalayas. In 2006 Bunting led an elite selection of climbers from the British Army on a groundbreaking expedition in an attempt to become the first British team to climb the formidable West Ridge of Mount Everest. As expedition leader, Dave headed up the planning, team selection and preparation, and he was a strong member of the climbing team. This highly publicised expedition earned Dave an MBE and was filmed for the televised documentary *Everest: Man vs. Mountain.*

John O'Hara, PhD, is a Senior Lecturer in Sports Performance Physiology within the Carnegie Faculty of Sport and Education at Leeds Metropolitan University. His PhD was on carbohydrate ingestion and endurance performance. He is a British Association of Sport and Exercise Sciences accredited sport and exercise scientist (Physiology – Scientific Support). His research interests are focussed on carbohydrate metabolism, hydration status, limiting factors for sports performance and the preparation of athletes for extreme sporting challenges. He has a keen interest in the outdoors, being a keen hill walker, mountain biker and climber. He has also been on two Himalayan Expeditions, Yala Peak (5,500 m) and with the Everest West Ridge 2006 team, climbed up to Camp 1 (6,100 m) on the lower slopes of Mount Everest. He has also summited Mount Killimanjaro (5,895 m). Through his accumulative experiences from academia and in the great outdoors, he led, developed, managed and successfully delivered the multidisciplinary support services provided to the Everest West Ridge 2006 team, which included physiological, nutritional and psychological support. Since then he has provided a similar level of support to other Army Mountaineering Association expeditions, as well as other sporting disciplines, such as a solo yachts women competing in the Vendee Globe 2008; around the world single hand sailing race.

About the Contributors

John Allan is senior lecturer in adventure education and psychology in the Carnegie faculty of Leeds Metropolitan University. His published research interests focus on adventure and personal growth with emphasis on the facilitation of psychological resilience through adventure programming. As an outdoor educator and practitioner, he has been instrumental in developing the world's largest database investigating the impact of residential adventure programmes on students' transition into higher education. As a member of the sport science research team supporting Everest West Ridge 2006, John undertook two trips to the Himalayas. This culminated in supporting climbers and collecting data on psychological resilience at base camp, particularly in the final stages of the expedition.

Steve Cobley, PhD, is a senior lecturer in skill acquisition and sport psychology in the Carnegie faculty of sport and education at Leeds Metropolitan University. In the faculty, Steve teaches at both undergraduate and postgraduate levels on a range of courses. He is a member of the Faculty Research Ethics Committee and coordinates the major independent study element of postgraduate provision. Steve's research interests focus on the developmental factors that constrain attainment. This has involved local and international collaborative research, which has subsequently been published in international peer-reviewed journals. Steve has been involved with coaching and performance consulting with amateur, varsity, representative, military, and international athletes in athletics, soccer, cricket, archery, and cycling. He was also a member of the multidisciplinary team that provided sport science support to the British Army's Everest West Ridge expedition in 2006.

John Doyle, MBE, has been a passionate rock climber, mountaineer, and general lover of the outdoors for over 30 years. He has climbed on major peaks all over the world, including the Cassin Ridge on Mount McKinley, the second

British ascent of Gasherbrum I (the world's 11th-highest mountain), the first British ascent of the southwest face of Kanchenjunga (the world's third-highest peak) without supplementary oxygen, and the Army Everest West Ridge expedition in 2006, in which he was the climbing leader. A former Royal Marine Commando, in 2001 John was awarded the MBE for his contribution to services mountaineering. In recent years he has focused on delivering training and development packages through challenging activities in an outdoor environment at individual and corporate levels. Equally at home in the boardroom or outdoors teaching his children to ski, John now co-directs the organisational development company My Peak Potential in the Bavarian alps of southern Germany, allowing his clients to unlock potential and maximise performance.

Theocharis Ispoglou, PhD, is a senior lecturer in the Carnegie faculty of sport and education at Leeds Metropolitan University. His primary research interests include the study of nutritional and exercise interventions on human performance and body composition. The focus of his PhD was the investigation of specific amino acid supplements on strength and body composition of athletes and non-athletes. Theocharis also has a special interest in athletics (sprinting), Olympic weightlifting, and sport performance. He is an accredited member of the UK Strength and Conditioning Association (UKSCA) and is a UK athletics coach.

Stevan Kenneth Jackson, FRGS, FInstLM, FCMI, MCGI, Chartered MCIPD, Royal Navy (rtd), is a seminal figure in the armed forces mountaineering community. In over three decades of service to the Royal Navy and Royal Marines Mountaineering Club, of which he became the chairman, he was involved in climbing expeditions to the Alps, Arctic Norway, Kenya, Tanzania, California, Peru, Bolivia, Argentina, Pakistan, Nepal, and Tibet. In 1987 and 1989 he led expeditions to Peru and Bolivia that carried out research on altitude illness conducted by Dr James S Milledge, FRCP, MD, co-author of *High Altitude Medicine and Physiology*. The findings of this research were published in the *British Medical Journal, Journal of Clinical Science,* and *European Journal of Respiration.* The research has led to increased understanding of hypoxic ventilatory response, microvascular fragility, and the role of atrial natriuretic peptide hormone in humans at altitude. In 1996 he was deputy leader of the British Services Gasherbrum I expedition. In 2000 he led an expedition to Kanchenjunga, the world's third-highest mountain; it was only the second British ascent of the southwest (Yalung) face of the mountain, still one of the most significant achievements by a service mountaineering team.

Roderick FGJ King, PhD, is Carnegie professor of sport and exercise biochemistry at Leeds Metropolitan University. He trained as a biochemist at Bath and obtained a doctorate in medical biochemistry at Leeds. Rod has spent over 35 years in academic life both as a lecturer and a researcher and has worked with the Open University both as a tutor and consultant. He has extensive experience in research with participants in a variety of contexts. Rod specialised in wet chemistry techniques and led the laboratory team in the academic unit at the Leeds General Infirmary. He has conducted quantitative research in chemical pathology, in the MRC neutron activation facility at Leeds, and in surgical procedures. He gained experience in innovation applied to nutrient products, which led to industrial and commercial involvement between and with patent agents, suppliers, plant manufacturers, ingredient producers, marketing agents, product consultants, retail organisations, and others on a national and international scale. His current research focuses on carbohydrate and hydration for sport performance. Rod joined the School of Leisure and Sports Studies at Leeds Metropolitan University in 2000.

Pete Longbottom, in the spring of 2003, was approached by Dave Bunting to participate as a climber with the British Army Everest West Ridge 2006 expedition. Because of persistent injuries,

Pete was forced to decline the invitation. But so insistent was Dave that Pete accepted the position of base camp logistics and communications manager.

Pete's first taste of climbing was on a school trip at the age of 10. He joined his college's climbing club in 1979. In 1983, Pete joined the British Army, where he completed 24 years service. In 1993, Pete was fortunate enough to attend and pass the prestigious German Army Mountain Guides Course (Heeresbergführe Lehrgang) in Mittenwald, Bavaria. On completion of the course, Pete spent much of his remaining service career providing training for British and other national armed forces military mountaineering and arctic warfare. In this capacity, his work has allowed him to pursue his main interest. He has planned trips to and climbed or skied on every continent except Antarctica. He insists that the crag climbing of his early climbing exploits are his fondest memories.

When he is not with his children, Pete spends his time developing interest in mountaineering in the Far East. He is currently planning expeditions to China and Kyrgyzstan.

Chris Low, PhD, is currently a senior lecturer in biomechanics at Leeds Metropolitan University. His research interests lie in the area of sport technique analysis. He completed his doctoral degree in 2005, researching the biomechanics of rock climbing movement. He has climbed and bouldered around the world for over a decade. As a high-performance gymnastics coach, he has provided consulting on body preparation exercises for the British climbing team.

Jim McKenna, PhD, is professor of physical activity and health at Leeds Metropolitan University and leads the Active Lifestyle Research Centre. He has a wide portfolio of research interests centred on behaviour change in a range of settings and contexts. Matching his diverse interests, his recent publications include exercise in ageing, promotion of workplace walking, community-wide promotion of physical activity, and development of personal growth through positive psychological approaches. He regularly reviews for various academic journals and research agencies.

Adrian Mellor, MBChB, FRCA, earned a medical degree specialising in anaesthesia from Leeds University in 1990. He is a surgeon commander in the Royal Navy and has seen service on submarines and aircraft carriers and in field hospitals in Iraq and Afghanistan. He has also worked as a consultant at James Cook University Hospital in Middlesbrough and with the Great North Air Ambulance Service. He is a military rock climbing instructor, mountain expedition leader, and Alpine mountain leader. Adrian started caving and climbing while at university in Leeds in 1986. His experience includes rock climbing in Europe and Australia and the Alps in summer and winter. In 2007 he led an expedition to Aconcagua in Argentina with a group of military medics and later in the year made the first ascent of a 4,800-meter peak in Kyrgyzstan with a Royal Marines team. He has been to the Himalayas twice to attempt 8,000-meter peaks (Broad Peak in 1992 and Makalu in 2004). Home is in North Yorkshire with his (very understanding) wife, Nicola, and daughters Poppy and Scarlett. He also has three children from a previous marriage: Victoria, James, and Harriette.

Paul (Chip) Rafferty, often labelled as "the fittest bloke in the Army," spent most of his coaching career in the Army Physical Training Corps training athletes in numerous sports as well as preparing soldiers, including the elite SAS, to be fit for duty. In the past three decades his achievements have included a top 20 finish in the London Marathon, winner of ultradistance races on road and fell, silver medallist in the Long Course World Duathlon Championship (Austria 2003), and World Championship Ironman qualifier Canada in under 11 hours. Adventurous highlights include leading the first descent of Low's Gully Borneo and exploring many of the world's most challenging caves and mountain ranges. He has a master's degree and is a high-performance coach with the English Institute of Sports, which has supported his work with Leeds Metropolitan University as endurance coach and climber on three major Himalayan expeditions, including the Services Everest West Ridge expedition in 2006.

Mark Robinson is director of Carnegie Great Outdoors and is responsible for outdoor adventure activities at Leeds Metropolitan University. Mark has a passion for the outdoors and is an experienced kayak coach, climber, and skier. He graduated from the University of York with a BA (honours) in educational studies before joining Leeds Metropolitan in 2000 to pursue a career as a lecturer and outdoor instructor. He has been instrumental in developing their academic curriculum, outdoor activity, and residential programmes, which are now accessed by thousands of students annually. In 2006 he received the Chancellor's Award in recognition of his many achievements and contributions to outdoor education at the university. Mark still lectures on the outdoors to a variety of audiences and remains an active coach. Currently he is director of Carnegie Great Outdoors, where he manages an extensive network of strategic partnerships that ensure the delivery of leading outdoor programmes in the UK and abroad.

Louise Sutton is a performance nutritionist and a principal lecturer in sport and exercise nutrition at Leeds Metropolitan University with a particular interest in the practical application of sport dietetics. She manages the Carnegie Centre for Sports Performance and Wellbeing, is a member of the Health and Fitness Technical Expert Group of SkillsActive (the Sector Skills Council for Active Leisure and Learning in the UK), and is an advisor to the Register of Sport and Exercise Nutritionists. Her research interests focus on the practical application of dietetics in elite sports and extreme environments. Louise led the provision of nutrition support to the British Army in their preparations for their attempt to ascend the West Ridge of Everest in 2006 and their ski mountaineering attempt on Mount Shishapangma in 2007. Over the past 15 years she has advised many elite sports professionals in athletics, orienteering, tennis, cricket, football, and rugby.

Known for her practical approach to nutrition problems and solutions, Louise regularly contributes to nutrition features in popular outdoor magazines.